D0892063

After the Heavenly Tune

Medieval & Renaissance Literary Studies

After the Heavenly Tune

English Poetry and the Aspiration to Song

Marc Berley

Duquesne University Press
Pittsburgh, Pennsylvania

Library of Congress Cataloging-in-Publication Data

Berley, Marc.
    After the heavenly tune: English poetry and the aspiration to song /
by Marc Berley.
        p. cm. — (Medieval & renaissance literary studies)
Includes bibliographical references and index.
    ISBN 0–8207–0316–8 (alk. paper)
    1. English poetry—History and criticism—Theory, etc.   2. Music and
literature.   3. Greek poetry—Appreciation—Great Britain.   4. English
poetry—History and criticism.   5. Lyric poetry—History and criticism.
6. English poetry—Greek influences.   7. Metaphor.   8. Poetics. I.
Title. II. Medieval & Renaissance literary studies
    PR508.M75 B47 2000
    821.009′357—dc21

                                        00–008592

A portion of chapter 3 was published as "Milton's Earthy Grossness" in *Milton Studies* 30, ed. Albert C. Labriola (Pittsburgh: U Pittsburgh P, 1993).

A portion of chapter 2 was published as "Jessica's Belmont Blues: Music and Merriment in *The Merchant of Venice*" in *Opening the Borders* (U Delaware P, 1999).

For Mort

Contents

Preface

A former student, a pianist, invited me recently to the Cosmopolitan Club, where he was giving a recital to inaugurate the club's new piano. The chairwoman of the music committee began her introduction of the all-Chopin program by calling Chopin "the most poetic" of composers. After the performance, she complimented the pianist by calling his playing "pure poetry." I remark her comments because they address the subject of this book: a reciprocity that has long been basic to conceptions of poetry and music in our culture. Despite Walter Pater's assertion that "all art constantly aspires towards the condition of music," composers and musicians sometimes aspire to poetry. As Giuseppe Giacosa once declared: "While *La Bohème* is all poetry and no plot, *Tosca* is all plot and no poetry." But Pater is right. Composers do not aspire to poetry in the way poets aspire to song. For poets, the aspiration to a condition of music is nearly universal. It takes a central role in a poet's conception of the general possibilities of poetry, and becomes the basis of an elaborately articulated theory of poetic. Valéry's desire to transcend the limits of poetry led him to identify his goal of "pure poetry" with the "music of poetry." To achieve poetry that is purely musical is likely impossible. Goethe avowed that "music begins where words end." Music, poets suggest, is better than poetry. The fact is variously a source of dependency ("Sing Muse ..."), longing ("I shall sing a fuller tune ..."), anxiety ("When the lute is broken ..."), and triumph ("I sing the body electric ..."). So goes an important story in the history of poetry and poetics.

Why do almost all of the world's greatest poets, from Virgil to Wallace Stevens, write that they "sing" when in fact they are writing? What precisely makes poetry musical? And what are the terms of poetic aspirations to song? *After the Heavenly Tune* examines various poets' aspirations to song, as well as their diverse ideas about the relationship between music and poetry. It reveals very quickly that these relationships are more complex than conventional considerations of meter, pitch, and rhythm. Poets as different as Shakespeare, Milton, Dickinson, Shelley, and Whitman, to name a few, return to the dialogue about speculative music begun by Socrates in Plato's dialogues — the music of the soul, the harmony of the spheres, the struggle between *musica speculativa* and *musica instrumentalis*. What is more, in struggling to turn words into music, these poets come to realize the greater "speculative musical" value of words.

This book begins by studying the complex relationship between music and poetry in the West — the mythical teachings of Pythagoras and Socrates, the writings of Plato and Aristotle, and the influential treatises on music and poetry by writers such as Augustine, Boethius, and Sir Philip Sidney. It then focuses on the poetry of the English Renaissance, a period distinguished by remarkable developments in the ways poets conceived the condition of music toward which they aspired. From Sidney to Milton, the more closely poetry approaches music, the bolder the claims poets can make for it. But what is most compelling about the aspiration to song is the way it becomes a means of exploring, defining, scrutinizing, and redefining poetry itself, as chapters 2 and 3, which focus on Shakespeare and Milton, show. Shakespeare made it possible to think that the English language, because graced by "the touches of sweet harmony," served as an instrument of the heavens. Milton, in contrast, knew that he wrote "After the heavenly tune, which none can hear/ Of human mold with gross unpurged ear." The last two chapters focus on Romantic and Modern aspirations to poetic song. To sing, for most of these poets, is in some measure as impossible as it is necessary. As Wordsworth writes, "My last and favourite aspiration, mounts,/ With yearning, tow'rds some philosophic Song/ Of Truth that cherishes our daily life . . .," the enjambment enacting a moment of erotic aspiration. In poetry, writes Stevens, we seek "A tune beyond us as we are,/ Yet nothing changed by the blue guitar. . . ." By the time of Stevens, the aspiration to song was still the best way to articulate what had become the difficult requirements of Modern poetry: to transcend without believing in transcendence, to change everything while changing nothing. Finally, the conclusion relates poetic claims to song to comparable aspirations of philosophers and composers such as Adorno, Schoenberg, and Wittgenstein.

We may get an idea, even from this briefest sketch, of the various forms poetic aspirations to song may take. The developments form an important aspect of the history of poetry. I attempt here to contribute to our understanding of what a number of poets mean and do when they refer to themselves either as singers or as poets who aspire to sing. By examining the aspiration to song in English poetry, and the various contexts that give it meaning, I aim to further both our understanding of an important aspect of the history of poetics and our appreciation of those poets who most aspire to and best achieve a condition of song.

Acknowledgments: Much thanks to those who gave me their attention and wisdom as I was writing this book: Andrew Thomas Armstrong, Harry Berger, Jr., Carolyn Betentsky, Margaret Ferguson, Allen Gimbel, Michael Mack, Charles E.

Mercier, James V. Mirollo, Anne Lake Prescott, Sandra Pierson Prior, Laura Slatkin, V. R. Sussman, and Richard Wollman. And to Albert Labriola, Susan Wadsworth-Booth and Sonja Embree of Duquesne University Press. Many thanks to Edward W. Tayler, who read numerous versions of this book and entreated me sweetly, from beginning to end, to get it right. The disgrace of error is everywhere mine. More thanks to: Lee, Hank, and Jackie; May and Seymour; Gordon; Joannah; Selma, Mom, Arnold, Amy, Nancy, Jennifer, and Phil. And to Vered, my wife, last and most.

Poets from Homer to Wallace Stevens have claimed for their poems not the status of poetry but of song: "Sing, goddess," "Let us begin to sing," "Of arms and a man I sing," "More safe I sing with mortal voice," "I sing the body electric," "I shall keep singing! . . . I shall sing a fuller tune."[1] There are differences, of course, among Homer and Hesiod in Greece, Virgil in Rome, and John Milton in England; between Walt Whitman and Emily Dickinson in their Americas; between invoking a muse and claiming to do one's own singing. But the declaration is common in part because long ago, before Homer, and not only in ancient Greece, a poet was an actual musician, a singer who sang to the accompaniment of a musical instrument — Orpheus, for instance. But whereas for Homer poetry was still some form of actual song, likely a melodic and rhythmic chanting, it was not for Virgil, nor later for Milton or Stevens. Composing orally, Homer would have intoned his epic over a number of nights, whereas Virgil, as the legend goes, wrote and polished a line a day. Once poets became writers, the claim to song became a trope — a revealing one. For many poets since Homer, it is evidence of mere compliance with a longstanding convention, likely established in Mesopotamia, that was gorgeously developed and fervently examined in ancient Greece. In the hands of certain poets, however, the claim to song declares a singular aspiration peculiar to the poet who recounts it. In numerous cases, it is a notable moment — whether of crisis or triumph — in the history of poetry and poetics.

The aspiration to song is central to many poets' conceptions of themselves and their poems, and it raises important questions. Why is song an inevitable goal of written poetry? Why would poets far removed from an oral tradition persist in claiming they are singing when in fact they are not? Of course, even after poets ceased to be actual singers, poetry and music were still conceived as sister arts. But this association is too tenuous to advance our appreciation of individual claims to song and our broader understanding of their importance. The association has led us to overlook the important differences between poetry and song. As Montaigne observes, "Resemblance does not make things so much alike as difference makes them unlike," and it is in the differences that a poet's aspiration to song is rooted.[2]

Whereas for Homer the claim to song is as near as possible to a literal statement, for Virgil it is already a revealing and troubling fiction. In the first clause of Virgil's *Aeneid*, "*Arma virumque cano*," the poet's claim to be singing is a conspicuous lie. Aiming to outdo the "arms" of Homer's *Iliad* and the "man" of his *Odyssey*, Virgil does not vie with Homer in the manner of the singing shepherds in the idyls of Theocritus — or, indeed, in the eclogues of Virgil. Rather, Virgil brandishes a manipulation of syntax and diction that would be impossible for an oral poet to achieve. Virgil aims not to *outsing* Homer but to *outwrite* him, to form new criteria by which his written epic must be judged. Although Virgil's wrought verse demonstrates the ways that written poetry excels oral poetry, within his complicated rivalry with his Greek precursor, Virgil's claim to song is a regressive affirmation that it is better to be a singer than a poet.

For the next 1,500 years, the tradition of oral, musical

poetry continued in Europe. But the history of English literature offers the interesting counterexample of *Beowulf*, a poem
that commits to writing a story long developed in oral, musical form, thus challenging the tradition in which it was better
to be a singer than a poet. The *Beowulf* poet describes the
"scop" who "sang, clear-voiced in Heorot," a "man skilled at
telling adventures, songs stored in his memory, who could
recall many of the stories of the old days, wrought a new tale
in well-joined words." But the author of *Beowulf* is not a
"scop." Unlike Virgil, rather than begin his poem by claiming
to be a singer, he announces the oldness of his story, boldly
declaring his ability to tell a familiar tale better than the last
teller. The *Beowulf* poet undertakes "with his art to recite . . .
and skillfully to tell an apt tale" — so well that his written
poem might stand as the last, triumphant version: "Yes, we
have heard of the glory of the Spear-Dane's kings in the
old days — how the princes of that people did brave deeds."[3]
A proud storyteller rather than an aspiring singer, he makes
no pretension to singing, distinguishing himself clearly from
the *scop* who sings to the music of his harp. The aspiration
to song is not central to the *Beowulf* poet's conception of
himself as a poet. He wishes to establish that it is he, not a
divine muse, who remembers and renders the story. He does
not claim the divine inspiration of song because he declares
storytelling a human skill.

The conflict between divine inspiration and poetic skill,
which Socrates discusses in Plato's *Ion*, is one that chapter 1
considers in detail. For the moment, let us only remark a distinction between two kinds of poets: (1) those for whom the
claim to song is an important trope that serves to define their
conceptions of themselves as poets and (2) those for whom
the claim is either merely a literary convention or a matter
to be examined hardly at all. Virgil, for example, is far less
concerned with the matter of singing than either Milton or
Stevens.

This book examines those poets for whom the claim to song is crucial, part of their conceptions of themselves and their poems. Homer and Hesiod, far more than the authors of *The Aeneid* or *Beowulf*, provide poets such as Shakespeare, Milton, Keats, and Stevens, among others, with models of aspiration to a condition of song. For these poets, it is the ancient Greek poets who establish the complex relationship between poetry and song.

Even in ancient Greece, when poetry was actually a form of music, a poet had to establish the divine origin of his ability to sing. Hence, Hesiod begins his *Theogony*, as Wesley Trimpi observes, "by giving an account of how he became a singer. One day near Mount Helicon, [Hesiod] says, the Muses, who first declared to him that they could not only feign things which seemed to be true but could also speak the truth, taught him to compose his songs." As Trimpi explains, Hesiod claims that the Muses "'breathed' into him a voice which had the divine power to tell of things to come as well as of what had passed and told him that he must praise the blessed life of the gods, but, most of all, he must sing about the Muses themselves." He must, that is, sing about his aspiration to song.

Hesiod describes the nine Muses "at their birth as being 'of one mind' . . . in their freedom from care and their desire to express themselves in song. This 'single-mindedness' unites them, as in a harmonious chorus, and enables them to perform those offices which are pleasing to the mind of Zeus." As Trimpi writes, "the Muses, together, provide . . . and express this coherence as mutually dependent principles of order." These principles "give direction to the various disciplines which define and exercise the speculative, the prudential, and the productive activities of [human] consciousness."[4] Such coherence, however, was destroyed with the fall away from the Golden Age; and the "freedom from restraint of cares" once provided by the Muses was transformed into restraint and care. Plutarch, as Trimpi remarks, "reveals the later fragmentation of Hesiod's conception" of the "function" of the Muses, and of "the original division of all discourse into three types of disciplines."[5] The ancients "considered them to be the gracious gifts of three goddesses, whom they named Muses," writes Plutarch. "Later, in Hesiod's day, by which time these faculties were being more clearly seen, they began to distinguish different parts and forms." According to Plutarch,

> they then observed that each faculty in its turn contained three different things. The mathematical genus includes music, arithmetic, and geometry, the philosophical comprises logic, ethics, and natural science, while in the rhetorical it is said that the original laudatory kind was joined first by the deliberative and finally by the forensic.[6]

According to these divisions, poetry — as Aristotle makes clear — is a rhetorical and philosophical art. Music, in contrast, is a mathematical discipline. While there was harmony among the Muses, the claim to song was an honest, literal expression of a cosmic truth. With the fragmentation of the Muses, however, music and poetry were separated, and a poet's claim to song was transformed into a trope.

The complex relationship between poetry and music is rooted in a crucial distinction — established by Pythagoras and developed by Socrates and Plato — between two disciplines corresponding to two ways of conceiving music: speculative music (*musica speculativa*) and practical music (*musica practica*). The distinction between speculative and practical musical study is discussed by Boethius in his momentous *De Musica*, which became the required book on music in universities throughout Europe during the Middle Ages and Renaissance. Boethius distinguishes three types of music: (1) *musica mundana*, the music of the heavenly spheres; (2) *musica humana*, the music of the human soul; and (3) *musica instrumentalis*, the music of instruments produced by man, which includes the human voice and therefore poetry.[7] The practical study of music concerns mainly the technical ability (in the sense of Aristotelian *techne*) to make instrumental music (*musica instrumentalis*); concerned with the production of actual sounds, the practical study of music served to link poetry and music as sister arts. The speculative study of music, in contrast, concerns the cosmic relationship of these three types of music. Concentrating on the musical structure of the universe and the musical nature of man, speculative music was associated with arithmetic and geometry, and it served in many ways to dissociate music and poetry as separate, and even contrary, disciplines.

These separate but related disciplines influenced the ways philosophers thought about poetry. Thinking in speculative terms, Plato distinguished strictly heavenly music and earthly poetry. Thinking chiefly in practical (rhetorical) terms, Aristotle linked them. As the fragmentation of the Muses pervaded the consciousness of poets, these diverse ways of thinking about the relationship between music and poetry produced a critical tension that could not be avoided. Although they possessed practical musical skills they clearly valued, poets aspiring to be singers sought the transcendent qualities of *musica mundana*. They sought a condition of music that — given the speculative distinction between heavenly music (*musica mundana*) and poetry (*musica instrumentalis*) — was the goal of a discipline too far removed from their own.

The "original division of all discourse" has been a central topic in literary theory for over 2,000 years. Only resolution of the "original division" could restore the order that made poetry and song indistinguishable. Trimpi's excellent study documents the attempt of classical literary theory to restore the fragmented function of the Muses.[8] This book, in contrast, examines the attempts of individual poets who, from the time of Hesiod, have confronted a mythological division that serves to differentiate — rather than link — poetry and song. Despite its concentration on the discord between heavenly music and earthly poetry, speculative music has, as we will see, been attractive to many poets. For it provides a way of speaking about poetry (*musica instrumentalis*) that is also a way of speaking about the order of the cosmos (*musica mundana*) and the muscial activity of a poet's soul or consciousness (*musica humana*) within it. Whereas practical music concerns primarily the matter of human skill, speculative music concerns the very link between divine inspiration and human skill that can authorize a poet's claim to song.

One example of an intense attraction to speculative music is the poetry of John Milton, which reveals the extent to which a desire once again to unify the discordant activities of human consciousness (speculative, prudential, and productive) may consume a poet. In "On Time," Milton, recalling a phrase from Lorenzo's speech about the "touches of sweet harmony" in *The Merchant of Venice*, uses the phrase "Earthy grossness" to designate the inability of humankind either to hear or to sing the harmony of the heavens. When he writes in "Arcades" about the time "After the heavenly tune, which none can hear/Of human mold with gross unpurged ear," Milton at once declares his speculative aspiration and questions his ability to join "such music."[9]

Milton early tells us about the seriousness of his speculative aspiration to a condition of music when he writes with irony in "On the Music of the Spheres" that he is "avoiding trite and commonplace subjects" (602). Milton tells us that what he says he says "in jest," but the prolusion is filled with sober observations about the relationship between the discordant human soul and the harmony of the heavenly spheres. The young Milton who wrote the prolusion was already deeply interested in, if not obsessed with, the relationship between *musica mundana* (the music of the spheres), *musica humana* (his soul), and *musica instrumentalis* (his poetry):

For what sane man would suppose that Pythagoras, that god of philosophers, at whose name all the men of his times rose up to do solemn reverence — who, I say, would have supposed that he would have brought forward so well grounded a theory? Certainly, if he taught a harmony of the spheres and a revolution of the heavens to that sweet music, he wished to symbolize in a wise way the intimate relations of the spheres and their even revolution forever in accordance with the law of destiny. (603)

Linking his poetic career and the speculative study of music, Milton offers this insight about the questions he confronts as a poet who wishes to hear and echo "the heavenly tune": "In this [Pythagoras] seems to have followed the example of the poets — or, what is almost the same thing, of the divine oracles — by which no sacred and arcane mystery is ever revealed to vulgar ears without being somehow wrapped up and veiled" (603). Milton was considering the cause, consequence, and possible restoration of the fragmentation of the Muses. He asked himself, for instance, whether there is "ground for believing that everything beyond the moon's sphere is absolutely mute and numb with torpid silence." His answer, moreover, is not in jest. "On the contrary," he writes, "let us blame our own impotent ears, which cannot catch the songs or are unworthy to hear such sweet strains" (604).

Milton follows Plato in many of his beliefs about the harmony of the spheres and the fragmentation of the Muses. Plato's formulations both worried and sustained Milton when he considered what they meant for him as a Christian and a poet: "The greatest of Mother Nature's interpreters, Plato, has followed [Pythagoras], for he has told us that certain sirens have their respective seats on every one of the heavenly spheres and hold both gods and men fast bound by the wonder of their utterly harmonious song" (603). Milton focused upon "that universal interaction of all things, that lovely concord among them, which Pythagoras poetically symbolized as harmony," which "was splendidly and aptly represented by Homer's figure of the golden chain which Jove suspended from heaven" (603). Milton desired to make use of such a chain, for it offered the potential reunion to an "earthy" singer.

The desire to reunite speculation and practice in a way that would once again link earthly poetry and heavenly music, thus allowing him at once to hear and echo, led Milton to shape his poetic career by striving toward the goal he defines at the end of "On the Music of the Spheres":

> Our impotence to hear this harmony seems to be a consequence of the insolence of the robber, Prometheus, which brought so many evils upon men, and at the same time deprived us of that felicity which we shall never be permitted to enjoy as long as we wallow in sin and are brutalized by our animal desires. For how can we, whose spirits, as Persius says, are warped earthward, and are defective in every heavenly element, be sensitive to that celestial sound. If our hearts were as pure, as chaste, as snowy as Pythagoras' was, our ears would resound and be filled with that supremely lovely music of the wheeling stars. Then we should be immune to pain, and we should enjoy the blessing of a peace that the gods themselves might envy. (604)

Milton's speculative agon implicates, as we will see, the agons of future poets writing in English. Milton first declares his goal — to purge his ears and hear "the heavenly tune." He then remarks this conflict:

> But now the hour cuts me short in mid-career, and very fortunately too, for I am afraid that by my rough and inharmonious style I have all along been clashing with this very harmony which I am proclaiming, and that I myself have impeded your hearing of it. And so I shut up. (604)

Even in this early exercise, Milton — the "lady" — was serious about the relationship between chastity and the speculative (theological) causes and consequences of his "inharmonious style." Milton's conception of speculative music governs, as we will see, his conception of poetry and music — as well as his conception of the relationship between poetry and prophecy, eloquence and truth. For Milton, the idea of a musical cosmos of once harmonious concentric spheres was no mere trope, much as for Sir Thomas Browne: "but to call our selves a Microcosme, or little world, I thought it onely a pleasant trope of Rhetorick, till my nearer judgement and second thoughts told me there was a reall truth therein."[10]

Milton is but one example. The claim to song is a trope, but it is one a number of poets use and examine in the hope of reclaiming a "reall truth therein." The aspiration to song involves a complex, arduous attempt to unite speculative and practical harmony, and it produces new pressures upon the ways poets conceive and use the trope of song. Poets worry that the trope itself may ring horribly false, but the desire to sing is overwhelming, worth every risk — except, in the end, the horrible risk of falsehood itself. The possibility of "clashing" with the tune to which he aspires is the paramount worry for any poet who aspires to a condition of music.

For Yeats in "Adam's Curse," as generally for Milton and Stevens, an attempt to achieve a harmony of "sweet sounds together" is the center of a poet's hard labor and restraint of cares:

> Better go down upon your marrow-bones
> And scrub a kitchen pavement, or break stones
> Like an old pauper, in all kinds of weather;
> For to articulate sweet sounds together
> Is to work harder than all these, and yet
> Be thought an idler by the noisy set
> Of bankers, schoolmasters, and clergymen
> The martyrs call the world.[11]

As with the fall begins the labor of human beings, so with the fragmentation of the Muses begins the labor of poets:

> I said, "A line will take us hours maybe;
> Yet if it does not seem a moment's thought,
> Our stitching and unstitching has been naught".

What for Yeats constitutes the seeming ease of "sweet sounds together" is very different, of course, from what constitutes "harmonious song" for Milton. Their conceptions of success and failure are also different: whereas one might be thought an idler, the other might be accused, as Andrew Marvell knew, of "ruin[ing] . . . The sacred truths."

Milton and Yeats identify the same goal, but with crucial differences. Whereas Yeats must achieve what must *seem* like the singing of a moment's thought, for Milton, singing must *be* "unpremeditated." The difference between *seem* and *be* occupied Stevens throughout his career, especially as he sought to sing "A tune beyond us as we are,/ Yet nothing changed by the blue guitar."

We must consider the way poets use the trope of song — the crucial differences between *be* and *seem* — within the context of the relationship between literal and metaphorical language. For different poets in different times, as we will see, the trope of song functions anywhere between the poles of literary hyperbole and literal truth. A claim to song is for some poets merely a figurative literary gesture; for others it is as near as possible to a literal expression of what a poet is and does — a deep examination of the potential musical activities of human consciousness. Susanne K. Langer, remarking her attempt to render a certain idea "more literally and logically," formulates a useful way to think generally about the relationship between figurative and literal language, and it is particularly useful in thinking about the trope of song:

> The process of philosophical thought moves typically from a first, inadequate, but ardent apprehension of some novel idea figuratively expressed, to more and more precise comprehension, until language catches up to logical insight, the figure is dispensed with, and literal expression takes its place. Really

> new concepts, having not names in current language, always
> make their earliest appearance in metaphorical statements;
> therefore the beginning of any theoretical structure is inevita-
> bly marked by fantastic inventions.[12]

The same movement is typical in the process of poetry,
whether during the thousands of years between Homer and
Wordsworth, or even during the careers of individual poets
such as Stevens. No idea demands "more and more precise
comprehension" than the idea of moving from speech to song.
The trope of song demands distinctive forms of scrutiny, new
ways of determining the relationships that may obtain between
literary hyperbole and literal truth.

Two ineluctable facts — metaphors belie truth; literal language never seems to catch up to logical or emotional insight —
motivate a poet to ply his trade, pushing literal expression
toward metaphor, and metaphor toward literal expression,
in the hope of expressing some real truth therein. Hence, when
a poet does the impossible — making it seem for a moment
that language has indeed caught up — we rightly designate
the occurrence a moment of genius. For these are moments
when, as Stevens writes in "Notes Toward a Supreme Fiction," "the language suddenly, with ease,/Said things it had
laboriously spoken."

From Homer to Stevens these are often moments in which,
as Langer observes, there is sudden movement from meta-
phoric to literal statement. The grandness of Homer is evident in the epic similes, but his genius is evident when Hector's
mother "[runs] out of the house *like* a raving woman with
a pulsing heart, and her two handmaidens with her," when
the swift movement toward literal statement razes the simile.
Or when Hermes says to Priam, "You seem to me *like* a be-
loved father," who soon in turn, newly a suppliant, says to
Achilles, "Achilles *like* the gods, remember your father, one
who is of years *like* mine, and on the door-sill of sorrowful
old age."[13] If, as Stevens says, "identity is the vanishing point

of resemblance," the allure of resemblances can seem to protect one from the painful recognition of identity. Later, when Priam says to Achilles, "I put my lips to the hands of the man who has killed my children,"[14] Achilles finally learns the lesson about identity that his *grammaticus*, Phoinix, could never teach him.

Book 9 of Homer's *Iliad* recounts the beginning of this lesson, as well as its deep relation to an aspiration to song. When Phoinix arrives with the embassy, Achilles reveals himself as a young man too able to delight himself with his lyre. Achilles is singing about the fame of other men, deluding himself both that the fame achieved by song means everything and that he himself will enjoy it without having to suffer the labor of its achievement. Phoinix tries unsuccessfully to influence Achilles by telling him the story of Meleagros, a sheer analogy (a trope that is not a trope) that Achilles will not comprehend. An obdurate reader, Achilles is bent toward his lyre, seduced by the lie that song is better than life — corrupted by the deeper lie that the songs he may sing are identical to the life he may live. In the end, the lecture by Phoinix turns out to be a lesson learned only through one's suffering of experience. Eventually, Achilles puts down his lyre, and by book 24 his likeness to a god proves only to emphasize his difference from a god. Finally, a father is a father and a son is a son. As Homer knew, moving from resemblance to identity, is to move from speech to song. Yet this movement is also labor.

Poetry is frequently the labor of pursuing unwelcome identities within the world of alluring tropes and posited resemblances. A metaphor compares two dissimilar objects in an attempt to highlight their similarity. The sentence "John is a tiger" tells us not that John is actually a tiger but that he is in some ways tiger-like. But the same sentence, depending on context, may also remind one just how much John is not a tiger, indeed how much he is like a lamb. As I. A. Richards observes, "there are very few metaphors in which disparities between tenor and vehicle are not as much operative as the similarities."[15]

In part for this reason, Aristotle states in his *Poetics* that he could not teach the use of metaphor, for "this alone cannot be learned from others and its use is a sign of genius, for to use metaphors well is to see resemblance." So, too, it is a sign of genius when a poet, say Stevens, discerns that "identity is the vanishing point of resemblance." Just as there is genius in the good use of metaphor, and a corresponding lack in bad use, so there is genius in comprehending the need to push metaphors toward their vanishing points, to shun metaphors that, however ingenious, lead poets to say something false — especially that they are singing when they know they are not. But a poet who aspires to be a singer can take a lifetime to achieve — and accept — such recognitions. Such moments, and the means to express them, come only to poets who experience the pains and labors of life for which there are no adequate metaphors, for which literal language is a better, perhaps heroic, choice.

Still, as Stevens knew, all language, even literal language, is finally metaphorical. Which is all the more reason a poet must be "a more severe,/ More harassing master."[16] To achieve a plain sense of things, one must supply what Stevens calls the "more urgent proof that the theory/Of poetry is the theory of life/As it is, in the intricate evasions of as." One must work to evade the evasions. And where one attends to one's identity as a poet and a human being, one will think first to harass the trope of song.

But as severe and harassing as the poet may be, there is still an urgent need to assert one's own identity as a singer — or resemblance to a singer — even while knowing one is only a poet, much as Lear feels a need to assert his former identity of king when he discovers he is only a man. So may a poet, even while eloquently divulging how it was lost, refuse to lose forever the harmony of speculative and productive activities — or consciousness otherwise conceived — that would make the poet a singer. The large question remains: how truly to transform speech into song — and how, meanwhile, to persist in claiming to sing. To keep the name of singer one has to reconceive poetic song; one has to reconstitute metaphors, forging resemblances where more differences exist.

"What really separates music from poetry," Lawrence Kramer writes, "is a complementarity in the roles that the two arts assign to their connotative and combinatory aspects: each art makes explicit the dimension that the other leaves tacit." What's more, "a critic who tries to find genuine elements of sonata form in the repetitions of Eliot's *Four Quartets* might as well be on a snipe hunt."[17] And looking generally at the motives of composers, it is clear that "vocal music always seems to be struggling against a latent impulse to dissolve its language away." Composers "seem caught up by what Nietzsche describes as 'a musical excitement that comes from altogether different regions' than does poetic excitement."[18] True, and while poets are slow to give up the power of their "region," they are quick to aspire to a musical condition of excitement, beauty, and truth.

The aspiration to song causes poets to liken speech to song precisely because they know the great degree of difference. One of the major points in Sir Philip Sidney's *An Apology for Poetry* is his assertion that "verse [is] but an ornament to poetry and no cause to poetry."[19] Yet we find Sidney, more famously than any poet of the Renaissance, placing great importance on versification. Derek Attridge asks why "so much of the Elizabethan theoretical and critical writing on literary topics . . . revolves around the question of quantitative versifiers?"[20] We find the answer in Sidney:

> For if *oratio* next to *ratio*, speech next to reason, be the greatest gift bestowed upon mortality, that cannot be praiseless which doth most polish that blessing of speech, which considers each word not only (as a man may say) by his forcible

quality, but by his best measured quantity, carrying even in themselves a harmony (without (perchance) number, measure, order, proportion be in our time grown odious).

Quantitative verse is, according to Sidney, "the only fit speech for music."[21] Observing that the resulting poetry appears to us as applications of force rather than of polish, Attridge wonders shrewdly "why the results seemed far more successful to . . . his immediate audience than they have to later generations."[22] It is because Sidney's contemporaries believed in a harmonious universe of musical spheres, and this fond belief put on them a burden to be antique — to claim identity where it would be better to renounce anything but slight resemblance. On the other hand, as we will see, one may, in the various manners of Milton and Stevens, become a harassing master who sees that any effort to forge every last resemblance where it does not exist only obscures the true and inevitable vanishing point one labors so long and hard to achieve.

We may consider individual reconceptions of poetic song, and the labors to effect them, only after considering further the relationship between figurative and literal language and its relevance to the ways various poets use the trope of song. A poet's claim to song may occur on two levels, conceived from either of the two perspectives we will be considering: speculative or practical. When one examines the trope of song from a practical perspective, the statement "I sing" could literally be true; it is merely the case that it is false.[23] Considered in practical terms, that is, the trope of song constitutes an unsuccessful attempt to make a literal statement, rather than a conceptual metaphor: the poet claims to be singing, but the poet is not even reciting. When a poet conceives the trope in speculative terms, in contrast, its metaphorical (or conceptual) force becomes clear: the claim to song is a conceptual metaphor that expresses an aspiration to speculative harmony, not an ability to achieve the pleasing effects of vocal rhythm and pitch that are achieved by an actual singer.

"It is a prerequisite to any discussion of metaphor," as George Lakoff and Mark Turner observe, "that we make a distinction between basic conceptual metaphors, which are cognitive in nature, and particular linguistic expressions of these conceptual metaphors." Although "a particular poetic passage may give a unique linguistic expression of a basic metaphor, the conceptual metaphor underlying it may nonetheless be extremely common." As Lakoff and Turner explain, "a given passage may express a common conceptual metaphor in a way that is linguistically either commonplace or idiosyncratic," but "an idiosyncratic conceptual metaphor is another matter. By its very nature," they argue, "it cannot yet be deeply conventionalized in our thought, and therefore its linguistic expression will necessarily be idiosyncratic in at least some respect. Modes of thought that are not themselves conventional cannot be expressed in conventional language. In short," they observe, "idiosyncrasy of language may or may not express idiosyncrasy of thought, but idiosyncratic thought requires idiosyncratic language."[24]

The expression "I sing" is extremely common. But the conceptual metaphor that is the basis for the poetic expression becomes, in its idiosyncratic treatment by a speculative poet, unique. Milton's conceptual metaphor is different from Whitman's, and both are idiosyncratic. But the linguistic expression of neither is "necessarily . . . idiosyncratic"; both use the verb *to sing*. The trope of song presents an intriguing exception to linguistic practice: the phrase "I sing" is idiosyncratic precisely in the way it expresses a poet's desire to make the vehicle and tenor identical. Speculative poets either invoke or seek to develop a context (aesthetic or religious) that makes their claim to song an idiosyncratic expression.

When a poet writes with only practical musical effects in mind, in contrast, the poet claims to achieve by one form of *musica instrumentalis* (poetry) the esteemed qualities of another form of *musica instrumentalis* (music). Such poets wish merely to attribute to their transcriptions of vocal effects certain qualities of actual singing. When such poets write "I sing," neither their conception nor their expression is idiosyncratic; there is, moreover, no conflict between literal and metaphorical meaning. This is possible because a practical conception of poetry either holds the Muses to be still harmonious or sees their fragmentation as inconsequential.

For a poet with either of these practical conceptions, poetry *is* a kind of music, for poetry is composed of rhythm, pitch, and a number of other musical elements. During the early part of the Renaissance in England, for example, one was likely to think the Muses once again united, and a poet was likely to be an actual singer. Thomas Campion is a poet for whom there is no fragmentation of the Muses, for whom poetry and music are literally — and joyously — one:

> Come, let us sound with melody the praises
> Of the kings king, th'omnipotent creator,
> Author of number, that hath all the world in
>   Harmony framed.[25]

Like Campion, Milton was an accomplished musician, but Milton could not satisfy himself with his practical musical skill, however considerable he knew it to be. A deep speculative belief in the fragmentation of the Muses led Milton to what became a crucial question in English poetry: how might a man, by means of his practical poetic art (*musica instrumentalis*), achieve the speculative harmony (between *musica humana* and *musica mundana*) that would transform the metaphor of song into a literal expression of the speculative harmony he wishes to achieve? For Milton, the question reaches a grand pitch, and it perseveres, as we will see, through myriad changes, in romanticism and modernism.

Poets as different as Milton and Stevens aspire to transform their claims to song into literal statements of a conceptual truth. A poet concerned with such speculative questions cannot merely assert the practical resemblances between poetry and song. He must, rather, attend to the differences between poetry and song.

In the most general, practical sense, poetry is — for the reasons expressed by Aristotle — "musical." But the musicality of language and poetry is still a mystery that has not been adequately described by any treatise. It is perhaps most adequately described by the hyperbolic idiom of its culture. Among other contemporaries who praised Shakespeare for his music, Richard Barnfield lauded his "honey-flowing vein," and John Weever called the poet "honey-tongu'd."[26] And which of us is not seduced first by the "honey" of Shakespeare, or the "sound" of Stevens, even before we are moved by their spectacular plots and supreme fictions? The pleasing effects of musical language exert a mysterious power that cannot be fully analyzed or explained, whether by Neoplatonism, rhetorical theory, or metrical and tonal analysis. Musical speech is a chief reason for seeing Shakespeare performed, an indispensable aspect of performance that is itself too widely neglected, as Yeats bemoaned in a remark about a school for players at Stratford: "Th[e] chief players will need to bring but few of their supporters, for the school will be able to fill all the lesser parts with players who are slowly recovering the lost tradition of musical speech."[27] Such a loss is a shame. And there is the possibility of further loss, which this book attempts to forestall: the loss of an appreciation of the wonderful ways poets from Shakespeare to Stevens reconcile speculation and practice as part of a larger attempt to tune real speech into transcendent song. The triumph of a poet's musical speech may best be appreciated, I am suggesting, within the speculative context furnished by the poet.

In English poetry, Shakespeare was the first poet to make speculative music a subject inseparable from questions about poetic authority and the status of human speech as music. Milton took this relationship to another level. But neither Shakespeare nor Milton left behind a separate, explicit statement of his poetic that would help us to read his poems — as did Sidney, Daniel, Ronsard, Du Bellay, and others before them. At the beginning of her attempt to provide one, Ruth Wallerstein writes that "we still have too little understanding" of "the poetic art of the seventeenth century. . . . We do not yet pick up most seventeenth century poems with that sense of being at home in their modes and patterns which would give us a unified impression of their substance and beauty."[28] One such pattern in the poetry of Shakespeare and Milton is use of allusions to speculative music to define the potential and limitations of poetry to achieve a condition of music.

Much has been written about the relationship between actual music and poetry, but little has been written about the relationship between speculative music and poetry, general literary interest in speculative music having peaked and declined in the 1970s. In the few studies of poetic allusions to speculative music we do have, moreover, the writers consider the relationship between poetry and speculative music mainly from the perspective of practical music. And scholars who examine the importance of speculative music tend to see only impersonal "treatment" of an idea.

The "treatment" to which scholars most frequently — and rightly — refer is Lorenzo's speech about "the touches of sweet harmony" in Shakespeare's *The Merchant of Venice.* James Hutton greatly influenced criticism of Lorenzo's speech and of Shakespeare's "view" of music, as well as general discussions of the relationship between poetry and music. Hutton reduces Shakespeare's view to Lorenzo's speech, and Lorenzo's speech to Neoplatonic "shorthand." He also reads later poets — his chief example is Milton — merely as "followers" of this "tradition," using the same arguments to explain musical passages in both poets, and others as well.[29] Other scholars who have done valuable work — John Hollander and S. K. Heninger, for example — follow Hutton's assumption that Shakespeare's "shorthand treatment" typifies the thought of an age that extends to Milton.[30] This view diminishes the achievements of both Shakespeare and Milton; it also obscures their diverse influence on later poets.

Several scholars have provided us with valuable studies of allusions to speculative music, but they have perpetuated two general errors that this book, as part of its study of the aspiration to song, attempts to amend. Literary scholars tend to look too much to Neoplatonic philosophy for universal explanations of speculative allusions; and historians of ideas, in their attempts to cull poetic examples "treating" the "idea of cosmic harmony," show insufficient concern for historical and biographical contexts, for important shifts within poetic periods and individual careers. In the end, both groups conclude that speculative music was a contemporary "Neoplatonic" tradition that Shakespeare and Milton alike appropriated or followed.[31]

Such views, taken loosely, may seem at first to suffice for a general reading of Shakespeare, in whose work we witness an extraordinary ability to make poetry of Neoplatonic commonplaces. But the reductive view that Shakespeare merely appropriated Neoplatonic doctrine needs to be revised. In *The Merchant of Venice*, we will see, Shakespeare subtly juxtaposes opposing theories of music to complicate and mediate the extreme views that compose the drama of the play. Contrary to what scholars have long suggested, Lorenzo speaks for neither Shakespeare nor the play. Jessica, to a degree, does. She recommends paying a new kind of attention to both the powers of actual music and the importance of an anti-Neoplatonic speculative perspective. Other plays further reveal Shakespeare's interest in using contrary practical and speculative theories to explore the power of poetry and its relationship to "the sweet power of music." The mistake of applying

Neoplatonic answers to Platonic questions leads, we will see, to a blurring of differences between Platonism and Neoplatonism that were crucial to both Shakespeare and Milton.

As Leo Spitzer warns with insight in the introduction of his invaluable study *Classical and Christian Ideas of World Harmony*, "the treatment of the peculiar subject of world harmony involves a special danger: the harmonizing habit of thought which historically underlies this concept may encroach upon the mental processes of the historical semanticist who seeks to study the conception. . . ."[32] The "harmonizing tendency" Spitzer warns against has tended to accompany a kind of humanism in which scholars merely endorse remarkable conceptual metaphors rather than analyze what is truly remarkable (or idiosyncratic) about them. John H. Long, for example, writes that Shakespeare referred to "common ideas" "when he had John of Gaunt . . . refer to the 'music of men's lives' — *musica humana* as the theorists called it — the harmony of the four humors that was but an echo of the divine harmony of God and His angels."[33] In his study of speculative music, Heninger sees this "common idea" as common not only to Shakespeare and Sidney but also to an age including Milton: "Sidney is not alone in his assumption that Pythagorean cosmology provides the proper patterns for beauty in our lives."[34] The idea is common, but the comparison of Shakespeare and Sidney deserves a more flexible argument than Heninger, among others, has made. For Milton, this "common idea" was common and necessary, but no longer true, the fall having torqued human souls — and indeed the universe — out of tune. No other single theological or cosmological truth more greatly affects Milton's conception of himself as a poet, and of his poems as song.[35] Milton confronts the fragmentation of the Muses more vigorously than any poet before him. Writing after Shakespeare, Milton developed remarkable means of both setting into profound conflict and reconciling Aristotelian rhetorical theory and Platonic speculation.

While this study does not offer a critique of Neoplatonism or Orphism, or any other philosophies or theories, it does caution against broad misapplication of philosophy to specific questions about the relationship between music and poetry raised by individual poets — especially when they threaten our ability to appreciate fully the complexity of and tensions within their poetic achievements. Even Spitzer is not fully attentive to the idiosyncratic development of the "idea of world harmony" in the work of individual poets. He does not distinguish, for example, Shakespeare's use of "the idea of world harmony" from Milton's. Nor does he remark important differences between Milton's and Goethe's conceptions of the relationship between heavenly music and earthly poetry.

Poets, as Aristotle asserted when considering the case of Empedocles, do not engage in mere philosophy. But certain philosophical concerns are at the center of many poets' conceptions of themselves and of their poems. Great poets borrow from and revise various and conflicting poetic and philosophical traditions, and they rarely effect clear, unambiguous reconciliation. Stevens's observation "that the probings of the philosopher are deliberate, but the probings of the poet fortuitous" offers, Frank Kermode points out, "another reason why it is so hard to make lasting matches between poetry and systematic thought."[36] This study attempts neither to assign ideas to poets or to trace the history of ideas. While it addresses these matters, it focuses on the spectacular ways poets continually harass and reconceive the trope of song. In its attempt to analyze the different relationships established by different poets between poetry and song, this book does at times engage the ancient and ongoing debates relating poetry to rhetoric, philosophy, and theology. The relationships between poetry and music, music and philosophy, and poetry and philosophy are fruitfully complex, and I attempt to consider the ways in which aspects of these relationships affected certain poets. I ask the reader to keep in mind the large background to which this study attempts to add its part.

Chapter 1, an analysis of ancient, medieval, and Renaissance theories of speculative music, provides an historical perspective from which to consider important old and recent debates. It examines the complex relationship between music and poetry in the West, focusing on the important relationship between Plato's notion of a "true musician" and the aspiration to heavenly song. Chapter 2 focuses on Shakespeare's brilliant and inventive use of commonplace ideas about practical and speculative music, and examines his influential view of the "sweet power" of poetry and music. Chapter 3 examines the poetry and career of Milton, who made the trope of song not only a central subject of his poems but the central principle of his remarkable theological poetic. As these chapters demonstrate, Shakespeare and Milton shaped the possible course of future aspirations to song in English poetry. Chapter 4 focuses on the distinctively romantic reconceptions of poetic song advanced by Blake and Wordsworth, as well as the "mute music" of Shelley and the triumphant song of Keats in his great odes. Chapter 5, which first considers the similarities and differences between romantic and modern aspirations to song, focuses on the poetry of Yeats and Stevens. Stevens effects a remarkable turn in the long tradition of aspirations toward music, demanding, finally, that

> Poetry
>
> Exceeding music must take the place
> Of empty heaven and its hymns,
> Ourselves in poetry must take their place,
> Even in the chattering of your guitar.[37]

Stevens, as we will see, brings the musical speculation of the ancients to a modern pitch, reconceiving in his own musical terms Plato's articulation of the "ancient cycle" of *eros*.

Although for every individual poet there are other concerns, other roles to consider, the role of singer is the first and favorite role of self-definition and evaluation for almost every great poet from Homer to Stevens. Some appear to resolve with ease the problems brought about by the fragmentation of the Muses. Others, however considerable their poetic skills, refuse to conceal an ineluctable speculative discord behind the practical harmony of poetic utterance. These refusals not only constitute remarkable aspirations to a condition of transcendent music; they reveal confidence in the speculative role of language to define and approach a condition of music.

For reasons this book attempts to explain, desire itself — especially erotic pursuit of a condition of music — can never truly be historicized, whether by new historicisms or postmodern critical practices, whether sociological or musicological. What these and related approaches reveal is the value of going back and examining further the history of musical ideas and their relationship to poetic forms of individual desire. Recent critical practices betray the erotic — and epistemic — displacements critics hazard when they "culturally produce" the subjectivity of others and invalidate their terms of desire.[38] As we will see, attempts to translate the desire for a harmonious self capable of song to social or other terms only confirm such desire to be immutable.

Doubtless, the aspiration to become a heavenly singer might strike a twentieth century reader as mere poetic convention, mere hyperbole, mere mythology. And doubtless it is. But it is hyperbolic convention that Shakespeare accepted as well as debunked; hyperbolic truth upon which Milton based his theological poetic; mythology that Stevens struggled candidly to make his own. The trope of song is central to Milton's theory of prophecy and deeply related to romantic theories of imagination and vision. It is basic to romantic concerns about the inefficacy of any poetic song that is a "product of consciousness,"[39] and crucial to Stevens's conception of a supreme fiction. For the poets who are the subjects of this book, a speculative conception of poetry does not produce mere philosophical deliberation. It leads, rather, to new poetic styles, new ways of aspiring to a condition of song. In English poetry, we will see, the most intense devotions to musical speculation have produced some of the greatest and most practically innovative achievements of poetic song.

ONE

ᚱᚨ

Plato's "True Musician" and the Trope of Song

It is commonly believed that Homer sang his epics to the accompaniment of a phorminx, yet it is likely that even Homer was not actually singing when he used the verb "to sing." The ancient Greeks made distinctions between speech, recitative (παρακαταλογή), and song. Homer's "song," as M. L. West writes, was delivered in recitative: "Classical writers distinguish rhapsodes from citharodes. The latter sang the poetry of Homer and others to melodies of their own, accompanying themselves on the cithara, and they looked back to Terpander as the famous exponent of this art." Homer, West observes, "was thought of as a rhapsode, and a rhapsode was evidently less of a musician than a citharode. ἀείδειν ["to sing"] can be used of him, but more often it is λέγειν ["to speak"]. He does not normally seem to play an instrument." For these reasons, as West writes, "he was noted for histrionic rather than musicianly qualities. Such was the rhapsode of

27

the classical period, and it was considered that he descended from the poet-rhapsode such as Homer."[1] Homer used the verb "to sing" (ἀείδειν) to designate the activity produced by the Muses in his body and soul, but he was as distinguishable from the actual singers of his day as Wallace Stevens was from Louis Armstrong.

From Homer's invocation of his epic muse to Stevens's mention of his fictive music and blue guitar, our acceptance of seemingly conventional claims to song is based partly on a myth involving Homer that explains little about later uses of the trope. A brief study of the relationship between poetry and music in ancient Greece might help us better to understand why so many poets have expressed the aspiration not to write a poem but to sing a song. Such aspirations originate not in the similarities but rather the differences between poetry and music.

Plato's "True Musician"

"The Western world inherited from the ancient Greeks," as Nan Cooke Carpenter writes in her examination of the study of music in the Middle Ages and Renaissance in Europe, "a culture comprising two different traditions of musical studies: music in connection with poetry, the two inseparable and originally allied with religious practices; and music related not to literature but to mathematics, being one of the four mathematical disciplines (all having a common basis in ratio and proportion) which preceded the study of philosophy."[2] Distinguishing two ways poets could think about unifying the activities of human consciousness, the two disciplines (*musica practica* and *musica speculativa*) link poetry and music in disparate ways that correspond to two distinct traditions.

In the tradition of Pythagoras, which Socrates and Plato developed,[3] practical and speculative music were inextricably linked while also clearly distinguished.[4] The study of music is said to have been initiated by Pythagoras on his Samian monochord. At the practical level, the student was taught — by the manipulation and plucking of a single string — musical and mathematical relations. It was believed, in turn, that these musical relations constituted the organizing principles of the universe. Influenced by a complex of assimilated ideas from the East and the West that is difficult if not impossible to trace, Pythagoras contributed to the West the grand and lasting metaphor of a musical universe — much as Thales gave us water and Heraclitus gave us fire and, of course, strife. Like the other pre-Socratic thinkers, Pythagoras was not a *philosopher* in the modern sense, but rather an ancient composite of scientist, theologian, and mythmaker, a man set upon the task of deriving an explanation of the universe and offering cultic prescriptions for ethical conduct that could help make one a harmonious part of it.

In the Pythagorean tradition, practical music was taught as part of a program of study associated with what later became the medieval trivium — grammar, logic, and rhetoric — and was closely linked to the study of poetry and eloquence. Speculative music, which was taught as a second program of study, was associated with the subjects that became the medieval quadrivium — arithmetic, geometry, astronomy, and music. Contemplative, mathematical, and ethical in its focus, the speculative study of music developed systematically by Plato was central to his philosophy.[5] Socrates makes the case for the "sovereignty" of music within his system of education in the third book of the *Republic*:

> And is it not for this reason . . . that education in music is most sovereign, because more than anything else rhythm and harmony find their way to the inmost soul and take strongest hold upon it, bringing with them and imparting grace, if one is rightly trained, and otherwise the contrary? And further, because omissions and the failure of beauty in things badly made or grown would be most quickly perceived by one who was

> properly educated in music, and so, feeling distaste rightly, he
> would praise beautiful things and take delight in them and
> receive them into his soul to foster its growth and become him-
> self beautiful and good.[6]

The speculative study of music is, says Socrates, the archetypal study of beauty, which (as Keats, for both similar and
different reasons, would later observe) is truth:

> By heaven, am I not right in saying that by the same token we
> shall never be *true musicians*, either — neither we nor the
> guardians that we have undertaken to educate — until we are
> able to recognize the forms of soberness, courage, liberality,
> and high-mindedness and all their kindred and their opposites
> too . . .? (402b–c)[7]

Soberness, courage, liberality, and high mindedness, not
lessons on a lyre, are the concerns of the "true musician."
The "true musician" is an ethical philosopher who strives to
achieve the proper tuning of "the inmost soul." One studies
the "actual" sounds made by the monochord only to begin
one's study of the abstract speculative principles of *cosmos*.
In the speculative tradition of Plato, harmony is not a metaphorical explanation of the universe; it is a literal statement
about what the universe is, and it becomes the basis for an
ethical, metaphysical, cosmological program of study in which
the human body and soul may strive to achieve harmony with
the music of the heavens. Hence, in the *Republic* and other
dialogues, just as poetry is sternly considered inferior to philosophy, training in practical music is considered inferior to
training in speculative music.

These passages in the *Republic*, along with the myth of Er
and passages in the *Laws* and *Timaeus*, are related to Socrates'
comment in Plato's *Phaedrus* on the difference between earthly
poetry and heavenly song: "Of that place beyond the heavens," Socrates declares, "none of our earthly poets has yet sung,
and none shall sing worthily."[8] It is a harsh statement, one
many would readily attribute to Socrates' or Plato's aversion

to poetry. But Socrates offers a warning to those who would evade its truth:

> But this is the manner of it, for assuredly we must be bold to speak what is true, and above all when our discourse is upon truth. It is there that true being dwells, without color or shape, that cannot be touched; reason alone, the soul's pilot, can behold it, and all the true knowledge is knowledge thereof. Now even as the mind of a god is nourished by reason and knowledge, so also is it with every soul that has a care to receive her proper food; wherefore when at last she has beheld being she is well content, and contemplating truth she is nourished and prospers, until the heaven's revolution brings her back full circle. (247c–d)

The last clause, which concerns the soul's potential completion of the cosmic circle, receives elaboration in the *Timaeus*.[9] Socrates' claim that "[no poet] shall sing worthily" is concerned with the human potential for just such an accomplishment.

More than affirming that no poet yet sings worthily of heaven ("οὔτε ποτὲ ὑμνήσει κατ᾿ἀξίαν"), Socrates is explaining that those who aspire to song must confront with soberness and courage the difference between earthly poetry and heavenly song:

> of the other souls that which best follows a god and becomes most like thereunto raises her charioteer's head into the outer region, and is carried round with the gods in the revolution, but being confounded by her steeds she has much ado to discern the things that are. (248a)

As in the *Republic*, Socrates here devalues poetry because it is three times removed, ontologically, from Truth. This ontological argument addresses the dangerous resemblance between heavenly song and earthly poetry. Continuing the metaphor of the steed, Socrates maintains that "many have their wings all broken, and for all their toiling they are balked, every one, of the full vision of being, and departing therefrom, they feed upon the food of semblance" (247d–248d). These are matters that concern poets as different as Milton and Stevens. The aspiration to song, as Socrates could see, is central to a poet's aspiration to turn *seem* into *be*. And the attempt involves worries about "clashing" and broken wings.

Socrates next recounts, in descending order, the nine levels of disharmonious consciousness (and mere semblances of being) to which a soul may fall:

> In her first birth she shall not be planted (φυτεῦσαι) in any brute beast, but the soul that hath seen the most of being shall enter into the human babe that shall grow into a seeker after wisdom or beauty, a follower of the Muses and a lover; the next, having seen less, shall dwell in a king that abides by law, or a warrior and ruler; the third in a statesman . . .; the fourth in an athlete, or physical trainer, or physician; the fifth shall have the life of a prophet or a Mystery priest. (248d–e)

This well-wrought passage is worthy of a poet. But Plato would not have welcomed such a comparison. Arriving at the "soul" of "a poet or other imitative artist," Socrates concludes the list of the first five categories, which are governed in the Greek by the verb φυτεῦσαι. He then begins a new sentence that is governed by the verb ἁρμόσει:

> To the sixth that of a poet or other imitative artist shall be fittingly given (ἁρμόσει); the seventh shall live in an artisan or farmer; the eighth in a Sophist or demagogue; the ninth in a tyrant.[10]

The precision of the grammatical construction serves emphatically to debase poetry by distinguishing it strongly from the first five categories and associating it with the last three.[11] The first five categories are, significantly, ones of which Socrates approves, whereas the last four are not. The verb ἁρμόσει, moreover, enacts an interesting juxtaposition of connotations.

The word ἁρμόσει, a form of the verb ἁρμόζω, means "to fit together" or "to join" (as in "to the sixth . . . shall be *fittingly* given." The verb ἁρμόσει not only denotes *fittingly*; it carries with it also a playfully derogatory connotation. A poet, Socrates implies, is a kind of "joiner," and is thereby to be associated with the artisan (δημιουργικός) and to be distinguished, on account of his removal from being, from the follower of the Muses (μουσικοῦ), as well as, certainly, from god as demiurge.[12] But another sense of the word is actualized here, an ironic one: the verb ἁρμόσει and the word for harmony (ἁρμονία) are verbal and nominal forms from the same Greek root. By using the verb ἁρμόσει to allude to the poet's role as a joiner and distinguish him from a follower of the Muses, Socrates emphasizes the degree to which the soul of a poet has fallen away from the harmony (ἁρμονία) of which it was once a part. Using the same root to actualize antithetical meanings, Socrates locates the speculative basis — and anxiety — of a poet's aspiration to song.

By locating the sixth kind of soul in the poet, Socrates confirms his reputation as an enemy of poetry. But he is so scrupulous a critic he makes himself a potentially constructive friend. Socrates is universally strict: even "the soul that hath seen the most of being" shall possess neither wisdom nor the power of heavenly song until it completes its circle.[13] Whereas a soul far removed from being is *fitted* for a poet, the most nearly harmonious soul, "the soul that hath seen the most of being," is born a "seeker after wisdom or beauty, a follower of the Muses and a lover" (φιλοσόφου ἢ φιλοκάλου ἢ μουσικοῦ τινος καὶ ἐρωτικοῦ).[14] Such a soul is devoted to reattuning itself with the harmony of the heavens. This it can do only when — upon the completion of the cosmic circle — the soul "discerns justice, its very self, and likewise temperance, and knowledge, not the knowledge that is neighbor to becoming and varies with the various objects to which we commonly ascribe being, but the veritable knowledge of being that veritably is" (247d–e). To desire to move from resemblance to identity is to desire to join the Muses in song.

What is notable about Socrates' consideration of poets, although more subtle than his renowned contempt for poetry, is his understanding of the poetic aspiration *to sing* (ὑμνῆσαι). Socrates compares poetry and singing not because they are markedly similar but because they are so different — because he understands that heavenly song will forever be the goal of poets who aspire not to become "joiners" or "mimetic artists" but "true musicians." "True musicians" — and poets who would sing "worthily" — confront their removal from being and truth in speculative terms. This strictness of Socrates, as we will see, exerts a large influence on a number of English poets.

"Training in practical music," as Carpenter points out, "was preliminary to the second kind of musical culture which grew up among the Greek philosophers; rationalistic explanations of music as a part of mathematics, of universal harmony — indeed, the harmony of the universe in a form perceptible to man."[15] Carpenter overlooks, however, the crucial detail most often overlooked by scholars concerned with the "treatment" of the "topic" of speculative music in Renaissance poetry. As Plato stated — in a central tenet of his speculative philosophy — heavenly harmony is a form *not* perceptible to human beings until they complete the cosmic circle. And even Socrates had not yet completed his.

Although he censures them for their failure to admit their removal from the heavenly harmony, Socrates owes a large part of his conception of the "true musician" to what he observes poets themselves aspiring to do. In the invocation to his *Theogony*, for example, Hesiod asserts a certain principle of moral ordering by the phrase ἀρχώμεθ᾽ ἀείδειν (let us begin to sing): "From the Heliconian Muses let us begin to sing . . ." (Μουσάων Ἑλικωνιάδων ἀρχώμεθ᾽ ἀειδειν . . .).[16] In the active voice the verb αρχω means "to govern"; in the middle voice it means "to rule yourself." An important moral principle underlies the grammatical structure of the language, *cosmos* and *logos* being related: to rule yourself *is* to begin. Self-rule is initiative; and initiative requires self-rule. In his Third Pythian Ode, Pindar emphasizes this important link between the two meanings of ἄρχω, *ruling* and *beginning*.[17] Before he can begin to compose his song, the singer has himself to be composed —has, as Milton would later write, "himself to be a true poem."

Whatever his stern view of their imitations of matters divine, Socrates shares with the early Greek poets a deep understanding of this relationship between self-rule and singing. As Socrates says in the *Republic*, after linking harmony and justice: "But the truth of the matter was, as it seems, that justice is indeed something of this kind, yet not in regard to the doing of one's own business externally, but with regard to that which is within and in the true sense concerns one's self, and the things of one's self." Wisdom is not knowledge one might acquire about phenomena in the world but the just, harmonious relation between the soul and the universe:

> a man . . . should dispose well of what in the true sense of the word is properly his own, and having first attained to self-mastery and beautiful order within himself, and having harmonized these three principles, the notes or intervals of three terms quite literally the lowest, the highest, and the mean, and all others there may be between them, and having linked and bound all three together and made of himself a unit, one man instead of many, self-controlled and in unison, he should then and then only turn to practice. (443d)

Socrates' concern is the speculative process of making oneself a follower of the muses, a true musician — a true singer.

When Socrates declares "Of that place beyond the heavens no poet has yet sung, nor shall sing worthily," he distinguishes mimetic poetry and heavenly song by a line as fast as the one that divides the earth from the heavens, appearance from truth.[18] Socrates draws attention to the distinction between earthly music (which may be harmonious to our ears but is always variable) and "the [heavenly] song" (τοῦ νόμου), which is Plato's invariable standard of harmony. As G. M. A. Grube observes, "Plato is playing on the double meaning of the Greek word νόμος which means both a *song* and a *law*."[19]

Making clearer our understanding of Plato's conception of the trope of song, we may restore the meaning and force that future poets would give it. Socrates' strict speculative philosophy engages the deep desire — common to poets from Homer to Stevens — to transcend merely practical aspects of music, to achieve a condition of transcendent song, thus making of themselves not merely poets among men but singers who sing with — or to — the gods.

Beyond Aristotelian Praxis: *Singing to the Gods*

Socrates and Plato doubtless set exorbitant goals, and becoming a "true musician" is perhaps their highest. Speaking of the orators who "will never attain such success as is within the grasp of mankind," Socrates asserts that the true capability of mankind is greater than the ability afforded by rhetorical *praxis*. Aspiring to go beyond rhetorical *praxis*, Socrates speaks toward the end of *Phaedrus* of the "competence which the wise man should exert not for the sake of speaking to and dealing with his fellow men, but that he may be able to speak what is pleasing to the gods" (273e). Socrates speaks here of a human power (δυνατὸν ἀνθρώπῳ), which his antirhetorical, dialectical program will cultivate.[20] Anticipating not only the impatience of his interlocutor, Phaedrus, but also that of a long history of philosophers and literary critics unwilling to stay his course, Socrates warns about the difficulty of his program: "So don't be surprised that we have to make a long detour; it is because the goal is glorious, though not the goal you think of" (274a). Socrates never says the goal — rejoining "the song" — will be achieved. He asserts only the paradox

that limitation must be recognized as part of human potential. As Montaigne writes, quoting Amyot's translation of
Plutarch's *Life of Pompey*: "*D'autant est tu dieu comme/ Tu
te recognois homme.*"[21] "You are as much a god as you will
own/ That you are nothing but a man alone."[22]

Despite Socrates' adjurations about settling for a less lofty
goal, Phaedrus suggests to Socrates that language should be
used for recreation: "How far superior to the other sort is the
recreation that a man finds in words, when he discourses about
justice and the other topics you speak of" (276e). Perceiving
Phaedrus's misinterpretation of most of what he has said,
Socrates responds: "Yes indeed, dear Phaedrus. But far more
excellent, I think, is the serious treatment of them, which
employs the art of dialectic" (276e), which Socrates then proceeds to define:

> The dialectician selects a soul of the right type, and in it he
> plants and sows his words founded on knowledge, words which
> can defend both themselves and him who planted them, words
> which instead of remaining barren contain a seed whence new
> words grow up in new characters, whereby the seed is vouch-
> safed immortality, and its possessor the fullest measure of bless-
> edness that man can attain unto. (276e–277a)

The human power (δυνατὸν ἀνθρώπῳ) to strive is "the best of
one's ability," and such strife leads to "the fullest measure of
blessedness that man can attain unto."[23] Knowing from experience its connection to the song of the soul, Emily Dickinson
believed in this power:

> "Hope" is the thing with feathers —
> That perches in the soul —
> And sings the tune without the words —
> And never stops — at all —

"I shall keep singing!" she declares, and with even more
desire to complete herself: "I shall bring a fuller tune." She
will do so when she comes, in good Platonic fashion, full circle

back: "Vespers — are sweeter than Matins — Signor — /Morning — only the seed of Noon —."[24]

In Plato's *Phaedrus*, Socrates attacks the Sophistic valuation of rhetorical persuasion: "One who would learn to speak . . . should only resort to me after he has come into possession of truth" (260e). And although one may not expect to apprehend the transcendent Truth of the Forms in one's lifetime, one must not satisfy oneself with anything less than a lifetime's attempt, the dedication of the ἐρωτικός to pursue one's completion of the cosmic circle.

Socrates established a profound link between the philosophical and musical desires for poetic authority. Indeed, the etymology for the word *muses* offered in the *Cratylus* confirms and underscores his conception of the speculative aspiration to song: "The name of the Muses and of music would seem to be derived from their making philosophical inquiries (μῶσθαι)" (406a). In his analysis of this passage, Trimpi observes that "[t]he word μῶσθαι (from μῶμαι), meaning 'to strive after,' 'to long for,' or 'to desire eagerly,' shares with 'philosophy' (φιλοσοφία) the conception of 'loving' and with 'searching' (ζήτησις) the conception of 'inquiry.'"[25]

The Aristotelian rhetorical tradition offers invaluable learning about plot and persuasion, but it does not address the speculative aspects of poetic authority considered by Socrates. Rather than a program for immediate practical success, Socrates offers Glaucon the prospect of surer authority in *The Republic*:

> You, said I, are speaking of the worthies who vex and torture the strings and rack them on the pegs, but — not to draw out the comparison with strokes of the plectrum and the musician's complaints of too responsive and too reluctant strings — I drop the figure, and tell you that I do not mean these people, but those others whom we just now said we would interrogate about harmony. Their method exactly corresponds to that of the astronomer, for the numbers they seek are those found in these

heard concords, but they do not ascend to generalized problems and the consideration of which numbers are inherently
concordant and which not and why in each case.

A superhuman task, he said.

Say, rather, useful, said I, for the investigation of the beautiful and the good, but if otherwise pursued, useless. (531b–c)

The task of the "true musician" is good, Socrates claims, not
for its transcendent achievement but for its approach to a difficult task:

And what is more, I said, I take it that if the investigation of all
these studies goes far enough to bring out their community
and kinship with one another, and to infer their affinities, then
to busy ourselves with them contributes to our desired end,
and the labor taken is not lost, but otherwise it is in vain.

I too so surmise, said he, but it is a huge task of which you
speak, Socrates.

Are you talking about the prelude, I said, or what? Or do we
not know that all this is but the preamble of the law itself, the
prelude of the [song] that we have to apprehend? (531d–e)[26]

"True musicians" see personal strife as "the prelude" of the
songs they wish to rejoin. Those who do not seek to become
"true musicians" are only poets, Sophists, rhetoricians — they
"vex and torture strings," concern themselves with the
effects of sounds on the body, rather than with the potential
harmony of "the inmost soul."

Of course, we really have no idea what kind of practical
music Plato was objecting to. Was it the ancient Greek version of Led Zeppelin? Would he have objected to a composer
such as Beethoven? Perhaps Beethoven would have caused
even Plato to alter his speculative program. We cannot know.
But the value of Plato's speculative conception of the relationship between heavenly and earthly music is clear. It would
become central to Shakespeare, Milton, Keats, and others.

Because it offers only *eros*, *dialectic*, and *aporia*, the speculative musical program of Socrates and Plato is not only

difficult — it is forbidding, reserved for the "worthies." Socrates does, however, have a practical side. For Socrates, practical music is the public, ceremonious (religious and or social) kind of music considered to be the sister art of poetry and dance. In the *Republic* and *Laws*, Plato suggests that practical music is a necessity for those who are not fit for speculative study. Plato writes in the *Laws* that the lyre is to be taught for three years in order to make good citizens.[27] This practical study is, as we see in the *Republic*, like a patriotic guitar lesson in which one learns to play the National Anthem without distortion. In ancient Greece, the main purpose of the practical study of music was to educate young men in the performance of rituals that would preserve its system of ethical, religious, and social values. The study of music was similar in the universities of the Christian world in the Middle Ages and the Renaissance. During the Renaissance in England, for example, the universities followed a program of practical musical education in which most students were simply taught according to an acceptable standard of mimicry to chant a tune with a similarly trained chorus.

The effect of this practical ritual is that students sing without knowing what they are singing, solely for the purpose of fulfilling religious ceremonies. In England there were statutes requiring students to learn music so that academic services could be performed. Carpenter observers that "[T]he Elizabethan Statutes, the *Nova Statuta* of 1564–65, 'set out afresh the rules for reading, disputations and degrees . . . reverting apparently to the old ideas which the Edwardian Statutes had varied.' The *forma* to be fulfilled before attaining the baccalaureate . . . specified four years (16 terms) in grammar, rhetoric, dialectic, arithmetic, and '*in musica Boetium*,' giving the length of time to be spent in each, including '*duos (terminos) deum musicae*.'" Citing Charles Mallet and Strickland Gison, Carpenter points out that "not only were undergraduates to hear lectures in music, but so were bachelors studying for the master's degree." But the Caroline Code established by Archbishop Laud in 1636 under the authority of King Charles I did not require any books to be read. All it did was "make attendance at public lectures obligatory for both bachelors and masters."[28]

Socrates endorses this kind of forced practical study in the *Republic*, but he also points out that the usefulness of practical musical education is its ability to force a lesser social order upon those who cannot achieve spiritual order for themselves. It is far better, Socrates repeatedly makes clear, for one to achieve the justice of one's soul without the fetters of the state: if individuals achieve justice — harmony — the state will function well. But it is difficult to order one's soul, and this difficulty is the basis for social and political hierarchy in the *Republic*. Indeed, the link underlies the transition in the second book of the *Republic* from the discussion of the just state of the individual soul to the discussion of justice in the republic. Socrates, who asserts that to know the good is to do the good, suggests that those who do not know the good may at least, by inducement to practical rituals, be habituated to march to a certain tune, and thus to do good and be kept from doing harm. Aristotle would pursue this aspect of habituation. Poets such as Milton, in contrast, would devote themselves, in the manner of Pindar, to achieving speculative self-rule.

Antipoetical and antimusical in statement — although not in style — as Plato's dialogues appear to be, they articulate elements of a speculative program that has been attractive to many poets. For the goal of a great poet is not merely a fineness of imitation and adroitness of plot but full authority, the attainment of a voice "such as the gods have," a voice like the one attributed by Homer to Phemius, the Ithacan bard whose life Odysseus spares during his slaughter of the suitors.[29] Whereas the Sophistic (and later Aristotelian) rhetorical theories are concerned with the techniques that allow men better to speak to men, Socrates is concerned with the reattuning of the human soul that will make him, in Milton's words, "a man who possessed every kind of virtue, who was worthy to consort with the gods themselves." And as Phemius says later, what is good for the gods is good enough also for people: "I sing to the gods and to human people . . . I am such a one as can sing before you as to a god."[30]

Plato and Aristotle do not disagree about what "human limits" are as much as they disagree about how to exceed them. Whereas Socrates strives "to speak what is pleasing to the gods," Aristotle is concerned with a speaker's ability to persuade his "fellow men." Socrates' assertion that one must attempt first to achieve knowledge of the truth and only then to speak it struck Aristotle as not merely impractical but impossible. Rather, Aristotle argues, the rhetorician and poet must concern themselves with what is probable, for what is probable is all it is humanly possible to know.[31] According to Aristotle, audiences neither demand epistemological certainty nor satisfy themselves with what is true but are duly persuaded by imitations of what is probable. Aristotle's *The Art of Rhetoric*, along with that fortuitous student notebook recording his comments on the art of poetic, offers, as Kathy Eden points out, "Aristotle's answer to [Plato's] charges."[32] By arguing, against Plato, that mimesis is the imitation of human action according to probability and that probability, moreover, reveals causes, Aristotle provides poets with a strategy to confront the Platonic assertion of man's separation from divine, eternal, and unknowable things.

Whereas Plato juxtaposes the speculative musical goal of the "true musician" to what he views as the inferior practical goals of the poets, Aristotle venerates the "art" of poetry in part by linking it with practical music. In his *Poetics*, Aristotle likens poetry to music and dancing because it uses meter, rhythm, and melody, furthering with his staunch authority the perception of poetry and music as friendly sister arts.[33]

Aristotle's comments on the art of poetic praise the formal musical aspects (meter, rhythm, and melody) that constitute poetry and distinguish it from rhetoric. In his companion work on the art of rhetoric, Aristotle fixes poetry firmly in the trivium, where it may be studied also as the (practical) sister art of logic and rhetoric, in which knowledge of syllogisms is the chief concern. "Rhetoric," Aristotle asserts, "is a kind of division or likeness of Dialectic, since neither of them is a science that deals with the nature of any definite subject, but they are merely faculties for furnishing arguments."[34] In Aristotelian terms, the art of poetic is a rhetorical art, and hence also chiefly a means of "furnishing arguments." While rhythm and melody distinguish poetry from rhetoric, it is argument, according to Aristotle, not rhythm and melody, that makes poetry what it is.

When Aristotle states that *ethos* is the most important inartificial proof, moreover, he does not prescribe a moral program commensurate with the Platonic one.[35] Aristotle argues only that rhetorical *ethos* is what makes a speaker believable, and that if he does not have it, he may not be believed even when he speaks the truth. When Quintilian writes, "*Neque enim esse oratorem nisi bonum virum iudico, et fieri etiamsi potest nolo,*" claiming that *ethos* is the most important inartificial proof, he does not prescribe *how* to be good, and he proceeds to offer, whatever his intention, the Socratic system of values stated in reverse.[36]

Quintilian subjugates the philosophical quadrivium (arithmetic, geometry, astronomy, music) to the rhetorical trivium (grammar, logic, and rhetoric), in which music is taught as a (practical) sister art. He also substitutes the theory of musical composition (the most intellectual aspect of practical study) for speculative study, which it is not:

> Nor can [the orator's] training be regarded as complete if it stop short of music, for the teacher of literature has to speak of meter and rhythm; nor again if he be ignorant of astronomy, can he

understand the poets; for they, to mention no further points, frequently give their indications of time by reference to the rising and setting of the stars. Ignorance of philosophy is an equal drawback, since there are numerous passages in almost every poem based on the most intricate questions of natural philosophy. . . .[37]

Rhythm and harmony are the means of persuasion. "Ignorance of philosophy is [a] . . . drawback" only in the sense that speculative music is a topic, much like others, of which the good rhetorician will have good rhetorical command. The orator must read philosophy, according to Quintilian, only to acquire something like what E. D. Hirsch calls "cultural literacy."[38]

For Quintilian, speculative music is conceived for its "practical" applications as a topic, as learning that might serve the orator. A source for later theories about music often cited as an example of the continuity between Orpheus, Pythagoras, Socrates, Plato, and Neoplatonists such as Ficino, Quintilian is actually an example of an early departure from Plato's speculative program. When Quintilian writes of "the knowledge of the principles of music, which have power to excite or assuage the emotions of mankind,"[39] he offers a rhetorician's view of the "principles of music," not the view of Plato's "true musician." The "true musician" is interested in the harmony of his soul, not in the ability of the man who does not necessarily understand his own role in the cosmos to persuade others of theirs.

Whereas Plato establishes self-rule as a means to achieving speculative harmony, Aristotle is concerned not with the harmony of his soul but mastery of his argument and control of his audience. His is a practical skill conceived not in accordance with heavenly harmony but rather with probability and other requirements for accommodation. A poet, in Aristotle's view, need not worry about harmony, about the relationship between earthly poetry and heavenly music, or about the musical condition of his soul.

Quintilian's view of the relationship between poetry and music derives from this practical perspective that Aristotle's authority established with unstoppable force. Even today, the persistent critical custom is to follow Aristotle and Quintilian in linking the "practice" of poetry to the trivium on the basis of its use of logic and rhetoric to persuade and delight. But as Carpenter writes, the tradition of speculative musical study is "related not to literature but to mathematics," music "being one of the four mathematical disciplines which preceded the study of philosophy."[40]

The Middle Ages and Renaissance were both generally shaped by Aristotle more than by Plato, but not where a poet's aspiration to a condition of music is concerned. Given the development of speculative musical study by Pythagoras, Socrates, and Plato, it is inaccurate to link poetry only with the trivium. Poets such as Shakespeare and Milton would not, nor would poets such as Keats and Stevens. To align practical music so strictly with poetry — and speculative music with philosophy — is to ignore the basic poetic desire to sing.

Platonic Self-Rule and Neoplatonic Frenzy

A consideration of the diverse influences of Platonic, Aristotelian, and Neoplatonic theories of speculative music is crucial to understanding English poets who aspire to song, especially during the Renaissance. The aspiration to a condition of music is central to Neoplatonism, which makes large claims for the human ability to achieve that condition. Sharing much with the Aristotelian rhetorical defense of poetry, Neoplatonic claims for music differ in important ways from Plato's speculative musical program on the matter of self-rule. According to Neoplatonists such as Marsilio Ficino, one may simultaneously lose control of oneself and be put into harmony by the heavenly power of earthly music.

We may locate important differences between Neoplatonism

and Platonism, as well as some of the similarites between Aristotelian rhetorical theory and Neoplatonic theories of music, in the work of Ficino, who, in a letter to Peregrino Agli, glosses Plato's *Phaedrus*:

> The minds of men, while they are [in heaven], are well nour-ished with perfect knowledge. Souls are depressed into bodies through thinking about and desiring earthly things. Then those who were previously fed on ambrosia and nectar, that is the perfect knowledge and bliss of God, in their descent are said to drink continuously of the river Lethe, that is forgetfulness of the divine. They do not fly back to heaven, whence they fell. . . . The divine philosopher considers we achieve this through two virtues, one relating to moral conduct and the other to con-templation; one he names with a common term "justice," and the other "wisdom." For this reason, he says, souls fly back to heaven on two wings, meaning, as I understand it, these vir-tues; and likewise Socrates teaches in *Phaedo* that we acquire these by the two parts of philosophy; namely the active and the contemplative. Hence, he says again in *Phaedrus* that only the mind of a philosopher regains wings.[41]

Ficino alters the main point of Plato's speculative program. Nowhere does Socrates say the philosopher is divine; nor does Socrates say that "the mind of a philosopher regains wings," nor that the philosopher *possesses* wisdom. In an attempt to suggest only his "love of wisdom" rather than his possession of it, Pythagoras was the first to call himself a *philosopher*. Similarly, Socrates makes it clear in the *Republic* that even he is not a philosopher-king, that even he does not have knowl-edge of the Forms, that even he must strive to be good.[42] In *Phaedrus*, Socrates says only that he is "a follower of the Muses and a lover" — a φιλοκάλος, an ἐρωτικός. Socrates maintained the distinction between striving in a speculative sense and possessing in a practical one. He maintained it stubbornly at his trial.[43] It was this distinction, as much as the stubborness, that got him killed.[44]

Whereas Plato wrote about striving to achieve justice of the soul by achieving self-rule, Ficino wrote about ecstatic frenzy that put one in possession of divine beauty: "On recovery of these wings, the soul is separated from the body by their power. Filled with God, it strives with all its might to reach the heavens, and thither it is drawn. Plato calls this drawing away and striving 'divine frenzy'. . . ." According to Ficino, Plato "thinks that the harmony which we make with musical instruments and voices is the image of divine harmony, and that the symmetry and comeliness that arise from the perfect union of the parts and members of the body are an image of divine beauty."[45] Plato saw a slow return, a great circle; Ficino saw the immediate power of music and poetry.

Unlike Plato, Ficino ascribed powers to actual music and poetry (*musica instrumentalis*) because he did not consider the human soul (*musica humana*) discordant:

> By the ears, as I have already said, the soul receives the echoes of that incomparable music, by which it is led back to the deep and silent memory of the harmony which it previously enjoyed. The whole soul then kindles with desire to fly back to its rightful home, so that it may enjoy that true music again.[46]

Whereas Plato demands that speculative "interrogation of harmony" replace the practical use of one's ears,[47] Ficino's Neoplatonism, like Aristotle's rhetorical theory, situates power *in the music itself* and identifies a magical effect with our hearing it. This aspect of Neoplatonism develops not by way of Plato but rather by way of Aristotle and Al-Farabi, the Arabic translator, commentator, and philosopher who instructed much of Europe when he asserted, writing on the existence of the inaudible music of the spheres, that no music exists that we cannot hear. Al-Farabi, who argued against the Pythagoreans' claims that the motions of the planets cause harmonious sounds, concerned himself with only the effects of actual music on a listener.[48] If there was no effect upon the soul, according to Al-Farabi, there was no music. Working from Aristotelian sources, Al-Farabi attacked the distinction between speculative and practical music that was so important in the philosophy of Plato. This fundamental departure from Plato (which began with an assimilation of Aristotle) was developed fully by Neoplatonists such as Ficino.

Nevertheless, as popular as Ficino's theory was, Plato's speculative program remained strong throughout the Renaissance. Supporting the authority of Raymond Klibansky in *The Continuity of the Platonic Tradition*, C. A. Patrides observes that "until the Renaissance the inestimably influential *Timaeus* was known in Chalcidius's fourth century version, which was not displaced even by Ficino's popular translation."[49] Chalcidius's redaction of Plato's *Timaeus* preserves the difference between hearing actual music and contemplating the relationship between man and divine harmony in strict speculative terms:

> the original modulation of the soul is lost through association with the body (*ob consortium corporis*) and forgotten, and hence the souls of the majority are inharmonious. The cure is music; not, however, vulgar music, but divine intelligible music, which recalls the straying soul to its pristine harmony. The best harmony in our moral nature is justice.[50]

The original harmony of the human soul is lost, as Milton recounts in his prolusion, and a cure, as Plato explains, is provided not by listening to actual music but by speculative study of music one cannot hear. For Ficino, actual music retains its power to elevate the soul (by penetrating the ear). Plato, in contrast, attributes power neither to music nor to the ear but rather to the soul, which must strive to reattune itself to "the [heavenly] song" (τοῦ νόμου). As Chalcidius relates, the harmony is not to be found in actual music, but in *justice*, which is the object of study and moral aim of the "true musician."[51]

Plato could not command the direction of Neoplatonism,

but he had tried to forestall any shift of emphasis from the soul to the ear. It is for this very reason that the musicians are commanded to leave in *Symposium*. The dialogue recounts not a festive symposium but an anti-symposium, taking place on the following day, dedicated to discussing *eros* and achieving self-rule. The anti-symposium, which prohibits music and restricts the intake of wine, is a "sober" version of the festive party on the previous night. One point is clear: music will not reattune one's soul, just as sexual union will not make one whole. Only by speculation may one complete one's cosmic circle.

Ficino attributes a raw magical power to music, abandoning Plato's stricter emphasis on moral speculation. Ficino's theory of music is rooted in a mythic view of the relationship between the Pythagorean-Platonic tradition of speculative music and practical music such as poetry and song. "Origen asserts, against Celsus, that there is great power in certain words, and Alchindus and Synesius, discussing magic, agree; likewise Zoroaster, who forbids the chanting of strange words, and Iamblichus, too," writes Ficino. "The Pythagoreans used to do wonderful things in the manner of Phoebus and Orpheus with words, songs, and sounds. The ancient doctors of the Hebrews considered this most important, and all poets sing and make wonderful things with their songs."[52] A great mythmaker, Pythagoras himself became a myth. Ficino associates him with Orpheus, the Thracian singer whose music is reputed to have had magical powers.[53]

During the Renaissance, the magical Neoplatonic solution of the penetrable ear became more popular than the philosophical Platonic problem of the discordant soul. Ficino's writings served many poets during the Renaissance. In France, Pierre de Ronsard made conventional the power of music celebrated by Ficino. But some poets, Shakespeare and Milton, for example, saw reasons to question deeply, and in some cases reject, Neoplatonic solutions. The magical power of music

was a fruitful obsession with Renaissance poets such as
Ronsard, but neither this Orphic version of Pythagoras nor
the Neoplatonic revision of Plato's musical teachings was central to poets as different as Milton, Wordsworth, and Keats.[54]
Each had a peculiar attraction to the strictness of Plato —
to questions about the musical condition of the human soul,
the efficacy of poetry, and the possibility of restoring a link
between earthly poetry and heavenly song.

Sidney's An Apology for Poetry

Given the antispeculative bias of a musician and writer as
important as Thomas Morley,[55] as well as the proliferation of
Aristotelian rhetorical manuals in the sixteenth century, there
are reasons for one to turn to the tradition of practical music
rather than to Plato for a poetic program.[56] Plato was the pli-
able source of Neoplatonic myth, but he was also the rigid
enemy of poetry and rhetoric that the Aristotelian treatises
were trying still to subdue. And although they both attempt
to reconstruct Plato, Aristotelianism and Neoplatonism
diverge in important ways. Plato's speculative philosophy,
Aristotle's rhetorical poetics, and Neoplatonism's theories
of orphic power presented conflicting sources of inspiration
and explanation for any poet who aspired to song. There are
revealing tensions among the three traditions in Sir Philip
Sidney's *An Apology for Poetry*.[57] Sidney, we will see, makes
two contradictory claims for poetry: one speculative, one practical. The speculative claim is based in a Neoplatonic belief
that was well stated by Thomas Hoby in his 1561 translation
of Castiglione's *Il Cortegiano*: "it hath been the opinion of
most wise Philosophers, that the worlde is made of musike,
and the heavens in their moving made a melodie, and our soule
is framed after the verie same sort and therefore lifteth up it
selfe, and (as it were) reviveth the vertues and force of it selfe
with Musicke."[58] According to this Neoplatonic view, poetry

is divine music. But for Sidney, the power of poetry is chiefly rhetorical, in the Aristotelian sense. Sidney links poetry not to divine inspiration but to Aristotle's definition of practical skill. Renouncing Plato's speculative assertion that one must strive to attain a knowledge of truth and only then to speak it, Aristotle set the goal of persuading people, not singing heavenly music with or to the gods.

Relinquishing the supernatural (Neoplatonic) power of actual music, Sidney's Aristotelian rhetorical program asserts instead the practical program of teaching, delighting, and moving. From this rhetorical perspective, poetry moves not because a poet is "made of musike," but because a poet, like an orator, makes a vivid and moving argument. And yet, although Sidney writes mainly from the rhetorical perspective, he also affirms a link between earthly poetry and heavenly music throughout his *Apology*. Nor does he reconcile these contrary perspectives.

Sidney's *Apology* articulates brilliantly the prevailing rhetorical poetic in England during the Renaissance, but he does not provide a consistent treatment of speculative music that accounts for the views of Shakespeare and Milton, contrary to what Heninger suggests in his valuable study. Heninger writes that Sidney's phrase "the Planet-like Musicke of *Poetrie*" is fraught with recondite meaning. "It implies," Heninger writes, "not only that poetry is measured in quantity like music, but also that poetry 'should' echo the cosmic order inherent in the music of the spheres. Just as each planet generates a note contributing to the harmony of the heavens to comprise an all-inclusive diapason which represents the cosmos in musical terms," Heninger explains,

> so *must* the elements of a poem fit together to comprise a comprehensive whole which reflects the universal order. Only then will poetry reproduce the "Planet-like Musicke" that Macrobius so greatly admired, and that Sidney takes to be a reasonable expectation for a poem. To epitomize the rich tradition which

Sidney assumes we recognize and accept, we might say that Pythagorean cosmology *should* determine poetic theory.[59]

For a speculative poet, however, the condition of the human soul was more complex a problem than Sidney could solve. Although Renaissance poets agree that "poetry *should* echo the cosmic order" and that "so *must* the elements of a poem fit together . . .,"[60] they may also find, as Milton in his pro-lusion, that they are incapable of "reflect[ing] the universal order," or participating in it. Heninger does not consider this conditional element — in part because he harmonizes diverse aspects of a "rich tradition."

Sidney does not demonstrate the speculative interest in Pythagorean cosmology that Heninger claims for him. The subject does not receive full and serious attention in his *Apology*. Sidney mentions the "planet-like music" only in his conclusion, which effects a hyperbolic and humorous tone. He concludes his defence by deriding any "idle tongues" who "bark" at poets (20): "But if (fie of such a but) you be born so near the dull-making cataract of Nilus that you cannot hear the planet-like music of poetry," Sidney writes,

> if you have so creeping a mind that it cannot lift itself up to look to the sky of poetry, or rather, by a certain rustical dis-dain, will become such a mome as to be a Momus of poetry; then, though I will not wish unto you the ass's ears of Midas . . . nor to be rhymed to death . . . yet thus much curse I must send you in the behalf of all poets, that while you live, you live in love, and never get favor for lacking skill of a sonnet. (89)

This humorous moment at the end of Sidney's *Apology* can-not make us forget his main argument. The point is, Sidney jests, if you lack practical poetic skill, you will suffer unre-quited love. A skillful poet, says Sidney, can keep a playful distance from the pain of *eros*: Plato's true-musician, in con-trast, lives a life devoted to the endless pain of an erotic pur-suit of truth.

Throughout his *Apology*, Sidney exalts the (practical) music of poetry, but — guided by Aristotelian rhetorical theory rather than Neoplatonism — he does not claim a "planet-like music" for the contemporary poetry he defends. Sidney's *Apology* has a clear purpose and structure that reveal why. After briefly considering the history of poets and admiring the powers of the ancient prophet-singers, Sidney begins his defense by considering "poesy" as "an art of imitation, for so Aristotle termeth it in this word *mimesis*" (17). Basing his Aristotelian defense on the fast Platonic distinction between heavenly song and earthly poetry, Sidney early distinguishes "three several kinds" (18) of poet. The "chief both in antiquity and excellency were they that did imitate the inconceivable excellencies of God" (18): they are singers of the *Hebrew Bible*. The second kind are not even "properly" poets (19), Sidney suggests: they are natural philosophers who write in verse, verse being "no cause of poetry" (21). The third kind are "indeed right poets" (20) who "most properly do imitate . . . to delight and teach, and delight to move men to take that goodness in hand which without delight they would fly as from a stranger . . ." (20). Sidney's "right poets," although they excel at teaching and delighting, may make no claim to the "excellency" with which David and Solomon were able to sing about "the inconceivable excellencies of God."

David, rather, is a prophet-singer much in the manner of Plato's "true musician":

> For what else is the awaking his musical instruments . . ., when he maketh you, as it were, see god coming in His majesty, his telling of the beasts' joyfulness, and hills leaping, but a heavenly poesy, wherein almost he showeth himself a passionate lover of that unspeakable and everlasting beauty to be seen by the eyes of the mind, only cleared by faith. (12)

To call David a heavenly singer is easy. But to link David to a "right poet" would be to assume a tenuous association, and

Sidney does not. Sidney makes clear that only prophet-poets such as David had such power, and "in this kind, though in a full wrong divinity, were Orpheus, Amphion, Homer in his Hymns . . ." (19). By distinguishing David so clearly from "right poets," Sidney affirms that there was once a time when the human soul was able to join in God's heavenly harmony, but when that time ended poets had to resort to lesser, and less truly musical, skills. The poets Sidney ably defends, "right poets," do not possess this ability to sing divine songs.

Like Aristotle, Sidney ably refutes Plato's charge that a poet's imitation even of earthly things is dangerously removed from reality, but he does not confront Plato's charge that poets cannot tell the "inconceivable" truth about the gods. Nor does Sidney confront in the speculative musical terms of Plato the conflict between divine inspiration and poetic skill. Sidney, like Aristotle, was less interested in that conflict than in establishing the superiority of poetry to history and philosophy in its ability not only to teach and delight but also to move.

Nevertheless, Sidney's *Apology* discloses a telling reluctance to surrender the claim to heavenly song. This reluctance is built into the structure of the essay. Sidney skirts any explicit comparison of the first and third — or "chief" and "right" — kinds of poet. "Betwixt" the second kinds of poet and the "right poet," Sidney asserts, "is such a kind of difference as betwixt the meaner sort of painters . . . and the more excellent . . ." (20). In contrast, although he early betrays them, Sidney never examines the differences between the first and third kinds of poet.

Sidney's reluctance to pursue these differences is rooted in the difficulty of reconciling speculative and practical conceptions of poetry. This, in turn, is related to the difficulty of reconciling conflicting biblical notions of the creation of man: one based on analogy, one based on synecdoche. The analogical creation of man in God's image is the basis of Sidney's practical rhetorical poetic, whereas the synecdochal creation is the basis of Christian applications of *musica speculativa*. Throughout his *Apology*, Sidney struggles between asserting the sanguine analogical relationship between God and man and accepting the harsh musical effects of a synecdochal cosmic relationship gone awry. The former sanctions bold assertions about "right poets"; the latter occasions wistful thoughts about participating in a formerly harmonious cosmos.

Sidney cannot safely compare "right poets" to David, nor can he reasonably suggest that the "art" of the Aristotelian poet can equal the "excellency" of divine inspiration. Instead, he offers a comparison he tellingly asks us not to deem "too saucy":

> Neither let it be deemed too saucy a comparison to balance the highest point of man's wit with the efficacy of nature, but rather give right honor to the heavenly Maker of that maker, who having made man to His own likeness, set him beyond and over all the works of that second nature, which in nothing he showeth so much as in poetry, when with the force of a divine breath he bringeth things forth far surpassing her doings, with no small argument to the incredulous of that first accursed fall of Adam: sith our erected wit maketh us know what perfection is, and yet our infected will keepeth us from reaching unto it. (17)

In this analogical conception, earth is still considered to be a mirror of heaven, and the human being is still considered a maker in the image of the heavenly maker. The poet is distinguished (analogically) as a maker, but not (synecdochically) as a singer. Wit, the source of logic and rhetoric (or trivium), is erected. But the will is infected. In the speculative musical terms of Pythagorean-Platonic cosmology, that is to say, the human soul is still discordant.

To reconcile the analogical and synecdochal conception of the universe is clearly not easy. The difficulty comes, as Edward W. Tayler's examination of the "two contrasting creations in Genesis" shows, when "the Christian must assume that his soul retains its divine essence even when 'in' the body . . . the 'breath of life' remains somehow radically opposed to the 'dust of the ground.'" The tension, writes Tayler, is "in its largest aspect a tension between dualistic and monistic views of the world." The second creation, Tayler observes, provides "no guarantee of likeness, congruence, between the creator and creature, any more than there is between potter and pot." The tension between rhetorical and speculative views of the universe, like the "redundant creations," presents Sidney with a conflict he does not try to resolve.[61] Milton encounters the same problem, as we will see, but, unlike Sidney, he deals with it directly, making it central to his theological poetic.

Whereas Milton submits the dilemma to his peculiar theological scrutiny, Sidney keeps his *Apology* to the empowering terms of rhetoric. Sidney attempts mainly to demonstrate that "of all the writers under the sun the poet is the least liar" (56) precisely because he feigns "pictures" of "what should be" rather than of what is. Right poets imitate, attempting to teach, delight, and move: "Uttering sweetly and properly the conceits of the mind . . . is the end of speech" (85). Sidney puts great emphasis on the poet's ability to achieve music, music being "the most divine striker of the senses." But his *Apology* falls short of making the speculative argument that humankind can still sing. Sidney's mention of Plato is enough to introduce tension, but his examination of Plato is not deep enough to confront it.

If we consider briefly the three views of *musica instrumentalis* — Platonic, Aristotelian, and Neoplatonic — we have been considering, we see profound distinctions that were crucial to Sidney, as well as to Shakespeare, Milton, and future ages of poets. Plato writes of the need not to recreate or transport the soul but rather to reattune it, whereas Aristotle and

Renaissance Aristotelians maintain that music, like rhetoric, is earthly recreation that teaches and delights.[62] Renaissance Neoplatonism, diverging from both of these views, maintains that poetry has a heavenly power that can transport the soul. While Sidney wishes to claim for poetry more than Aristotle would allow, he is unwilling to claim as much as Neoplatonism asserts — namely, that poets might hold the greater hope of regaining their wings. The poetic feet of the "right" poet must be sufficient for Sidney. To claim those magical wings would be to contradict the Aristotelian assertion of human art. Sidney does not claim Neoplatonic musical powers in his "saucy" comparison, but "erected wit," which he conceives in the terms of the rhetorical tradition ("by knowledge to lift up the mind"). Above all, Sidney claims for poetry the status of art — indeed, the status of the supreme human art.

Sidney's "saucy" attempt to bolster one regnant Renaissance philosophy with another is brilliant, but not without tensions he cannot resolve. His reluctance to give up a poet's claim to song leads him to hedge. Late in his *Apology*, he slips in a notable claim to divine inspiration precisely when — not coincidentally — he tries to declare Plato a friend rather than a foe: Plato "in his dialogue called *Ion*, giveth high and rightly divine commendation to poetry. So as Plato, banishing the abuse, not the thing, not banishing it, but giving due honor unto it, shall be our patron and not our adversary" (66–67). The attempt to hedge is significant. It is Plato, after all, not Aristotle, whom Sidney ranks "of all philosophers . . . the most poetical."

Plato does not, of course, "giveth high and rightly divine commendation to poetry." Truly divine inspiration, as Socrates admits in *Ion*, would be absolute commendation. But Socrates denies that Ion is divinely inspired. Distinguishing divine frenzy from poetic skill, Socrates interrogates Ion and arrives at the conclusion that a divine poet is a light and winged thing, and holy, and never able to compose until he has become inspired, and is beside himself and reason is no longer in him. So long as he has [reason] in his possession, no man is able to make poetry or to chant in prophecy. Therefore, since their making is not by art, when they utter many things and fine about the deeds of men, just as you do about Homer, but is by lot divine [θεια μοίρᾳ] — therefore each is able to do well only that to which the Muse has impelled him [ἡ Μοῦσα αὐτον ὥρμησεν]. (534b3–534c3)

Socrates argues that Ion, as a rhapsode, aspires to possess not an art (τέχνη) but a divine power (θεία δύναμις):

This gift you have of speaking well on Homer is not an art; it is a power divine, impelling you like the power in the stone Euripides called the magnet. . . . This stone does not simply attract the iron rings, just by themselves; it also imparts to the rings a force enabling them to do the same thing as the stone itself, that is, to attract another ring, so that sometimes a chain is formed, quite a long one, of iron rings, suspended from one another. For all of them, however, their power depends upon that loadstone. Just so the Muse. She first makes men inspired, and then through these inspired ones others share in the enthusiasm, and a chain is formed, for the epic poets, all the good ones, have their excellence, not from art, but are inspired, possessed. (533d1–e9)

Emphasizing the "gift" and "power" of the "lot divine" (536a2–3), Socrates asserts that Ion is a middle ring [μέσος]. He is neither possesed of an art nor inspired directly by the Muse but by Homer. The role of the "middle ring" is important, as Socrates makes clear, but he holds that neither the rhapsode nor even Homer possesses an art, for one cannot at once be possessed by divine frenzy and at the same time possess an art. Socrates admits that Ion's "spirit dances," but Ion ends the dialogue by ignoring Socrates' distinction between inspiration and art (as well as between philosophical knowledge and rhetorical imitation), asserting comically that as a rhapsode he possesses even the art of a military general.

Taking up Ion's general cause, Aristotle does not claim that poets are divinely inspired; he claims that they have an art, a human skill. Sidney chooses to advance Aristotle's argument, but not without fostering contradictions Aristotle was careful to avoid. Why doesn't Sidney avoid them, like any good "Aristotelian"? Likely because he is too attracted to the speculative aspiration to song articulated by Plato:

> for some that thought . . . felicity principally to be gotten by knowledge, and no knowledge to be so high and heavenly as acquaintance with the stars, gave themselves to astronomy; others, persuading themselves to be demi-gods if they know the causes of things, became natural and supernatural philosophers; some an admirable delight drew to music; and some, the certainty of demonstration, to the mathematics. But all, one and other, having this scope, to know, and by knowledge to lift up the mind from the dungeon of the body to the enjoying his own divine essence. (22)

Sidney's Aristotelian defense does not permit him to pursue the aspiration fully. As attractive as they may be to one who aspires to sing like David, moreover, Sidney cannot embrace Neoplatonic claims for the power of instrumental music. Sidney himself mentions the claims to speculative knowledge and felicity by those devoted to the subjects of the quadrivium — the astronomer, supernatural philosopher, musician, and mathematician — only to deflate them:

> But when by the balance of experience it was found that the astronomer, looking to the stars, might fall into a ditch, that the inquiring philosopher might be blind in himself, and the mathematician might draw forth a straight line with a crooked heart, then lo did proof, the overruler of opinions, make manifest that all these are but serving sciences, which, as they have each a private end in themselves, so yet are they all directed to the highest end of the mistress knowledge, by the Greeks called *architectonike*, which stands (as I think) in the knowledge of man's self, in the ethic and politic consideration, with the end of well doing and not of well knowing only. . . . (22–23)

Sidney, like Quintillian, maintains that the rhetorician needs to know how to *exercise* knowledge: "For as Aristotle saith, it is not *gnosis* but *praxis* must be the fruit" (37). The quadrivium, says Sidney, only serves the trivium, for Socrates was wrong to assert that to know the good is to do it. Curiously, however, while the second passage mocks the foibles of the astronomer, philosopher, and mathematician, it excludes a second mention of the musician. Sidney, it appears, does not wish to remind us once again that to raise the practical poet above the speculative musician he must belittle the preeminent role of the speculative musician in Platonic philosophy — that "most poetic" of antipoetic philosophies.

While Sidney demonstrates his greater interest in comparing "right poets" to philosophers and historians than to prophet-poets, the aspiration to a condition of divine song is a needling, ambiguous, and even destabilizing theme throughout Sidney's *Apology*. However forceful Sidney's defense of poetry when considered in the context of the rhetorical tradition of which it is a monumental flourish, one cannot locate in Sidney a uniform and inclusive Renaissance solution to a difficult and long-disputed problem. Sidney's *Apology* offers a remarkably compelling and influential defense of the rhetorical powers of the "right poet," but Sidney leaves Shakespeare and Milton to devise their own speculative poetics. Shakespeare has much to say on the matter that is not found in Sidney; and it is Milton, we will see, not Sidney, who first made "planet-like music" an expectation for a poem.

Following the Muses

Boethius had confronted Sidney's conflict long before Sidney, and he had come to an important conclusion. The problems of the soul are not solved by actual music or rhetoric, Boethius tells Philosophy in *The Consolation of Philosophy*: "You have made a persuasive argument . . . and presented it with sweet music and rhetoric. But it satisfies only while it is being spoken."[63] The spiritual wound is deep, and the musical cure is superficial: "Those in misery have a more profound awareness of their afflictions, and therefore a deep-seated pain continues long after the music stops."[64] Boethius alludes to the subject with which this book will conclude: the temporality of sound — the nature of earthly music to disperse into silence. It is silence that Socrates addresses so poigniantly in Plato's *Phaedrus*. Some speech is patently false, and some speech aspires to apprehend what is true; but all speech ends. A speaker should therefore try, as Socrates says, to speak in such a way that "words . . . instead of remaining barren contain a seed whence new words grow up in new characters, whereby the seed is vouchsafed immortality, and its possessor the fullest measure of blessedness that man can attain unto" (276e–277a). Given its determination to resist the silence that comes with death, it is purposefully ironic that the speculative musical program developed by Socrates induces one to become not a writer but rather a speculative "follower of the Muses."

In resisting the silence that comes with death, as well as the noise that comes with life, both Pythagoras and Socrates strove to achieve a speculative harmony. But in confronting the threat of eternal discord, they chose the inevitable silence of speech over the lasting discord of writing. The paradox, which goes beyond Derrida's notion of the death of the letter, is one we will consider in subsequent chapters. For the moment, it is useful to observe that when a poetic program places speculative (ethical) considerations before the achievement of practical ones (such as persuasion and fame), and when it induces even a poet such as Milton to speak of shutting up, the program is likely to become unpopular for its difficulty.[65]

Efforts to reject the teachings of Socrates have therefore been rather successful. The most successful was Cicero's charge that Socrates is to blame for the severing of eloquence and truth.[66] But the separation was not made by Socrates. It was made within the rhetorical tradition itself. Cicero's observation, not Socrates' teachings, constitutes the split. The separation of eloquence from truth denounced by Cicero is comparable, in fact, to the separation of the study of practical music from the study of speculative music.[67] Whereas Socrates was demanding a form of literary discourse that did not differentiate among speculative, prudential, and practical aspects, Cicero was defending a rhetorical and poetic art that limited itself to the prudential and practical activities of consciousness.

Although Socrates remarks most strictly the differences between poetry and song, he also most strenuously refuses to accept a poetic that accepts the fragmentation of the Muses. Socrates' life, not merely his philosophy, is a remarkable attempt to align the speculative ("true"), the prudential ("just"), and the practical ("beautiful") activities of human consciousness. The rhetorical "theorists," in contrast, accepted the fragmentation of the Muses, and they proceeded from a rhetorical perspective to pursue "responses of style in search of decorum." It is Plutarch, as Trimpi remarks, who points out Hesiod's "differentiation of rational discourse into philosophical, rhetorical, and mathematical disciplines, which frequently competed with one another." Most important, "such rivalry," as Trimpi observes, "encouraged the separation and antagonism between the cognitive, judicative, and formal intentions of literature," leading "to more restricted conceptions of literary discourse itself."[68]

Trimpi, who aims "to describe the nature of these restrictions placed upon the literary analysis of experience and of the ever-recurring efforts to overcome them," agrees with Cicero's charge that Socrates "narrowed the contemporary conception of philosophy, a discipline which had originally included 'the whole study and practice of the liberal sciences. . . . By his efforts, Socrates separated the science of wise thinking from that of elegant speaking, though in reality they are closely linked together.' From him, therefore, 'has sprung the undoubtedly absurd and unprofitable and reprehensible severance between the tongue and the brain, leading to our having one set of professors to teach us to think and another to teach us to speak.'"[69] But if the "differentiation" and "restrictions" are inherent in Hesiod's invocation, then it cannot be Socrates who is responsible for them. Nor is Hesiod. No one person, after all, can be responsible. Such "differentiation" and "restrictions" are deep mysterious elements of the Greek mythology, just as they are a part of the mythologies of most cultures, for they are part of life. What we see, really, are two ways of confronting them. Whereas the rhetorical tradition concentrates on ways to overcome the "restrictions" caused by "differentiation" it accepts, Socrates, in contrast, refuses to accept that they are permanantly sundered. Whereas the Aristotelian rhetorical tradition subsumes speculation under practical concerns, Socrates insists on striving to unify the speculative, prudential, and practical activities of consciousness. Indeed, in his battle with the Sophists, Socrates' chief difficulty was that he could not allow himself to "[separate] the science of wise thinking from that of elegant speaking."

Aristotle's transformation of Socratic dialectic into a form of Aristotelian dialectic that is the basis of the rhetorical and poetic arts is the greatest achievement of ancient literary theory in the West. To say it has been influential and valuable to future writers is an understatement. Aristotelean rhetorical theory has offered a good deal more to the practical aspects of literary discourse than Socrates' speculative philosophy. But that is no cause to redefine the debate in rhetorical terms and to hold Socrates responsible for a "differentiation" that was made, identified, and accepted by the rhetorical tradition.

Socrates' view of the Muses, along with his harsh criticism of the poets, has been more attractive to many poets — Milton, Wordsworth, Shelley, Keats, Dickinson, and Stevens, to take some examples — than the view offered by the rhetorical tradition. Unfortunately, scholars guided by the rhetorical tradition portray negatively Socrates' reluctance to employ rhetorical techniques. They do this in part because it is part of human nature to desire to be seduced by sounds and persuaded by plots. Aristotle understood this desire and devised a rhetorical poetic that would use it to an advantage.

Socrates understood it, too. Refusing to placate this desire, thinking, rather, to martyr himself for *eros*, he handed himself over to a jury that would likely kill him if he failed to tell them what they wanted to hear. Knowing that speaking the truth would likely get him killed by people who like to hold opinions rather than to accept the task of producing a condition of harmony in their souls, Socrates begins his defense in the *Apology* by addressing the very pressure put on him to persuade by means of logical and rhetorical proof: "I do not know, men of Athens, how my accusers affected you; as for me, I was almost carried away in spite of myself, so persuasively did they speak. And yet, hardly anything of what they said was true." Socrates will not allow them to call him "an accomplished speaker," he says, "unless indeed they call an accomplished speaker the man who speaks the truth." Socrates insists that the Athenians conceive eloquence in the speculative tradition developed by him, rather than the practical terms of the Sophists:

> From me you will hear the whole truth, though not, by Zeus, gentlemen, expressed in embroidered and stylized phrases like theirs, but things spoken at random and expressed in the first words that come to mind, for I put my trust in the justice of what I say, and let none of you expect anything else. It would not be fitting at my age, as it might be for a young man, to toy with words when I appear before you. (17a–c)

Just as he is known to have lived by it, so Socrates appears to have died by his speculative program.

In Plato's account, Socrates playfully uses rhetorical skills to demonstrate that he possesses them in abundance but does not value them, refusing to substitute rhetorical triumph for moral struggle. Aristotle knew, partly from the example of Socrates, that the believable speaker will more likely be believed than the truthful one. Plato addresses this point in *Crito*: Crito represents a devoted but not altogether promising student of Socrates, for, much in the manner of the jury who convicts Socrates, he fails to comprehend and accept what Socrates tells him, trying instead to persuade his teacher to flee his death sentence. Plato is likely having fun at the expense of his less capable peer, but he seems also to be making an important point: namely, that it is fitting that even Socrates' faithful student could be incapable of understanding and keeping Socrates' standards. From the perspective of the Sophistic and rhetorical tradition, of course, Socrates has a bad rhetorical *ethos*; he does not do what he can to appear believable.

From a practical perspective, Socrates is a brazen speaker with intentionally bad rhetorical *ethos*. From a speculative perspective he is merely truthful, and whereas what is believable (τὸ πιθανόν) is believable, mere truth, as Aristotle knew, is not. But as Socrates says in the *Republic*, by claiming to be wise when in fact he is not, he would bring his friends down with him (*Republic*, 451a–b). By offending his jury, just as by wandering around Athens demonstrating that people who claim to be wise are not, Socrates performs his cosmic housekeeping ("service to the gods"[70]), making it likely that fewer souls will be diverted from completing the cosmic circle he describes in the *Phaedrus*.

The subjugation of eloquence to truth is the chief element of the Platonic speculative musical program, for it is the only way to keep from splitting eloquence and truth. Socrates' words are sealed as truth with the sacrifice of his earthly life into the clench of an opining mob. Cicero, nevertheless, sees the subjugation of eloquence to truth as a splitting:

For in the old days at all events the same system of instruction seems to have imparted education both in right conduct and in good speech; nor were the professors in two separate groups, but the same master gave instruction both in ethics and in rhetoric, for instance the great Phoenix in Homer, who says that he was assigned to the young Achilles by his father Peleus to accompany him to the wars in order to make him "an orator and man of action too". . . . [A]nd whereas the persons engaged in handling and pursuing and teaching the subjects that we are now investigating were designated by a single title, the whole study and practice of the liberal sciences being entitled philosophy, Socrates robbed them of this general designation, and in his discussions separated the science of wise thinking from that of elegant speaking, though in reality they are closely linked together; and the genius and varied discourses of Socrates have been immortally enshrined in the compositions of Plato, Socrates himself not having left a single scrap of writing.[71]

Phoenix, of course, did not persuade Achilles to follow his ethical instruction. Nor did Socrates fail to see the link between truth and beauty. Unlike Cicero, Socrates and writers of the New Testament determined that the subjugation of eloquence under truth is the only way truly to link the two. In his defense of poetry, Sidney could not agree with Socrates, and could therefore say only that of philsophers Plato was the most poetical. Shelley, in contrast, in his exultant language, tells of the complex mixture of a love of truth and a love of eloquence that is obvious to those who read Plato in his Greek: "Plato exhibits the rare union of close and subtle logic with the Pythian enthusiasm of poetry, melted by the splendour and harmony of his periods into one irresistible stream of musical impression, which hurry the persuasions onward, as in a breathless career." Not surprisingly, in defending Plato, Shelley has no mind for the rhetorical career of Cicero: "[Plato's] imitator, Cicero, sinks in the comparison into an ape mocking the gestures of a man."[72] The criticism of Cicero is doubtless extreme, but Shelley's contribution to the controversy is notable. Like poets before and after him, Shelley honors the value and power of speculative aspiration.

De Musica: *Augustine and Boethius*

Pythagoras himself is said not to have made the distinction of music into three types but only two, practical and speculative. The formulation by Boethius into three types of music helps us to understand both the points of confluence and difference between the two ways of thinking about music and poetry. After the fall from the golden age, *musica humana* was changed in its relation to "the [heavenly] song" (*musica mundana*).[73] The triadic system of Boethius introduced the potential mediator of *musica instrumentalis* into the old dyadic scheme. Instrumental music, whether music or poetry, offers a potential link between earth and heaven, beauty and truth.

As important as Boethius's disinctions were, it is important to realize that while all Renaissance poets were interested in truth and beauty, not all of them were equally interested in speculative music. The inability of *musica instrumentalis* to participate in "the heavenly tune" (*musica mundana*) was a source of some good speeches in Shakespeare's plays, diverse speeches that consider the relationship between poetry and song with ingenuity. They were central concerns, even obsessions, as we will see, for Milton. The status of *musica instrumentalis* was not, however, a comparable concern for Dante and Edmund Spenser; they not only pay much less attention to speculative music but also pay it a different kind of attention. When Dante claims to see "the heavenly tune" in canto 10 of *Paradiso*, his synesthetic apprehension is conventional.[74] I do not want to risk simplifying Dante. I wish only to remark that Dante recalls certain conventional themes but does not care to conceive himself as a poet in speculative terms.

"*Lo bel stilo*," refers to Dante's place within the canzone tradition; "*La dolce stil novo*" refers to the movement of his style toward God, but not in speculative musical terms. Dante's poetic is firmly rooted in the rhetorical tradition. Dante may write about "the relation between the cosmos and the soul," about "ideas originated in Plato's *Timaeus*" and "assimilated and transformed by neoplatonic and Christian thinkers,"[75] but he is not determined to define a link between "lo bel stilo che m'ha fatto onore" (*Inferno*, 1.87), the "*dolce stil novo*" (*Purgatorio*, 24.57), and "*tin tin sonando con sì dolce nota.*"[76]

Spenser, throughout his poetic career, maintains chiefly a pastoral conception of song. According to this pastoral conception, humankind has not yet lost its ability to communicate musically with nature and heaven. Birds sing. Shepherds pipe and sing. There are passages in which Spenser alludes to the difference between his poetry and what would be "an heavenly Hymne, such as the Angels sing,"[77] but Spenser, like Dante, advances no speculative discussion of his aspiration to be a singer. It is important, for reasons subsequent chapters will make clear, to realize the difference between the narrative use of "images" or discussions of the "topics" of speculative music and a poetic rooted in important aspects of Plato's speculative program.

Boethius's *De Musica*, the required textbook on music throughout Europe until the Renaissance, made clear the importance of musical speculation. With his introduction of instrumental music as a mediator of earth and heaven, he made clear the practical power of music and poetry and the importance of thinking about the relationship between music and poetry in speculative terms.

Because scholars still tend to view poetry and music in practical terms, seeing them as practical sister arts, there are far more studies of the relationship between poetry and practical music than of the relationship between poetry and speculative music. Even in the finest of these few studies, moreover, scholars such as Hollander seek to associate "actual" music and poetry rather than attend to the important distinctions between them:

> Today we are closer to one kind of understanding of the common ground of music and poetry than has been hitherto possible. Purely formalistic analysis, cleansed on the one hand of the incipient platonism and, on the other, of the polemical intentions that have traditionally encumbered stylistic studies, has been gradually increasing its scope.

Hollander suggests further that:

> As our knowledge of the nature and uses of language and of the structure of musical configurations increases, the materials that ultimately comprise both music and poetic language may become more and more susceptible of identification in terms of the mathematical concept of information.[78]

The differences between music and poetry generally, and between speculative and practical music more specifically, which Plato distinguishes so clearly, make two of Hollander's suggestions particularly troubling. The first is his assertion that his goal is to get closer to an "understanding of the common ground of music and poetry." The second is his claim that analysis is better if it is cleansed of "incipient platonism." I am not sure what Hollander means by "platonism" here (the second page of his introduction, nor does it become clear enough later in the book), but I am aware of the confusion the term creates when it is used without very specific reference to a specific Platonism. Such a Platonism ought to be explicitly referred to and adequately explained, preferably first by mention of Plato's Platonism and thereafter by mention of the relevant version, perversion, or subversion of it. Otherwise, when one writes about Renaissance poetry, one is liable to fail to keep the "platonism[s]" straight, the analysis clean.

We need generally to distinguish speculative poets — poets

who aspire to be "true musicians" — from poets who either assume the permanent separation of earthly poetry and divine song or who presume to bridge the gap by rhetorical or other means. We need to distinguish poets who desire to sing "what is pleasing to the gods" from poets who desire only to persuade their "fellow men." In brief, we need to appreciate the moments when poets, by their use of conceptual metaphors of song, demonstrate attraction to either a speculative or practical poetic, or to a combination of the two. As we will see, a poet who derives a poetic from Plato's considerations of speculative music may make gorgeous use of rhetorical techniques, much in the manner of Plato as described by Shelley.

Recent work in musicology has also attempted to smooth the differences between music and language. "Whether inflected dryly, to create the necessity of positivist and formalist musicology, or fervently, to invest music with the glamour of what Derrida calls the metaphysics of presence, the opposition of music and language is untenable from a postmodernist perspective," writes Kramer. "Neither linguistic constatation nor musical immediacy can empower that opposition," he continues. "Once music and language are understood, not as antitheses divided by the lack or possession of constative power, but as common elements in the communicative economy, their differences become practical, not radical."[79] To say what happens once music is understood in a different way is to beg the question. The opposition between music and language may be untenable from a postmodern perspective, but it holds for poets, at least until Stevens, and even beyond. To redefine dichotomies and say the differences become merely "practical" is to reduce a rich and complex part of the history of poetry and of musical ideas. As we will see, Stevens must struggle against the "constative" power of words and keep from settling for the immediate power of music. Stevens's modern conception of poetic song has its basis in a radical devotion to speculation; and this begins in Shakespeare.

It has been hard — improbable really — for scholars to re-sist the habit of thinking of the relationship between music and poetry chiefly in the practical terms of Aristotle or the ecstatic terms of Neoplatonism advanced in the work of Aris-totle, Cicero, Ficino, Sidney, and Ronsard. It is a further loss when literary scholars and historians of ideas consider the "idea of world harmony," and then its exemplary *use* by an array of dissimilar poets, and without paying close attention to poetic context and career. Lionel Trilling, in "The Sense of the Past," observes this general problem in Arthur O. Lovejoy's *The Great Chain of Being*: "[A] regression was made when Professor Lovejoy, in that influential book of his, assured us that 'the ideas in serious reflective literature are, of course, in great part philosophical ideas in dilution.'" As Trilling writes, "Certainly we must question the assumption which gives the priority in ideas to the philosopher and sees the movement of thought as always from the systematic thinker, who thinks up the ideas in, presumably, a cultural vacuum, to the poet who 'uses' the ideas 'in dilution.' We must question this," Trilling urges, "even if it means a reconstruction of what we mean by 'ideas.' And this leads to another matter about which we may not be simple, the relation of the poet to his environ-ment. The poet, it is true, is an effect of environment, but we must remember that he is no less a cause. He may be used as the barometer, but let us not forget that he is also part of the weather." Trilling's cultural criticism relates the question of environment to the question of influence and provides a su-perb formulation of the checks that must be put upon the corruptible powers of the critic:

> Corollary to this question of environment is the question of influence, the influence which one writer is said to have had on another. In its historical meaning, from which we take our present use, *influence* was a word intended to express a mys-tery. It means a flowing-in, but not as a tributary river flows into the main stream at a certain observable point; historically the image is an astrological one and the meanings which the

Oxford Dictionary gives all suggest "producing effects by *insensible* or *invisible* means" — "the infusion of any kind of divine, spiritual, moral, or *secret* power or principle."[80]

Influence is a complicated matter, as Trilling suggests. Denis Donoghue, reacting to Lucien Febvre's warning that the word *influence "ce n'est pas un mot de la langue scientifique mais la langue astrologique,"* suggests replacing the idea of influence with the more determinable fact of "relation."[81] Whatever the word we use, we confront in the case of Plato the fact of his having been insightful — or correct — rather than influential. As Milton affirms in his prolusion, Plato is "the greatest of Mother Nature's interpreters." Plato was the first author in the West to put into writing a "divine, spiritual, and moral power or principle" that would seem to produce "effects by *insensible* or *invisible* means." Poets aspiring to song could hardly help but reveal a deep relation to Plato in this matter, as in others.

We witness the power of such *insensible* and *invisible* means of influence in the superb example of the life and work of Augustine, whose deep relation to Christian poets in the English Renaissance is extraordinarily rich and complex. Early in his career, when he was a teacher of rhetoric, Augustine paid more attention to practical music than he himself would later approve. In his *De Musica*, Augustine devotes five books to the study of rhythmics and metrics — roughly in the Aristotelian tradition that views poetry and music as (practical) sister arts — and a sixth and final book to the study of cosmic harmony. The first five books consider aspects of music associated with the trivium, whereas the last book considers the aspects of music associated with the quadrivium. Observing the disparity, Robert Taliaferro writes:

At first glance, we are tempted to consider the great concern of Augustine with [the] details of rhythm and meter as something of a tragedy. If we think of the comparable mathematical

concerns of Plato, those of Augustine seem trivial, unworthy
vehicles of the weighty dialectical truths they are supposed to
carry. We think of Augustine as the victim of a period which
had lost the profound mathematical insight of the great Greek
age and could offer little for those living in it to reason on.
There was not much a deep and sensitive soul could avail
itself of, to escape the all-pervading rhetoric. But such a view
is, perhaps, too simple, true in part though it may be.[82]

With his last, qualifying statement, Taliaferro is more rev-
erent than perhaps he ought to be. His view does not seem
too simple.

Augustine was embarked upon a program that would have
him complete seven treatises, one each on all of the seven
liberal arts. Our possession of the treatise on music is a boon,
for most of the seven were not completed, or are not extant.
But it seems a loss to have Augustine devote so much tedious
attention to the study of metrics. The work is most interesting and valuable for its sixth, and last, book, which describes
Augustine's attitude toward practical and speculative music.
In a prologue to the sixth book, Augustine himself comments
on the tediousness of his practical study. He aims to distinguish the sixth book from the previous five:

> (1) M. We have delayed long enough and very childishly, too,
> through five books, in those number-traces belonging to time-
> intervals. And let's hope a dutiful labor will readily excuse our
> triviality in the eyes of benevolent men. For we only thought
> it ought to be undertaken so adolescents, or men of any age
> God has endowed with a good natural capacity, might with
> reason guiding be torn away, not quickly but gradually, from
> the fleshly senses and letters it is difficult for them not to stick
> to, and adhere with the love of unchangeable truth to one God
> and Master of all things who with no mean term whatsoever
> directs human minds.

While Augustine apologizes for the tedium and waste, he also
indicates that it is part of a necessary process:

And so, whoever reads those first books will find us dwelling with grammatical and poetical minds, not through choice of permanent company, but through necessity of wayfaring. But when he comes to this book, if, as I hope and pray, one God and Lord has governed my purpose and will and led it to what it was intent upon, he will understand this trifling way is not of trifling value, this way we, too, not very strong ourselves, have preferred to walk, in company with lighter persons, rather than to rush with weaker wings through freer air.

Augustine maintains the Platonic distinction between practical and speculative music and manifests a Platonic disdain for practical matters, which, like Plato, he deems to be merely a necessary "prelude" to becoming a part of "the heavenly tune":

> For if by chance the other crowd from the schools, with tumultuous tongues taking vulgar delight in the noise of rhythm-dancers, should chance upon these writings, they will either despise all or consider those first five books sufficient. But this one the very fruit of those is found in, they will either throw aside as not necessary, or put off as over and above the necessary.[83]

"For anyone reading the treatise *On Music* and then books 10 and 11 of the *Confessions*," Taliaferro remarks, "the dovetailing of the themes is striking. Augustine remains a rhetorician. But, from the frivolous rhetorician that he was before his conversion, he becomes the real rhetorician, he who wins the outer to the inner man, the world to number, and the soul to its Redemption."[84] It is perhaps misleading to call the convert "the real rhetorician," but Taliaferro's remark is apt, much like Kenneth Burke's description of Augustine's "development from the selling of words to the preaching of The Word."[85]

In the prologue to the sixth book, Augustine's interest in practical matters, though it remains, is subjugated to his spiritual concerns. Eventually, toward the end of the book, he is able to rejoice: "And so that verse proposed by us, '*Deus creator omnium*,' sounds with the harmony of number not only to the ears, but even more is most pleasing in truth and wholeness to the soul's sentiment."[86]

His faith finally firm, Augustine made the exemplary journey from a life of practical (literary) concerns to a life of speculative ones. For this reason — and others — Augustine, like Pythagoras and Socrates, was a model for any poet who wished to entertain seriously the tensions between practical and speculative views of the relationship between song and poetry, especially for any Christian poet in the Renaissance who sees "reall truth" in the metaphor of a musical universe — George Herbert, for instance:

> O cheer and tune my heartlesse breast,
> > Deferre no time;
> That so thy favours granting my request,
> > They and my minde may chime,
> > And mend my ryme.[87]

The Music of Poetry

In both Platonic and Christian terms, a heavenly singer must be a wordsmith, but the smithy must be in the service of a song beyond words. For Augustine, the service demanded the constant conversion from words to The Word. Despite the reliance on rhetorical technique, and the basis of Renaissance humanist education in classical rhetoric, no serious religious poet of the seventeenth century wanted to be a mere word-merchant. The struggle was to become a "true musician," to make of one's self, of one's life, a "true poem," which is to say a song — or perhaps only a "prelude to that song."

Seeing his life as a prelude, Socrates wrote nothing. At the end of *Phaedrus*, Socrates explains why writing has less value than speech, and the point is related to poetry having less value than song. Writing, he says, removes language from the erotic pursuit of meaning, for it puts an end to discourse, disguising it as an arrival at truth. Montaigne understood this problem: "What shall we do with this people that admits none but printed evidence, that does not believe men unless they are in a book, or truth unless it is of competent age? We dignify our stupidities when we put them in print. It carries very different weight with this people if you say 'I have read it' than if you say 'I have heard it.'"[88] Socrates disparages writers who value their ability to turn phrases more than the pursuit of truth: "[O]ne who has nothing to show of more value than the literary works on whose phrases he spends hours, twisting them this way and that, pasting them together and pulling them apart, will rightly, I suggest, be called a poet or speech writer or law writer." But a writer that "can defend his statements when challenged, and can demonstrate the inferiority of his writings out of his own mouth . . . he would be a 'lover of wisdom.'"[89] And a lover of wisdom is a follower of the Muses.

Plato, going further than Socrates, affirms the value of writing — especially his writing. It is good precisely because it removes us from what we seek. As in *Phaedrus* and *Symposium*, Plato loves erotic narrative structure in which the object of inquiry is removed by a series of ironizing levels. Plato asserts the value of putting one's love of wisdom onto paper — of containing the pursuit of stasis in the psuedostasis of written dialogues. He shows us that the more we seek an object through written language, even a definition of *eros* itself, the more we desire it. This tension between the Socratic and Platonic programs is central to the aspiration of poets such as Milton, Wordsworth, Keats, and Stevens.

Silence, especially when a response to imperfect attempts at enjoying heavenly music on earth, can indicate its own deceptive failure. Shakespeare, we will see, makes this point in *The Merchant of Venice*. The relationship of Socrates to Plato is crucial on this point. Despite his reputation as an enemy of

poets, Plato gives to writing precisely the kind of speculative value poets who aspire to be singers seek. The point is
expounded by Milton in "Apology for Smectymnuus," where
he writes that "he who would not be frustrate of his hope to
write well hereafter in laudable things, ought himself to be a
true poem." Milton understood that for one to be "a true
poem" was not simply a question of achieving, in Aristotelian terms, good *ethos*, or effecting a good plot and good
rhythm, but rather a question of redefining writing as an erotic,
speculative commitment to completing his cosmic circle.
Concluding his prolusion by pointing to an "inharmonious
style" that clashes with "the very harmony" he seeks to join,
and finally asserting "And so I shut up," Milton hints — with
an ability for grim laughter that will flourish in *Paradise
Lost* — that in striving to achieve a condition of harmonious
song both Pythagoras and Socrates wrote nothing. Fortunately,
Milton could not shut up. As the Athenian in Plato's *Laws*
observes: "No young creature . . . can keep its body or its voice
still; all are perpetually trying to make movements and noises"
(653e). Plato has a deep relation to the movements and noises
future ages of poets would make.

In writing on a subject that urges shameless silence as an
alternative to noisy shame, Plato and Augustine are not only
useful in the consideration of Christian poets. They help us
to understand the dilemma of any poet who seeks to turn the
musings of a "true musician" into noisy solutions achieved
in language. Augustine's difficulties in the last book of his
treatise on music demonstrate how challenging it is to use
language either to speak about or aspire to a condition of
music. They also indicate just how fiercely great wordsmiths
can aspire to a condition of music conceived in speculative
rather than practical terms.

The differences between speculative and practical music
are perhaps far greater for a poet than for a composer. This may
lead us to ask why certain poets did not become composers?

Milton, who was a musician, answers this question best, as we will see. But it is useful first to consider the question in the general terms of this chapter.

The composer Allen Gimbel describes music as "philosophy made palpable," for a composer can make "pure philosophy" or "pure mathematics" into sound. He means by this that music is Pythagorean speculation made audible. As Edward Rothstein explains in *Emblems of Mind*, the connection between sounds and number is "not arbitrary. It is not a metaphor: if we interpret the words properly, sound is simply heard number; number is latent sound."[90] Whereas the difference between speculative and practical music can make even a poet such as Milton talk about "shutting up," composers can make speculation and practice one. But if the most exalted music can begin in the realm of "pure music," as it doubtless can, poetry cannot. Poetry attempts not to make "pure philosophy" or "pure mathematics" palpable, but to confront life, in all its dirtiness, and somehow purify it, raising it to a level of "music." In the words of Karl Kraus, "My language is the univeral whore whom I have to make into a virgin."[91]

Composers would confront a similar difficulty, but they would largely confront the more nearly "pure" problem of turning music theory into song. Unlike poets, they could begin in the realm of music, taking as their task to make speculation ornately audible, as Bach does in his fugues. Playing for his God, and also to people, Bach could make even the tonic dissonant, and could turn, reassuringly, that dissonance into consonance. Later, Mozart would think to take us far away from the tonic, moving to a key we shouldn't wish to be in, then moving quickly — and perhaps effortlessly on his part — back to the tonic, which our ears have been hankering to achieve. And Beethoven would play yet more intensely with the possibilities and problems of purifying resolution — taking us further and further away from where our resolute ears are heading before finally redirecting our entrance home.

Especially when writing about the impure relationship between poetry and music, Shakespeare and Milton are interested in delaying, complicating, or refusing resolution — chiefly because for poets the nature of poetry as song was not merely in flux but always in crisis.

The battle between poetry and music has always been fierce, and the rest of this book examines it from the perspectives of various poets, chiefly those with the most claim to triumph. But we must remember, from beginning to end, the nature and complexity of the battle — and the degree to which it becomes an idiosyncratic, personal agon, informed in part by the larger struggle of finding idiosyncratic language to depict it. Ironically, one could say this about poets and composers alike. Both need continually to create anew — and always recreate — distinct structural bases for their chief conceptual metaphors. Both composers and poets have to define and redefine what "song" is. It is a difficult, and different, task from each side, and creating metaphors that articulate differences in an attempt to posit identity — namely the identity of song — always takes, to quote Aristotle, "genius." And the skill is a mystery that cannot be taught.

In Richard Strauss's opera *Cappriccio*, La Roche responds to the assertion that poetry and music are sister and brother arts by calling it "a bold metaphor." His is a bold, but apt, assertion, questioning with humor the ancient association. *Capriccio* at once shows that the two are so different not truly to be siblings, and at the same time best when linked. The opera ends by declaring opera the supreme art because it combines the two. But putting poetry to music, as Kramer oberves, almost always means making poetry subservient to it — making poetry "musical" because it is not musical itself.

Poetry is "musical." It is simply not musical in the ways music is — and can never be, short of being subsumed by it.[92] As Liszt writes, juxtaposing the self-sufficiency of music and the inferiority of poetry, one cannot "assert that the heavenly art does not exist for its own sake, is not self-sufficient, does not kindle of itself the divine spark, and has value only as the representative of an *idea* or as an exaltation of language."[93] What is most significant is that Liszt thought the defense necessary.

Kramer suggests that "once separated, music and poetry tend to become nostalgic for each other."[94] But envy, not nostalgia, I think, is often the appropriate word, for it is not so much a desire to be recombined with the other but a need to succeed on its own. Each sister art envies qualities possessed with seeming ease by the other.

Liszt notwithstanding, composers do envy a certain ability for articulating ideas. And poets, like it or not, envy music, its superior — perhaps "pure" — musicality. This is the central issue for any poet who aspires to a condition of music.

Poetry is, as Aristotle said, musical, but even Valéry could not make it "musical" in the "purely musical" way music is. Words can be musical, but they are not music. "By diction," Aristotle writes, "I mean the actual composition of the verses, while the effect of music is clear to all." But we know it is not. Most mysterious, finally, is what the "musicality" of poetry actually is. Poetry doubtless has rhythm, assonance, alliteration, rhyme, and even pitch. But there are no pure musical tones. And the question arises: how to conceive "ditties of no tone" — unheard melodies — as "sweeter" than heard melodies. Keats is suggesting that poetry can better "pipe to the spirit" than music can. The question is why? What could poetry have on music?

It is best to begin by acknowledging, along with the greatest — indeed, most musical — poets, why poetry must aspire toward music. Only then may we begin, along with poets, to assert, describe, and define the ways poetry may exceed music. Poetry may exceed music in its Socratic ability for discourse — for speculative discussions that are less than "purely musical," unavoidably representative, and therefore, as both Shakespeare and Stevens knew, inextricable parts of life and art.

Music can move us to ineffable feelings and lead us to miraculous, metalinguistic ideas, but poetry can surpass music in the complex articulation of certain ideas. Poetry is "representative" in ways music cannot be. Language can further speculative discussions in ways music cannot. This does not mean, however, that the "music of poetry" is reduced to articulations of ideas. There is a kind of music specific to poetry, a music of language, however mysterious in nature, that even music does not have.

In the rivalry of sibling arts, Shakespeare cannot beat Beethoven. But neither can Beethoven beat Shakespeare. If we imagine a tug of war, composers and poets will line up on opposite sides, each entrant with his or her feet grounded in friendly theoretical soil, each with wonderful, tugging explanations for why his side wins. But viewed from the muddy middle, the knot in the rope will never move. Neither side could possibly lose. And so neither side could ever win. At the end of the day, both sides can only hope not to be challenged and vanquished on their common field by another sibling art, say painting, which could easily canvass the derisible scene.

While the sibling rivalry has no end in sight, poets acknowledge the superiority of music to poetry much more frequently and with much greater consequence than composers do the opposite. Why don't poets become musicians or composers? The answer is they view the matter in speculative terms. Composers may hold that music is the only pure and immediate art; but this, we know, is not altogether true. "Music suffers from its similarity to language and cannot escape from it," writes Theodor Adorno. "Only music that has once been language transcends its similarity to language."[95] While Adorno's assertion is a call to a certain aspiration on the part of composers, it is also a justification of poetic aspirations toward a condition of music. It even suggests the potential superiority of poetry to music.

The "music of poetry" is a difficult metaphor, and for poets the relationship between speculative and instrumental music is at the heart of what this metaphor means, or can mean. Poets who grapple with the Platonic view of the relationship between earthly poetry and heavenly music will not accept conventional rhetorical poetics as solutions to their speculative dilemmas. Their inventive speculative poetics consider the stark differences between poetry and song. In fact, they tend to be those few poets who have been rightly credited with changing forever the practical possibilities of addressing new subjects and achieving new sounds. Shakespeare, Milton, Wordsworth, Keats, Stevens — each is a poet who saw a need to fashion a speculative poetic for himself, one that addresses in the practical terms of poetic form the deep tensions between poetry and song, between the accomplishments accessible to a poet and the aspirations of a "true musician."

TWO

꙾

Shakespeare and the "Sweet Power of Music"

Shakespeare put into dramatic conflict all of the competing theories considered in the previous chapter. Platonic speculation, Aristotelian *ars*, and Neoplatonic magic all have a place not only in dramatic and lyric poetry, Shakespeare knew, but in the contemplation and enjoyment of life itself. Living in a nation hungry for musical language, he dramatized not only individual poetic aspiration to a heavenly tune but also the complex aspiration of an entire nation at once to enjoy the music he could give them and examine their proper enjoyment of it. The importance of music — both practical and speculative — in Shakespeare's plays is rooted in an intense need both to engage people in their aspirations toward musical merriment and show them how pursuits of merriment might come to either harmonious or clashing ends. Shakespeare made it possible, indeed necessary, at once to enjoy the inscrutable magic of poetic music and contemplate its potential dangers.

Enjoyment of the wrong kind of earthly music, many in Shakespeare's England knew, could lead one away from the heavenly tune. But dissonance, Shakespeare consistently shows us, is part of the rich harmony we may know on earth.

The conflict between speculation and practice is related to the grandest themes in Shakespeare's plays — a way of speaking about the mediation of appetite and reason, frenzy and self-rule, evasion of shame and painful self-reflection. An insuperable champion of "the sweet power of music" and musical language, Shakespeare was also critical of naive (Neoplatonic) assertions of that power. He was unique in using the charms of music and musical language subtly to involve audiences in complex speculative debates about their power and value. With an abiding interest in the conflict between speculative and practical music and his ability to complicate or resolve it with his honeyed tongue, Shakespeare fashioned the condition of music to which future poets could aspire.

Shakespeare's interest in speculative music is most famously represented by Lorenzo's dazzling speech about heavenly harmony in the last scene of *The Merchant of Venice*. With Lorenzo's speech, Shakespeare offers, as he often does, his uncommon treatment of a Renaissance commonplace.

James Hutton first identified Lorenzo's speech as merely a conventional mixture of speculative (chiefly Neoplatonic) musical theories in praise of music.[1] "Much has been written . . . about Lorenzo's almost too familiar lines," Hutton writes. "Everyone recognizes that the topics are traditional, but, if I am not mistaken, it is always assumed that Shakespeare himself has brought them together. . . . [I]t has not . . . been made clear that this speech not only contains traditional topics, but that the arrangement is traditional. . . . [I]n short," Hutton concludes, "we have here to do with a coherent literary theme that Shakespeare has taken bodily into his play . . . [s]o familiar a theme, indeed, that Shakespeare permits himself to treat it in a kind of shorthand." As Hutton writes:

The following topics appear in this order, though much expanded, in Gioseffo Zarlino's *Institutioni harmoniche* 1.2–4 (1558): The Pythagoreans said that the world is musically composed, the heavens produce harmony, and that the human soul, formed on the same principle, is moved and vivifies its virtue by music; music is an important ingredient in the other arts and disciplines . . . and is the only art practiced in Paradise; the earth is full of natural music; man the microcosm should respond to music, since even insensible things do so, and Linus and Orpheus tamed beasts and birds, moved rocks, and checked streams; the Pythagoreans and others cured ills of mind and body with music; one who does not delight in it must be of base character, and nature has failed to provide him with the organ that judges of harmony.

Quoting Ronsard on the subject of the "unmusical man," Hutton concludes that "It is as one more of these *laudes musicae* that an Elizabethan audience would hear Lorenzo's familiar words."[2]

Lorenzo's speech is rightly the *locus classicus* for discussions of speculative music in the Renaissance, but it is so for a number of wrong reasons. Scholars have long agreed that Lorenzo's speech is merely a traditional (Neoplatonic) praise of music that enacts dramatically the play's fully harmonious resolution. But the musical and dramatic meanings of his speech are more complicated than scholars have suggested. Lorenzo's speech is doubtless filled with Neoplatonic elements, but it is not a disembodied summary of Neoplatonic treatises that "Shakespeare has taken bodily into his play."

Hutton's valuable study influenced the criticism of Lorenzo's speech, and Shakespeare's allusions to speculative music in general, in two important ways. First, scholars — John Hollander, S. K. Heninger, and Lawrence Danson, among others — furthered Hutton's reductions: of Lorenzo's speech to Neoplatonic "shorthand"; of Lorenzo to Shakespeare; and of Shakespeare's view to Lorenzo's speech.[3] Second, they followed

Hutton's assumption that Shakespeare's "shorthand treatment" typifies the thought of an age that extends from Ronsard
to Milton.[4] Such readings of Lorenzo's speech fail to account
for the considerable innovations not only of *Merchant*, but,
more generally, of Shakespeare and Milton.[5]

Shakespeare's interests and "views" go far beyond what
Lorenzo says, or what has been said about Lorenzo's speech.
Lorenzo speaks for neither Shakespeare nor the play. Lorenzo,
we will see, speaks for himself, not for Shakespeare. For too
long, many fine critics have based their interpretations of
Merchant on a fixed Neoplatonic reading of Lorenzo's speech.
C. L. Barber asserted long ago that "No other comedy, until
the late romances, ends with so full an expression of harmony
as that which we get in the opening of the final scene of *Merchant*. And no other final scene is so completely without irony
about the joys it celebrates."[6] This is still a standard reading
of Lorenzo's speech and the final scene. The play, however,
does not fully support it, for a number of reasons this chapter
will examine. A harmonious resolution "completely without
irony" requires the harmonious assimilation of Jessica in
Belmont, but Jessica perhaps excludes herself from the celebration with her response to Lorenzo's speech: "I am never
merry when I hear sweet music" (5.1.69).[7] The meaning of
this line rests, ultimately, upon the context of discussions
about music and merriment that take up much of *Merchant*
to this point. Either Jessica is hinting, darkly, that she is never
"pleased," or "joyous," when she hears music that should
make her so, or she is asserting with ironic humor that she is
never "facetious," or merely "amused," when she hears music that should make her contemplative. Either way, we will
see, Jessica's last line presents us with an engaging problem
that centers on the conflict between practical and speculative
approaches to music.

Critics have been hesitant to see the darker aspects of Jessica's last line, hearing it as mere prattle in a playful relationship. But there is much more to Jessica and her response.

Shakespeare built into *Merchant* a pattern of responses to music that culminates in Jessica's response to Lorenzo and the celebratory music. In a number of ways, the play is a less-than-merry, troubling comedy that questions with ironic dissonance the joys most of its characters celebrate too forcibly.

The relationship between Jessica and Lorenzo and the pattern of allusions to music and merriment throughout *Merchant* provide, we will see, the larger context in which not only Lorenzo's speech but also the general harmony of Belmont and resolution of *Merchant* must be considered. The harmony of Belmont must be examined, moreover, within a theoretical musical context: the conflict between speculative and practical music on which Shakespeare bases a number of the play's dramatic tensions.

What exactly does Jessica mean when she says, "I am never merry when I hear sweet music"? What, generally, is the relationship between music and merriment — and between speculation and practice — within the play? And what is the relationship between these questions and the central issues of the play? On these important matters, Jessica, as much as Lorenzo, speaks for the play. In *Merchant*, men attempt to control women by controlling their reactions to music. Shylock and Lorenzo live according to competing theories not only of religion and life but also music. By living with both, Jessica learns more about their competing truths than anyone else in the play.

One of many reactions to music and talk about music within *Merchant*, Jessica's last line is the most important; for too long it has been attuned by scholars to the dazzling speech that surrounds it. During the last 40 years, various critics and diverse schools of criticism, paying little attention to Shakespeare's interest in the conflict between speculative and practical music, have either ignored Jessica or fit her into their readings. Even recent feminist studies do not give Jessica the attention she demands.[8] Some critics have suggested that the harmony of Belmont is suspect, but the matter — like Jessica —

has still not been adequately considered, in large part because the speculative context has not been fully examined. The aspiration to a condition of song brought Shakespeare to remarkable insights for which commonplaces would not do.

Shakespeare was, among other things, a brilliant and subtle orchestrator of dramatic form, and by the time of *Merchant* he was already getting very good. He was beginning to write comedies in which problems resist the dramatic resolution of the play, using not only dramatic but also thematic tensions to involve his audience in its own moral and cultural dilemmas. Throughout *Merchant*, reactions to music form a coherent pattern, building tensions that climax in Lorenzo's speech and Jessica's reaction to it. Shakespeare, we will see, not only develops and complicates the idea of harmony within the history of ideas; he does so with complex theoretical and dramatic contextualizations.

As Cynthia Lewis points out, taking further the observations of Norman Rabkin, "a sensible reading of [*Merchant*] begins not with formulating quick judgements that reduce its meaning, but with observing 'patterns,' like those in a 'dance,' which recur throughout the work."[9] Reactions to music in *Merchant* reveal a large, coherent pattern that helps us to understand the play. Reactions to music — and talk about music — reveal the quality of merriment achieved by its characters. Finally, the reaction of an audience to Lorenzo's speech reveals a good deal about the quality of merriment that audience may achieve for itself.

Although Shakespeare never reveals directly his desire to sing with the angels, even in his sonnets, he everywhere exhibits it. What is perhaps most important, he often plays with our aspiration, sometimes delighting us with the heights of his music just after he has warned us of the power of false music to delude and corrupt. So, too, he often tells us about the power of music to heal by bringing us to truth. A study of *Merchant*, followed by a brief look at Shakespeare's broader theoretical and dramatic interest in competing theories of music, will help us better to appreciate Shakespeare's innovative articulations of the "sweet power" of music and poetry, as well as the ways they shaped profoundly both the opportunities and limits of future poets who would aspire to turn poetry into song.

Music and Merriment in The Merchant of Venice

One can say with good reason, along with Frank Kermode, that *Merchant* is a play about justice, but it is also chiefly a play about characters who seek, in their various ways, merriment.[10] The pursuit of merriment — and its relation to a Platonic sense of justice, or temperance — is the subject of the first three scenes. Antonio begins the play by saying, "I know not why I am so sad," confessing wisely that he has "much ado to know myself." His friend Solanio offers tautology as counsel, "Then let us say you are sad/ Because you are not merry . . ." (1.1.47–8). In the second scene, Nerissa has to tell Portia, who has long been seeking merriment, to be careful not to let eagerness to achieve it keep her from striking a happy mean: "It is no mean happiness . . . to be seated in the mean; superfluity comes sooner by white hairs, but competency lives longer" (1.2.6–8). With her choice "curbed by the will of a dead father," which requires certain reactions to music, Portia reveals that such pressure can further thwart one's judgement. Musing upon two bad choices and rejecting "mean happiness," Portia proposes an intemperate choice, "I had rather be married to a death's-head with a bone in his mouth than to either of these. God defend me from these two" (1.2.47–49). In the third scene, Shylock sets up the extreme requirements of his "merry sport."

In the first three scenes, Shakespeare quickly establishes the context in which we must see the choices characters make in their attempts to be merry. Whether merriment is to come from within or without is a central question, and it is related to the difference between Platonic and Neoplatonic approaches to the power of music.

The question whether "sweet music" should make Jessica "merry" contains within it the larger question on which the play is centered: what does it mean to be "merry?" *Merchant* is a play about conflicting attempts to be "merry" — and the antipodal worldviews on which these attempts are based. The crux of the play is that Antonio and Shylock cannot both end the play "merry." There is the further suggestion that Christians and Jews cannot simultaneously be merry, and this is why Jessica's last utterance carries so much weight.

The Christians are, as Bassanio himself exclaims to Gratiano, "friends/ That purpose merriment" (2.2.189–90). For Shylock, who rejects such purposing, the possibility for merriment exists only in the "merry sport" of his "bond" (1.3.139–47). It is clear that the "sport" of Shylock's bond is not "merry." It is less clear, although clearly as true, that forcible conversion of "the Jew" is another form of "merry sport" that is not truly "merry" or "gentle."

Merchant is a play about polarizing worldviews causing people to assert one as true and the other as the false pursuit of merriment. No character, moreover, is willing to be content with "mean happiness." But, as Maynard Mack observes in his essay "Engagement and Detachment in Shakespeare's Plays," the "usual lesson of comedy" is that "overengagement to any obsessive single view of oneself or the world is to be avoided."[11] *Merchant* depicts merciless Christians purposing merriment as well as a merciless Jew. The play considers not why one of the two pursuits is true, but why both are potentially destructive. And it is Jessica, a willing convert, I am suggesting, who most comes to understand the reasons why.

The pun on *gentle* and *gentile* made consistently in the play suggests that Shylock could improve his fortune by assimilating: by being *gentle* (by becoming a Christian). The plot requires that we accept not only Shylock's forced conversion as a comic resolution, but also his forced response to Portia's question: "Art thou contented, Jew? What dost thou say?" Shylock says, "I am content" (4.1.391–92), but we know he is not. Jessica, in stark contrast, not only converts willingly but twice accepts the promise that a change of religion will bring a change of fortune: "O Lorenzo,/ If thou keep promise, I shall end this strife,/ Become a Christian and thy loving wife"; and "I shall be saved by my husband. He hath made me a Christian" (2.3.20–22; 3.5.17–18). The first time we see her, Jessica says: "Our house is hell" (2.3.1). Jessica looks to conversion for salvation and merriment, for an alternative to her life "of tediousness" (2.3.3) with her repressive Jewish father. Whereas Shylock is forced to convert, Jessica is willing — but her willingness is a repressive flight from curbed choices more than it is a faithful leap to a good life. She gives away her father's turquoise ring, voiding with this gesture the union that made her a Jew, trading, symbolically, a rigid world of law for a lascivious world of choice. But the question of self-knowledge complicates her embrace of choice.

Whereas Shylock is forced to convert, Jessica is seduced by the offer of a merry life. Shylock's penultimate utterance in the play — "I am content" — is ironic. Jessica's last line — "I am never merry when I hear sweet music" — is also ironic. She cannot say *never*. Or can she? Is she saying she was not merry the first time she heard Lorenzo's sweet music? Or is she saying she will follow Lorenzo's speculative lesson with requisite seriousness? We know what Portia demands of Shylock when she asks, "Are you content, Jew?" But do we know exactly what Lorenzo demands of Jessica when he says, "Mark the music"?

The dramatic counterpoint created by the last utterances of father and daughter is significant. Lorenzo's "resolution" in Belmont hinges on whether or not Jessica is "merry" at the end of the play — and whether any failure to be merry is a result of a failure in her (a natural failure of her impenetrable Jewish soul?) or a failure in Lorenzo. Anyone interested in *Merchant* must arbitrate these matters, and this means taking a fresh view of the play, and of the dramatic and thematic contexts of Lorenzo's speech.

The immediate context of Lorenzo's famous speech is the echoic exchange of "In such a night . . ." that precedes it. The exchange centers on classical stories of love-turned-bitter; the subject speaks against the harmony of the echoic form. Lorenzo speaks of Troilus and Cressida, which turns Jessica to Thisbe. Lorenzo mentions Dido, which turns Jessica to Medea, and Jessica's insinuation that she has risked everything for him leads Lorenzo to their case:

> In such a night
> Did Jessica steal from the wealthy Jew,
> And with an unthrift love did run from Venice
> As far as Belmont.

Jessica speaks directly to the core of what seem to be real troubles:

> In such a night
> Did young Lorenzo swear he loved her well,
> Stealing her soul with many vows of faith,
> And ne'er a true one.
>
> (5.1.14–22)

If the other exchanges can be excused as playful literary allusions, Jessica's last charge — a direct one — cannot. Lorenzo responds: "In such a night/ Did pretty Jessica, like a little shrow/ Slander her love, and he forgave it her." But Jessica appears unforgiving, concluding the exchange by remarking her unwillingness to conclude it: "I would out-night you, did nobody come:/ But hark, I hear the footing of a man" (5.1.23–24). By 5.1, real trouble appears to be afoot.

The exchange ends with Jessica promising to "out-night" Lorenzo, interrupted by Portia's servant Stephano. Before

Stephano is gone, Lorenzo begins his speculative speech about musical harmony. Rather than an isolated piece of Neoplatonism, Lorenzo's speech is part of Shakespeare's intricate dramatic context. It appears to be an attempt to make Jessica merry once again. Lorenzo's speech is a seductive praise of the power of music, spoken by the play's hottest lover at a time when Jessica appears, with reason, to be getting cold.

The serious subject of the exchange pushes the limits of playful banter, signaling a conflict between beautiful form and ugly content, between the charm of sound and the trouble of its meaning. Lorenzo attempts to effect a transition to a better, more harmonious aspect of "such a night." He tries to get Jessica to see that "such a night" *becomes* "soft stillness" and "the touches of sweet harmony" rather than the will to "out-night." Any movement from embittered discussion to "sweet touches" would be good, and Lorenzo, an astute rhetorician, uses what he knows of musical theory to refashion the night.

Rather than mere Neoplatonic shorthand, Lorenzo's speech is a conspicuous translation of a lover's lofty new promises into exalted musical terms:

> Sweet soul, let's in, and there expect their coming.
> And yet no matter; why should we go in?
> My friend Stephano, signify, I pray you,
> Within this house, your mistress is at hand,
> And bring your music forth into the air.   [*Exit Stephano.*]
> How sweet the moonlight sleeps upon this bank!
> Here will we sit and let the sounds of music
> Creep in our ears; soft stillness and the night
> Become the touches of sweet harmony.
> Sit, Jessica. Look how the floor of heaven
> Is thick inlaid with patens of bright gold.
> There's not the smallest orb which thou behold'st
> But in his motion like an angel sings,
> Still quiring to the young-eyed cherubins;
> Such harmony is in immortal souls,

> But whilst this muddy vesture of decay
> Doth grossly close it in, we cannot hear it.
>   *[Enter musicians.]*
> Come ho, and wake Diana with a hymn!
> With sweetest touches pierce your mistress' ear
> And draw her home with music.
>   *Play music.*
>
>   (5.1.49–68)

Lorenzo first promises "the touches of sweet harmony," which appears, at first, to refer to actual music to be played (off stage) by the musicians — seductive sounds that might make Jessica happy to become soft and still, and receptive to Lorenzo's "sweet touches." But six lines later Lorenzo links "the touches of sweet harmony" to the heavenly harmony they cannot hear: "Such harmony" refers back to the "sweet harmony," but "whilst this muddy vesture of decay/ Doth grossly close it in," Lorenzo says, they cannot hear.

Six lines after offering Jessica some tangible music, he redefines it as heavenly harmony, only to explain one line later that they cannot hear it. In short, Lorenzo promises Jessica something he cannot provide, and the exchange of "In such a night . . ." suggests he has done this before. The speech is dazzling, but it reveals what appears to be a habit of breaking vows.

The "sweet power" of speech and music were deeply linked in Shakespeare's day. Both were considered modes of seduction, and in 5.1, Lorenzo has a need for grander, "sweeter" promises, bigger vows that might make Jessica forget about broken ones. Lorenzo, it appears, must elicit harmony from discord. After he tells Jessica that we cannot hear the music of the spheres, the musicians enter, and Lorenzo gives them specific directions. Speaking to Portia's musicians at Portia's house, Lorenzo tells them, literally, to draw her home. But he is also speaking, in Neoplatonic terms, about the theory according to which the actual "sounds of music" can pierce the ear, touch the soul, and reattune it, thereby drawing it home to the heavenly harmony. The Neoplatonic theory of the "sweet power of music," namely that music can penetrate one's soul and draw it to heaven, merely complicates the matter of wooing with false vows, for it is deeply related to seduction by false music, as well as, more generally, to penetration of Jessica's body.

Lorenzo attempts to placate Jessica not by winning an old argument, as in the exchange of "In such a night," but by dazzling her with beautiful new promises and lascivious music — both of which had worked well before. As Robin Headlam Wells observes, "a man of eloquence is capable of persuading people to do whatever he wishes. However, the real mark of his power is not his ability to *force* people 'to yeeld in that which most standth against their will,' but rather," as Thomas Wilson asserts in his influential *Arte of Rhetorique*, "his skill in inducing them 'to *will* that which he did.'"[12] Using the common association of music and rhetoric, Shakespeare juxtaposes the forced conversion of Shylock with Lorenzo's attempt to re-seduce Jessica in the final scene.

It is only within this dramatic context that we can appreciate the significance of Lorenzo's speech. It is not merely a traditional (Neoplatonic) praise of music. And it is surely not "the most purely religious utterance in the play," as John Gross suggests.[13] Shakespeare gives Lorenzo a seductive speech, but he also subtly reveals Lorenzo's purpose. Lorenzo not only applies the "sweet power" of speech; he exposes his motives by seizing every opportunity to throw in the adjective *sweet*. In Shakespeare's plays, such excess serves to mock precisely the subjects most relevant here. To be excessively "sweet" is to be not "sweet" at all. Music, like rhetorical seduction, can be an illusion, and the love it induces becomes a foible. The best example of such acrid sweetness is *Troilus and Cressida* 3.1, where Shakespeare links the hyperbolic use of the word *sweet* with excessive appetites that lead to "broken music."

As Ulysses says, "Take but degree away, untune that string,/ And hark what discord follows" (1.3.109–10).

In *Cymbeline*, Shakespeare has Cloten mock the hyperbole of both the Neoplatonic idea of penetration and the literary conventions derived from it. Cloten — like Lorenzo, but in direct language — alludes to the musicians as surrogate seducers: "Come on, tune. If you can penetrate her with your fingering, so; we'll try with tongue too." After the musicians play, Cloten hedges: "So, get you gone. If this penetrate, I will consider your music the better; if it do not, it is a vice in her ears which horsehairs and calves' guts, nor the voice of unpaved eunuch to boot, can never amend."[14] Comically rendering the difference between deceptively false and beautifully true music, Cloten razes the system of musical powers affirmed by Neoplatonists such as Ronsard. Music shall prove good and powerful, says Cloten, only when it shall have enabled him to penetrate his lady.

Shakespeare's interest in mocking Neoplatonic theory is part of his larger interest in the pursuit of merriment and its relationship to the conflict between specualtive and practical aspirations to music. It is evident as early as *Love's Labor's Lost*, which exalts an austere course of speculative musical study in the Platonic tradition only then to undercut it with Neoplatonic sublimations of rampant appetite. The King decrees that he and his lords will be "brave conquerors . . ./ That war against your own affections," devoted to a contemplative life: "Our court shall be a little academe,/ Still and contemplative in living art." Berowne, however, troubled by the prospect of there being no ladies, voices his doubt about the austerity: "But is there no quick recreation granted?" Offering a substitute, the King answers that in lieu of ladies the men shall recreate themselves by means of musical language:

> Our court you know is haunted
> With a refinèd traveller of Spain, ·
> A man in all the world's new fashion planted,

That hath a mint of phrases in his brain;
One who the music of his own vain tongue
Doth ravish like enchanting harmony;
A man of complements, whom right and wrong
Have chose as umpire of their mutiny.

(1.1.159–66)

Such a man is a rhetorician. He may be an umpire of mutiny, but his skill points to another mutiny: between "quick recreation" (wine, women, and song) and slow moral re-creation ("contemplation in living art"), between "purposing merriment" and enduring the "much ado" it takes to achieve the happiness of self-knowledge.

Merchant is a play that centers on this conflict. Neoplatonic theory promises momentary ecstasy, but, in the end, Jessica offers, in the manner of her father, rough idiom to Lorenzo's mellifluous "vows of faith." At first, Jessica engages in the echoic exchange of "In such a night," showing that it cannot contain and beautify ugly truths. But, finally, she returns blunt prose to Lorenzo's dazzling blank verse: "I am never merry when I hear sweet music."

Jessica's unmusical last line induces Lorenzo to deliver a stock Neoplatonic answer that, rather than resolve the matter, shows that he is in deeper trouble than commonplace (Neoplatonic) sweet-talk can get him out of:

The reason is, your spirits are attentive.
For do but note a wild and wanton herd
Or race of youthful and unhandled colts
Fetching mad bounds, bellowing and neighing loud,
Which is the hot condition of their blood:
If they but hear perchance a trumpet sound,
Or any air of music touch their ears,
You shall perceive them make a mutual stand,
Their savage eyes turned to a modest gaze
By the sweet power of music. Therefore the poet
Did feign that Orpheus drew trees, stones, and floods;
Since naught so stockish, hard, and full of rage

But music for the time doth change his nature.
The man that hath no music in himself,
Nor is not moved with concord of sweet sounds,
Is fit for treasons, stratagems, and spoils;
The motions of his spirit are dull as night,
And his affections dark as Erebus.
Let no such man be trusted. Mark the music.

(5.1.70–88)

Lorenzo's reply, his Neoplatonic theory of the "unmusical man," suggests the seriousness of Jessica's reply. He glosses Ronsard: "The man who, on hearing a sweet accord of instruments or the sweetness of the natural voice, is not delighted and is not moved and does not tremble from head to foot, sweetly ravished and transported, gives proof thereby that he has a crooked, vicious, and depraved soul, and is to be guarded against as one not happily born."[15] Lorenzo darkly suggests that Jessica has no music in herself, for the reason that she is "not happily born."

In both parts of his speech, Lorenzo speaks not for Renaissance humanism, not for Shakespeare, but for himself. At first, trying to make a smooth romantic transition where none seems possible, Lorenzo applies the grandeur of Platonic talk. Pressed by Jessica's response that what he offers her does not make her merry, however, Lorenzo shows the meaner side of the man who stole "her soul with many vows of faith." In the first part of his speech, Lorenzo tells Jessica that heavenly harmony — much like true love? — is impossible to experience in this life. But after Jessica speaks, Lorenzo demands, with the hyperbole and illogic common to Shakespeare's hot lovers, that she — hence they — experience it. In the first part, while he is trying to charm Jessica, Lorenzo blames a universal human nature, the "muddy vesture of decay." What they have, he appears to be saying, is as good as can be had, given the "gross" nature of the world. But after Jessica says she is not merry, Lorenzo, shifting to a Neoplatonic argument, blames Jessica specifically.

Shakespeare has Lorenzo allude to two traditions (or conflicting aspects of a larger one). Whereas Plato maintains the unmusicality of all human souls (even Socrates'), Neoplatonists maintain that only unmusical souls are incapable of being pierced.[16] According to the strict speculative tradition developed by Plato, the soul must reattune itself.[17] According to Zarlino and other Neoplatonists, in contrast, instrumental music possesses the "sweet power" to refresh or "recreate" the human soul, to induce ecstasy, to lift the soul temporarily out of the body — to "draw it home."[18] Revealing the limits of Neoplatonic powers — especially the "sweet power" of "sweet music" — is part of the drama of the last scene.

Merchant is a play about contrary systems of values, and competing theories of music — like competing religions — are central to its dramatic structure. Lorenzo and Shylock offer competing theories of music, as well as competing beliefs about what will make Jessica merry. Lorenzo speaks the grandest, most eloquent speech about music in *Merchant*, but Shakespeare places it among plainer voices, voices he arranges to achieve the grand counterpoint of his dramatic logic. Despite his contempt for Christians and misplaced passion for his daughter, and despite the vile language in which he issues it, Shylock early offers Jessica what turns out to be a useful warning about music.

Sensing "some ill a-brewing towards my rest," Shylock warns, "Jessica my girl,/ Look to my house" (2.5.15–17). Informed by Launcelot about "a masque," Shylock warns, more specifically, about the danger of music:

> What, are there masques? Hear you me, Jessica:
> Lock up my doors; and when you hear the drum
> And the vile squealing of the wry-necked fife,
> Clamber not you up to the casements then,

> Nor thrust your head into the public street
> To gaze on Christian fools with varnished faces;
> But stop my house's ears — I mean my casements;
> Let not the sound of shallow fopp'ry enter
> My sober house. By Jacob's staff I swear
> I have no mind of feasting forth to-night;
> But I will go. Go you before me, sirrah.
> Say I will come.
>
> (2.5.27–38)

Fearful of the sexual allure of a Christian fool, Shylock commands Jessica not to "thrust" her "[maiden]head" into "the public street." The music played by Christians, warns Shylock, is like the "vile squealing" of pigs. Shylock commands Jessica to "stop [his] house's ears." Jessica's ears are the doors to her maidenhead, and such doors are his, for "Jessica [his] girl" is part of his house. With words that anticipate, in both form and matter, the first words of Lorenzo's speech in act 5, Shylock gives his daughter his last command: "Let not the sound of shallow fopp'ry enter/ My sober house."

Music has power, according to Shylock — not the deep, true power claimed by Neoplatonists, but the shallow power to corrupt decried by Puritans. That Shylock the Jew with his emotive Jewish music should make this charge only shows how complex the musical discussion in *Merchant* is. Shakespeare leaves us much to mark. Shylock has no "mind of feasting" on the "vile squealing" of "sweet music." Jessica does. But after feasting, she says, in her last line, that she "is never merry" when she hears "sweet music."

"Mark the Music"

Unlike Lorenzo, Shakespeare is not one to tell us simply to "mark the music." Shakespeare urges us to examine ourselves — to know what music we mark and how we mark it. We should not be surprised that *Merchant*, a comedy that plays on an audience's willingness to side emotionally with one tradition against another, concludes not with a traditional praise of harmony (*laudes musicae*) but rather with an ambiguous speech that borrows antithetical views from opposing traditions. Much like *Measure for Measure*, a play with which it has much in common, *Merchant* juxtaposes not only Judaism and Christianity but also Platonism and Neoplatonism. Both *Merchant* and *Measure* depict the opposition of merciless appetites for merriment and law, and both depict mediation by a Duke whose power it is either to be too merciful or too severe. Just as justice depends on temperance, as *Measure* shows, so does merriment. The way one listens — the expectations one has — determines how one will hear the music, and what kind of power it will have to make one happy.

That Shylock cannot be happy is a basic fact required by the plot of *Merchant*. But Jessica's happiness is a different matter: its uncertainty is a central part of the play. One reason "Shylock's enforced baptism is disconcerting," as Gross observes, "is that it is contrary to predominant Christian tradition. . . . The treatment meted out to Shylock belongs at the harsh end of the spectrum."[19] Jessica's unhappiness, if the result of a seduction that belongs at the kinder end of the spectrum, stands as a significant, ironic counterpoint to Shylock's defeat. Jessica converts willingly, yet still Lorenzo accounts early for the possibility of her eventual misfortune. Indeed, the likely failure of Jessica's assimilation is registered with irony in every scene in which she appears before 5.1.

In 2.4, even before the two appear together in the play, Lorenzo warns that Jessica might come to misfortune even as his bride:

> If e'er the Jew her father come to heaven,
> It will be for his gentle daughter's sake;
> And never dare misfortune cross her foot,
> Unless she do it under this excuse,
> That she is issue to a faithless Jew.

(2.4.33–37)

The "excuse" will be Jessica's Jewish nature, which, despite Jessica's hope that marriage and conversion will change it, Lorenzo says plainly cannot be changed. Similarly, Launcelot helps Jessica to leave her father, but not without telling her that "the sins of the father are to be laid upon the children" and "truly I think you are damned" (3.5.1–6).

Long before it seems that something has changed for the worse between Jessica and Lorenzo in 5.1, the play hints consistently at the likelihood of such trouble. As early as the elopement scene, the first scene in which Jessica and Lorenzo appear together, Gratiano and Salerio preface the elopement with foreboding truisms about love. As Salerio says, "O ten times faster Venus' pigeons fly/ To seal love's bonds new-made than they are wont/ To keep obligèd faith unforfeited" (2.6.5–7). Gratiano replies with his speech on the effects of "the strumpet wind," including his maxim "All things that are/ Are with more spirit chasèd than enjoyed" (2.6.12–13). And as soon as Jessica reenters, Lorenzo confirms that, as Gratiano had said, "lovers ever run before the clock" (2.6.4): "What, art thou come? On, gentlemen, away!/ Our masquing mates by this time for us stay" (2.6.58–59). It is time, says Lorenzo, to be in time for music and merriment.

The elopement scene shows Jessica too eager for merriment. It imparts misgivings about Jessica's self-knowledge, as well as deeper matters of shame and conscience that might come to her one day when she knows herself better. Jessica has expected Lorenzo to change her Jewish identity and thus her fortune, as she says to Launcelot before leaving Shylock's house:

> Alack, what heinous sin is it in me
> To be ashamed to be my father's child.
> But though I am a daughter to his blood,
> I am not to his manners. O Lorenzo,
> If thou keep promise, I shall end this strife,
> Become a Christian and thy loving wife!
>
> (2.3.16–21)

Jessica puts all her hope for future merriment in Lorenzo's "promise" and the associated promise of her conversion. Jessica confuses strife, which can end, with facts about her nature that cannot be erased — facts which, if she refuses to acknowledge them, would seem to promise to increase her strife.

In saying farewell to her father, Jessica tries to change her identity, and hence her fortune: "Farewell; and if my fortune be not crost,/ I have a father, you a daughter lost" (2.5.54–55). But in the elopement scene, Jessica shows herself to be very much "to his manners": while trying to rid herself of the shame of being her father's child, Jessica "gilds" herself with her father's ducats.

Whether a Jew can change her fortune by assimilating, by changing her manners, is a question central to the play. Jessica's "Here, catch this casket" (2.3.33) suggests her possession of an unburdened, merry spirit. She thinks she is trading tedium for merriment. The rest of what Jessica says in the elopement scene, however, is laden with dark meanings: "I am glad 'tis night — you do not look on me — /For I am much ashamed of my exchange" (2.6.34–35). She then offers a truism that hints at future troubles: "But love is blind, and lovers cannot see/ The pretty follies that themselves commit" (2.6.36–37). Since Jessica sees the shame of cross-dressing ("my exchange"), the lines register a latent concern that what she does not see might in the future be of greater consequence.

Jessica uses the word *shame* twice in this scene, and both times it resonates with her earlier mention of the "heinous sin . . . To be ashamed to be my father's child":

> What, must I hold a candle to my shames?
> They in themselves, good sooth, are too too light.
> Why, 'tis an office of discovery, love —
> And I should be obscured.
>
> (2.6.43–44)

The lines have their obvious as well as a deeper meaning. Clearly, Jessica wishes to hide her cross-dressing from her lover — and this seems natural. But Jessica appears more generally concerned with her "shames." There is disparity between Jessica's worry "I should be obscured" and Lorenzo's playful assurance, "So are you, sweet,/ Even in the lovely garnish of a boy." Lorenzo knows what he is getting — a pretty Jewish girl who is wearing pants and sporting the ducats of her "father Jew" (2.6.22). What Jessica seems anxious to obscure, rather, is a general need to obscure herself. Lorenzo tells Jessica to "come at once," but Jessica — thinking her shames "too too light" — delays, risking, in effect, a greater light, the sun: "I will make fast the doores, and gild myself/ With some moe ducats, and be with you straight" (2.6.49–50). Jessica appears worried about the exchange she makes with Lorenzo; to gild herself further with ducats is worth the risk. Jessica's identity — as a woman, as a lover, as a convert — appears to be in flux in 2.6. One problem is that she knows too little about the nature of "exchange" (her father's hated skill).[20] She does not know the true value of what she is giving in "exchange," and worries too little about what she is getting in Lorenzo.

Gilded in her father's ducats, Jessica endeavors to close forever behind her the doors of her father's house. But the scene suggests that Jessica may not quit her father's house with the mere consequence of the shame that comes from one episode of cross-dressing. On a deeper level, Jessica is ashamed to be ashamed of shame. This is a common proto-Freudian theme in Shakespeare, and it usually means trouble.

The notion that love is an "office of discovery" suggests that in time, through the foibles of blind love, there is truth to be known by Jessica — both about Lorenzo and about herself. Jessica also stands to learn about two very important subjects about which Launcelot proffers his clownish wisdom: the practical concerns of leaving one's Jewish master and the conscience that attends an attempted flight from one's identity as one's father's child. Launcelot has an easier time than Jessica, for the two concerns are not one for him. "Certainly my conscience will serve me to run from this Jew my master" (2.1.1), he says in his first line. He then encounters his father, Old Gobbo, and proceeds to ask him "Do you know me, father?" The Launcelot-Gobbo subplot suggests, however glibly, that where identity, conscience, shame, and fathers are concerned, "Truth will come to light . . . in the end truth will out" (2.2.74). Not only is love an "office of discovery"; music is a means toward revelation.

The relationship between Jessica and Lorenzo develops offstage. Shakespeare tells us little about them, but he composes what he does tell us with his consummate ability to use themes to build dramatic conflict. Jessica and Lorenzo appear together in only three scenes: 2.6, 3.5, and 5.1. The first two establish a pattern of hinting at trouble that is sure to come, at truth that is sure to come out. In 2.6, Salerio ends his discussion with Gratiano about the fickleness of lovers. In 3.5. Lorenzo appears ready to defend Jessica from the charge he himself makes in 2.4, namely "that there's no mercy for [Jessica] in heaven because [she is] a Jew's daughter," as Launcelot says. Evading the serious charge against his wife, Lorenzo chooses instead to defend the comic assault on his own reputation, namely that he is "no good member of the commonwealth" (3.5.29–33) because by converting Jews he raises the price of pork. Lorenzo's tone with the clown is appropriately playful, but Lorenzo's focus on himself is suspect. He spends very little time talking with Jessica. Finished with Launcelot, Lorenzo asks, "How cheer'st thou, Jessica?" The question is central to our understanding of the banter in act 5. Lorenzo does not, however, wait for an answer. Instead, he elicits her opinion of Portia. When Jessica replies that "the poor rude world/ Hath not her fellow" (3.5.75–76), Lorenzo takes her answer as an opportunity to assert his opinion of himself: "Even such a

husband/ Hast thou of me as she is for a wife" (3.5.77–78).
The ensuing dialogue is the only conversation between the
couple since 2.6, and it is last we hear from them until 5.1:

> Jessica: Nay, but ask my opinion too of that!
> Lorenzo: I will anon. First let us go to dinner.
> Jessica: Nay, let me praise you while I have a stomach.
> Lorenzo: No, pray there, let it serve for table-talk;
>   Then howsome'er thou speak'st, 'mong other things
>   I shall digest it.
> Jessica: Well, I'll set you forth.
>
> (3.5.78–83)

The banter is playful, but the talk about appetite broaches
darker matters. The transformation of appetite to dyspepsia
is a common theme throughout Shakespeare, most notably in
Troilus and Cressida, the play in which, not coincidentally,
Shakespeare shows with the greatest detail the way excessively
"sweet" music and speech become sour. In *Merchant* the
theme is initiated by Nerissa — "they are as sick that surfeit
with too much" (1.2.5) — and continued, as we have seen, by
Gratiano and Salerio in 2.6. The short dialogue between Jessica and Lorenzo in 3.5 alludes to the correlation between
moving from appetite to digestion and from opinion to knowledge. It registers hints of difference between the lovers that
begin to seem serious in 5.1.

And there are significant differences: Lorenzo would eat
first; Jessica would praise him while she has a stomach. Jessica appears set on giving her opinions; Lorenzo appears ready
to digest them, "among other things." Digestion, like the
calculated rendering and shifting of opinions, is the stuff of
lovers after they have ceased to "run before the clock," after
they have "feasted," as the excessive urge to taste gives way
to disgust. Music sounds different when the stomach is full of
food and the ear full of compliments. As Shakespeare's Cleopatra knows, the ear is lusty. But it also gets full.

The two brief discussions between Jessica and Lorenzo in 2.6 and 3.5, along with the exchange of "In such a night . . ." at the beginning of 5.1, compose the context of Lorenzo's famous speech about harmony. The pattern is vital. Just as there is irony in Jessica's last response to Lorenzo, so is there irony in Jessica's first response to Lorenzo in the play, in the balcony scene: "Who are you? Tell me for more certainty,/ Albeit I'll swear that I do know your tongue" (2.6.26–27). As the play goes on, it appears that Jessica knew the tongue, the dazzling vows, but not the man. By 5.1, there is the strong suggestion that something has happened since 2.6, that a shrewd woman (shrewd like her father) confronts a sweet-talking man who appears to have failed to keep his vows, that Lorenzo is the main reason Jessica is not merry when she hears "sweet music." Self-knowledge and conscience appear to be other reasons.

Shakespeare develops a pattern showing that blame is to be placed on both Jessica and Lorenzo. On Jessica, not because her soul is Jewish, but because she intemperately avoids the truth that it is. Jessica is an inversion of Antonio. Antonio considers self-knowledge a precondition for merriment and merriment a necessary precondition for love. Jessica, in contrast, has less need to hide her shames from the public street than from herself. Antonio knows enough to reject Solanio's suggestion that repression leads to happiness: "Then let us say you are sad/ Because you are not merry; and 'twere as easy/ For you to laugh and leap, and say you are merry/ Because you are not sad" (1.1.47–50). Jessica thinks that because she is unhappy in her father's house she will be happy if she leaves it — with Lorenzo. With an "unthrift love," she goes as far as she thinks she has to ("As far as Belmont," as Lorenzo says), which turns out, it seems, to be at once not far enough and too far from home.

Following the description of the serious consequences of failing to be made merry by music, Lorenzo speaks his last words to Jessica: "Mark the music." These last words, in the form of a command, do not suggest mere playful banter. Recalling Shylock's commands when he senses trouble with his daughter, Lorenzo's last words to Jessica suggest that there is, and is going to be, trouble between him and his wife. By the last scene of the play, Jessica appears to know that merriment is not determined according to religious dogma or musical theories but according to the faith of one's lover.

Just when Lorenzo's vows may turn to lies, his seductive exhortations turn to commands. Lorenzo's commands replace Shylock's. They are more subtle, made mellifluous by the music of his speech, but they are commands: "Sit, Jessica. . . . Mark the music." Jessica's reaction to Lorenzo's speech and the music of Portia's musicians is her form of resisting once again the man who commands her, her rejection of a world-view that would govern her reaction to music, and thereby her reactions to all things. Jessica's answer that she is "never merry" when she hears "sweet music" reveals, moreover, that Shylock's view of music turns out to be more nearly true for her than Lorenzo's view.

Jessica must not only choose between the antithetical views put forth by her father and her lover; twice she is called upon to see through the discrepancy between form and content apparent in the articulation of each view. In the first instance Jessica shuns her father's disharmonious "manners" and is led to a kind of merriment by the "vile squealing" of Lorenzo's music. Finally, however, at Belmont, music — and musical speech — lose their formerly seductive power. Lorenzo's speech about "the sweet power of music" becomes a useless lesson about harmony, for an untrue lover cannot teach it, having already taught a lesson about discord.

Whether or not *Merchant* expresses a cogent theory in which Shakespeare himself believed may not be determined from Lorenzo's speech alone. What is clear from Lorenzo's speech is that Shakespeare was learned enough to make Lorenzo speak in a way that fit his clear dramatic design.[21]

The question whether "sweet music" should make Jessica "merry" contains within it the larger question on which the play is centered: what does it mean to be "merry?" Jessica may perhaps seem too "attentive" to discord, but contemplation, as Antonio declares at the beginning of the play, is the only means of achieving true and lasting merriment. This antithesis — between Platonic speculation and Neoplatonic magic — is a central theme of the play. Whatever the mystery of Antonio's sadness, Antonio's conception of merriment is Socratic in its basic terms: one needs to reattune (re-create) one's soul morally before one can achieve merriment (recreation). Jessica, in contrast, had thought that merriment might come as freely as the music of a tabor — as a result of the easy conversion from Judaism to Christianity. At first Lorenzo provides her with recreation; but eventually, it is clear that neither conversion nor marriage will re-create Jessica. She must do that herself. One has to mark not only the seductive music of another but the speculative music of one's life.

Harmony in Belmont

Jessica's response to Lorenzo's speech and the music of Portia's musicians in act 5 raises questions crucial to the resolution of the drama. Does Jessica's response confirm that a Jewish soul is "not unhappily born?" Or is Jessica's failure to be merry a good thing? Does she exhibit a noble melancholia that distinguishes her from those flighty wenches who, when they hear the strains of a lascivious lute, giggle, roll their eyes, and fall wholly for the man who brings the strains about — as Jessica once did? Do we listen to a woman who promises, after merely playful banter, that she will not be facetious in response to her husband's philosophical speech?

Or do we listen now to a young woman who has by now "discovered" herself through "love," a woman who is ready to register a view about music and theories about music that dissents from her husband's? And, if so, might we be listening to a woman who speaks loudly within the play? Or is Jessica's view marginal, as dismissible as her father's?

Jessica's response to Lorenzo's speech confronts, in musical terms, the complex systems of values — Jewish versus Christian, Platonic versus Neoplatonic — in which the play more generally involves its audience. Lorenzo's two-part speech and Jessica's response raise questions that further, rather than resolve, these dramatic tensions. How, precisely, does Lorenzo conceive the problem of hearing the heavenly tune (*musica mundana*), the nature of the human soul (*musica humana*), and the ability of instrumental music (*musica instrumentalis*) to tune the soul? Does Lorenzo think the relationship is different for him than for Jessica?

The musical accompaniment to Lorenzo's speech — from 5.1.65 to 5.1.88, throughout Jessica's reply and the second part of Lorenzo's speech — raises other vital questions: How is the effect of the music on Jessica related to the effect the music may have on Shakespeare's audience? Are we merry as we hear the music playing in Belmont? If so, what kind of merriment is it? Do we have cause to be truly merry? Or do we "purpose merriment" too much? Are we being too facetious? too serious?

Most of the critics who pay close attention to the music of *Merchant* close attention ignore most of the questions that Jessica's experience raises. Writing about Jessica and Lorenzo in *The Harmonies of The Merchant of Venice*, Lawrence Danson — following Hollander in assuming that Lorenzo speaks for Jessica — concludes that "[it is] this pair of lovers who speak about that music of the spheres which the play's other harmonies imitate."[22] Danson's conclusion is based on his assumption that the talk about false vows is merely "easy banter and serious intimacy." Danson sees Lorenzo's speech and Jessica's reply as plainly celebratory, a clear instance of dramatic "fulfillment and reconciliation":

> Now, in act 5, a sweeter sort of unheard melody is invoked by Lorenzo for the benefit of the attentive Jessica: the heard music that sounds throughout much of the last part of the play is a sensory approximation of that heavenly music which (as Lorenzo explains) sounds just beyond the threshold of our gross mortal perceptions.

Danson dismisses Jessica's reaction to Lorenzo's speech as that of a "gentle newcomer": "because Jessica is a newcomer, and because he loves her, Lorenzo tells Jessica about the musical wonders of this peaceful night."[23]

Danson concludes that "the intellectual history of the ideas out of which Lorenzo's speech on celestial music is made" is "embarrassingly rich. . . . But it is not necessary to dwell on it in order to appreciate the speech, so tactful is Lorenzo's pedagogy." According to Danson, "Lorenzo's treatment of music's role in human and in cosmic nature is at once description and demonstration: it enacts its meanings. It leaves us, as audience, as it does Jessica, prepared to mark the music."[24] Concluding that Lorenzo speaks for the play and for Shakespeare, Danson, it appears, is not prepared to mark what Jessica says. Nor does he allow an audience to feel ambivalence in its experience of the play. According to Danson, we, like Jessica, remain naive to our genuine feelings because Lorenzo is so "tactful" a pedant.[25] Charles Mosely offers a similar reading: "Lorenzo gives Jessica some elementary instruction in what her father, who was deaf to music and blind to Christian Grace, never told her."[26]

As we have seen, however, Lorenzo's Neoplatonic musical theory itself offers the darkest hints about Jessica's nature. Jessica's response that she is not merry is not a confirmation of her salvation — not even a playful one. We are reminded, rather, of the County Palatine, who "hears merry tales and smiles not" (1.2.44–45), whom Portia therefore deems unfit to marry. By the time Lorenzo speaks the second part of his speech, Jessica has already proven herself "fit for . . . stratagems," and there is the deep suggestion that she is unmusical, "not happily born." As Launcelot says about Jessica, she is "damned both by father and mother" (3.5.13–14).

In addition to these serious questions about Jessica's nature, there is also the question of Lorenzo's "moral fitness," which is, as Danson knows, crucial to "our response to teasing banter at the opening of the fifth act." Danson concludes that Lorenzo's fitness has "been established," but the only proof he adduces is the encomium of a hot lover, Lorenzo's praise of Jessica in 2.6.52–57. In Danson's view, Lorenzo "enacts" his moral fitness with harmonious words. This ignores the running conflict between speculation and practice, as well as the irony that the words of a vow-breaker make a mockery of those who believe in verbal enactment. It is for precisely this reason that Cordelia makes a dramatic point of acting before she speaks in *King Lear*. Too many people, she knows too well, manipulate the human desire to mistake mere words for the accomplishment of deeds.

Danson bases Lorenzo's moral fitness on an assumption that his famous speech in act 5 is itself an enactment of religious harmony: the "union of the Gentile husband and the daughter of the Jew suggests the penultimate stage of salvation history described by St. Paul."[27] But a Christian's theft of a soul "with many vows of faith/ And ne'er a true one" speaks, ultimately, not for the "harmony in his immortal soul" but for the impenetrable "grossness" of his "muddy vesture of decay."

Many critics have provided intelligent arguments for the dominant reading represented by Barber and Danson. *Merchant*, writes Kermode, "begins with usury and corrupt love" and "ends with harmony and perfect love."[28] And although Gross sees the darker aspects of Jessica's marriage to Lorenzo, and of the troubles broached in the dialogues preceding Lorenzo's speech, even he suggests "[o]ne should not make too much of" them.[29] But if troubles exist, I am suggesting, they must be accounted for, and examined more deeply than scholars intent on seeing harmony have been willing to go. Any harmony in Belmont must, if not resolve, at least include these discordant elements.

In "Love in Venice," Catherine Belsey appears ready to reverse the sway of the "harmonizing habit" that critics have brought to the play.[30] But while she questions the assumptions of Barber and Danson, Belsey offers a sweeping description of love in Venice that leads her to reduce Lorenzo's talk about the "muddy vesture of decay" to putatively historical truths about the body and desire. Belsey writes that "the older understanding of love leaves traces in the text, with the effect that desire is only imperfectly domesticated" and the "consequence" that "Venice is superimposed on Belmont." Belsey identifies the consequence accurately, but she ignores Jessica's important reactions to music and love in Belmont — as well as the exclusion of Jessica from the harmonies described by Lorenzo and effected by Portia.[31]

Scholars have for so long thrown Jessica over to the side of the Christians, despite what she says — and does not say.[32] Jessica's answer to Lorenzo's speech is central to the theme of merry resolution at Portia's house in Belmont, but Jessica's voice, like her father's, is curiously absent from the final celebration. Shakespeare subtly highlights the problem posed to the harmony at Belmont by Jessica's silence. Jessica is addressed by Portia, but Jessica never speaks again. Portia addresses Jessica precisely on the subject of exclusion, of "being absent":

> Go in, Nerissa.
> Give order to my servants that they take
> No note at all of our being absent hence —
> Nor you, Lorenzo — Jessica, nor you.
>
> (5.1.118–21)

Jessica does not say a word. Shakespeare taunts us with the disparity between harmonious form and real discord. The chiastic word order addresses a couple; but the repetition and reversal of word order ("Jessica, nor you") suggests, with incongruous neatness, the afterthought one gives to what remains.

Silence indicates trouble here, as does an unwillingness or inability to confront the roots of discord head on. Shakespeare clearly understands the implications, and value, of allowing unresolved tensions to threaten the larger dramatic resolution. Scholars such as Hutton, Hollander, and Danson see Lorenzo as a Neoplatonic philosopher. But although Lorenzo's speech raises many serious philosophical questions, Shakespeare clearly does not make Lorenzo a speculative musician capable of resolving the troubles he brings.[33]

As Rabkin has written, "As the entire critical history of the play has made equally apparent, the play's ultimate resolution of [its] conflicts is anything but clear or simple." But even Rabkin sees the critical challenge as a demand for allegiance on one of two sides. He, too, reads Lorenzo's speech as the signal of harmonious resolution of Lorenzo's side: "On the one side, as we have seen, we find Shylock, trickery, anality, precise definition, possessiveness, contempt for prodigality" as well as "distrust of emotion and hatred of music, bad luck, and failure." "On the other," writes Rabkin, "we find Portia, but also Antonio, Bassanio, Lorenzo, Jessica, and Gratiano; freedom, metaphorical richness of language, prodigality" as well as "love of emotion and music, supreme trickery, a fondness for bonds, good luck, success."[34] In this common reading, Jessica is thrown in — here just before Gratiano — as Lorenzo's happily instructed wife.

Building on the insight of Rabkin, Keith Geary articulates the burden we confront in seeing or reading *Merchant*: "We must, critics tell us, take sides either with Shylock or with Portia and the Christians, and stand by our choice." But such "black-and-white judgement seems peculiarly inappropriate to a play that argues the falsity of such neat and absolute distinctions." *Merchant*, as Geary writes, "deals in shades of grey and continually raises the problem of appropriate response and judgement, most acutely, of course, in relation to Shylock."[35]

Jessica, I am suggesting, is the character who most feels and portrays what becomes the obvious falsity of neat distinctions. For Jessica, the differences between "sweet music" and "vile squealing" appear to resolve, finally, to the differences between true and false vows. Music is "sweet" only if degree holds.

Merchant forces its audience to focus on the human tendency — regardless of sex or religion — to "purpose merriment." The play centers on a conflict between people who "purpose merriment" without mercy (Shylock and the Christians alike) and people with "attentive spirits." Jessica begins the play by purposing merriment and ends it with "attentive spirits." Whereas Shylock is compelled to say he is content, Jessica feels free enough — finally — to speak her truth. And we must not dismiss her dissenting opinion. It is a woman's merry sport with language, one Christian's ability to out-interpret a Jew, that brings about the comic resolution that keeps Shylock from the "merry sport" of his bond. Against Portia's ability must be seen Jessica's confidence at the end of the play that she can "out-night" Lorenzo.

For every question in *Merchant*, Shakespeare poses a counterquestion that is even more important and more difficult to answer. He also makes it easy for us to fail to see the latter. This problem, our problem, is in large part what *Merchant* is about.

Merchant considers the burden of choosing "a love song, or a song of good life" (2.3.32), as Feste puts it to Sir Toby Belch in *Twelfth Night*. In *Romeo and Juliet*, both are possible at once, but parents do the choosing when the lovers should. In *Twelfth Night*, the parents are out of the way; but the lovers at first have trouble with the burden of choosing. In *Merchant*, Shakespeare considers the ways in which two fathers attempt to control their daughters by controlling their reactions to music. Both daughters are hampered by their father's rules for choosing men, opposing sets of rules that specify different reactions to music, reactions that are central to the resolution of the play. Children prevailing against parental error is one aspect of comedy. *Merchant*, however, concerns the extent to which parents may be right, as well as wrong, in trying to check urges to be merry their children do not yet fully understand. Launcelot's theft of the doves from old Gobbo shows the importance of this theme within the play.[36]

Portia's father has seen to it that his daughter's suitors are unable to seduce her with sweet-talk; rather, they must show their good nature in their reaction to music. It is a Neoplatonic test: it determines if one is "happily born." The case of Portia is a precise inversion of Jessica's: Portia secures her man with the help of music. But these facts alone do not assure her future merriment. Bassanio appears to be a good match for Portia, for he chooses the right casket, but the words to Portia's song provide him with hints. It is possible her father's trust in music could fail to prove true. But if Portia cheats with her hints, her father's wisdom — like Shylock's — might prevail, and therefore not her love.

Portia's success must be examined alongside Jessica's failure. Showing a knowledge of the need to temper Neoplatonism with Platonism when Bassanio chooses the right casket, Portia knows she will be merry only if her love may "be moderate" and "allay thy ecstasy,/ In measure rain thy joy, scant this excess!/ I feel too much thy blessing. Make it less/ For I fear I surfeit" (3.2.111–14). Seen against Shylock's fear of music, Portia's fear of "surfeit" is perhaps the most healthy feeling in the play. It is precisely what Jessica lacks. Here the play points to Portia's success, which we are to weigh against Jessica's failure — not because Portia is Christian, but because she, unlike Jessica, early understands the danger of music. Nevertheless, even Portia is susceptible to its corruptive powers. And knowledge of Jessica's experience could help her.

Jessica early speaks against the character of Bassanio, and in the beginning of act 5 speaks generally, and from experience, against trusting the "sweet power of music." But Bassanio's speech about a world "still deceived with ornament" does show his value. He could perhaps turn out to be Portia's fellow, just as Lorenzo, if he would "keep promise," could turn out to be Jessica's fellow. During the celebration at Belmont, however, there is the suggestion that Jessica might be right in her early appraisal of Bassanio, correct that the poor rude world hath not Portia's fellow. The final scene broaches the possibility that "the sweet power of music" has helped to bring together another pair of lovers who do not know each other well enough; and one — or both — may purpose merriment too much. Portia, like Viola in *Twelfth Night*, remembers her lover from long ago. But whereas Orsino "unclasped" to Viola "the book even of my secret soul" (1.4.12–13), Portia has no access to Basanio's secret soul. It is clear Portia loves Bassanio, but it is not clear what he offers her. To this point, he has offered only deceit.

Portia, like Jessica, must deal with a man's inconstancy, and however well she fares, the lesson is that "the pledge to a woman," as Harry Berger, Jr. observes, "can be superseded by the debt of gratitude owed a man." Whereas "Shylock practices usury, Portia is the master mistress of negative usury," which Berger defines as "giving more than you get." I do not agree that "in her own way, Portia is no less an outsider than Shylock" because "her 'I stand for sacrifice' is finally not much different from Shylock's 'I stand for judgment.'"[37] But Berger's point about Portia's troubles is just — made larger when we consider the plight of Portia and Jessica as women, whether in Venice or Belmont. Portia is the character in the play who appears most capable of controlling her fortune. But Portia's superiority deflects attention away from her vulnerability.

More generally, the conflict between Christians and Jews deflects attention away from the problem between men and women that arises when one or both have insufficient knowledge of themselves. This problem is a large part of the intricate relationship between music and merriment the play addresses. As Portia returns home in the final scene, she hears the music of her own house without recognizing it. The music, Nerissa has to tell her, "is your music, madam, of the house." The error is comic, but also serious. Portia responds, "Nothing is good, I see, without respect" (5.1.99).

As Antonio says at the beginning of the play, there will be no merriment without "respect." It takes Jessica some time to learn what Antonio announces in the first lines of the play. Portia knows enough to handle Shylock and Bassanio, but it is not a good sign if Portia needs Nerissa to identify the music of her house. Likely there remains "much ado to know [her]self."

Self-knowledge and reactions to music are linked, moreover, to the crucial subject of *Merchant*: mercy. In *Measure for Measure*, a play with a trenchant message about the virtue of moving from Hebrew justice to Christian mercy, Shakespeare links concisely, in speculative terms, the Christian capacity for mercy and the subjects of self-knowledge, merriment, and temperance. Asked to describe the "disposition" of the Duke, Escalus says that he is "One that, above all other strifes, contended especially to know himself. . . . Rather rejoicing to see another merry, than merry at anything which professed to make him rejoice: a gentleman of all temperance" (3.2.217–23). Such temperance constitutes being "contemplative in living art" — not being prone to "quick recreation" by wine, women, and lascivious song. But so, too, such temperance necessitates not being too rigid, whether in the manner of Angelo or Shylock. Vincentio, the Duke, is reputed, if only by Lucio, to have "some feeling" of the merry "sport" of getting bastards. The Duke's temperance supports Lucio's claim, if not its truth. Angelo, in contrast, is a Christian version of Shylock. Exhibiting trickery, anality, precise definition, contempt for prodigality, distrust of emotion and hunger for justice, his sin is not so much the corruptibility of the Christian soul as his merciless ability to cover up his sin by imputing it to others. If Portia can force Shylock to purpose merriment falsely ("I am content") and derive from such force her own "merry sport," does not her lack of mercy speak not only generally against a lasting Christian merriment but also specifically against her understanding of what makes one truly merry? Hatred of "the Jew" can help, in this respect, to make the harmony of Belmont seem real, durable — indeed, blessed.[38] But there is the hint that Portia is susceptible to dangerous forms of displacement.

In many ways, *Merchant* is a precursor of *Measure for Measure* — a comedy with a troubling comedic resolution; a comedy about the virtue of moving from Hebrew justice to Christian mercy; a comedy about the difficulty Christians can have in being merciful as they seek merriment; a comedy about the difficulty an audience will have when a merciful Duke pardons a Christian scoundrel. Only a few years after *Merchant* Shakespeare would begin to write what we call his "problem plays."[39]

Merchant not only examines large speculative musical debates, but also their practical value in life. The play demands that we distinguish musical sweet-talkers who "purpose" but displace merriment from plain-talkers who are attentive to the preconditions of true merriment. *Merchant* contrasts the Christians' gift for musical speech with the rough idiom of Shylock. Lorenzo is dazzling. Shylock is blunt. Shylock's nasty "contempt for prodigality" and "hatred of music" is merely an extreme antithesis to the dangerous trust in music shown by the Christians. The Italians are puffed with rhetoric; they are prodigal with words because they can use them so well, and they demonstrate a Neoplatonic trust in music and musical language that becomes suspect. And so is their conception of merriment suspect. With Jessica's final words to Lorenzo, *Merchant* suggests that the "sweet power" of "sweet music" is a potentially destructive illusion for Christians as well as Jews.

In *Merchant*, as in other plays, Shakespeare induces us to distinguish between eloquence and truth, between form and content, between words and deeds. *Merchant*, in this respect, is complex, for it offers no explicit speeches on the subject; rather, it subtly pits the harmony of form ("In such a night . . .") against the force of real discord. At the same time, however, the play reveals — and involves — our inability to distinguish them. Similarly, the play also involves our ability — or inability — to discern true merriment.

When Lorenzo asks her opinion of "Lord Bassanio's wife" Jessica focuses on the two ways of defining and achieving merriment that are at odds in the play:

> Past all expressing. It is very meet
> The Lord Bassanio live an upright life
> For having such a blessing in his lady;
> He finds the joys of heaven here on earth,
> And if on earth he do not merit it,
> In reason he should never come to heaven.
>
> (3.5.63–68)

Jessica suggests that Bassanio achieves a merriment he may not merit. He "finds the joys of heaven here on earth," but "the poor rude world/ Hath not [Portia's] fellow." Portia, that is, may be settling for an illusive merriment that will not last. The Christians manifest, as Bassanio reveals (2.2.188–91), the human tendency to "purpose" a kind of merriment, aided by music and musical speech, that turns out — in its stubborn clinging to earthly judgements of divine things and pseudodivine judgements of earthly things — to be false.

Given her high view of Portia, it cannot be that Jessica flatly rejects the merriment of the Christian world as her father tried to teach her to do. In her last line, Jessica seems to remark not her unmusical Jewish soul but the unmusicality of a "poor rude world." This theme is common in Shakespeare. In this respect, Jessica speaks for Shakespeare as much as, if not more than, Lorenzo.

It is Shakespeare's genius to center the closure of *Merchant* in his audience's opinion of the power of "sweet music" — and to center our opinion of the power of "sweet music" in the speculative connections between music and merriment. It takes an openness to the possibility of drama to see that "ambivalent signals" are "built into the play," as Rabkin has observed: "one element or another in the play can come to seem like the center of the play's values and the focus of its allegiances is paradoxically the source of both its inexhaustible complexity and its vulnerability to powerful productions in which the play seems to belong completely to Shylock or to Belmont."[40] Lorenzo's speech is the last starkly "inexhaustible complexity" before the festivities at Portia's house. By failing to attend to the character of Jessica, to her important responses to music in the play, and to her significant exclusion and silence, one may dismiss the way in which Lorenzo's speech reproduces many of the "ambivalent signals" of the play, not in a traditional way, but with Shakespeare's ability to use a commonplace subject to effect uncommon and decided dramatic meanings.

In *Merchant*, Shakespeare involves the audience in the moral dilemma of the play. He compels us to take sides even as he warns of the dangers of doing so. He gives us a character whose middle position is, even more dangerously, easy to ignore. By living between "Antipodes," by reacting nakedly to music, Jessica learns the most in the play, and yet she is the least pedantic character in the play. She is, moreover, the least likely to seduce us: as a Jew, Jessica is eclipsed by her father;

as a woman by Portia; as someone who might tell us something about being merry, she is eclipsed by Antonio; as someone who might tell us something about the "power of music," by Lorenzo. By the end of the play, Jessica can neither be dissociated from nor identified with her father — or Lorenzo.[41] Jessica's is the strange suffering of one who dares to live between the "Antipodes." A tug on the audience from two sides can make for great drama, but Shakespeare does even better in *Merchant*. If all the other characters demand our taking one side or another, Jessica does not, for she herself is tugged by both. Launcelot says her mother and father are Scylla and Charybdis: "Well, you are gone both ways" (3.5.15–16).

The wonder of the play, I am suggesting, is its ability to bring the audience around to Jessica's experience as it keeps Jessica's view in the middle of what are depicted as undesirable extremes. In *Merchant*, one character, a minor character, Jessica, tries unsuccessfully to arbitrate the merciless extremes of Jewish rigidity and Christian frivolity, as well as Jewish frivolity and Christian rigidity. Shakespeare gives Shylock, not Jessica, the moving argument for the humanity of the Jew, for the essential identity of the Jewish and Christian soul (3.1.46–64). But if Shakespeare does not inspire much sympathy for Shylock because he so ably depicts his thirst for Christian blood, he does inspire sympathy for Jessica; and he gives her final view of music a competing authority.

The sympathy one has for Antonio precludes the sympathy one might have for Shylock; but one is likely to have similar sympathy for Antonio and Jessica. Shakespeare sets up the glaring antipodes of Antonio and Shylock, but he suggests the deeper similarities and differences between Antonio and Jessica.

Whereas Shylock and Antonio are the blatant "Antipodes" of the play, Jessica converts willingly, moving from one pole to another in an attempt to make herself "merry." This willingness makes Jessica a compelling case. Whatever the viciousness of the victory, the defeat of Shylock's "merry sport" is comic resolution. But it is not comic when Jessica, who willingly converts, must say "I am never merry when I hear sweet music." Shakespeare centers the great mystery of *Merchant* — what makes one "merry?" — in the minor character of Jessica.

Putting her stock in the salvation offered by a Christian husband, Jessica is a character whose attempt to be merry becomes a touchstone. Shakespeare gives us a neutral character to offset any sympathy we might feel either with Shylock or with the purposed and vengeful merriment of the Christians.

It is difficult not to side with Jessica in this play. Siding with Jessica, however, one does not know where one stands, for one may feel a particular sympathy for everyone. One may see that every individual may have a desire to let music creep in her ear, may put her trust in a seductive *if*, may depend upon a vow — may have a misfounded scheme to "purpose merriment" that is sure to go awry.

Act 5 begins (and *Merchant* ends) by developing the problems the play presents, not by fully resolving them in a traditional praise of musical harmony. Shakespeare offers the forced resolution of the conversion of Shylock, but not without subtly implying, in the case of Jessica, questions that the conversion of Shylock too-forcibly resolves. Lorenzo offers a dazzling speech by which we, like Jessica, are liable to be seduced. Thinking themselves to be seduced by Shakespeare himself, scholars have for a long time been seduced instead by Lorenzo, hearing his speech as an enactment of the univocal resolution of the play. But Shakespeare allows us to see through Lorenzo, and forces us to consider large and important questions raised both by Jessica and the dramatic themes and tensions within the play.

Merchant is a difficult play, and has long been a divisive one. Most critics, siding with Lorenzo, have praised a pristine harmony; only a few have remarked hints of discord.[42] A number of critics have argued intelligently for a complete celebration of joys without irony, but that requires an explicit and fully resolved harmony between Jessica and Lorenzo. And that is not what we get. Shakespeare appears to leave the matter of harmonizing to us, and we will each, he seems to suggest, do it in our own ways. Some of us will not hear Jessica fully. *Merchant* is a much deeper play, less purely enjoyable, but more ripe for ongoing contemplation, with Jessica as its dissonant center. It is not that Shakespeare is pessimistic here, but rather that he appears to be telling us that the achievement of harmony on earth is a process, not the celebration it will be one day in heaven.

Merchant demands that its audience mark both the music to which we aspire and the means we employ to mark it. To that end, Jessica's last line — like the second part of Lorenzo's speech — competes for our attention with the seductive sounds of Portia's musicians. *Merchant* is a play that pushes its dramatic content to the limits of comic form, a play that juxtaposes the harmony of form with the reality of discord and coerced harmonies. At its conclusion, we must enjoy with a hungry ear the seductive music of both Lorenzo's speech and Portia's musicians, with our soul bent all the while toward deeper, more speculative matters. Such temperance is, after all, the universal condition of aspiring toward the heavenly tune.

The "Sweet Power of Music"

While *Merchant* offers Shakespeare's most concentrated treatment of the power of music, it is by no means the only place we must look to understand his interest in the subject. "'Sweet' and 'sweetness,'" as Edward S. LeComte observes, "are words that [Milton] reserves, almost always, for music, for paradise, and for the originally perfect affection between Adam and Eve."[43] Shakespeare, in contrast, calls all music "sweet," for all music is powerful, and power — especially the power to seduce — is "sweet." In many of his comedies,

Shakespeare advances the idea that earth is infused with the "sweet" pleasures of heavenly music. There is, however, a larger pattern. Shakespeare not only seeks to please the spectators; he regularly sets forth discussions of what gives pleasure and how. And in many of these discussions what gives pleasure is carnal love, musical language, and instrumental music. The latter two may secure the first pleasure, or substitute for it, such substitution being either a propitious surrogate or a harmful delusion.

In *Twelfth Night*, the Duke's words seem to give him as much pleasure as the music about which he is speaking. Music and words are too adequate as substitutes for the love he is not getting. The Duke knows the rudiments of Renaissance love psychology well enough to wish that by getting too much of the substitute he might kill his appetite for the thing itself. But the Duke is so lovesick he cannot act on his knowledge. He is caught in the sensual music of his life.

In *The Taming of the Shrew*, Bianca must forgo the connubial pleasures denied her by her sister. In contrast to Shylock, Baptista, a resourceful father, knows that music can meanwhile give his younger daughter both pleasure and instruction:

> Go in, Bianca.   [Exit Bianca.]
> And for I know she taketh most delight
> In music, instruments, and poetry,
> Schoolmasters will I keep within my house,
> Fit to instruct her youth.
>
> (1.1.91–95)

And although his design to dupe his friend is his first motive, Hortensio — the potential teacher — reveals that his motive is not unlike Lorenzo's:

> Now shall my friend Petruchio do me grace
> And offer me disguis'd in sober robes
> To old Baptista as a schoolmaster

> Well seen in music, to instruct Bianca,
> That so I may by this device at last
> Have leave and leisure to make love to her
> And unsuspected court her by herself.
>
> (1.2.128–34)

Love — or sex — is the object desired, and music and language are the means of achieving it. Hortensio's lessons will not be only lessons in practical music; they will be practical. Hortensio will not merely speculate about the musical condition of her soul; he will lean over Bianca and teach her how to play a lute.

Hortensio's rival, Lucentio, in contrast, speaks from the perspective of a speculative musician when he comes to Padua:

> And therefore, Tranio, for the time I study
> Virtue, and that part of philosophy
> Will I apply that treats of happiness
> By virtue specially to be achieved.
>
> (1.1.17–20)

His servant, Tranio, objects, reminding his master of the "sweetness of ladies" by remarking the obvious excess of the "sweets of sweet philosophy":

> Glad that you thus continue your resolve
> To suck the sweets of sweet philosophy.
> Only, good master, while we do admire
> This virtue and this moral discipline,
> Let's be no stoics nor no stocks, I pray,
> Or so devote to Aristotle's checks
> As Ovid be an outcast quite abjured.
> Balk logic with acquaintance that you have
> And practice rhetoric in your common talk.
> Music and poesy use to quicken you.
> The mathematics and the metaphysics,
> Fall to them as you find your stomach serves you.
> No profit grows where is no pleasure ta'en.
> In brief, sir, study what you most affect.
>
> (1.1.27–40)

Tranio urges using speculative subjects — mathematics and physics — only as they serve practically to bring pleasure. The moral program of speculative music concerns some of Shakespeare's male characters, but it does not concern the bulk of them once they have seen a lady — Hamlet being the great exception whom it concerns too much.

With Lorenzo, Shakespeare gives us a character who fits into a discernible pattern. For many of Shakespeare's characters, rather than a "world-picture" in which they seem to believe, speculative music is chiefly a subject, like many others, to be used to achieve amorous effects, to give pleasure to others that will beget pleasure for oneself.

Music and poetry seduce, as Tranio says, and Shakespeare gladly uses both of them to seduce us. He expects us to delight in his seduction, but also to see it for what it is. Consider the exchange between Hortensio and Lucentio:

> Fiddler, forbear, you grow too forward, sir.
> Have you so soon forgot the entertainment
> Her sister Katherine welcomed you withal?

Hortensio replies:

> But, wrangling pendant, this is
> The patroness of heavenly harmony.
> Then give me leave to have prerogative,
> And when in music we have spent an hour
> Your lecture shall have leisure for as much.

Lucentio counters:

> Preposterous ass, that never read so far
> To know the cause why music was ordained!
> Was it not to refresh the mind of man
> After his studies or his usual pain?
> Then give me leave to read philosophy,
> And while I pause, serve in your harmony.

> (3.1.1–14)

In his attempt at once to seduce and instruct his audience, Shakespeare was determined neither to follow nor to set straight the history of an idea, ideas about poetry, music, and seduction. These lines were written to entertain us, to make us laugh at Shakespeare's wit, and celebrate his extraordinary ability to make music out of words.

Similarly, Bianca's rejoinder to her posing "schoolmasters" — "cunning men," as her father calls them — demonstrates that her wit is superior to the wit of her conniving suitors. Hearing or reading this exchange, we should not be interested in Lucentio's Neoplatonic view of music as much as in Bianca's response, which, rather than assert a philosophical point about tuning, declares her a "sweeter" rhetorician than either of her two suitors — and so proclaims her a superior lover to both of them:

> Why, gentlemen, you do me double wrong
> To strive for that which resteth in my choice.
> I am no breeching scholar in the schools.
> I'll not be tied to hours nor 'pointed times,
> But learn my lessons as I please myself.
> And, to cut off all strife, here sit we down.
> Take you your instrument, play you the whiles;
> His lecture will be done ere you have tuned.
>
> (3.1.16–23)

As Bianca wittily points out, the "lecture" is pedantic, and the "tuning" is practical, a fumbling passing of some fools of time. She'll learn her lessons as she pleases — and perhaps as she pleases herself. The case of Jessica is apposite. Self-knowledge allows for self-amusement, and both allow one to make good choices. There is a lesson here, and it concerns the relative values of speculative and practical music. Without self-knowledge, music can be dangerous. It can appear to offer "heavenly harmony" when it does not. With self-knowledge, music — including poetry — can be a recreating and re-creating pleasure.

In the world created by Shakespeare on the stage, musical language such as poetry and rhetoric is "sweet," much like a "lady." In *Love's Labor's Lost*, in contrast with *Twelfth Night* and *The Taming of the Shrew*, the "sweetness" of language is deemed an insufficient substitute for the "sweetness" of the "lady" it is intended to snare, but the point is the same in all three comedies: flowery speech "Doth ravish like enchanting harmony." One ought to enjoy the pursuit. But so, too, one may go astray in moral and psychological as well as purely aesthetic terms.

In Shakespeare's comedies, lust and mortality make the sexes excessively "sweet" to each other, and hence hyper-rhetorical. As Theseus says, lovers, like madmen, use "more than cool reason." And Shakespeare often takes the rhetoric of hot lovers to its logical extreme. Lust can become lechery, and rhetorical "sweetness" can become a "sour offense," as in *Troilus and Cressida* 3.1. Pandarus, who is "full of harmony," says he will make things "whole again." But Pandarus's music makes nothing whole; it seduces everything to decay. Pandarus calls Helen "my sweet queen, my very, very sweet queen." And she calls Pandarus her "honey-sweet lord." But Pandarus is long past "sweet," like a "humble-bee" who "hath lost his honey and his sting." Hence, in the end, "Sweet honey and sweet notes together fail." The power of "sweet music" and the puissance of a "honey-sweet lord" both miscarry. And Thersites knows a trope when he hears one: "No, but out of tune thus. What music will be in him when Hector has knocked out his brains, I know not; but I am sure none, unless the fidler Apollo get his sinews to make catlins on." So, too, he knows bitterly that the word *sweet* loses its meaning when used lightly: "Sweet draught! 'Sweet,' quoth 'a! Sweet sink, sweet sewer."[44]

Just as it was a Pléiade favorite, *sweet* is one of Shakespeare's favorite words. But whereas Ronsard appears to have believed in the Neoplatonic musical theories, Shakespeare does not.[45]

Shakespeare delighted, rather, in invoking a powerful trope with which he could at once create and mediate numerous conflicts, including the debate about the sweet power of music. As the Duke in *Measure for Measure* says, "music oft hath such a charm/ To make bad good, and good provoke to harm" (4.1.14–15).

"The Music of Men's Lives"

Shakespeare asks us not only to delight in his musical poetry, but also to consider its value in helping us to enjoy examined lives. On this subject, he is wonderfully sanguine — confident in the power of his music to work its mysterious as well as more definable charms.

Shakespeare generally exhibits less of a speculative, or philosophical, view of music and poetry than a poetic interest in philosophizing about speculative music, but he did create a number of speeches in which the character — and perhaps the playwright — has a speculative view of the role of the human soul and human voice in a musical cosmos.

In *The Tragedy of King Richard the Second*, John of Gaunt — perhaps getting close to Shakespeare's interests as a poet and a man — speaks about the relationship between language and life, music and truth:

> O, but they say the tongues of dying men
> Enforce attention like deep harmony.
> Where words are scarce, they are seldom spent in vain,
> For they breathe truth that breathe their words in pain.
> He that no more must say is listened more
>   Than they whom youth and ease have taught to glose.
> More are men's ends marked than their lives before.
>   The setting sun, and music at the close,
> As the last taste of sweets, is sweetest last,
> Writ in remembrance more than things long past.
> Though Richard my life's counsel would not hear,
> My death's sad tale may yet undeaf his ear.

(2.1.5–16)

"Sweet music" depends on a speculative perspective to give "degree" to its "sweetness." It takes the truth of oncoming death — not the truths of life, nor "sweet" sounds — says old John, to "undeaf" the ear, to "enforce attention like deep harmony." John offers something like Socrates' description of the soul's completion of the cosmic circle in *Phaedrus*: "music at the close," a "sweet" end to the music of a life.

The Duke of York answers John:

> No; it is stopped with other, flattering sounds,
> As praises, of whose taste the wise are fond,
> Lascivious metres, to whose venom sound
> The open ear of youth doth always listen;
> Report of fashions in proud Italy,
> Whose manners still our tardy apish nation
> Limps after in base imitation.
> Where doth the world thrust forth a vanity
> (So it be new, there's no respect how vile)
> That is not quickly buzzed into his ears?
> Then all too late comes counsel to be heard
> Where will doth mutiny with wit's regard.
> Direct not him whose way himself will choose.
> 'Tis breath thou lack'st, and that breath wilt thou lose.
>
> (2.1.17–30)

York sees a rude world ruled by "vain tongues" and rampant appetites, in which reason argues too long against the will about the truth of true counsel, which it hears — or accepts — too late.

An "open ear of youth" drinks in every vile vanity as it is buzzed: "vile squealing," "flattering sounds," "lascivious metres." Without early devotion to speculation, the deafing and undeafing merely happens, in the manner described by John and York. In the penultimate scene, Richard finally contemplates the sounds he hears:

> (*The music plays.*) Music do I hear?
> Ha — ha — keep time! How sour sweet music is
> When time is broke and no proportion kept!

So is it in the music of men's lives.
And here have I the daintiness of ear
To check time broke in a disordered string;
But for the concord of my state and time,
Had not an ear to hear my true time broke.

(5.5.41–48)

Shakespeare juxtaposes "sweet" and "sour" music through-out his work, but nowhere else is music described as "sour sweet." This is not mere rhetoric. "So is it in the music of men's lives. . . ."

Richard next reveals a twist on the Neoplatonic theory of musical cure:

This music mads me. Let it sound no more;
For though it have holp madmen to their wits,
In me it seems it will make wise men mad.
Yet blessing on his heart that gives it me!
For 'tis a sign of love, and love to Richard
Is a strange brooch in this all-hating world.
        Enter a Groom of the stable.

(5.5.61–66)

The comic deflation is grave. Shakespeare mocks the Neo-platonic theory of musical ecstasy by bringing in the reality of the stable at the moment of Richard's insight. Music brings Richard not to an ecstatic experience of heaven; it brings him to insights about the music of his life.

When we look at the dramatic use of musical allusions in various plays, we witness something much more complicated than a playwright taking "bodily" into his plays common themes of Neoplatonism. Shakespeare uses the competing views of large, competing traditions, mixing and transform-ing them, making of them the conflict of drama — and the drama of truth.

It is not the music itself but either a repressive need to stop one's ears or an unexamined desire to open them that gets one into trouble. Shakespeare is neither a Platonist nor a Neoplatonist, but he is closer to Plato than to Ficino: not the power of the music but the condition of the listener is the chief concern.

Shakespeare does offer a general theory of language throughout the plays, one that addresses both practical and speculative concerns. A lack of awareness to the music of one's life generally makes one susceptible to "flattering sounds." But it is also possible to be too attentive. Evincing his peculiar pedantry, Hamlet stops courting Ophelia on account of her "unmusical" nature; and innocent Ophelia is "unmusical" only because she was born into an unmusical world. In *Hamlet* we are all "not happily born"; an "unmusical" nature causes the kind of speculative trouble that leads to death. Lorenzo's speech about heavenly harmony succumbs to the earthly conflict it tries to resolve. In *Hamlet*, Shakespeare creates a character who acquires too deep a knowledge of "the music of men's lives." It is such knowledge, as Ophelia appears to observe after their dark exchange in act 3, that makes wise men mad. It causes Hamlet to lose his temperance.

The theme runs throughout *Hamlet*. Ophelia's temperance is destroyed by her desire to have Hamlet's music overwhelm the music of her life, which is so far guided by her unmusical father and brother. Earlier warned by Laertes what will happen "If with too credent ear you list his songs" (1.3.30), Ophelia describes the trouble with Hamlet in musical terms:

> O! what a noble mind is here o'erthrown!
> The courtier's, soldier's, scholar's, eye, tongue, sword,
> Th' expectancy and rose of the fair state,
> The glass of fashion and the mould of form;
> Th' observ'd of all observers, quite, quite down!
> And I, of ladies most deject and wretched,
> That suck'd the honey of his music vows,
> Now see that noble and most sovereign reason
> Like sweet bells jangled, out of tune and harsh,

That unmatch'd form and feature of blown youth
Blasted with ecstasy. O! woe is me
T' have seen what I have seen, see what I see!

(3.1.153–64)

It is Hamlet's knowledge of the world's discord — and the inevitable discord of his soul — that makes him the way he is. And doomed by human nature ever to be so. Hamlet's is speculation gone awry — for it has no ability to accept the human condition of "grossness," no ability to deal with relativism, or his own part in it.

The "gross" condition of earth and humanity causes, Hamlet knows, a doubleness in all things. Whereas most characters in Shakespeare's tragedies know this too late, Hamlet knows too soon. Such doubleness is the perversion of the analogy between humans and their Maker, which, like the synecdoche of microcosm and macrocosm, is ruined by the cosmic discord effected between *musica humana* and *musica mundana* after the fall. All language is affected, but doubleness shows itself most in rhetoric, whether the double-talk of Polonius or the anti-double-talk of Hamlet.[46] Obsessed with this sameness of consequence, itself a consequence of doubleness, Hamlet misplaces his anger accordingly. He accuses otherwise-innocent Ophelia of giving "nickname[s]" to "God's creatures." No speaker, according to Hamlet, is innocent; and given the severe cosmic view on which it is based, the charge is true. Hamlet becomes too interested in the precision of cosmic housekeeping — and thus not "sweet." In *Hamlet*, the musical discussion is always grave, not the source of comedy, not the stuff that dreams are made on — unless one has in mind Delmore Schwartz's idea of dreams.

The trouble with many characters in Shakespeare's comedies is that they purpose merriment at every cost, especially the cost of true merriment; but a comic structure keeps things merry in the end, holding them to few of their words and granting them all of the pleasures and effects of rhetorical language and lascivious music. Shakespeare's tragedies, conversely, commonly observe a need to root out people who merely "purpose merriment," earthly pretenders to heavenly truth. Still, the Hamlet-like attempt to subsume all practice under speculation can itself become an impediment to true merriment. When one's understanding of mortality, decay, and cosmic discord is too deeply speculative, one may become too much at war with the logic and rhetoric that one must use to think and feel. Such is the case of Hamlet, for whom words and deeds are never met, and *logodædaly* ceases to be "sweet." Bodies heap meaningfully upon the stage. Hamlet appears responsible for killing Ophelia with differences, precisely because she aspires to nothing but harmony — pure love and uncluttered truth. By the time Gertrude becomes a body on the stage, the differences between excessively speculative aspirations and miscreant practical schemes are very clear, but the sameness of their consequences leaves an audience to ponder over the differences between slings and arrows. Finally, there comes someone who is trying to purpose lasting good, a Horatio or an Edgar, an enduring speaker who may finally, if only for a moment, unify eloquence and truth.

For Shakespeare, speculation appears to give value to practical power. There is throughout Shakespeare's poetry the sanguine, transcending view of an erected speculative wit, which manifests itself in his remarkable, and always maturing, playfulness with language — even the early groping after puns that provoked Dr. Johnson to remark his "fatal Cleopatra." Where the opportunities for "words, words, words" are plentiful, there is doubtless opportunity for vanity. "Where words are scarce, they are seldom spent in vain,/ For they breathe truth that breathe their words in pain." We have so little evidence of Shakespeare's pain, but he was able to breathe many words as if they were his last. But he also saw some value in spending words in vain precisely because they are scarce.

The playful use of language, even when indecorous, is never, in the end, fatal. Only mortality, Shakespeare seems to tell us, is fatal. To the living, words in life are sweeter than the perfection of silence in death. It is this speculative truth that gives Shakespeare his sanguine practical view.

As Hamlet knows, only death can stop one from singing: "That skull had a tongue in it, and could sing once" (5.1.71–2). The prospect of death becomes more horrible, more palpable, indeed, when language becomes joyless. The ability to speak is plainly good, unless, as Hamlet also knows, "Words, words, words" become, as Troilus says, "Words, words, mere words, no matter from the heart." When there is matter from the heart, it is visible, and shows noble and "sweet." "Now cracks a noble heart," says Horatio, "Good night, sweet prince/ And flights of angels sing thee to thy rest." As Shakespeare knew, flouting a regnant trope of his day, any other music is an inadequate substitute for the true music of a person's plain speech — even the singing of angels. "Had I but time. . . . O, I could tell you . . .," says Hamlet. But the "sweet prince" could never bring "sweet" harmony to the rude world; that takes the louder speech of warlike noise. Finally, it is time for Fortinbras to say, "The soldier's music and the rites of war/ Speak loudly for him./ Take up the bodies."

Unlike Hamlet, Shakespeare saw in "grossness" an opportunity to thrive. There is the monumental example from *The Tempest*, in which the "sweet power of music" that is part of Prospero's magic appears to be not only beautiful and true but also associated with Shakespeare's own power as a poet. After putting it to much good use, Prospero relinquishes his "so potent art":

> graves at my command
> Have waked their sleepers, oped, and let 'em forth
> By my so potent art. But this rough magic
> I here abjure; and when I have required
> Some heavenly music (which even now I do)
> To work mine end upon their senses that

> This airy charm is for, I'll break my staff,
> Bury it certain fathoms in the earth,
> And deeper than did ever plummet sound
> I'll drown my book.
>
> (5.1.48–57)

Prospero's resolve to relinquish his quest to harness the power of heavenly music comes as a disappointment to the audience. It is, however, an assertion of what Socrates calls the limits of human power. The magic is rough. Prospero affirms our human reach toward God, not human achievement of heaven on earth.

The immediate application of Prospero's lines to Shakespeare should be resisted, but also considered, carefully. Because Shakespeare — even in the Sonnets — does not write about himself directly, we would have to perform the dubious task of putting him together the way we might put Chaucer together, by aligning him only with certain of his many characters. This leads to danger, as Kermode writes: "What we do is to make him in our own image and then call him unique."[47] It is one thing to invoke power of magic or the "sweet power of music" in one's plays, another to believe in them. It would be impossible to say just how close Shakespeare's view is to Hamlet's or Lorenzo's. But a broad examination of all of his plays allows us to see that Shakespeare had a general view of the relationship between speculative and practical music, and of the "sweet power" of music and poetry. Speculative music was more than a commonplace to Shakespeare. Some of his characters use the trope of a musical universe loosely, but Shakespeare's important characters invoke it in inventive ways that lead to important speculative insights.

Shakespeare neither makes unambiguous claims for a harmonious universe of which the poet is a harmonious part nor bemoans a world that is irremediably untuned. It is, of course, part of his genius to reveal skepticism about a worldview even as he uses that view to examine the world. Jonathan Dollimore

writes that "Every major theme of the plays which I explore . . .
transgresses or challenges the Elizabethan equivalent of the
modern obsession with a *telos* of harmonic integration."[48] But
the case of Shakespeare is far more complex than Dollimore's
obsession with transgression allows. Shakespeare at times
depends upon the Elizabethan World Picture; he at times shows
it flying apart; he at times breaks it apart himself; he at times
puts it back together. In most cases, moreover, we must confess that only his characters do. While for some characters the
idea of a musical universe is a destructive belief in deceptive
doctrine, for others it is a noble truth that cannot be destroyed
by the "poor rude world."

It is possible Shakespeare had a consistent personal view of
the role and power of music and poetry in the lives of his
audience, but it is not likely we will ever be able to describe it
fully. One thing, however, is clear: for Shakespeare the "grossness" to which Lorenzo alludes was not the dire theological,
cosmological, and hence literary consequence of original sin
it would become for Milton. Sonnets 8, 29, 38, 73, 78, 85, 100,
101, 102 and 146 suggest a general confidence in the speculative status of Shakespeare's poetry. He carries himself as a
poet sure that his poetry has achieved the condition of song.

In Sonnet 73, Shakespeare alludes to the prospect of "bare
ruined choirs," but flaunts the "glowing" of his "fire," defy-
ing not only aging and death but also the "grossness" that
sets limits upon music and poetry:

> That time of year thou mayst in me behold
> When yellow leaves, or none, or few, do hang
> Upon those boughs which shake against the cold,
> Bare ruined choirs where late the sweet birds sang.
> In me thou seest the twilight of such day
> As after sunset fadeth in the west,
> Which by and by black night doth take away,
> Death's second self that seals up all in rest.
> In me thou seest the glowing of such fire

> That on the ashes of his youth doth lie,
> As the deathbed whereon it must expire,
> Consumed with that which it was nourished by.
> > This thou perceiv'st, which makes thy love more strong,
> > To love that well which thou must leave ere long.

This remarkable poem embraces at once two starkly different ways of confronting a poet's aspiration to song. Shakespeare asserts the confidence of the great singers of antiquity even as he anticipates a central dilemma of romanticism.

For Shakespeare, fallenness, or "grossness," is not a desperate poetic condition that needs God's grace or a naive return to the blithe and innocent vision of youth. It is a human limitation that can be jostled, if not overcome, by the adroit manipulations of diction, syntax, and rhythm. Showing no worry that his soul and thereby his art were out of tune with the music of the heavens, Shakespeare reveals the extraordinary attuning of his heart and voice to the noise and motion of the world in which he lived. He made discord a subject he could write about with defiant optimism about his craft. A man of the world who appears to have understood the music of his life, Shakespeare had no need to stop his ears to its creeping sounds. Nor did he reveal a cramping desire to escape the reality of a discordant world for the harmony of an ideal one.

Shakespeare appears to have felt very confident about his status as a singer, divinely inspired by a God who tuned his musical cosmos, but he also left, through the mouths of some of his characters, speculative musings that would cause future poets to examine with scrutiny their authority as heavenly singers on earth. For just as Shakespeare tells us that the end of speech is the only death, so he alerts us to the speculative conviction that it is worse than death to speak before one's time:

> For he's no man on whom perfections wait
> That, knowing sin within, will touch the gate.
> You are a fair viol, and your sense the strings;

> Who, fingered to make man his lawful music,
> Would draw heaven down, and all the gods to hearken;
> But being play'd upon before your time,
> Hell only danceth at so harsh a chime.[49]

Pericles offers Shakespeare's most sober speculative articulation of the music of life. Far more than Lorenzo, Pericles alludes to the consequences that would concern Milton.

Shakespeare never suggests he believed himself one who played before his time. As a dramatic poet, Shakespeare gives us, among others, the struggles of Lear and Hamlet, but he never gives us any indication that he struggled to consider himself a singer. In the sonnets, we perhaps get closer to Shakespeare the man, although never close enough. The topic clearly intrigued him, but Shakespeare appears not to have considered the problem of speculative discord as in any way a serious threat to his ability to turn words into song. He played with the confidence of one who was tuned, or who played in a world made for the earthly purpose of celebratory, preludic fingering.

Shakespeare was the first poet to link the conflict between speculative and practical impulses to the aspiration of a poet to song. But as much as he must be admired for his speculation, it is still Shakespeare's peerless practical skill that is most remarkable. Shakespeare's poetry is as heavenly "sweet" as human utterance could be; and it was his strong embrace of his "human mold" in the face of speculative aspiration that made him so daunting an influence on later poets. Shakespeare's reflections on the relationship between music and poetry exerted strong influences on later poets. They left Milton to speculate further; they anticipated the "Philosophic Song" of Wordsworth, the triumphant silence of Keats, and the playful speculation of Stevens.

THREE

Milton's "Earthy Grossness"

ॐ

Music and the Condition of the Poet

Renaissance commonplaces, many of them, receive their most inventive and eloquent treatment in the poetry of Shakespeare, their most notable refinement in the poetry of Milton. This is especially true of the trope of song. Shaping the idea of speculative music into a personal, Christian poetic, Milton defined his task as a poet.[1] What was that task? Nothing less than to turn the trope of song into a literal truth: to hear and rejoin "the heavenly tune."

As Milton writes in "Arcades," however, he lived at a time "after the heavenly tune, which none can hear/ Of human mold with gross unpurged ear."[2] Like "Comus," "Arcades" has as one of its aims to instruct the aristocracy in certain aspects of the reformist programs that would interest Milton for years to come. This includes purging their ears, enabling them to hear God's Word. Remarking the "clash of values between the earnest young poet and his aristocratic audiences," Cedric C. Brown suggests that "there are patterns of responsibility to be traced, above all in the poet's sense of his own role" as a shepherd in "Arcades," "Comus," and "Lycidas."[3] Indeed there are, the same patterns of reformist responsibility for the people of England that are later written large in Milton's prose and poetry.

But the earnest poet began to exhibit in his early poetry another pattern of responsibility. He was not only a Christian eager to reform the English people, but also a young poet who understood his aspiration to song to be rooted in a profound Christian responsibility that he would have himself to shape. "Arcades" offers only one of many allusions to speculative music in which Milton questions not only the ability of his fellow Englishmen to hear and rejoin "the heavenly tune," but also his own. As a Christian, Milton was his whole life concerned with reading Providence, for it was required of anyone striving to live in tune with God's law. As a poet, Milton was greatly concerned with purging his speculative ear of the inability to rejoin God's heavenly tune. Statements concerning this inability — which Milton, in "On Time," calls "Earthy grossness" — recur throughout his career.

Milton was himself a fine musician, and from a young age knew himself to be a gifted poet, but it troubled him, even in *Paradise Lost* (hereafter *PL*), that poetry is a form of *musica instrumentalis*.[4] In *PL*, Milton makes singular and brilliant use of prophetic modes, to be rivaled by few poets, equaled by none. Clearly, between the time of his ludic prolusion and his great epic poem, Milton had arrived at a high degree of confidence in his skill as a poet, but there remained for him deep questions about the vocation of a poet in a fallen world. Inspiration and skill are, for reasons considered in chapter 1, not easily reconciled in either the literary or prophetic traditions in which Milton wrote.

Did Milton consider himself a divinely inspired singer in the same way many of his readers do? To answer this important question, we must consider the matter of divine inspiration in Milton's terms. Milton's conception of himself as a singer, his understanding of the relationship between inspiration and skill, is deeply related to his theory of prophecy. His theory of prophecy, moreover, reveals influence by the writings of Moses Maimonides, whose quest for prophetic authority mirrors Milton's. An examination of Milton's thoughts about prophecy will help us to appreciate the speculative poetic he developed throughout his career.

Milton's poetic rendering of his reattuning is intense and beautiful. But underlying his account of his spiritual reattuning is Milton's understanding that his poetic aspiration to song runs the risk of "clashing with this very harmony which I am proclaiming" (604). It is one thing to try to live as a Christian in tune with God's law, all the while teaching one's fellow Englishmen to do the same. It is quite another to sing with "the heavenly tune," to claim to add to a world that contains God's holy scripture another book, a divinely inspired prophetic poem written by an English poet who, "long choosing" and "beginning late," had also in mind the great epics of Greece and Rome as his literary models. It is one thing to write an epic poem that teaches the ways of God to humankind, quite another to claim, implicitly and explicitly, to achieve a condition of music on par with that of the biblical prophets.

Milton knew that "all the instruction necessary for self-government, and societal government, can be found in the precepts of the moral law and the preachings of the prophets," as Joan S. Bennett writes.[5] Milton faced a dilemma: to be an interpreter of God's scripture is to be his dutiful servant. To be a poet claiming prophetic song, in contrast, is perhaps not only to clash loudly with God's song but also to offend his law. "Whoever keeps the whole law, and yet offends in one point, is guilty of all," writes Milton in *The Christian Doctrine*. As this chapter aims to show, Milton's conception of speculative music provides a way to mediate his chief concerns as a Christian poet and thereby keep the law whole.

Milton renders the most remarkable poetic solution to what he himself devises as poetry's greatest dilemma. Of all poets writing in English, Milton expresses the greatest desire to participate in God's heavenly harmony, and he possessed practical ability to achieve it that few, if any, poets could rival. But rather than claim prophetic authority, we will see, Milton mediates in new ways the tensions between practical and speculative music, between being a divine singer and a reformist, a prophet and a poet. These tensions, fully developed with Miltonic wit, are part of the drama of Milton's verse. Part of the drama of Milton's account of paradise lost is the responsibility of the reader freely to read in the poem both his own complicity and salvation. Included in, and compounding, this drama is the responsibility to consider the speculative condition of the poet as he makes his own attempt to reattune himself. The authority of the poet as singer is always under exquisite, edifying scrutiny in *PL*. The music of Milton's poetry engages the reader in Milton's own speculation about the relationship between the music of heaven and earth, involving us in his complex movement toward God's heavenly tune.

The beauty and power of Milton's poetic song is clear, and by examining it in the speculative terms Milton devised, we may broaden our appreciation of what he boldly attempted and grandly achieved. Milton renders the process of his reattuning like no other poet. His speculative musical conception of his role as a prophetic poet aspiring to heavenly song is a salient aspect of both his achievement and the history of English poetry. Still, scholarship has yet to describe it. By examining his early poems and great epic, this chapter attempts to show how Milton's abiding interest in speculative music creates a richer poetry, a fuller tune. Engaging in speculative musical scrutiny of one's authority as a singer, Milton makes clear, is a necessary part of God's better music.

Early Poems

Milton's early poems, like the rest of his work, are often still read in the light of biographies that portray a monumental Milton who, knowing always, from a young age, what he wanted to do — become a poet of prophetic epic song — eventually matured and accomplished his lofty goal.[6] Scholars have long privileged late works and undervalued early poems such as "L'Allegro" and "Il Penseroso" by marking them "immature" or judging them less than profound. E. M. W. Tillyard calls them "poems of escape, of fancy," which, if typical of Milton at all, are "typical of only a part, and not a large part." F. W. Bateson maintains that "the conflict between reason and passion that dominated the later Milton has not yet made its appearance."[7] Milton surely became a better poet with age, but his early poems demonstrate less concern with a lack of poetic skill than a lack of "inward ripeness." Milton expresses in *PL* the same unripeness he describes in his early poems. There is clearly usefulness in defining early and mature work, but when such definition too clearly divides Milton's "hasting days" and "full career" it results in paying too little attention — and often the wrong kind — to Milton's consistent allusions to the relationship between earthly poetry and heavenly song.

"At a Solemn Music," an early poem about the difference between earthly music and heavenly harmony, is perhaps Milton's most concise statement of his desire to rejoin the divine harmony that fallen man lost the ability to hear. It expresses Milton's understanding of his task as a Christian poet, and it indicates the way Milton would deal with this important concern throughout his career. The poem is composed of 2 sentences; the first, 24 lines, contains 3 commands:

> *Wed* your divine sounds, and mixt power *employ*
> Dead things with inbreath'd sense able to pierce,

And to our high-rais'd fantasy *present*
That undisturbed Song of pure concent,

(3–6)

but the sentence is divided by a semicolon at line 16; the description of the harmony ends with

. . . the Cherubic host in thousand choirs . . .
Hymns devout and holy Psalms
Singing everlastingly;

(12; 15–16)

then and only then does the wish behind the commands become clear:

That we on Earth with undiscording voice
May rightly answer that melodious noise;[8]
As once we did, till disproportion'd sin
Jarr'd against nature's chime, and with harsh din
Broke the fair music that all creatures made
To their great Lord, whose love their motion sway'd
In perfect Diapason, whilst they stood
In first obedience and their state of good.

(17–24)

For Milton the circle of perfection is not broken because of the new science but rather lost to man because of sin. "[D]isproportion'd sin . . . broke the fair music," and "At a Solemn Music" is a consideration of the problem of restoring it.[9] Before the fall, heavenly harmony was truly echoed on earth; after the fall, according to Milton, each of us has a "gross unpurged ear" (the consequence and symptom of "disproportion'd sin"). Each of us is a discordant soul unable to echo "the heavenly tune," for God has not yet renewed "that Song."

Instrumental music cannot produce harmony that accords with God's heavenly tune. "Earthy grossness" is a speculative conception of the poet's postlapsarian condition: it

describes the certain wait for (uncertain) grace and the renovation (certain if grace comes) of the soul that would restore
to the poet the ability to sing "that Song of pure concent."
Milton is not the kind of Calvinist who believes grace to be
inscrutable and uninstrumental. But he did need to devise,
as no poet before him had, a way to enact and represent the
instrumentality of practical music in a fallen world.

Typical of Milton's poems about divine music, "At a Solemn Music" expresses the poet's state of "Earthy grossness"
by devising a grammar of gross poetry. This means rendering
the poet's speculative condition, his wish to be reattuned, and
his devotion to effecting his own reattuning. Transitions from
commands to clauses of purpose ("That we on Earth . . . May")
and finally to exhortations express not only the poet's present
condition but also the conditional status of the redemption of
his soul and thereby the purging of his ear and voice:

> O may we soon again renew that Song,
> And keep in tune with Heav'n, till God ere long
> To his celestial consort us unite,
> To live with him, and sing in endless morn of light.
>
> (25–28)

The second sentence of the poem advances the movement of
the first; the (subjunctive) exhortation makes all successive
clauses conditional. Surely we would live with him, writes
Milton, but we are waiting "till God ere long" brings us to
him. This grammatical enactment is common to many of
Milton's early poems.

Milton writes of keeping in tune with the laws of heaven
until the time when God rejoins us with God's own heavenly
tune. Accepting his "Earthy grossness" is part of the process
of reattuning. "At a Solemn Music" does not celebrate the
celestial music in the tradition of *laudes musicae*.[10] And
Milton does not consider instrumental — "earthly" — music
a cause of either Neoplatonic ecstasy or purgation; rather, he

maintains that purgation and regeneration must come first.[11]

"At a Solemn Music" describes a music Milton longs to hear. Hearing "the heavenly tune" is, according to Milton, a sign that one has a chaste ear; and having a chaste ear is a sign that purgation and regeneration have occurred. This is a good Miltonic tautology; it expresses at once the problem of election and the further problem of waiting for grace.

The difficult question for Milton is what the waiting means for a poet who is possessed of remarkable poetic skill and ambition. In "At a Solemn Music," Milton is asking for the grace that will allow him to enjoy once again (as did Adam and Eve before the fall) what James Hutton calls the "harmonious structure of the universe reflected in the human soul."[12] Similarly, in "Sonnet VII," a poem written near in time to "At a Solemn Music," Milton worries that the "semblance" of adroit poetry "might deceive the truth" of a poet's discordant soul. But if "inward ripeness" (harmony) is a requirement not yet achieved, and completed only in God's "strictest measure" (in God's musical time), Milton's poetry can nevertheless be instrumental in his reattuning. Both "On the Music of the Spheres" and "Sonnet VII" consider waiting silently to have one's soul and voice reattuned, but Milton understands the opportunity to write one's way out of inward unripeness.

As Joan S. Bennett writes about the "radical English humanists" who, like Milton, were "utterly committed to building a holy society, to responding to God's call for his kingdom's coming on earth," they were "simultaneously aware that they must not either act precipitously or fail to act."[13] Writing poetry was, in Milton's speculative terms, its own kind of action. Milton's brilliant solution was to make his impatience a central subject of his poetry and to make his speculative musical dilemma the basis of his practical poetic. His poetic career, he iterates in many early poems, will constitute an attempt to mediate the differences between "earthy" poetry and heavenly song.

Poetic ambition, speculative *eros*, and Christian patience are the central subjects of many of Milton's early poems. His chief poetic task is to reconcile them, to devise a poetic that enacts his desire in a way that accords with both God's law and his eternal music. In "Ad Patrem," as in "Sonnet VII," Milton conceives "earthy" poetry within the hard terms of God's "strictest measure." The young Milton is nowhere more concerned with earthly fame than in "Ad Patrem," the poem to his father in which he defends his chosen trade. As in "At a Solemn Music," Milton uses a conditional statement (*Nunc . . . cupiam . . . ut surgat*) to express his aspiration to a condition of song:

> *Nos etiam, patrium tunc cum repetemus Olympum,*
> *Aeternaeque morae stabunt immobilis aevi,*
> *Ibimus auratis per caeli templa coronis,*
> *Dulcia suaviloquo sociantes carmina plectro,*
> *Astra quibus geminique poli convexa sonabunt.*
>
> (29–34)

[When we return to our native Olympus and the everlasting ages of immutable eternity are established, we shall walk, crowned with gold, through the temples of the skies and with the harp's soft accompaniment we shall sing sweet songs to which the stars shall echo and the vault of heaven from pole to pole.]

Milton does more than describe the problem of time through syntax, mood, and tense. Concentrating on the relationship between "now" and "when" (*"Nunc quoque . . . nos etiam . . . cum repetemus"*), he begins to enact his "Earthy grossness." Milton seeks to attain an "undiscording voice." He will when the Golden Age returns. The poem, however, broaches this question: what to do *now* on earth?

After first describing the laudable qualities of epic song, Milton poses an antipoetical question: *"Denique quid vocis modulamen inane iuvabit/ Verborum sensusque vacans, numerique loquacis"?*[14] Milton's answer is significant:

> *Silvestres decte iste choros, non Orphea, cantus,*
> *Qui tenuit fluvios, et quercubus addidit aures,*
> *Carmine, non cithara, simulacraque functa canendo*
> *Compulit in lacrymas; habet has a carmine laudes.*
>
> (52–55)

[Such music is good enough for the forest choirs, but not for Orpheus, who by his song — not by his cithara — restrained rivers and gave ears to the oaks, and by his singing stirred the ghosts of the dead to tears. That fame he owes to his song.]

When the young Milton describes the poetic power of Orpheus, he praises not the outward power effected by his cithara (*musica instrumentalis*) but the inward harmony of his song (*musica humana*). In Milton's words, "*Carmine, non cithara.*"

This speculative conception of poetry builds upon an earlier passage:

> *Nec tu vatis opus divinum despice carmen,*
> *Quo nihil aethereos ortus, et semina caeli,*
> *Nil magis humanam commendat origine mentem,*
> *Sancta Prometheae retinens vestigia flammae.*
>
> (17–20)

[You should not despise the poet's task, divine song, which preserves some spark of Promethean fire and is the unrivalled glory of the heaven-born human mind and an evidence of our ethereal origin and celestial descent.]

"Ad Patrem" is a poem by a loving son to his father, but the nascent speculative disputes between father and son are significant. The practical father's wish would seem to require the son to sully the very ears he wishes to purge: "*Iura, nec insulsis damnas clamoribus aures*" (72). The conflict here is not merely the ordinary one between the crude world of lucre and the fine world of art.

"Ad Patrem" is as much a speculative declaration of the difficulty of Milton's poetic aspiration as it is a filial justification of the attempt. Defending his sister art, Milton concludes by adverting not to his present achievement but to what "my juvenile verses and amusements" might dare to hope — "*sperare audebitis*" (116).

Milton examines the conditional terms of his reattuning in a number of early poems. In the "Nativity Ode," Milton again writes that only grace can return us to the time when man could hear divine harmony. In the thirteenth stanza Milton confirms that divine music itself *is* an agent of grace:

> For *if* such holy song
> Enwrap our fancy long,
>   Time will run back, and fetch the age of gold,
>
> (133–35)

but there is still the wait: "But wisest Fate says no/ This must not yet be so,/ The babe lies yet in smiling Infancy" (149–51). This counterfactual statement ("if," "but . . . not yet") expresses the theological condition that might keep the poet from singing. When Milton writes

> Say Heav'nly Muse, shall not thy sacred vein
> Afford a present to the Infant God?
> Hast thou no verse, no hymn, or solemn strain,
> To welcome him to this his new abode,
>
> (15–18)

he might seem to blame the "Heav'nly Muse," but in fact, with subtle irony, he implicates himself. The thirteenth stanza has the same effect:

> Ring out ye Crystal spheres,
> Once bless our human ears,
>   (If ye have power to touch our senses so).
>
> (125–27)

Milton's dilemma is that his unchaste ear, which is not yet blessed by grace, not yet purged, lacks the power to hear, not that the "Crystal spheres" lack the power "to touch our senses so."

The "Nativity Ode" looks ahead to "The Passion," that poem Milton could never finish.[15] One reason for not finishing the poem is the premeditation of Milton's muse:

> Yet on the soft'ned Quarry would I score
> My plaining verse as lively as before;
>   For sure so well instructed are my tears,
> That they would fitly fall in order'd Characters.
>
> (46–49)

There is also the further possibility of forcing his song into tune, his earthy vision into divine truth:

> Or should I thence hurried on viewless wing,
> Take up a weeping on the Mountains wild,
> The gentle neighborhood of grove and spring
> Would soon unbosom all thir Echoes mild,
> And I (for grief is easily beguil'd)
>   Might think th'infection of my sorrows loud
> Had got a race of mourners on some pregnant cloud.
>
> (50–56)

To write one's verse "on viewless wing" is to write without divine inspiration — and here about the subject for which one needs it most.

Milton's recurrent thoughts on chastening his ear do not appear to be hyperbole. Milton's thoughts about how he could regain the lost ability to participate in "the heavenly tune" were derived from Pythagorean theory, as in "Elegy VI":

> *Et nunc sancta canit superum consulta deorum,*
>   *Nunc latrata fero regna profunda cane,*
> *Ille quidem parce Samii pro more magistri*
>   *Vivat, et innocuos praebeat herba cibos.*
>
> (57–60)

> [And he who sings now of the sacred counsels of the gods on high, and now of the infernal realms where the fierce dog howls, let him live sparingly, like the Samian teacher; and let herbs furnish his innocent diet.]

Milton writes that if his heart "were as pure, as chaste, as snowy as Pythagoras's was," then his "ears would resound and be filled with that supremely lovely music of the wheeling stars." In other words, "all things would appear to return to the age of gold."[16]

Looking ahead to that time, Milton set strict rules of conduct — innocent of crime, chaste, with "upright heart and pure" — that could make him fit to hear and sing divine song:

> *Additur huic sclerisque vacans et casta iuventus,*
> *Et rigidi mores, et sine labe manus.*
>
> (63–64)

> [Beyond this, his youth must be innocent of crime and chaste, his conduct irreproachable and his hands stainless.]

With Pythagoras as his model, Milton saw chastity as a precondition to hearing, a prelude to the song. Only the good soul might hear the divine harmony, and in the absence of the sign that he was good (hearing), Milton thought instead to make himself ready to receive it. He had to prepare.

Sigmond Spaeth suggests that the theory of "measured music" — which Spaeth identifies as Pythagorean — might have offered the earthly singer a way of reaching heaven by numbers.[17] But the theory of "measured music" attributes to practical music a Neoplatonic power that Milton clearly denies. Spaeth does, however, provide a useful account of Milton's theory of music as Christian cosmos: "To Milton the significance of music lies in its relation to the entire universe — to man first of all, to nature as affecting man and possibly affected by him, and finally to God as controlling both Nature and man."[18] Milton considered nature doubtless (not *possibly*) affected by humankind. According to book 9 of *Paradise Lost*, the three worlds (the universe, the earth, and humankind) fell together:

> Earth trembl'd from her entrails, as again
> In pangs, and Nature gave a second groan,

Sky low'r'd, and muttering Thunder, some sad drops
Wept at completing of the mortal Sin
Original.

(1000–04)

"Music to Milton," as writes Spaeth, "represents law and order."[19] But Milton's concern is more complicated than Spaeth allows, as we see in the following passage from "Arcades":

But else in deep of night, when drowsiness
Hath lockt up mortal sense, then listen I
To the celestial *Sirens'* harmony,
That sit upon the nine infolded Spheres
And sing to those that hold the vital shears
And turn the Adamantine spindle round,
On which the fate of gods and men is wound.
Such sweet compulsion doth in music lie,
To lull the daughters of *Necessity*,
And keep unsteady Nature to her law,
And the low world in measur'd motion draw
After the heavenly tune, which none can hear
Of human mold with gross unpurged ear.

(61–73)

As a prelapsarian spirit conceived in the context of a pastoral mask, the Genius of the Wood possesses precisely the power that — in addition to his aristocratic audience, and the English people more generally — Milton himself lacks. In the tradition of *laudes musicae*, Milton celebrates the music of the heavenly spheres, but he emphasizes the human inability of his "gross unpurged ear" to hear it.

From this speculative dilemma Milton derives not merely the subject but also the poetic structure of many poems. Many of his early poems express — in speculative terms he would continue to develop — his determination to use poetry to move toward "the heavenly tune." One way is patiently to enact the theological terms of his reattuning. Rather than prohibit him from engaging the powers of instrumental music, as we will see, his speculative poetic enables Milton to devise, like no other poet in English, a precise grammar of aspiration and future fulfillment.

"L'Allegro" and "Il Penseroso"

"L'Allegro" and "Il Penseroso," both of which end with passages about music, are early poems in which Milton makes skillful use of allusions to speculative music. The poems are read by many critics as descriptions of two different sorts of music — one mirthful, one melancholy — that evoke two different responses from one who hears them. They are, rather, companion poems in which the poet is both asking for the reattuning of his soul and enacting the condition under which it will be reattuned.

Critics who attempt to identify the divine music about which Milton is writing in the companion poems (and elsewhere) are usually divided into two schools: one claims that Milton was writing about music he merely contemplated; another claims that Milton was writing about music he actually heard.[20] Both schools pay too little attention to Milton's deep interest in speculative music. Milton knew the harmony was sounding, and he knew he could not hear it; the subject of the poems is the ear that would hear it — or rather, the soul that would join it.[21]

In a famous passage about music from "L'Allegro" we find Milton asking unsubtly for the reattuning of his soul:

> And ever against eating Cares,
> Lap me in soft *Lydian* Airs,
> Married to immortal verse,
> Such as the meeting soul may pierce
> In notes, with many a winding bout
> Of linked sweetness long drawn out,
> With wanton heed, and giddy cunning,
> The melting voice through mazes running;

> Untwisting all the chains that tie
> The hidden soul of harmony;[22]

(135–44)

The plea for "Untwisting all the chains that tie/ The hidden soul of harmony" is close to the view recounted by Simmias in Plato's *Phaedo*:

> You might say the same thing about tuning the strings of a musical instrument, that the attunement is something invisible and incorporeal and splendid and divine and is located in the tuned instrument, while the instrument itself and its strings are material and corporeal and composite and earthly and closely related to what is mortal. Now suppose that the instrument is broken, or its strings cut or snapped. . . . You would say that the attunement must still exist somewhere just as it was, and that the wood and strings will rot away before anything happens to it.[23]

The "hidden soul of harmony," untied from the body's "grossness," would be *musica humana* in harmony with *musica mundana*, as it was in Paradise, as it is in books 4 and 5 of *Paradise Lost*; and *musica instrumentalis* would then be a perfect echo of divine harmony, the product of *carmine* — *musica humana* in harmony with *musica mundana*.

As in the other early poems, Milton employs telling conditional statements: "Such as . . . may pierce." But only the renovated soul may be pierced, since it alone is reattuned with the harmony of the spheres. Milton does not describe a Platonic or Neoplatonic ascent but rather asks to be rid of the "muddy vesture of decay," to be purged that he *might* ascend. The two events would be coterminous but are as yet unfulfilled. We see the same sort of request also in "Il Penseroso":

> And as I wake, sweet music breathe
> Above, about, or underneath,
> Sent by some spirit to mortals good,
> Or th'unseen Genius of the Wood.

(151–54)

The music is sent only "to mortals good." "'Sweet' and 'sweet-ness,'" we recall, "are words that [Milton] reserves, almost always, for music, for paradise, and for the originally per-fect affection between Adam and Eve,"[24] and "L'Allegro" and "Il Penseroso" remind us of the sweetness of heavenly har-mony and love in earthly Paradise precisely to remind us more strongly of the bitter discord brought about by "dispro-portion'd sin."

Announcing the condition of discord, "Il Penseroso" begins with a depiction of the limits of the human senses:

> Hail divinest Melancholy,
> Whose Saintly visage is too bright
> To hit the Sense of human sight;
> And therefore to our weaker view,
> O'erlaid with black, staid Wisdom's hue.
>
> (12–16)

The combination of metaphors of hearing and seeing to dis-cuss the subject of fallen human senses has its roots in classi-cal discussions of the harmony of the spheres: "'But this mighty music, produced by the revolution of the whole uni-verse at the highest speed, cannot be perceived by human ears, any more than you can look straight at the sun, your sense of sight being overpowered by its radiance.'"[25] A result of the poet's "weaker view" or "gross unpurged ear," all seeing or hearing is conditional. The subject of the companion poems is the present inability of the soul to be pierced by music: in "L'Allegro" "that may pierce"; in "Il Penseroso" "as may pierce." Critics who read these passages — and the poems — as examples of Neoplatonic ascent or ecstasy do so because they pay little or no attention to the importance of the condi-tional couplets that end both poems.[26]

Samuel Johnson was apparently the first to notice that more is conditional in the companion poems than their final couplets:

> Both his characters delight in musick; but he seems to think
> that cheerful notes would have obtained from Pluto a com-
> pleat dismission of Eurydice, of whom solemn sounds only
> procured a conditional release.[27]

Indeed, the poems are similar in their tendency to express
things conditionally. "L'Allegro" and "Il Penseroso" share with
"At a Solemn Music" a grammatical structure common to
many of Milton's early poems — a command followed by a
purpose or result (subjunctive) clause. In "L'Allegro" —

> That *Orpheus'* self may heave his head
> From golden slumber on a bed
> Of heapt *Elysian* flow'rs, and hear
> Such strains as would have won the ear
> Of *Pluto*, to have quite set free
> His half-regain'd *Eurydice* —
>
> (145–50)

Milton employs a subjunctive ("may heave"), a past contrary
to fact ("as would have won"), and another past contrary to
fact dependent on the first ("to have quite set free"). The
"quite" provides nice emphasis when we read "half-regain'd."

The companion passage from "Il Penseroso" reminds us that
this is only half the story:

> But, O sad Virgin, that thy power
> Might raise *Musaeus* from his bower,
> Or bid the soul of *Orpheus* sing
> Such notes as, warbled to the string,
> Drew Iron tears down *Pluto's* cheek,
> And made Hell grant what Love did seek.
>
> (103–08)

What love did seek was only "half-regain'd," not because
poetry failed but because the poet, lacking the fortitude not
to turn back, failed to do what would have secured the return
of Eurydice. Orpheus did not obey the god's command, and
so Pluto did not grant what would have been something like

Christian grace. Thus the poet bids "the soul of *Orpheus* sing." But this is an Orpheus who has, like Adam, disobeyed a god. The power of his music was subjected to a greater law, which, when disobeyed, rendered it ineffective. Without his *carmine*, Orpheus's *cithara* is powerless to control all that he once controlled. The image of Orpheus recurs throughout Milton's early poems, for the example of the "ineffective" Orpheus is a model of caution for Milton's own case. When Milton bids Orpheus sing "such notes as," he asks that poetry (*cithara*) succeed where the will of the poet (*carmine*) failed. It is the weak command of a strongly Christian poet. Milton is not commanding; he is asking God for grace.

The tendency to write about these passages and many other passages concerned with divine music as examples of Neoplatonic ascent or ecstasy, as well as the inclination to consider these passages as examples of ascent or of mirth and melancholy, has accompanied the inclination to pay little or no attention to the importance of the conditionality expressed by Milton's grammatical constructions.[28] Throughout the long history of criticism of the poems too many critics have ignored what Milton painstakingly shows us in the urgent command, the plaintive exhortation, and the conditional clauses — his grammatical enactment of waiting.

The history of reading these passages as actual ascent, ecstasy, or purgation centers on the mistake of ignoring the importance of the phrase "as may."[29] Ascent is precisely what the young Milton desires to achieve in "Il Penseroso" (and elsewhere). Milton desires to hear with his ears and see with his eyes the universal harmony of the spheres.[30] But the desire is immediately unfulfillable. For this reason, both poems begin with commands that eventually, and subtly, shift into hortatory subjunctives and finally into the conditional couplets that conclude both poems.

The prolonged conditional structure within the companion poems constitutes the grammatical enactment of asking and waiting for grace. In "Il Penseroso" the shift becomes noticeable at line 147: "me Goddess bring" (132); "Hide me" (141); "And let" (147); "But let" (155); and finally:

There let the pealing Organ blow
To the full voic'd Choir below,
In Service high and Anthems clear,
As may with sweetness, through mine ear,
Dissolve me into ecstasies,
And bring all Heav'n before mine eyes.

(161–66)

Il Penseroso does not *experience* the "ecstasies"; he exhorts ("There let") that he may ("*as may*") be pierced ("through mine ear") and dissolved into "ecstasies." Nor is heaven brought before his eyes. There is poignant ambiguity in "And bring." Is it another imperative? Or does it depend on "as may," a contingency of the optative? The ambiguity emphasizes that the occurrences are conditional.

Not only is nothing achieved and nothing chosen, not only are the demands of the conditional couplets not satisfied — but that is the point of the poem. "Il Penseroso" expresses the poet's condition and his attitude toward it: his relation to divine harmony. Just as he contrasts his urgent "now" and God's eternity in "At a Solemn Music," so too in the companion poems does Milton express his condition as both man and poet by making an urgent command that secures only the condition of waiting.

Milton expresses this condition within each poem in the grammatical structure built by the sequence of conditional couplets that unites the poems. In addition to the two conditional couplets with which the poems conclude there is, of course, a third. It occurs early in "L'Allegro":

And if I give thee honor due,
Mirth, admit me of thy crew.

(37–38)

In this, the first conditional couplet to appear in the companion poems, the poet places the burden of giving on himself. The second conditional couplet concludes "*L'Allegro*":

> These delights if thou canst give,
> Mirth, with thee I mean to live.

> (151–152)

Here the reversal of the earlier couplet marks strongly the poet's movement from a plaintive stance to a demanding one. But the three couplets work as a triad, the third couplet drawing to a close the rhetorical development of the companion poems:

> These pleasures *Melancholy* give,
> And I with thee will choose to live.

> (175–76)

The grammatical development within the three conditional couplets expresses a parallel development in the attitude of the poet.

Within the development there are two shifts: from giving (in the first couplet) to receiving (in the second). But the most important shift in attitude (from the second couplet to the third) is expressed by a change from one type of conditional statement to another. The first two are present simple conditionals; both the protases and apodoses are in the present tense: the first, "if I give" (present), "admit" (imperative); the second, "if thou canst give" (present), "I mean" (present). The third, unlike the first two, is an odd sort of mixed conditional: "give" (imperative), "and I will choose" (future). The mixed condition has the force of expediency (imperative) in the protasis and certain uncertainty (future) in the apodasis. Moreover, Milton does not write "and I will live" but rather "I will choose to live." He urgently commands ("give"), yet the completion of this command is the condition not for immediate action or choice but only for the postponement of choice;

only then (in the future) he *"will* choose." The urgent uncertainty confirms now what the poet seems earlier reluctant to acknowledge: there is no possibility of fulfilling the conditions but only of stating them.[31]

Together, by means of the progression of these commands, the poems enact the condition of the poet: waiting — till grace purges his "grossness" and brings the music and light of heaven to his ears and eyes. Before the music may be heard, there must be grace, remission of sin, and renovation. As Milton writes in *The Christian Doctrine*, quoting from and interpreting Exodus 33.19: *"I will be gracious to whom I will be gracious*, that is, not to enter more largely into the causes of this graciousness at present, Romans 9.18. *he hath mercy on whom he will have mercy*, by that method, namely, which he had appointed in Christ" (919). At that time there will be "the remission of sins, even in his human nature," Milton writes, quoting Isaiah 35.4–6: *"behold, your God will come with vengeance, even God with a recompense, he will come and save you: then the eyes of the blind shall be opened, &c."* And there will be "renovation," writes Milton, quoting 2 Corinthians 5.17–18: *"behold, all things are become new, and all things are of God, who hath reconciled himself to us by Jesus Christ"* (958–59).

Arthur Barker has shown that the three movements of "Lycidas" begin with "invocation[s] of pastoral muses" and end with "perfectly controlled" Christian "crescendos."[32] In the companion poems, we see a similar movement in the triad of conditional couplets. As in "At a Solemn Music," a poem in which Milton writes not about the *nunc stans* of the "Nativity Ode" but about himself as a poet and his earthly "now," Milton here expresses *his* condition in the movement of the conditional couplets, and in a way that demonstrates his acceptance of it. With the movement from urgency to uncertainty in the final couplet, Milton completes his grammatical enactment of waiting, to which we must contrast the *nunc stans.*[33] In the "Nativity Ode," Milton writes about the time for which all are waiting, the time when the golden age will be brought back:

> And then at last our bliss
> Full and perfect is . . .

when, as Edward Tayler has written, "instead of the expected future ('will be'), the poet writes in a kind of eternal present, for as Joseph Fletcher says, 'God . . . needeth not the distinctions of Time' — the notion stated most memorably by Sir Thomas Browne: 'in eternity there is no distinction of Tenses.'"[34] But Milton lives in time, not in eternity; and poetry is subject to the laws of time. Time is the awful part of "grossness" — the punishment for original sin.

With nothing available to the poet but tenses, Milton therefore chooses them differently when writing about God than when writing about himself. For in God's eternal time Christ has already come, whereas Milton must wait, and may express himself only in the temporal terms he knows on earth. Only by ridding himself of time, Milton writes in "On Time," will he rid himself of his "Earthy grossness":

> When once our heav'nly-guided soul shall climb,
> Then all this Earthy grossness quit,
> Attir'd with Stars, we shall for ever sit
>   Triumphing over Death, and Chance, and thee
>   O Time.
>
> (19–23)

Milton describes the good end of time with an ironic temporal clause: "When once." The soul is unable to be "pierced" until it is made immortal again — in Milton's terms, until it is purged, renovated, and drawn home, when, "Triumphing over Death, and Chance, and thee/ O Time," the poet may sing about himself as he would sing about heaven. All will be one. This long wait, Milton knows, will require much patience.

As in a number of early poems, the eagerness must give way to patience. Eager to receive immediately his poetic fate, Milton concludes in "Sonnet VII":

> All is, if I have grace to use it so,
> As ever in my great task-Master's eye.

The sense conveys patience and resignation while the syntax, which enacts the temporal uncertainty it expresses, reveals anxiousness. There is the thought of waiting "Till old experience do attain/ To something *like* Prophetic strain" (173–74).[35] But Milton need not wait to write, not if he can make the process of his reattuning the subject and structure of his verse. To do this is to live in tune with God's law and move, with instrumentality, toward "the heavenly tune."

In the companion poems, Milton brilliantly expresses this tension between anxiousness and patience by means of the series of conditional invitations modeled cleverly upon the tradition of pastoral invitation and reply that emerged with Marlowe and Raleigh. Milton seems to have adopted not Marlowe's invitation but Raleigh's mock acceptance, which is acceptance on the grounds that a whole list of counterfactual conditions be satisfied. Raleigh answers Marlowe's promises of future delights — "Come live with me, and be my love/ And we will all the pleasures prove" — by turning Marlowe's "will" into a counterfactual "could" and conditional "might":

> But could youth last, and love still breede,
> Had joyes no date, nor age no neede,
>
> Then these delights my minde might move
> To live with thee, and be thy love.[36]

Milton seems to have picked this up and built into the progression of the three conditional couplets of the companion poems something like Marlowe's promise and Raleigh's mocking reply. In the final couplet of the companion poems —

> These pleasures *Melancholy* give
> And I with thee will choose to live

— the series of invitations culminates in its own reply (a rejection) to itself by ending with the indefinite postponement of choice. Milton effectively rejects both the pagan goddess and the pastoral (the Marlovian) invitation, suggesting instead that he has begun his wait for Christian grace.

In the companion poems (and elsewhere), Milton doubts not the power of music to draw us home; he doubts the power of his ear to hear it and his discordant soul to be drawn. Milton writes that until one receives grace and undergoes renovation music can neither pierce the "grossness" nor draw the soul out of the body. Does all this mean that music (*musica instrumentalis*) draws us only to awareness of the impenetrable, "gross" decaying house of clay, or can it still draw us up to God? The companion poems and "At a Solemn Music" provide the same answer:

> O may we soon again renew that Song,
> And keep in tune with Heav'n, till God ere long
> To his celestial consort us unite,
> To live with him, and sing in endless morn of light.
>
> (25–28)

According to Milton, music itself does not have the Orphic power to draw one home; one must first be drawn home to God in order to hear "the heavenly tune."

In the last conditional statement of the companion poems, Milton first commands the heaven that could make him chaste, but not boldly; he then softens the commands, changes them to exhortations, that heaven might stoop to him. For the hope is, as the final lines of *Comus* state: "Or if Vertue feeble were,/ Heav'n itself would stoop to her" (1022–23). finally, Milton transforms his exhortations to heaven into hard conditional statements to himself: for surely he would live with God, but he knows he must wait "till God ere long" brings him to Him. Throughout his career, Milton attempted to moderate his poetic zeal with speculative temperance. His genius was to develop a poetic — a theological conception of poetry based in speculative preparation — that would enact simultaneously his earthly dilemma and its divine solution.

"To Something Like Prophetic Strain"

Between the writing of his early poems and *PL*, there is much in Milton's prose that tells us about his aspiration toward "the heavenly tune." Before we turn to *PL* and consider Milton's achievement of prophetic song, we should examine the important relationship between his aspiration to song and his theory of prophecy.

Literary scholars, whether interested in the method or influence of Milton's prophetic mode, tend to take as a starting point the similarity between Milton's poetic style and the methods of the biblical prophets.[37] Biblical scholars, in contrast, begin by remarking the differences between poets and prophets, pointing out the need to confront with reasonable skepticism any post-biblical poet's claim to prophecy. "That poets and prophets have something in common with each other is an idea with a long history," as James L. Kugel writes. "Certainly anyone acquainted with the Western literary tradition knows that some of its greatest poets — Dante, Milton, Blake (to name only three of the most celebrated examples) — have in one way or another viewed themselves, and presented themselves to the world, as endowed with prophetic gifts or divinely inspired speech. What is perhaps less well known," Kugel points out, "is that such figures were themselves the inheritors of an earlier tradition associating poetry and prophecy," a tradition "that winds back through the Middle Ages in Christian Europe and Muslim Spain and the East, and back still further to ancient Greece and biblical Israel. This tradition," as Kugel cautions, "hardly speaks with one voice":

> At times, it seems, there have been those who would utterly separate the offices of poet and prophet, sometimes seeking

quite consciously to exalt the latter through specific contrast with the former. At other times, quite the opposite operation has been performed, and the prophetlike nature of the poet — indeed, the identity of poet and prophet — has just as willfully been asserted. In either case, the position of poetry vis-à-vis prophecy has not infrequently been the subject of debate or polemic: the makers of poetry have more than once been attacked as usurpers or falsifiers of the Divine Word, and defended as following nothing less than Scripture's own dictates and models of prescribed behavior. . . .[38]

When they examine the "separate . . . offices of poet and prophet," many scholars willfully assert the identity of poet and prophet, granting the poet divine inspiration.[39] But Milton himself looked at the matter as much with the reason of a biblical scholar as with the zeal of a Christian poet aspiring to heavenly song.

In considering seriously the separate offices, Milton was instructed by, among other writers, the greatest expert on prophecy in the West, Moses Maimonides.[40] Using distinctions codified by Maimonides, Milton conceived of himself — and presented himself — as capable of a kind of prophecy very different from those that literary scholars have so far described.

Since the work of Fletcher, Saurat, and Baldwin, Milton's knowledge of Hebraic writings has been debated, but his familiarity with Maimonides' *Doctor Perplexorum* is indisputable. In Maimonides, Milton saw a theologian who could instruct him on matters such as divorce, Edenic polity, and natural and Mosaic law. What is more important, Milton also encountered a thinker whose very personal understanding of the requirements for achieving divinely inspired prophecy were strikingly similar to his own. "Even in his youth," as Abraham Joshua Heschel writes, "Maimonides felt he knew when prophetic illumination, which had been lost for centuries, would be possible again. Its time was not far off, [Maimonides] said; he himself might live to see the era of grace."[41] And might not. Milton thought his era might be the "new and great period" of Jerusalem and England, as he writes in *Areopagitica*: "What does he then but reveal himself to his servants, and, as his manner is, first to his Englishmen?" (743).

Most striking is the similarity between Milton and Maimonides on the matter of preparation: "This expectation [of that era], this inner preparation marked [Maimonides'] youth. . . . His family preserved a tradition that was handed down from father to son since the Destruction of the Temple: as of the year 1216, the spirit of the illumination would return to the world." Maimonides could not help "being seized with a yearning to reach the level of prophecy, the uninhibited way in which his prophetiological views penetrate the most diverse aspects of his writings," writes Heschel. "At a very early point, he decided to write a 'book on prophecy.'" After having written a part of it, however, Maimonides "was displeased with the method of his explanations. He feared being misunderstood by the masses," for "they would 'resent his interpretation.' Finally, he gave up writing the book altogether and contented himself with allusions in his presentation of the basic teachings of religion and the universal truths, which he was working on at the same time. To make up for this," writes Heschel, Maimonides "seems to have primed himself all the more intensely for receiving prophetic inspiration. He was convinced that personal qualities are the foundation on which to construct the prophetic man, 'that no one receives the gift of prophecy until all intellectual and most of the moral virtues, the most unshakable ones,' like wisdom, courage, and moderation, are part of him."[42] Maimonides lived in a tradition that obliged him to give up his book on prophecy and take up more basic teaching of religion, but although he would not consider himself the beneficiary of God's gift of prophecy, he would not stop writing about prophecy. He would not stop preparing.

The striking biographical similarities between Milton and Maimonides are part of a deeper relation. Most relevant to

Milton is Maimonides' painstaking account of the principles of prophecy. "There are three different opinions [on Prophecy] held by those who believe in God," writes Maimonides in *Guide for the Perplexed*. First, "there are some ignorant people who believe as follows: God selects any person He pleases, inspires him with the spirit of Prophecy, and entrusts him with a mission. It makes no difference whether that person be wise or stupid .. .; provided he be, to some extent, morally good." Second, "[t]he philosophers hold that prophecy is a certain faculty of man in a state of perfection, which can only be obtained by study. Although the faculty is common to the whole race, yet it is not fully developed in each individual." And "it is impossible that it should not be perfect in some individual of the class." More important, "if a person, perfect in his intellectual and moral faculties, and also perfect, as far as possible, in his imaginative faculty, prepares himself in the manner which will be described, he must become a prophet; for prophecy is a natural faculty of man." And most important, in the view of the philosophers "it is impossible that a man who has the capacity for prophecy should prepare himself for it without attaining it."[43]

Milton nowhere demonstrates a willingness to hold the view of the philosophers. Like Maimonides, rather, he held a third view, which complicated the view of "the philosophers" by adding consideration of God's will:

> The third view is that which is taught in Scripture, and which forms one of the principles of our religion. It coincides with the opinion of the philosophers in all points except one. For we believe that, even if one has the capacity for prophecy, and has duly prepared himself, it may yet happen that he does not actually prophesy. It is in that case the will of God [that withholds from him the use of the faculty].[44]

We have already begun to consider Milton's treatment of this conflict in his poetry, but his theory of prophecy also receives treatment in his prose.

Although "Milton was profoundly indebted to a long theological tradition of defining and categorizing the kinds of prophetic inspiration in the Bible," William Kerrigan is "convinced that Milton developed his prophetic stance as a private response to an unusually various tradition." Kerrigan concludes that Milton "believed himself a prophet" and "never examined his belief in prophecy as he examined his belief in mortalism or divorce."[45] But Milton clearly did examine his claim to prophecy, with an urgency that deserves our attention.

Whatever his attempts to defray worry with bold assertions against his enemies in *The Reason of Church Government Urged against Prelaty* (hereafter *CG*), the concerns about prophecy expressed by Maimonides were shared by Milton:

> For the laws of Nature demand that every one should be a prophet, who has a proper physical constitution, and has been duly prepared as regards education and training. If such a person is not a prophet, he is in the same position as a person who, like Jeroboam (1 Kings 13.4) is deprived of the use of his hand, or of his eyes, as was the case with the army of Syria, in the history of Elisha (2 Kings 6.18). As for the principle which I laid down, that preparation and perfection of moral and rational faculties are the *sine quâ non*, our Sages say exactly the same. . . . We have explained these words in our commentary on the Mishnah, and in our large work. We have stated there that the Sons of the Prophets were constantly engaged in preparation. That those who have prepared themselves may still be prevented from being prophets, may be inferred from the history of Baruch. . . . There are . . . numerous passages in Scripture as well as in the writings of our Sages, which support the principle that it depends chiefly on the will of God who is to prophesy . . ., and at what time; and that he only selects the best and the wisest. . . . [W]hen these have created the possibility, then it depends on the will of God whether the possibility is to be turned into reality.[46]

Preparation is always necessary, but the granting of prophecy is always conditional. Even the prepared may be prevented by God's will. Always preparing for prophecy, Milton, like Maimonides, appears always prepared for God to say "no."

Milton addresses the matter in the autobiographical discussion of poetry in *CG*, published 25 years before he published *PL*. There he discusses the distinct qualities of divinely inspired prophecy and addresses the foremost question of his *duty*. When Adam and Eve spoke before the fall, "prompt eloquence/ flow'd from thir lips." Thereafter, as Milton writes in *CG*, God "sends out his seraphim with the hallowed fire of his altar, to touch and purify the lips of whom he pleases" (671). Given the rarity of the gift of prophecy, Milton declares his "concernment," or "duty," as "the enforcement of his conscience only and a preventive fear lest the omitting of this duty should be against me" (667). The question is: what exactly is his "duty"? Milton understands his "duty" as "the furtherance or contribution of those few talents which God at that present had lent him" (666). Does this mean it is his "duty" to receive and deliver divine prophecy? No, "few talents" are skills that, in the absence of the kind of inspiration a biblical prophet receives, enable one person to teach another to live a Christian life. Milton had in some respects to choose between earthly duty and preparation for divinely inspired prophecy.

Milton's onerous question is how to "further" or "contribute" — whether to speak or be silent. The risk? He would, he writes, "hear within myself, all my life after, of discourage and reproach":

> Timorous and ungrateful, the church of God is now again at the foot of her insulting enemies, and thou bewailst. What matters it for thee, or thy bewailing? When time was, thou couldst not find a syllable of all that thou hadst read or studied, to utter in her behalf. Yet ease and leisure was given thee

for thy retired thoughts, out of the sweat of other men. Thou hadst the diligence, the parts, the language of a man, if a vain subject were to be adorned or beautified, but when the cause of God and his church was to be pleaded, for which purpose that tongue was given the which thou hast, God listened if he could hear thy voice among his zealous servants, but thou were dumb as a beast; from henceforward be that which thine own brutish silence hast made thee. (666)

The reason for silence here recalls Milton's prolusion: "I should not write thus out of mine own season when I have neither yet completed to my mind the full circle of my private studies, although I complain not of any insufficiency to the matter in hand . . ." (666). Now, however, given the urgency of political and religious circumstances, silence turns out to be "brutish," and the "purpose" of his tongue greater than any worry about its noise. But there is yet vacillation. In the long personal digression, Milton worries that even "were I ready to my wishes, it were a folly to commit anything elaborately composed to the careless and interrupted listening of these tumultuous times" (667). The unpreparedness of his listeners — unfit audience — is one concern. But the central concern is Milton's preparedness for his task:

> Next, if I were wise only to mine own ends, I would certainly take such a subject as of itself might catch applause, whereas this hath all the disadvantages on the contrary, and such a subject as the publishing whereof might be delayed at pleasure, and time enough to pencil it over with all the curious touches of art, even to the perfection of a faultless picture; whenas in this argument the not deferring is of great moment to the good speeding, that if solidity have leisure to do her office, art cannot have much. (667)

And there is the further problem: preparedness itself is insufficient. Part of Milton's "concernment" is to consider deeply the looming contradiction between inspiration and art, between God's and Milton's "ends."

Making good use of his skill for progressive negations, striving to keep himself from every possible kind of fault, Milton manifests his "preventive fear." Milton considers himself a vigorous, reasonable voice chosen by God to speak to His Englishmen. But with equal vigor Milton scrutinizes his authority to speak. At his "moment" in history and time, whatever the deferred status of his inspiration, Milton has quickly to lead his country on a timely matter. At this "moment" in his prose, however, Milton turns, not coincidentally, to the subject of great poetry. Milton's "not deferring" here looks ahead to the "long choosing" and "beginning late" he would address in *PL*.

Milton's apology for the biographical nature of his prose turns *CG* even more biographical. Indeed, it turns Milton directly to his concern about inspiration:

> For although a poet, soaring in the high region of his fancies with his garland and singing robes about him, might without apology speak more of himself than I mean to do, yet for me sitting here below in the cool element of prose, a mortal thing among many readers of no empyreal conceit, to venture and divulge unusual things of myself, I shall petition to the gentler sort, it may not be envy to me. (667)

For Milton, the achievement of prophetic song is not as simple as donning "singing robes," for he may merely soar "in the high region of his fancies."[47] While it seeks to defend the personal remarks in *CG* "in the cool element of prose," Milton's discussion of poetry passionately considers his ambitions:

> I began thus far to assent . . . not less to an inward prompting which now grew daily upon me, that by labor and intent study (which I take to be my portion in this life) joined with the strong propensity of nature, I might perhaps leave something so written to aftertimes, as they should not willingly let it die. (668)

"These thoughts" of achieving earthly fame by means of the labor of art "at once possessed me, and these other; that if I were certain to write as men buy leases, for three lives and downward, there ought no regard be sooner had than to God's glory, by the honor and instruction of my country" (668). As Milton confronted the conflict inherent in "these thoughts," he appears to have found as much resolution as he could find in Maimonides.

As Maimonides writes, "the words, 'In order that the people hear when I speak with thee' (Exodus 19.9), show that God spoke to Moses, and the people only heard the mighty sound, not distinct words. . . . It was only Moses that heard the words, and he reported them to the people."[48] Without the authority of Moses, Milton could not think to invade God's office. Instead, he could interpret truths already revealed in Scripture; he could instruct his country.

Milton maintains the important distinction between biblical prophecy and preaching made by Maimonides, between the rare gift of divine prophecy and the "duty" of being "an interpreter and relater." It is Milton's hope to do for England "what the greatest and choicest wits of Athens, Rome, or modern Italy, and those Hebrews of old did for their country, I, in my proportion, with this over and above of being a Christian . . ." (668):

> For which cause, and not only for that I knew it would be hard to arrive at the second rank among the Latins, I applied myself to that resolution which Ariosto followed against the persuasions of Bembo, to fix all the industry and art I could unite to the adorning of my native tongue; not to make verbal curiosities the end, that were a toilsome vanity, but to be an interpreter and relater of the best and sagest things among mine own citizens. (668)

To be "an interpreter and relater" does not require hearing God's Word, or boldly invading God's office.

Whether Milton is a divinely inspired poet or an interpreter is a valid debate, and it is necessary to consider the tensions

Milton confronted in its historical context. In 1683, Matthew Poole, a biblical commentator, regarded Milton as an "'ingenious and learned' expositor rather than poet" and the last books of *PL* as "biblical exegesis rather than epic," as Jason P. Rosenblatt writes.[49] When we consider Milton dutifully engaged in the prophetic activity of interpretation, we should, I think, appreciate Rosenblatt's association of Milton with Josiah rather than with Moses, as well as his suggestion that "Milton sees himself as a moral archaeologist, picking up shards of truth buried for years in custom and error."[50] As he writes in his *Doctrine and Discipline of Divorce*, Milton sees himself as

> Bringing in my hands an ancient and most necessary, most charitable and yet most injured, statute of Moses: not repealed ever by him who only had the authority, but thrown aside with much inconsiderate neglect under the rubbish of Canonical ignorance; as once the whole law was by some such like conveyance in Josiah's time. (697)

Milton goes on to make a less than subtle claim for himself: "And he who shall endeavor the amendment of any old neglected grievance in church or state, or in the daily course of life, if he be gifted with abilities of mind that may raise him to so high an undertaking, I grant he hath already much whereof not to repent him" (697).[51] Milton juxtaposes his view of Moses' authority and his conception of his authority as an "interpretor and relator."

If Milton were boldly to claim divine inspiration, he would cross a line he himself had drawn and redrawn. The writing of *CG* is, however open to the errors of human reason, dutiful civic instruction in the service of "God's glory," but the writing of poetry is another matter. Milton's dilemma was clear: to be an expositor is to be a dutiful servant, whereas to be a poet making claims to prophecy is potentially to clash with God's law as well as his song.

As Milton writes in *The Christian Doctrine*, "whoever keeps the whole law, and yet offends in one point, is guilty of all." In the writing of Maimonides, Milton found a way to relate his largest concerns as a Christian poet: his Platonic conception of speculative musical preparation, his conception of grace, his understanding of divine inspiration, and his strict personal moral code. Milton was able to combine these personal theories into what I have been calling his speculative musical poetic — and thereby to keep the law whole.

Milton, like the Mosaic code, argues against trying to sing without the authority of God's certain inspiration.[52] But although Milton observed the consequences of his "disproportion'd sin," he could not subdue his highest hope. The mention of poetry in *CG* leads tellingly to a discussion of the obstacles to his "hardest attempting": "Time serves not now, and perhaps I might seem too profuse to give any certain account of what the mind at home in the spacious circuits of her musing hath liberty to propose to herself, though of highest hope and hardest attempting" (668). The practical considerations — "whether that epic form whereof the two poems of Homer and those other two of Virgil and Tasso are a diffuse" (668) — are circumscribed by ardent speculation. The impediments are largely speculative:

> Or if occasion shall lead to imitate those magnific odes and hymns wherein Pindarus and Callimachus are in most things worthy, some others in their frame judicious, in their matter most an end faulty. But those frequent songs throughout the law and prophets beyond all these, not in their divine argument alone, but in the very critical art of composition, may be easily made appear over all the kinds of lyric poesy to be incomparable. (669)

Milton is concerned with the question of genre, upon which many scholars have focused, but he is more concerned, as he goes on to write, with the question of inspiration — with the speculative differences between divine song and "earthy" poetry.

Numerous scholars have compared Milton's verse to the biblical models, as Kerrigan does when analyzing the first invocation of *PL*: "[t]he Spirit 'know'st' and can therefore properly inspire a literary creation about Creation, whether by Moses or by Milton."[53] But for Milton the songs of the biblical prophets are "incomparable," songs by those whose "Earthy grossness" it pleased God to purge:

> These abilities, wheresoever they be found, are the inspired gift of God rarely bestowed, but yet to some (though most abuse) in every nation; and are of power beside the office of a pulpit, to inbreed and cherish in a great people the seeds of virtue and public civility, to allay the perturbations of the mind and set the affections in right tune, to celebrate in glorious and lofty hymns the throne and equipage of God's almightiness, and what he works and what he suffers to be wrought with high providence in his church, to sing the victorious agonies of martyrs and saints, the deeds and triumphs of just and pious nations doing valiantly through faith against the enemies of Christ, to deplore the general relapses of kingdoms and states from justice and God's true worship.[54] (669–70)

Milton knows he demonstrates practical abilities, but "the inspired gift of god" is "rarely bestowed," and assertion of "high providence" is more than he may at present assert. Inspiration is "of power beside the office of a pulpit."

When Milton is brashly confident in *CG* and other prose, he is merely asserting the right of his reason, not his acceptance of the gift of prophecy that would signal the end of his preparation. Milton writes in *Areop* that, "God uses not to captivate under a perpetual childhood of prescription, but trusts him with the gift of reason to be his own chooser; there were but little work left for preaching, if law and compulsion should grow so fast upon those things which heretofore were governed only by exhortation" (727). The "talents" provide his "power to examine our spiritual knowledge and to demand from us in God's behalf a service entirely reasonable" (641). The "two" most important "principles," in Judaism and

Christianity, Maimonides explains, "the existence of God and His Unity, can be arrived at by means of reasoning, and whatever can be established by proof is known by the prophet in the same way as by any other person; he has no advantage in this respect."[55] As Maimonides makes clear, even if he lacks divine inspiration, the preparation of a prophet — perfection of faculties of reason and imagination — makes him capable, by virtue of his "reason," of the kind of prophetic exposition that is identical with good preaching. The gift of reason demands discipline, as well as contemplation of the differences between speculation and practice.

Milton's preparation, his conception of Pythagorean "discipline" remained constant throughout his career:

> whatsoever power or sway in moral things weaker men have attributed to fortune, I durst with more confidence (the honor of divine providence ever saved) ascribed either to the vigor or the slackness of discipline. Nor is there any sociable perfection in this life, civil or sacred, that can be above discipline; but she is that which with her musical chords preserves and holds all the parts thereof together. (642)

In *CG*, Milton later records his hope to "leave a calm and pleasing solitariness, fed with cheerful and confident thoughts to embark in a troubled sea of noises and hoarse disputes, put from beholding the bright countenance of truth in the quiet and still air of delightful studies . . ." (671). Milton condemns "noises and hoarse disputes," and declares his concern about bringing his own voice to such discordant raspiness, but "he who would take orders must subscribe slave and take an oath withal, which unless he took with a conscience that would retch, he must either straight perjure or split his faith; I thought it better to prefer a blameless silence before the sacred office of speaking" (671). Kerrigan observes that "[t]ranquility was the dearest luxury of this age. And if the disharmonies of war threatened all poetic creation, they were particularly dangerous to inspired creation." Milton certainly "associated prophetic inspiration with mental calm," but the question is what precisely distracted him when he was "distracted by the barbarous dissonance of a noisy age."[56]

For Milton the prose writer, the brutal distraction by this time was political and religious. For Milton the poet, the distraction was always largely speculative. Writing *CG* is necessary; one must put one's "few talents" in service. But even in the matter of such necessity, Milton cannot assuage his "preventive fear." He questions his "right . . . to meddle in these matters, as before the necessity and constraint appeared" (671).

But the "troubl'd sea of noises and hoarse disputes" makes his own troubled noises and hoarse dispute necessary. Otherwise, he were "'dumb as a beast.'" It is, finally, not "better to prefer a blameless silence." To "shut up" is to clash, too. Silent speculation is clearly better than noisy discord, but when service is necessary silence is not blameless.

Observing himself in God's musical time, his "strictest measure," Milton considered himself unripe as a prophetic singer, but he also considered himself called upon, in his time, to exercise his "talents":

> And if any man incline to think I undertake a task too difficult for my years, I trust through the supreme enlightening assistance far otherwise; for my years, be they few or many, what imports it? So they bring reason, let that be looked on: and for the task, from hence the question in hand is so needful to be known at this time, chiefly by every meaner capacity and contains in it the explication of many admirable and heavenly privileges reached out to us by the gospel, I conclude the task must be easy: God having to this end ordained his gospel to be the revelation of his power and wisdom in Christ Jesus. (641)

The task in which Milton has confidence here is biblical exposition — not yet the task of "higher argument" that later obliges him at the beginning of the second book of *CG* to doubt his preparation and to worry that he clashes with the harmony he is contemplating.

Milton appears to have made an important distinction between the biblical prophets and those, like him, who sought to achieve as firm an authority. Going beyond the rhetorical concerns of Sidney, Milton writes of those who, lacking that divine authority "were such men as with authority enough might give it out to be so" (643).

Milton doubted precisely because he conceived prophecy in strict biblical terms. When God speaks through a biblical prophet, the matter is clear. There is no wait. God is merciful and instantly purges him: "And he laid *it* upon my mouth, and said, Lo, his hath touched thy lips; and thine iniquity is taken away, and thy sin purged," says Isaiah. Such a prophet speaks God's harmonious song at precisely the moment he hears God's voice. He hears and rejoins "the heavenly tune" on earth, in this life: "Also I heard the voice of the Lord, saying, Whom shall I send, and who will go for us? Then said I, Here *am* I; send me."[57] Milton was unable to make this claim, and no other fact is more central, we will see, to Milton's claims to prophetic song in *PL*.

Paradise Lost

Milton's grammatical enactment of his aspiration toward God's music in his early poems obeys God's law, and his verse assuredly moves the poet, and his readers, toward "the heavenly tune." The same is true, more gloriously so, of *PL*. In *PL* Milton does, of course, render paradise, but he also renders, if more subtly than in his early poems, a further developed acceptance of his "grossness." In the early poems, Milton writes directly about his awareness that only grace can bring the restoration of his soul that will make his singing an echo of "the heavenly tune." But truly to render paradise requires the actual renewal of "that Song of pure concent." Many of the invocations in *PL* might seem at first to suggest that Milton believed he had purged his "grossness," but Milton never

makes this claim. The solutions offered in the four invocations of *PL* are Milton's remarkable way of rendering paradise
while continuing to examine his condition as a singer. Milton
highlights the dangers of singing his bold song while enacting, with the magnificent music of his verse, the speculative
poetic that keeps him safe.

Milton addresses his postlapsarian condition with directness in the invocation of book 3:

> Hail holy Light, offspring of Heav'n first-born,
> Or of th' Eternal Coeternal beam
> May I express thee unblam'd? since God is Light,
> And never but in unapproached Light
> Dwelt from Eternity, dwelt then in thee,
> Bright effluence of bright essence increate.
>
> (3.1–6)

It might seem that something had changed in Milton's life,
that he interpreted his blindness as a sign of his election, a
physical manifestation of a call to true prophecy. But nothing,
in fact, seems to have changed. Milton sings, he says, "with
bolder wing" (13),

> Yet not the more
> Cease I to wander where the Muses haunt
> Clear Spring, or shady Grove, or Sunny Hill,
> Smit with love of sacred Song.
>
> (3.26–29)

Milton is "smit with love of sacred Song," and it is precisely
this "love," Milton is aware, that might make him "wander"
in the postlapsarian sense.

Throughout the invocation of book 3, Milton carefully distinguishes his speculative condition from the one to which
he aspires — showing clearly the differences between his poem
and God's "Celestial Song." Milton seeks to "feed on thoughts,
that voluntary move/ Harmonious numbers" (378). The heavenly tune is "innumerable," as The Son tells The Father:

> O Father, gracious was that word which clos'd
> Thy sovran sentence, that Man should find grace;
> For which both Heav'n and Earth shall high extol
> Thy praises, with th'innumerable sound
> Of Hymns and sacred Songs, wherewith thy Throne
> Encompass'd shall resound thee ever blest.

$$(3.144-49)$$

Milton's poem, in contrast, is, as Andrew Marvell writes, "created like thy Theme sublime,/ In Number, Weight, and Measure, needs not Rime" (210). Whereas such proportion was a practical achievement for Ben Jonson and Marvell, one that reflected, through the splendor of an analogous creation, God's proportion in man, Milton would not claim that poetry echoes "the cosmic order inherent in the music of the spheres."[58]

Milton observes this distinction between earthly and heavenly song throughout book 3, and throughout the rest of the poem, especially in the invocations of book 7 and book 9. The distinction provides a context for his requests for divine inspiration:

> But cloud instead, and ever-during dark
> Surrounds me, from the cheerful ways of men
> Cut off, and for the Book of knowledge fair
> Presented with a Universal blanc
> Of Nature's works to me expung'd and ras'd,
> And wisdom at one entrance quite shut out.
> So much the rather thou Celestial Light . . .
> Shine inward, and the mind through all her powers
> Irradiate, there plant eyes, all mist from thence
> Purge and disperse, that I may see and tell
> Of things invisible to mortal sight.

$$(3.45-55)$$

As in "L'Allegro" and "Il Penseroso," celestial light and celestial song are interchangeable. Here, too, Milton contrasts his "lapsed powers" with the condition to which he aspires ("So much the rather . . ."). He begins with a command ("shine") that he transforms into an exhortation ("that I may see and tell"). This exhortation is soon put into its clear theological context by words from the Father:

> Man shall not quite be lost, but sav'd who will,
> Yet not of will in him, but grace in me
> Freely voutsaf't; once more I will renew
> His lapsed powers, though forfeit and enthrall'd
> By sin to foul exorbitant desires.
>
> (3.173–77)

An ambitious poet, Milton knew, might turn "love of sacred Song" into "foul exorbitant desires," claiming to hear what he, as yet, cannot. As God says,

> for I will clear thir senses dark,
> What may suffice, and soft'n stony hearts
> To pray, repent, and bring obedience due.
> To Prayer, repentance, and obedience due,
> Though but endeavor'd with sincere intent,
> Mine ear shall not be slow, mine eye not shut.
> And I will place within them as a guide
> My Umpire *Conscience*, whom if they will hear,
> Light after light well us'd they shall attain,
> And to the end persisting, safe arrive.
>
> (3.188–96)

An account of Milton's safe arrival, *PL* is brilliantly designed to draw our attention to the dangers. In a postlapsarian world, where God's ear is quick but the poet's is unpurged, it remains for the poet to hear the "Umpire *Conscience*" that will help him one day to hear the heavenly tune. Awareness of dangers can bring one to safety. A poet must persist in the condition of "grossnes" until the end to arrive safe, and this makes aspiration to divine poetic song dangerous.

Here — and in later books — Milton hints that he may not be safe. In book 7, he declares, "More safe I Sing with mortal voice" (7.24), where the comparative "more safe" suggests still *unsafe*. There are, moreover, dangerous consequences: "But

hard be hard'n'd, blind be blinded more,/ That they may
stumble on, and deeper fall" (3.200–01).

At the end of book 6 of *PL*, Raphaël warns Adam about
"the deep fall/ Of those too high aspiring": "firm they might
have stood,/ Yet fell; remember, and fear to transgress." The
aspiration to heavenly song is a high aspiration. To represent
his dilemma, Milton consistently contrasts the lapsed powers
of an "earthy" poet with the sweet power of the heavenly choir:

> No sooner had th'Almighty ceas't, but all
> The multitude of Angels with a shout
> Loud as from numbers without number, sweet
> As from blest voices, uttering joy, Heav'n rung
> With Jubilee, and loud Hosannas fill'd
> Th' eternal Regions.
>
> (3.344–49)

The Angels sing "as from numbers without number":

> Then Crown'd again thir gold'n harps they took,
> Harps ever tun'd, that glittering by thir side
> Like Quivers hung, and with Preamble sweet
> Of charming symphony they introduce
> Thir sacred Song, and waken raptures high;
> No voice exempt, no voice but well could join
> Melodious part, such concord is in Heav'n.
>
> (3.365–71)

Milton's voice, in contrast, is "exempt." Milton's verse may
be well proportioned in practical terms, but "disproportion'd
sin" *disjoins* him from the "sacred Song." As the narrator
explains in book 10,

> Some say he bid his Angels turn askance
> The Poles of Earth Twice ten degrees and more
> From the Sun's Axle; they with labor push'd
> Oblique the Centric Globe.
>
> (10.669–72)

"Some say" that the earthly sphere — and so its music — is twisted out of tune with the heavenly spheres. The number of degrees is in dispute (disputation over number being part of the condition of "grossness," a punishment for sin), but the fact is certain. The fall brings these changes, and "[t]hese changes in the Heav'ns, though slow, produc'd/ Like change on Sea and Land" (10.692–93), the kind of climatic changes Milton recounts in the invocation of book 9.

The speculative dilemma confronted by Milton in "Sonnet VII" remained for the mature Milton. As Milton suggests in "Sonnet XIX," his practical talent as a poet is less important than the speculative condition of his soul:

> When I consider how my light is spent,
>   Ere half my days, in this dark world and wide,
>   And that one Talent which is death to hide,
>   Lodg'd with me useless, though my Soul more bent
> To serve therewith my Maker, and present
>   My true account, lest he returning chide;
>   "Doth God exact day-labor, light denied,"
>   I fondly ask; But patience to prevent
> That murmur, soon replies, "God doth not need
>   Either man's work or his own gifts; who best
>   Bear his mild yoke, they serve him best; his State
> Is Kingly. Thousands at his bidding speed
>   And posts o'er Land and Ocean without rest:
>   They also serve who only stand and wait.

Failure to wait, insistence on singing, could mean failure to stand.

Throughout *PL*, Milton calls attention to himself as a postlapsarian narrator in a fallen world and tells us something important about the potential consequences of aspiring betimes to heavenly song.[59] The invocation of book 7 reveals the potentially transgressive aspects of Milton's poem:

> Thou with Eternal Wisdom didst converse,
> Wisdom thy sister, and with her didst play

In presence of th'Almighty Father, pleas'd
With thy Celestial Song. Up led by thee
Into the Heav'n of heav'ns I have presum'd,
An Earthly Guest, and drawn Empyreal Air,
Thy temp'ring.

(7.9–15)

The narrator is an early and "Earthly Guest." *Presum'd* suggests "taken early," on "bold wings" (*audacibus alis*), before
receiving the grace that would restore one to the harmony of
heaven. In book 8, Raphaël explains to Adam how

God to remove his ways from human sense,
Plac'd Heav'n from Earth so far, that earthly sight,
If it presume, might err in things too high,
And no advantage gain.

(8.119–21)

This makes us reconsider the invocation of book 7, which
Milton fills with some of the most loaded words in the poem
("presume," "safety," "fall," "erroneous," "wander"):

with like safety guided down
Return me to my Native Element:
Lest from this flying Steed unrein'd, (as once
Bellerophon, though from a lower Clime)
Dismounted, on th' *Aleian* field I fall
Erroneous there to wander and forlorn.

(7.15–20)

There is the safety of "Lest," but the phrase "like safety" —
like "more safe" — calls attention to the danger that remains.
It is a momentous instance of Miltonic *negando*.

"Half yet remains unsung," says the narrator, "but narrower
bound/ Within the visible Diurnal Sphere;/ Standing on Earth,
not rapt above the Pole,"

More safe I Sing with mortal voice, unchang'd
To hoarse or mute, though fall'n on evil days,
On evil days though fall'n, and evil tongues. . . .

(7.21–26)

Milton denies having either a hoarse mortal voice or muteness — the two choices remarked in his prolusion, where
"mortal voice" is by nature "hoarse," and therefore, he jests,
perhaps better "mute." As the notes turn tragic, Milton, with
irony, turns most bold. He is singing his song anyway. It must
include, however, the truth about his aspiration. And he must,
eventually, mediate and temper his claims before he is done.
He must sing standing on earth. The sequence of the invocations dramatizes his safe arrival at earthy song that strives
patiently to rejoin the music of heaven.

The invocations of books 1 and 3 begin to call attention to
the dangers of Milton's project. The invocations of books 7
and 9 refocus on the matter with increasing directness:

> Say Goddess, what ensu'd when *Raphaël*,
> The affable Arch-angel, had forewarn'd
> *Adam* by dire example to beware
> Apostasy, by what befell in Heaven
> To those Apostates, lest the like befall
> In Paradise to *Adam* or his Race. . . .
>
> (7.41–46)

Milton is forewarned by Adam's dire example, just as Adam is
forewarned by "those Apostates." As a postlapsarian narrator, Milton, "knowing good by evil," has greater ability to be
forewarned than innocent Adam. But Milton raises the possibility that he is perhaps "smit with love of sacred Song," much
in the way Adam is smit with love of Eve.

Book 7 emphasizes the contrast between Adam's prelapsarian ears and Milton's, between Raphaël's divine interpretation to Adam and Milton's interpretation to his "fit audience":

> Great things, and full of wonder in our ears,
> Far differing from this World, thou hast reveal'd
> Divine Interpreter, by favor sent
> Down from the Empyrean to forewarn
> Us timely of what might else have been our loss,
> Unknown, which human knowledge could not reach. . . .
>
> (7.70–76)

The "timely" forewarnings of apostasy ring, now untimely, in Milton's ear in the invocation of book 9.

As Milton writes in *Areop*, appraising the vantage of our postlapsarian condition, "And perhaps this is that doom which Adam fell into of knowing good and evil, that is to say, of knowing good by evil" (728). But in book 11 of *PL*, God makes clear that humankind would have been happier knowing only good:

> O sons, like one of us Man is become
> To know both Good and Evil, since his taste
> Of that defended Fruit; but let him boast
> His knowledge of Good lost, and Evil got,
> Happier, had it suffic'd him to have known
> Good by itself, and Evil not at all.
>
> (11.84–89)

One Miltonic paradox readers must accept — along with its consequent ironies — is the need to maintain at once the postlapsarian view of knowledge expressed by Milton in *Areop* and the preferable epistemology asserted by God in *PL*. Had he stood, man would not have fallen into the doubleness of language. He would not, moreover, need to search for words to describe things both unknown and ineffable.

Tayler's examination of the "two (contrasting) creations in Genesis" — one in God's image, one from the dust of the earth — shows that they "exemplify clearly, and from the beginning, the predicament of the Christian poet who feels he must attempt to utter the ineffable, must therefore try to fabricate analogies in which one term is by definition unde-finable. Troubled by real or apparent dualisms," as Tayler writes, "the Christian seeks the unity of one God: and the language of the Christian poet cannot but betray his aware-ness of the dangers of his task."[60]

The invocation of book 9, in which the narrator says he must "change/ Those Notes to Tragic," offers no proof of the safety he desires. Milton offers instead his famous statement that his principal challenge is to obtain "answerable style":

> If answerable style I can obtain
> Of my Celestial Patroness, who deigns
> Her nightly visitation unimplor'd,
> And dictates to me slumb'ring, or inspires
> Easy my unpremeditated Verse:
> Since first this Subject for Heroic Song
> Pleas'd me long choosing, and beginning late.
>
> (9.20–26)

One clear problem is the falsity of any claim to "easy . . . unpremeditated Verse." One need not agree with Ezra Pound to see exactly how premeditated this verse is, nor to tell us that premeditation is a poet's ineluctable postlapsarian condition. Milton's "Heroic Song" involves choices about choices, premeditation. God's "Celestial Song," in contrast, enjoins one. "No voice exempt, no voice but well could join/ Melodious part, such concord is in Heav'n" (3.365–71). And so Adam and Eve, before the fall, echo God's music "With Heav'nly touch" (4.686).

Milton's aspiration, like Adam's, is something from which we may learn a lot — especially about the difference between heaven and earth. The point is that Milton's verse cannot be unpremeditated. There are significant differences between Milton's speculative condition and that of the angels in heaven, Adam and Eve on earth, and even Satan and the apostate angels in hell. They trouble Milton throughout *PL*, and especially in the invocations. Furthering his attention to these concerns, Milton makes a less than subtle comparison between his poetic project and the apostasy of the fallen angels. Moloch, who "rather than be less,/ Car'd not to be at all" (2.47–48), speaks, for instance, of those who "longing wait/ The signal to ascend," while they "sit ling'ring here/ Heav'n's fugitives" (2.55–57). I am not suggesting that Milton was consciously more free than William Blake allowed. I am merely remarking the way Milton alludes to the danger of refusing to accept the delay of his reattuning — the danger of singing anyway.

In rich, musical lines, Milton offers a number of comparisons suggesting danger. Both full of ambition and devoted to patience, Milton himself was "long choosing, and beginning late." He could not decide quickly what kind of epic to write. But once he chose to write a prophetic Christian epic, his theological lateness — or "grossness" — became more significant than his late beginning.

The association of Milton and the narrator of *PL* is more than close, and Milton uses speculative musical distinctions to compare himself to Satan. "Th' Assembly" of fallen angels speaks "now with hoarse cadence," and Beëlzebub's statement of his vain hope is perilously close in many aspects to Milton's poetic project:

> perhaps in view
> Of those bright confines, whence with neighboring Arms
> And opportune excursion we may chance
> Re-enter Heav'n; or else some mild Zone
> Dwell not unvisited of Heav'n's fair Light
> Secure, and at the bright'ning Orient beam
> Purge off this gloom. . . .
>
> (2.394–400)

"Th' ascent is easy then" (2.81), says Moloch, getting Virgil wrong much in the way Satan earlier gets Homer wrong.[61] The way down is easy, the way up is hard. We cannot help but think about these hopes and errors when we read Milton's invocation in book 3, and Milton develops the comparison throughout the epic.[62] The ability of the fallen angels to sing exceedes Milton's. If the fallen angels are hoarse, how can Milton not be?

Surely it is difficult for us to see the music of Milton's poetry as anything but transcending, but we are obliged to consider it in the speculative context established so clearly by Milton. One of the profound ironies of Milton's cosmology is that Satan is in a better speculative musical condition than even the most dutiful postlapsarian poet. Where divine singing is concerned, Milton is even more *disjoined* than Satan. The narrator reveals his envy of Satan's speculative lot in his description of the fallen angels' ability to make divine song. They may have "troubl'd thought," but, unlike Milton, they cannot help having "solemn touches" of sweet harmony:

> Anon they move
> In perfect *Phalanx* to the *Dorian* mood
> Of Flutes and soft Recorders; such as rais'd
> To highth of noblest temper Heroes old
> Arming to Battle, and instead of rage
> Deliberate valor breath'd, firm and unmov'd
> With dread of death to flight or foul retreat,
> Nor wanting power to mitigate and swage
> With solemn touches, troubl'd thoughts, and chase
> Anguish and doubt and fear and sorrow and pain
> From mortal or immortal minds.
>
> (1.549–58)

Their music is closer than Milton's poetry to the kind of music to which Milton aspires:

> Thir Song was partial, but the harmony
> (What could it less when Spirits immortal sing?)
> Suspended Hell, and took with ravishment
> The thronging audience.
>
> (2.552–55)

"Thir song" is a perverse part of the heavenly harmony, for it *ravishes* a devilish throng. Nevertheless, it is — what could it less? — more than any earthly poet can achieve.

The last invocation in *PL* does not assert the poet's ability to rejoin the "sacred Song." The last invocation further establishes the poet's link not to the harmony of the "sacred Song" in heaven but rather to the "cold/ Climate" that *may* "damp" the speaker's "intended wing." The possibility of a "damp . . intended wing" recalls the claim "Thee I revisit now with bolder wing," as well as the young careerist's "*audacibus alis*" in "Ad Patrem." The discussion of climate recalls Satan's early speech to "his Legions" in Hell:

> Is this the Region, this the Soil, the Clime
> Said then the lost Arch-Angel, this the seat
> That we must change for Heav'n, this mournful gloom
> For that celestial light?
>
> (1.242–45)

This dilemma leads Satan to his empty romantic consolation, to himself and "his Legion":

> One who brings
> A mind not to be chang'd by Place or Time
> The mind is its own place, and in itself
> Can make a Heav'n of Hell, a Hell of Heav'n.
>
> (1.252–55)

Milton must confront and solve the problem of his displacement and disproportion in a manner far different from Satan's.

The full irony is even more painful: Satan never suffers for his transgression anything near the *disjoining* Milton suffers for the first sin. The perverse trinity is not only a precise parody of the holy trinity but also a source of perverse envy for a Christian poet who aspires to join God's heavenly tune. Like the Son, Satan's daughter, Sin, enjoys a harmonious relationship with her father. She speaks of "My Heart, which by a secret harmony/ Still moves with thine, join'd in connexion sweet . . ." (3.358–59). Whereas Sin is still "join'd" to her father and creator, Milton is *disjoined*, musically, from his father and creator.

The condition of Adam and Eve before the fall is a source for more saddening comparison between the harmonious souls of others and the condition of Milton's own:

> All these with ceaseless praise his works behold
> Both day and night: how often from the steep

> Of echoing Hill or Thicket have we heard
> Celestial voices to the midnight air,
> Sole, or responsive each to other's note
> Singing thir great Creator: oft in bands
> While they keep watch, or nightly rounding walk,
> With Heav'nly touch of instrumental sounds
> In full harmonic number join'd, thir songs
> Divide the night, and lift our thoughts to Heaven.
>
> (4.679–88)

Obeying the enjambment of "each to other's note/ Singing thir great Creator" we, as readers, lift our thoughts from earth to heaven; from the thought of earthly music to the thought of its original correspondence with divine music; from the thought of echo on earth to the thought of earth as an echo of heaven; from a practical to a speculative conception of the fragmented activities of human consciousness.

The music and beauty of his verse can make us slow to attend to them, but Milton's aspiration to a condition of heavenly music leads him to ever finer speculative distinctions. These distinctions are the source of even further irony — putting Milton at once in the Satanic position of desiring for humanity more than God gave it and in the Chrisitan position of being grateful for the promised return of what he no longer has.

Even before the fall, moreover, there was a difference between the heavenly harmony and the human voice:

> Thir Orisons, each Morning duly paid
> In various style, for neither various style
> Nor holy rapture wanted they to praise
> Thir Maker, in fit strains pronounct or sung
> Unmeditated, such prompt eloquence
> Flow'd from thir lips, in Prose or numerous Verse,
> More tuneable than needed Lute or Harp
> To add more sweetness, and they thus began.
>
> (5.145–52)

"Thir Orisons" are "numerous" like the narrator's verse, not "innumerable" like the "sacred Song." Adam and Eve never had what Satan could never lose. But they had everything to which the narrator aspires; the human voice was true, harmonious, eloquent, sweet. Unlike Milton's verse, Adam and Eve's "prose or numerous Verse" is "unmeditated." Adam and Eve possess precisely the power Milton attributes to Orpheus, *carmine*. They did not need to "add" the sweetness of the *cithara*. Their prayers are "More tuneable than needed Lute or Harp/ To add more sweetness." The kind of sweetness an "earthy" poet can achieve — with the premeditative practical skills of *musica instrumentalis* — is for Milton an insufficient substitute, and potentially dangerous addition. Trying to add what Adam and Eve never had to add, a poet "smit with love of sacred Song" might add the authoritative sweetness of a prophetic mode to an "empty dream" — might add a specious book to God's two books. As in the "The Passion," there is the danger of being "hurried on viewless wing."

Recalling the fate of Orpheus in book 7 of *PL*, Milton aptly juxtaposes his aspiration to song with concern about its consequent speculative danger:

> In darkness, and with dangers compast round,
> And solitude; yet not alone, while thou
> Visit'st my slumbers Nightly, or when Morn
> Purples the East: still govern thou my Song,
> *Urania*, and fit audience find, though few.
> But drive far off the barbarous dissonance
> Of *Bacchus* and his Revellers, the Race
> Of that wild rout that tore the *Thracian* Bard
> In *Rhodope*, where Woods and Rocks had Ears
> To rapture, till the savage clamor drown'd
> Both Harp and Voice; nor could the Muse defend
> Her son. So fail not thou, who thee implores:
> For thou art Heavn'ly, shee an empty dream.
>
> (7.27–40)

By asking for "fit audience," one that will read him without ripping him apart, Milton might seem to imply the fitness of his song, and doubt only the fitness of his audience. But his subsequent allusion to Orpheus expresses the complexity of his request. When the power of song is his subject, Milton always returns to the example of Orpheus. Orpheus meets his fate, we must remember, because he loses his *carmine*, and he loses his *carmine* because he is impatient to see Eurydice — because his will is weak.

Orpheus is the chief figure of the conditional powers of the poet throughout Milton's career. Recalling the companion poems, Milton here bemoans the defense by the Muse Calliope. In the last line of this invocation, Milton contrasts Calliope's deficient defense with the sufficient power of heavenly grace to restore his *carmine*. As in his early poems, Milton here offers a flourish of urgent commands: "still govern thou"; "But drive far off"; "fail not thou." The first ("still govern thou") is a declarative statement; the second ("But drive far off") adds a condition to it; the third ("So fail not thou") effects an exhortive stance. Together, they confirm the urgency of Milton's request.

This movement culminates in the last invocation of *PL*, where Milton addresses, in a conditional statement, the same speculative concerns we witness in his early poetry:

> Mee of these
> Nor skill'd nor studious, higher Argument
> Remains, sufficient of itself to raise
> That name, unless an age too late, or cold
> Climate, or Years damp my intended wing
> Deprest; and much they may, if all bee mine,
> Not Hers who brings it nightly to my Ear.

(9.41–47)

The last words of general invocation in the poem, they carry great force. The narrator admits the possibility that he lacks divine inspiration, that all may possibly be his. We need not doubt that Milton believed he actually heard something, but we must consider that it is in keeping with his speculative theology not to trust his "Ear." The phrase "and much they may" depends on the "if" of "if all be mine," which in turn depends on the poet's ability to hear.

"Shepherds are honest people: let them sing," writes George Herbert in "Jordan (I)." Milton wished to be an honest singer, but a postlapsarian honesty demands not pastoral simplicity but postlapsarian speculation, including acceptance of one's current inability to hear and simply echo "the heavenly tune." Milton's brilliant solution is to build the complex grammar of his condition into a style that calls attention to the "earthy" need to add premeditated sweetness.[63] While the Edenic gift for song may be lost, God gave humankind the gift of reason, which is nowhere more evident than in Milton's ability to use grammar at once to dramatize and reconcile the differences between earthly and heavenly music. Within the context of Milton's speculative poetic, those differences move, with honesty, toward majestic resemblances. If the requirement for achieving heavenly song is an inward tuning only God can ultimately effect, there is no more instrumental a way for a poet to prepare for that gift in Milton's view than to highlight the "earthy" condition of his soul and turn the most discordant aspects of earthly music into a decidedly postlapsarian echo of "the heavenly tune."

"Singing Robes about Him"

The invocations of *PL* are clearly not the "short digressions" that "might doubtless be spared," as Samuel Johnson once suggested. They establish, as Anne Davidson Ferry writes, "the identity and characteristic tone" that is "sustained throughout the epic" and serves to "control our interpretation of its meaning."[64] Milton aspired to divinely inspired prophetic song, and the invocations of *PL* follow a conception of prophecy, inseparable from Milton's speculative conception of heavenly song, that keeps him from claiming the authority of an inspired prophet.

Scholars have been quick to share the zeal of Milton the Christian poet but slow to follow the circumspection of Milton the biblical scholar. That Milton was a prophet was early expressed by D. Masson, "The author is, in a real sense, an inspired man."[65] William R. Parker, E. M. W. Tillyard, and A. S. P. Woodhouse, among others, contributed to this view. According to Woodhouse, Milton early resolved the tensions between poetry and prophecy, talent and inspiration, artistic maturation and grace.[66] But to reduce these tensions is to render a less original poet than Milton is. This is still a dominant view, chiefly because, to borrow Kerrigan's observation of early patristic writing, "prophetic inspiration [is] always assumed and its nature rarely discussed with any precision."[67] The editors of *Milton and the Art of Sacred Song*, for example, devote the volume to the way Milton's poetry "reveals its author's tendency to draw inspiration from sacred writings and then to compose his own sacred poetic music in the service of his Creator."[68] Milton, like Kugel, would want us to be precise: the drawing of poetic inspiration is one thing; the drawing of divine inspiration, another. The drawing of divine inspiration, moreover, may not be reduced to an "author's tendency."

J. H. Hanford was, as Kerrigan observes, the first to treat "divine inspiration in any detail. . . . [P]erhaps the [other] embattled Miltonists feared that an extended discussion of prophecy and inspiration might deliver Milton into the hands of the anti-Miltonists."[69] But Kerrigan goes further: "Milton believed himself to be divinely inspired."[70]

Whereas I am cautioning against the assumption of divine inspiration, Kerrigan was defending his prophetic Milton from attacks such as the one put forward by William G. Madsen:

It is . . . difficult to understand what it means to say that Milton uses the *method* of accommodation in *Paradise Lost*, since he would hardly arrogate to himself a mode of understanding and expression that he denies to the human authors of the Bible and reserves to God alone. He of course uses the Biblical *language* by which God has accommodated Himself to our understandings, but this does not make him a Moses who has "looked on the face of truth unveiled." Nor does the fact that Raphael, as fictional character, tells Adam that he must use the method of accommodation in describing the War in Heaven mean that Milton thought that he himself was in possession of truths so ineffable that he had to "accommodate" them to ordinary human understanding by veiling them in myth and allegory.[71]

Though the rest of his argument went too far, Madsen was right that Milton would not arrogate such authority to himself.

It is not surprising that scholars who disagree on a matter only a god could decide tend to battle somewhat fiercely. As Kerrigan writes, "the epic Madsen describes is ungodly safe — no disturbing ambition, no horror, no misdoubting of the attempt." But whereas Madsen sees Milton as "ungodly safe," Kerrigan sees Milton as "godly safe." Kerrigan does see the danger of "if all be mine" in book 9, but he dismisses it. All cannot be Milton's, according to Kerrigan, because otherwise "his Satan would be a self-portrait drawn in perfect likeness to the hidden image of himself."[72] Well, yes. And this is a real danger, perceived by Milton, acclaimed by Blake. According to Kerrigan, however, *PL* documents actual ascendence for which there is merely the need for accommodation: "There is only one accommodation in the epic: the Muse accommodates divine truth for the narrator, who transcribes this accommodation for the reader. Both poet and reader are spectators at the heavenly court."[73]

Kerrigan's assertion of a prophetic Milton causes him to cloud the distinctions between the art of poetry and the artlessness of prophecy he articulates so well in the first part of his book. As Kerrigan himself observes, Milton is part of the tradition of prophecy in which the divinely inspired *furor* of the prophet is opposed to the art of the poet practiced in treating biblical themes by imitating rhetorical and poetic techniques found in the Bible.[74] Kerrigan's attempts to resolve the tension between art and inspiration lead him, however, to readings that fail to meet Milton on his terms. Kerrigan sees Milton divinely inspired from a young age, and concludes that the "method of the [Nativity] Ode became the method of *Paradise Lost*." In *PL*, "once again, the individual 'I' of the invocations reappears in a composite voice dignified with prophetic authority." Such willingness to assert a prophetic Milton sometimes leads to perverse, if jocular, conclusions: "This double voice," writes Kerrigan, "does not threaten orthodox conceptions of artistic creation — everyone attributes this poem to John Milton, and anthologies of Renaissance literature do not include poems by the Heavenly Muse (1608–1674)." And "critics have yet to accuse Milton of schizophrenia."[75]

Kerrigan draws the conclusion Milton could never draw: "[Milton's] the singing, but the song is God."[76] According to Kerrigan, Milton "sings with the upright rectitude of pre-lapsarian Adam and sees with the authority of Moses. . . . . [T]he narrator [of *PL*] indicates his prophetic equality with John.[77] As Barbara Kiefer Lewalski points out, in contrast, "though I take Milton's conception of himself as poet-prophet to be central to his poetics, I do not find him claiming the direct divine inspiration or the transcendent visions afforded the biblical prophets."[78]

Indeed, comparison is necessary, but identification (or assertion of identical authority) must be made with care. Milton was himself very careful. In *CG*, he deems Moses unique among prophets:

> the only lawgiver that we can believe to have been visibly taught of God, knowing how vain it was to write laws to men whose hearts were not first seasoned with the knowledge of God and

of his works, began from the book of Genesis, as a prologue to his laws. (640)

That Milton considered himself called upon is not in question. What is in question is the degree of his calling and the kind of prophetic authority he might ultimately claim. On this point, Madsen is precise: "Milton could hardly have regarded himself as a Moses Anglicus who 'accommodated' his ineffable vision to the understanding of ordinary morals."[79]

Even scholars focusing on music fail to engage Milton fully on his terms.[80] Like Kerrigan, Heninger, too, suggests that Milton's task was merely to accommodate. Sidney's "concept of the poet as a creator analogous to the divine creator of our universe," he argues, provides Milton with his poetic. Analyzing the doctrine of accommodation in book 7, Heninger writes about "the role of the poet" as "vatic maker":

> In his fiction, using the medium of words, the poet renders knowable to our "earthly notion" that which "without process of speech" would remain ineffable. The maker, then, does not have license to create indiscriminately or even whimsically — as Sidney puts it, his "delivering forth . . . is not wholly imaginative, as we are wont to say by them that build Castles in the aire" (*Defence*, C1). He must stick to God's truth. His *raison d'être*, in fact, is to re-create in our terms "the Acts of God." Such a poetics predetermines the way in which a poem must be read.[81]

Heninger's claim that Milton actually sees heaven and uses words "to bridge the conceptual and the physical realms" suggests that human understanding is limited whereas Milton's is not. According to Heninger, Milton must stick to God's truth, and has no trouble doing so.[82] Milton nowhere claims to have it so easy.

When one considers the analogical view of "the vatic maker," it becomes clear that such a poetic is not Milton's. Milton knows he cannot claim to mediate divine truths he

actually received in accordance with the doctrine of accommodation expressed by Raphaël in book 7:

> Immediate are the Acts of God, more swift
> Than time or motion, but to human ears
> Cannot without prócess of speech be told,
> So told as earthly notion can receive.
>
> (7.176–79)

It is no coincidence that the doctrine of accommodation
is followed immediately by a description of great triumph,
rejoicing, and "God's glory," all of which take the unified
form of "the heavenly tune":

> Great triumph and rejoicing was in Heav'n
> When such was heard declar'd the Almighty's will;
> Glory they sung to the most High, good will
> To future men, and in thir dwellings peace. . . .
>
> (7.181–84)

Excluded from such triumph and rejoicing, Milton is a "future" man disjoined from participation in "the heavenly tune."
His future participation in heaven must await God's grace.

Milton renders paradise in *PL*, but asserts no claim to
divinely inspired prophecy. As he writes in *CG*:

> Neither do I think it shame to covenant with any knowing
> reader, that for some few years yet I may go on trust with him
> toward the payment of what I am now indebted, as being a
> work not to be raised from the heat of youth, or the vapors of
> wine, like that which flows at waste from the pen of some
> vulgar amorist, or the trencher fury of a riming parasite, nor
> to be obtained by the invocation of Dame Memory and her
> Siren daughters, but by devout prayer to that eternal spirit
> who . . . sends out his seraphim with the hallowed fire of his
> altar, to touch and purify the lips of whom he pleases. (671)

His spirit doubtless moves toward heavenly music, but, as
Milton understood, divine inspiration is clear. The purging is

instant. There is no wait. Milton could not claim that God had sent his seraphim to him. He could not claim *PL* to be the result of "hallowed fire" that purifies the lips.

Milton surely possessed the poetic and rhetorical ability to make a more direct claim to prophecy than he asserts in the invocations of *PL*. Had he chosen to evade his theological agon, Milton would be as unequivocal as Blake. But, as Northrop Frye points out, "Milton could never have uttered Blake's aphorism: 'Genius has no Error.'"[83]

With its remarkable reconciliation of speculation and practice, as well as of human instrumentality and God's grace, *PL* is hardly the "rough and inharmonious style" that "clash[es] with th[e] very harmony which" Milton aspired to join. Milton is not of the devil's party, nor wishes in the deepest recess of his consciousness to be. He knows, rather, that refusal to accept the consequences of his discordant soul would put him in that party, would make him clash with the harmony he aspires to join.

PL renders not only the reattuning only God provides, but also the instrumental waiting only a poet of Milton's ability and dedication could pursue. It reconciles Milton's ambition for poetic fame and devotion to civic and religious instruction; it unites his commitment to serve "God's glory" and his aspiration toward "the heavenly tune."

Milton's exemplary aspiration to heavenly song is a singular achievement in the history of English poetry. It would be an understatement to say it had a deep influence upon English romantic poetry, which is the subject of the next chapter. British romantic poets, as we will see, seek inward, individual harmonies, restored not by God but by the power of the imagination, or Poetic Genius, in which they might see the divinity within themselves. The romantics invert Milton's speculative musical conception of humankind: they attempt to collapse the large circle into themselves, attempting to expand themselves as universal centers.

Romantic readings of Milton have, of course, been fancifully loose with the facts of Milton's life and work:

> John Milton never stumbled about in a cosmological emptiness stretching between truth and meaning. He enjoyed the possession of a rocklike ego, and was persuaded that he incarnated truth, so that his life was rammed with meaning. Belief, for Milton, was the liberty exercised by his own pure and upright heart, and poetry is what he sublimely wrote, in loving but fierce competition with the Bible and Homer, Virgil and Dante, Spenser and Shakespeare.[84]

Harold Bloom's strong reading oversimplifies both Milton's poetic and theological agons,[85] but it is valuable if we correct misprisions:

> John Milton always stumbled about in a cosmological fullness stretching between truth and meaning. He was tormented by the wavering of a rocklike ego, and was persuaded that he did not always incarnate truth, so that his life was rammed with meaning, but perhaps not always God's meaning. Belief, for Milton, was the doubt he exercised with respect to the purity of his heart.

Milton boldly confronted the dilemma Sidney did not pursue — the difference between an analogical and synecdochal relationship to God. Whereas Sidney's analogical poetic (with its basis in "erected wit") might seem either to resolve or evade the conflict created by these contrasting creations, Milton's speculative conception of "disproportion'd sin," which is based on fallen humanity's relationship to God, boldy attempts to renew a synecdochal relationship "turn[ed] askance" (*PL* 10.669). It is in large part because of the complicated tension between the analogical and synecdochal conceptions of humankind as God's creation — a tension that erupted in the seventeenth century, with its epicenter in Milton — that Spensarians claim Milton as an heir while romantics claim him as a father.[86]

On the subject of turning English poetry into music, the centrality of Milton is clear, but how, finally, ought we to describe the peerless epic poet who aspired to prophetic song? Written 60 years ago, Hanford's essay "That Shepherd, Who first Taught the Chosen Seed: A Note on Milton's Mosaic Inspiration," still provides some of the deepest insight into the subject we have been considering.[87] Offering a brief account of Milton's "conception of his mission as a poet and the theory which he built up regarding the character and authenticity of his inspiration," Hanford goes directly to the crux of Milton's theory of inspiration: "when Milton was meditating the dramatic plans, he already had, in anticipation, 'his singing robes about him,' though, as we shall see, he was capable of checking himself before the 'spacious circuit of his musings' was complete."[88] At the end of Milton's career, as Hanford remarks, there is no supernatural Moses, no Urania, no Messiah, in *Samson Agonistes*. And *Paradise Regained* suggests that Milton made a more direct turn in his poetry to prophecy that is "ingenious and learned" exposition. Hanford writes elsewhere that "the personal passages" in Milton "were designed to exhibit the works of God in John Milton — to proclaim the fruits of faith, his own faith, not another's, in order that believers everywhere might be strengthened." He suggests that "the writing of this sort of spiritual autobiography, widely practiced among the Puritans, was the obligation of every man who felt conviction within himself, though ordinarily the record is less complicated by the secular and humanistic factors which are so strong in Milton."[89] I suggest we continue to explore the richness of the complication, keeping in mind the importance of Milton's abiding dedication to musical speculation.

We ought, finally, to reevaluate the dichotomous casting of Milton's career as early (immature) versus mature (late), of a young poet (immature), a writer of occasional verse, who matured into a great poet of grand themes who with the gift of divine inspiration wrote the epic he had always wanted to write. We should, I think, revise the view of Milton that sees him first as a young careerist who knew early what he wanted to achieve and sees him later as a mature poet-prophet who, having worked hard and long from an early age, finally received divine inspiration, and finally achieved what he had earlier set out to do: hear and echo his God's divine song — and rival Virgil and Homer as an epic poet while doing it. In the early poems, we read the epic of the poet trying to purge his "Earthy grossness." In his great epic, we read a poet — still "gross" — who learned to devise a speculative poetic that allows him safely to sing his song. His "earthy" song is different than his song will be in heaven, but his poetic aspiration to join "the heavenly tune," his glorious instrumentality, both early and late, is itself a part of God's merciful tuning. There is still the wait, but the achievement, God's and Milton's, is already immeasurable.

"In literature, ideas are merely raw matter, congealed feelings," as Denis Donoghue remarks. "The invention of a style is a far more considerable act in literature than the invention of an idea."[90] Beginning with a grand idea developed by Plato, Milton invented a complex, subtle, and expressive grammar by which he could teach not only the lesson of "God's glory," but also the more difficult lesson about the patience needed to endure the manner in which God brings about the slow reattuning of the human soul. Milton renders not only the process of reattuning his own soul, but also, potentially, the aspiring souls of his readers. As Milton seems to have known, he was responsible not only for a momentous movement in the history of the music of English poetry, but also for a glorious part of God's insuperable music.

FOUR

"Ditties of No Tone"

৵

Romantic Aspirations Toward
Song and Silence

Then, a wish,
My last and favourite aspiration, mounts,
With yearning, tow'rds some philosophic Song
Of Truth that cherishes our daily life;
With meditations passionate, from deep
Recesses in man's heart, immortal verse
Thoughtfully fitted to the Orphean lyre;
But from this awful burthen I full soon
Take refuge, and beguile myself with trust
That mellower years will bring a riper mind
And clearer insight.[1]

— William Wordsworth, *The Prelude*

The "Awful Burthen"

Romantic conceptions of imagination, nature, self, and God transformed the possibilities and requirements of English poetry, but the yearning to achieve song remained a "last and favourite aspiration" and an "awful burthen." The burden was awful because, unlike Milton, the major British poets we call romantic had to seek refuge without beguiling themselves with trust in something that either never was or would never be. This chapter examines the complexity of romantic aspirations to song and their centrality to romanticism's ability for self-critical anaysis of both its aims and its means of representing them.

Much as they replaced the conception of the mind as a mirror with the conception of the mind as a lamp, the poets discussed in this chapter transformed the aspiration to join a heavenly choir into personal modes of musical speculation that both put new demands upon and made new possibilities for poetic style. Whereas Milton could wait for God to rejoin him to "the heavenly tune," the romantics had not only to create their own music; they had also to invent the forms that music would take and the terms of their aspirations toward it. Aspirations to song distinguish the romantics not only generally from the world of Milton, the age of Pope, and from the coming age of poets in America, but also from each other.

Wordsworth, Coleridge, Shelley, and Keats had not only to keep up with the palpable philosophy of composers such as Beethoven; they had also to keep up with themselves, with the motives and theories of their aspirations, and their examinations of each. Any spiritual and poetic motions toward song had to be based in an informed debate about the relationship between poetry and song.

Despite their aspirations to unbidden song — to spontaneous harmony achieved by a unified consciousness — the poets who shaped the romantic movement embraced the intellectual,

psychological, and philological scrutiny required to turn mean-
ingless convention not only into meaningful utterance, but
into poetry worthy of the status of song. Coleridge, for example,
reports that his "sensible" though "very severe" headmaster
at the grammar school Christ's Hospital, the Reverend James
Boyer, denounced the use of conventional and evasive metaphors, especially claims to song:

> In our own English compositions . . . he showed no mercy to
> phrase, metaphor, or image, unsupported by a sound sense, or
> where the same sense might have been conveyed with equal
> force and dignity in plainer words. Lute, harp, and lyre, muse,
> muses, and inspirations, Pegasus, Parnassus, and Hipocrene,
> were all an abomination to him. In fancy I can almost hear
> him now, exclaiming "Harp? Harp? Lyre? Pen and ink, boy,
> you mean! Muse, boy, Muse? your Nurse's daughter, you mean!
> Pierian spring? Oh 'aye! the cloister-pump, I suppose!"[2]

Coleridge and the other romantics did not readily forsake the
glorious fiction of the Pierian spring for the dull and defeating
truth of the cloister-pump, and they persisted in attempting
to turn the poetic fiction into a glorious truth.

Boyer's concern was not unique. "To breathe," as Sir Henry
Taylor wrote in 1834 in his "Essay on the Poetical Works of
Mr. Wordsworth," had "become a verb poetical which [means]
anything but respiration."[3] Since then, critics have justified
the use of verbs "poetical" by explaining their glorified romantic meanings. Some of these explanations, however, need further investigation. In his essay "The Correspondent Breeze: A
Romantic Metaphor," for example, M. H. Abrams demonstrates that "the analogy between poetic mind and Aeolian
harp" is a part of a general romantic "revival of poetic inspiration which Wordsworth, going beyond Coleridge, equates
with the inspiration of the Prophets when touched by the
Holy Spirit." As Abrams explains, "The symbolic equations
between breeze, breath, and soul, respiration and inspiration,

the reanimation of nature and of the spirit, are not peculiarly romantic, nor in any way recent," but "older than recorded history" as well as "inherent in the constitution of ancient languages."[4] Abrams's valuable argument broaches the relationship between inspiration and song, but the passages he quotes, chiefly from *The Prelude*, do not indicate the kind or degree of confidence in the status of the poem as song he describes.

Wordsworth's articulations of his aspiration to song in *The Prelude* reveal conflicts common to the romantics. At the beginning, he defines for Coleridge the foundation of his "hope":

> Thus far, O Friend! did I, not used to make
> A Present joy the matter of a Song,
> Pour forth, that day, my soul in measured strains,
> That would not be forgotten, and are here
> Recorded: — to the open fields I told
> A prophecy: — poetic numbers came
> Spontaneously, to clothe in priestly robe
> A renovated Spirit singled out,
> Such hope was mine, for holy services:
> My own voice cheered me, and far more, the mind's
> Internal echo of the imperfect sound;
> To both I listened, drawing from them both
> A cheerful confidence in things to come.
>
> (1.46–58)

Recalling a former musical moment of "present joy," Wordsworth looks forward — with a "cheerful confidence in things to come" — to a better one, for a song that is truly both "measured" and "spontaneous" requires a renovated spirit. What comes, however, 50 lines later, is an account of "harmony dispersed":

> It was a splendid evening: and my soul
> Did once again make trial of her strength
> Restored to her afresh; nor did she want

Eolian visitations; but the harp
Was soon defrauded, and the banded host
Of harmony dispersed in straggling sounds;
And lastly utter silence!

(1.94–101)

In this notable peripeteia, restoration turns out to have been defrauding.

For Wordsworth, however, words embody a "Visionary power" by which a poet might turn the earth into a new paradise. His burden might be resolved, as Abrams suggests, by his conception of a "Visionary power," which is derived from an intimate relationship with nature:

Here must we pause: this only let me add,
From heart-experience, and in humblest sense
Of modesty, that he, who in his youth
A daily wanderer among woods and fields
With living Nature hath been intimate,
Not only in that raw unpractised time
Is stirred to ecstasy, as others are,
By glittering verse; but further, doth receive,
In measure only dealt out to himself,
Knowledge and increase of enduring joy
From the great Nature that exists in works
Of mighty Poets. Visionary power
Attends the motions of the viewless winds,
Embodied in the mystery of words:
There, darkness makes abode, and all the host
Of shadowy things work endless changes, — there
As in a mansion like their proper home,
Even forms and substances are circumfused
By that transparent veil with light divine,
And, through the turnings intricate of verse,
Present themselves as objects recognised,
In flashes, and with glory not their own.

(*The Prelude* 5.584–605)

It is difficult to sustain moments of spiritual harmony, but it is possible, through the practical labor of "intricate . . . verse," to turn "straggling sounds" into the timeless harmony of "immortal verse." Such turnings, however, take the time of the entire poem, and this is a problem. For the poem must report this process; and process, while part of God's glorious music for Milton, and part of the acquisition of "Visionary power" for Wordsworth, did not constitute sustained harmony for any of the romantics.

Wordsworth's burden is based in the romantic replacement of the musical cosmos affirmed by Milton with the psychic mythology of romantic philosophy.[5] "The ancient struggle for the blessedness of reconciliation with an alienated God becomes," as Abrams observes, "the attempt to recover in maturity an earlier state of integrity with oneself and the outer world, in a mode of consciousness for which the standard name is 'joy.'" As much as they moved the possibilities for redeemed integrity increasingly inward, they also moved outward, translating a myth of redemption into new terms. Imagination, replacing God, became the redeemer. If one had faith in the imagination, one could claim, as Wordsworth to Henry Crabb Robinson in 1812, "I have no need of a Redeemer."[6] But when the goal was a sustained condition of "ceaseless music" rather than moments of "splendid vision," one could quickly lose faith in the imagination. Imagination might redeem the person, but not the ability to become a singer.

Whereas Milton wished to rejoin the prelapsarian harmony of God's "Celestial Song," Wordsworth wished to achieve visions "of an organic universe" that might, he knew, turn out to "be a fiction of what never was."[7] Integrity might be restored by the "animating breeze," as Abrams observes, but such restoration, as Wordsworth makes clear, is sporadic and temporary. When his soul is momentarily restored, moreover, Wordsworth must go even farther. He must not only sustain it; he must be sure that the restoration he experiences is not defrauding. As Geoffrey Hartman suggests, "Modernism as we have come to know it — and Post Modernism too — is perhaps less conscious than Wordsworth of a contradiction that besets its desire for the unmediated. The new, quasi-erotic simplicity it claims is strangely apocalyptic in vigor of demand."[8] This contradiction is an important part of Wordsworth's poetry, and of romantic aspirations to song more generally.

There is no easy renewal of the once harmonious function of the fragmented Muses when such harmony is reconceived in the romantic terms of consciousness. The nature of inspiration and vision to disperse makes it impossible to base one's ability to sing on the power of either vision or renewed intimacy with nature.

A number of critics have shown that the relationship between Wordsworth and nature is far more complicated than "the revival of poetic inspiration" suggested by Abrams.[9] As Kenneth R. Johnston observes, for a long time romantic scholars maintained that the romantic poets, and especially Wordsworth, experienced transcendence through their relationships to nature, "in ways which assume that 'Nature' or 'transcendence' or 'relationship' is a metaphysical given that everyone knows and understands in common." But as Johnston writes, "the sense Wordsworth conveys of transcendence and relationship in Nature is earned, not given, and," what is most important, "his poems are the enactment or creation of a faith, not simply the expression of it."[10] As Hartman remarks in his 1971 preface to *Wordsworth's Poetry*, it was a large part of Wordsworth's goal to describe not only "the counterbalanced and ideal vision" but also "the labor necessary to achieve it."[11] As Wordsworth writes, "he who . . . hath been intimate" with Nature "doth receive,/ In measure only dealt out to himself." He does not arrive at "Visionary power" spontaneously, in "raw unpractised time." It is only "through the turnings intricate of verse" that he might deal out to himself the glory of such vision. Only through the laborious manipulation of words might he restore to himself the kind of speculative integrity that would allow him to sustain a renewed intimacy with nature.

Renewed intimacy with nature and confidence in the "Visionary power" of imagination are two concepts that distinguish romanticism. Both, however, are challenged when poets conceive themselves — and hence both their relationship with nature and their visionary powers — in musical terms. True and beautiful song is accomplished, for Wordsworth, Shelley, and Keats alike, only with "full-throated ease." Labor and process compromise one's ability to sing. Aspiration toward song reveals not only a debased relationship with nature but also a poet's delusions in trying to repair it. As we will see, Wordsworth's aspiration "tow'rds some philosophic Song" addresses these problems in remarkable ways.

Wordsworth and the other romantics aspire to spontaneous music, but one sees in Wordsworth's aspiration "tow'rds some philosophic Song/Of truth that cherishes our daily life" and devotion to achieving "Visionary power" a longstanding conflict of aims: artless inspiration and intricate craft. This conflict is the basis of the attempt to achieve "immortal verse/ Thoughtfully fitted to the Orphean lyre." The only way to sing is to engage the battle between the actual music of the world and the speculative music of the mind, to accept the impediments to unbidden song, and the damage it does to one's status as a singer.

The conflict between the means to vision and the requirements of song is a compelling aspect of British romanticism, and of the history of poetry generally. Plato had asserted that sight is the noblest sense, but he had also centered *eros* in the conception of a musical cosmos composed of potentially harmonious souls. This conflict is brought to an exciting level in the poetry of Wordsworth, and romanticism more generally. "Imagination," as Hartman writes, "is consciousness of self at its highest pitch."[12] I would point out further that while imagination is the source of "Visionary power" in Wordsworth, consciousness is the chief romantic source of — and obstacle to — glorious song.

The romantics seek to define themselves as singers as much as any poets before or after them, less systematically than Milton, but often with consistently revealing passion. While there remains a need to address this subject, there are also reasons why recent criticism has not. One is the view of all pursuits of harmony as escapist forms of ideology. Jerome J. McGann, for example, in *The Romantic Ideology*, disapproves of critics — his chief example is Hartman — who seek to define romanticism and write about romantic poetry in part by accepting "those issues in Romanticism which are fundamental precisely because they were declared to be fundamental by the earliest Romantics themselves."[13] The aspiration to a condition of music is doubtless a part of what McGann defines as romantic ideology, those ideas that exhibit "a repeated concern to achieve various types of harmonies, systems, and reconciliations and to establish these unified configurations in conceptual terms." Aspirations to song in romantic poetry do not represent, however, the uncritical kind of ideology that McGann warns against. McGann's admonitions to read all ideology historically actually reveal the exceptional function of romantic aspirations to song. Romantic ideology, he writes, often eschews "extreme cultural upheaval throughout Europe" in order to pursue its "obsession with restoring what was perceived . . . as a lost sense of total order."[14] But while McGann argues that "a critic must grant to Romantic works their special historical character," he also sees that a "history of ideas approach to Romantic Poetry and the Romantic Period" is not merely "traditional" but "necessary . . . for this reason: it represents the originary terms in which Romantic works sought to cast their historical relations."[15] There is a larger point here. The "awful burthen" does not represent an escape from historical indicia. The aspiration to song induces ineluctable critique of the fundamental ideals of romanticism. As McGann observes, *Lyrical Ballads* is "already laden with self-critical and revisionist elements," and Wordsworth's "greatest works . . . incorporate vision and its critique from the start."[16] McGann does not develop the point, but it is an important one. Aspirations to song register critically — in abstract aesthetic terms, rather than concrete social ones — the most important crises in each poet's version of romanticism; they are revealing analyses of their attempts to remake themselves into singers.

As McGann writes, the "emotional structure" of romantic poetry "depends upon the credit and fidelity it gives to its own fundamental illusions. And its greatest moments usually occur when it pursues its last and final illusion."[17] Wordsworth's "last and favourite aspiration" in no way constitutes a repressive attempt to retreat to idealism or ideology. We can say the same about Shelley and Keats. They do not attempt to hide the pains of social life behind idealism; they render the conceptual conflicts rooted in their greatest hope: to sing spontaneously in solitude and to sing a restorative, universal song.

Where the "awful burthen" becomes too great there is an urge to avoid it, or see its cause as social rather than individual, spiritual, or aesthetic. Wordsworth, Shelley, and Keats could neither avoid it nor transmute it. Many times in *The Prelude* a noisy crowd drowns out the possibility of calm thought, but outward noise, while it denotes the grave social problems of Wordsworth's London, does not constitute his chief challenge as a poet. The din of self-consciousness presents the great and destructive noise. Defrauding harmony, because less immediately destructive, is the chief danger.

Wordsworth's attempt to define himself as a singer conflicts with romantic ideals about harmony — as well as ideas about vision, unity of being, and unity of consciousness. It is a central agon in romantic poetry. Different ways of confronting it lead not only to triumph or despair, but also to different romantic conceptions of the possibilities and limits of poetic song. Wordsworth, Shelley, and Keats had to weigh the refuge of speculation against the burden of practice. Nor was speculation a refuge only. It was its own burden. And practice was a refuge only when defined in speculative terms.

Consciousness and "Straggling Sounds"

Whereas Milton thought that the theological fall untuned the soul, the romantics considered themselves untuned by their specific psychological falls into consciousness. They sought to restore participation in a harmony that is ceaseless, eternal, divine — a harmony of earthly sounds available to them in youth, when thought, feeling, and sensation were one. They had, moreover, to deal with consequences of their own devising, having replaced Hesiod's fragmentation of the Muses ("division of all discourse") with various divisions of the world — especially of the self.[18]

Wordsworth writes in *The Prelude* of "vacancy between" the poet and his "self-presence":

> so wide appears
> The vacancy between me and those days,
> Which yet have such self-presence in my mind,
> That, musing on them, often do I seem
> Two consciousnesses, conscious of myself
> And of some other Being.
>
> (2.28)

This psychological displacement — a fall away from one's former, true self — creates discord between one's soul and the true and beautiful songs of nature. Wordsworth and Shelley, like Blake in his early poems, refer back to a "time when" song was possible, but both believe they live in a time — "now" — when such song is not possible for them.

Unlike Milton, Wordsworth and Shelley can hear the music
to which they aspire. The earth of the romantics is still suf-
fused with the beautiful, sublime music of nature, and it brings
about discord in their souls. The discord brought about by
the transition from youth to maturity cannot, moreover, be
easily or absolutely remedied. The "vacancy" may be remedied, writes Wordsworth in *The Prelude*, only by the mind's
active creation of moments of unity:

> The Song would speak
> Of that interminable building reared
> By observation of affinities
> In objects where no brotherhood exists
> To passive minds.
>
> (2.383–87)

"The Song would speak," but the question Wordsworth poses
in various and demanding ways is whether it ever does. The
important objects here are the poet's true and present selves.

Wordsworth's aspiration to song required a painfully circular process of "interminable building" in which the soul must
produce an outward song that speaks of "affinites/ In objects
where no brotherhood exists/ To passive minds." The glorious solution brings its awful loss: "through the turnings intricate of verse," objects are "recognised/ In flashes," but "with
a glory not their own." An active imagination can create affi-
nites between disparate objects through "intricate turnings,"
but such turnings intricately change the objects. At issue is
the potentially defrauding verse that is produced by such turnings. Whereas objects in nature — birds and streams — can sing
themselves, poets face the need either to sing their imperfect
song or create a glory not their own. The poet hears so many
sounds, and whether they are the "straggling sounds" of the
poet's lute or the triumphant harmonies of nature, they
remind the poet of personal "vacancy."

Though Blake eventually achieved a forcible solution to the

problem of "vacancy," he, too, was early concerned with the relationship between the quality of his voice and the pressures of consciousness. In their youth, both Blake and Wordsworth maintain, they were joyous parts of nature's song, and therefore unaware of it. In Blake's poem "The Ecchoing Green," "care" is an enemy of life — and song.[19] And although one may try to "laugh away care," the need to do this brings, if not the end of song, at least the beginning of songs about the end of song. Once one is aware of the harmonious echo of the echoing green, the echo becomes discordant: "little ones weary/ No more can be merry." There is a clear difference between the laugh of Old John and the laugh of "the green woods . . . with the voice of joy" in "Laughing Song." Such is the difference between songs of innocence and experience, as we see in the companion poems called "Nurse's Song."

In the nurse's song of innocence, the nurse is part of the song; she does not hear it. The poem depicts the archetypal romantic conception of musical integrity: a timeless, quiet echo that denotes full presence of a poet's mind and body in a moment. In the nurse's song of experience, in contrast, echoes become "whisprings," which refer vividly to a physiological pressure put consciously upon the voice. In her attempt to hear what she hears, the nurse darkens "the voices of children." Full presence in a moment turns into memory, then into envy of a past time when the voices went unheard:

> When the voices of children, are heard on the green
> And whisprings are in the dale:
> The days of my youth rise fresh in my mind,
> My face turns green and pale.
>
> Then come home my children, the sun is gone down
> And the dews of night arise
> Your spring & your day, are wasted in play
> And your winter and night in disguise.

Envy is *eros* turned destructively outward. The wish for another's power leads to a loss of one's own. It must be rejected.

The romantic burden of singing, like its conception of untuning, has a number of potentially severe consequences. "The pains of psychic maturation" may become, as Bloom writes about Shelley, "the potentially saving though usually destructive crisis in which the imagination confronts its choice of either sustaining its own integrity, or yielding to the illusive beauty of Nature."[20] It is not, however, merely a choice, for to sustain one's integrity is its own formidable crisis.

From this awful burden one might think to take a beguiling form of refuge. Wordsworth, Coleridge, Shelley, and Keats did not. Wordsworth calls *The Prelude* a "song" throughout the poem, but he frequently examines what kind of song it is. Wordsworth offers, as Hartman writes, his "doubts, revisions, and vacillations — in short, the *temporalization* of insight as he moves from poem to poem or year to year."[21] Wordsworth pauses consistently in *The Prelude*, and other poems, to examine the status of his poem as song. It is one of Wordsworth's triumphs to create moments of harmony without delusion and to confront moments of "straggling sounds" without a disabling despair.

Against this burden, the romantics juxtapose the sounds of liberty, integrity, and innocence: birds singing effortlessly, the unbroken sound of streams, the joyous roar of children at play. A bird singing gloriously to itself in its sweet unpremeditated voice is the decided romantic revision of Milton's "heavenly tune," an instance of solitary success against which romantic poets measure their attempts to restore to their souls — and to their poems — the form, motion, and glory of harmonious being. Wordsworth, Shelley, and Keats aspire to the "music long" of what Shelley calls the "voice of his own soul/ Heard in the calm of thought." But their mature souls, beset by the discord of consciousness, are noisy. Against their defective inward music competes the outward "calm/ That Nature breathes among the hills and groves."

The choice between seeking to join a song not of one's making and insisting on creating an inward music is the central conflict of any romantic aspiration to song. Wordsworth confronts it numerous times in *The Prelude*:

> So sweetly 'mid the gloom the invisible Bird
> Sang to herself, that there I could have made
> My dwelling-place, and lived for ever there
> To hear such music.
>
> (2.125–28)

The "invisible Bird" sings its loud harmonies, but the human voice inevitably reproduces the "straggling sounds" produced by consciousness. Wordsworth thought to perfect his voice by achieving a "philosophic Song," turning devotion to speculative premeditation ("mediation passionate") into a practical exercise in sweet, unpremeditated singing.[22] But whereas Yeats would later remark in "Adam's Curse" that the labor must *seem* effortless, Wordsworth — along with Coleridge, Shelley, and Keats — maintained that the labor had actually to *become* effortless.

Noisy labor bespeaks the imperfection of a poet's singing. Hence, the paradoxical goal of musical silence is the basis of Wordsworth's aspiration toward some "philosophic Song," Shelley's defeating retreat into "mute music," and, finally, Keats's triumphant creation of "ditties of no tone." Each aspires to a condition of silence, but in various ways all see the silence of speculation as both unachievable and inferior to the harmony of actual music.

For Wordsworth, the silent solution of a purely speculative music must, inevitably, be rejected. He must instead mediate speculation and practice, hope and burden. The practice of poetry itself must redeem the soul, but speculation must inform the practice if it is to have anything but defrauding power. The practical process of composing poetry must become a means to confront the obstacle to song that is presented by consciousness.

Coleridge, Shelley, and Keats had hopes similar to Wordsworth's. Coleridge early considered his conditional achievement of song, as in "Kubla Khan," but he eventually felt chiefly the despair of its loss. Shelley, despite his singular music, is distinguished by his tendency to put more emphasis on his debased speculative condition than his poetic imagination could overcome. Keats, in contrast, was able to assert triumphantly in his great odes a newfound ability to join speculative and practical harmony in a way that makes a poem superior to an actual song.

Unlike Shelley, Byron allowed despair to keep him from taking the trope of song seriously. He saw speculative music as a mere trope of disillusioning rhetoric, which he mocks in "The Vision of Judgement": "The angels all were singing out of tune,/ And hoarse with having little else to do."[23] Byron's cynical despair, his manner of turning burden into bluster, is not only an important part of romanticism; it also signals a significant shift in the romantic aspiration to song. Like Blake, Byron refused in his way to be burdened. But his flight from song is its own illusive attempt at escape. For Wordsworth, Shelley, and Keats, in contrast, the loss of a certain condition of music engendered an awful burden that had to be confronted. Consciousness — indeed, time — did not allow the kind of natural songs they wished to sing. Poetry was the best, and necessary, means of attempting restoration.

Blake's Inward and Outward Song

Blake conceived a defiant, rather than harmonious, music, a fiercely anti-Miltonic definition of poetic song that would appear to preclude a number of emerging romantic burdens. But Wordsworth, Shelley, and Keats would have to reject his conception of poetic song.

Blake is unique among the romantics in aspiring not to

inward harmony but to an indomitable roar. He had seen that the very act of trying decorously to reattune oneself causes one to lose the very energy that defines a poet. In "To the Muses," an early poem from *Poetical Sketches* about the status of poetry as song, Blake blames the Muses for "forsaking Poetry":

> How have you left the antient love
> That bards of old enjoy'd in you!
> The languid strings do scarcely move!
> The sound is forc'd, the notes are few!

This and other early poems reflect not only Blake's view of the state of poetry during the eighteenth century but also his conception of an invigorated poetic voice, the imagination, and their relation to his task as a poet. "Languid strings" merely lack energy, which may be provided by imagination, Blake's True Man.

William Crisman reads "To the Muses" as an envoy in a sequence of eight early poems called "Song." With "To the Muses," he writes, "the series becomes a farewell to Lyricism."[24] Furthering terms used first by Northrop Frye, Crisman writes that this series registers "a tension between" the "oracular" and the "rhapsodic." The "selflessness and self-possession collide," and the result is "'howling' ('Mad Song,' line 18) in an isolated 'rage' ('Song 1') at the same time [Blake] is driven from without."[25] Facing the conflict between inspiration and craft, Blake knew he would have to free himself from what Crisman calls the "bind of self-conscious lyricism."[26]

Reactions against traditional ways of carrying out the debate between speculative ideas about inspiration and practical ideas about craft brought Blake to his major invigorations of poetic voice. Rejecting both the Miltonic conception of reattuning and the burdensome rules of poetic rhetoric and decorum of the eighteenth century, Blake replaced them with his theory of vision; and he replaced lyricism with the will to an indomitable visionary roar. According to Blake, it is not practical poetic skill but the inspiration of Poetic Genius that makes a poet a singer. We all have Poetic Genius, says Blake, and a True Poet is one who frees it from the "mind forg'd manacles" that enslave it.

Repudiating the theological doctrines according to which the human soul becomes discordant, Blake celebrates an inherently powerful self capable of singing a song of which it is the emanating, self-attuned center. Imagination comes "to signify," as Abrams writes, "not a sickly fantasy, but the faculty of vision and eternal truth."[27] By replacing the burden of reattuning with the liberating power of vision, Blake redresses what he sees as the defeating Miltonic requirement of future participation in a universal singing in heaven with the present possibility of an individual roar, which, given the nature of Poetic Genius, is itself a manifestation of universal truth.

Blake's bold innovation was to take the idea of God as the only True Poet — namely the notion of God as a sphere whose center is everywhere and whose circumference is nowhere — and attribute it, along with the Poetic Genius it defines, to his True Man. With this inversion, Blake declares that a True Poet must roar like Rintra and shake "his fires in the burdened air."[28] Air, of course, is the actual stuff of song — what the singer physically gives shape to. Whereas Wordsworth would later bear the "awful burthen" of his vocation, Blake first declared it is the free poet who burdens the air.

Seeking to fill the world with his irrepressible, visionary song, Blake took the association of bird and bard and twisted it into his precise inversion of Milton's poetic. For Blake, as C. M. Bowra writes, commenting on the couplet "A Robin Red Breast in a Cage/ Puts all Heaven in a Rage," "robin redbreast is itself a spiritual thing, not merely a visible bird, but the powers which such a bird embodies and symbolizes, the free spirit which delights in song and in all that song implies. Such a spirit," writes Bowra, "must not be repressed, and any

repression of it is a sin against the divine life of the universe."[29]
Indeed, Blake would allow no repression:

> I am perhaps the most sinful of men! I pretend not to holiness!
> yet I pretend to love, to see, to converse with daily, as man
> with man, & the more to have an interest in the Friend of
> Sinners. Therefore [*Dear*] Reader, [*forgive*] what you do not
> approve, & [*love*] me for this energetic exertion of my talent.

Blake offers a powerful new conception of poetic song for which
we are to love the poet, seeing "energetic exertion" as the
way to free one's latent "talent" from "languid strings."

Blake's inversions allow him not only to trust his ear but to
trust his ear alone — and therefore to trust no other voice but
his own. Even when he claims to hear God's voice, Blake must
fashion what he hears in his own image:

> Even from the depths of Hell his voice I hear,
> Within the unfathomd caverns of my Ear.
> Therefore I print; nor vain my types shall be:
> Heaven, Earth & Hell, henceforth shall live in harmony[30]

Blake's ear has "unfathomd caverns." He would sooner imagine harmony than seek to apprehend it. Nor would he succumb to "the modern bondage" of English poetic style:

> Of the Measure, in which
> the following Poem is written

> We who dwell on Earth can do nothing of ourselves, every
> thing is conducted by Spirits. . . . When this Verse was
> first dictated to me I consider'd a Monotonous Cadence
> like that used by Milton & Shakespeare & all writers of
> English Blank Verse, derived from the modern bondage of
> Rhyming. . . . I therefore have produced a variety in every
> line, both of cadences & number of syllables. Every word
> and every letter is studied and put into its fit place:
> the terrific numbers are reserved for the terrific parts
> — the mild & gentle. . . .

Blake links practical poetic concerns with spiritual bondage. His desire for inward song requires him to assert not only his own solutions but also his own requirements:

> I must Create a System, or be enslav'd by another Mans
> I will not Reason & Compare: my business is to Create[31]

Blake's need to change the style of his muse declares his unwillingness to acknowledge merely another form of bondage.

Like Blake, Goethe inverted the traditional conception of a musical cosmos established from Plato to Milton. Goethe, too, was concerned with the inevitable depletion of a poet's song-producing spirit. As The Poet asks in the Prelude of *Faust*:

> How does the poet stir all hearts?
> How does he conquer every element?
> Is it not the music welling from his heart
> that draws the world into his breast again?
> When Nature spins with unconcern
> the endless thread and winds it on the spindle,
> when the discordant mass of living things
> sounds its sullen dark cacophony,
> who divides the flowing changeless line,
> infusing life, and gives it pulse and rhythm?

Concern about cosmic untuning is replaced by a greater worry about the probability of a depletion of the poet's being:

> Then let me live those years again
> when I could still mature and grow,
> when songs gushed up as from a spring
> that ceaselessly renewed itself within.[32]

The spring of inward song ceases to renew itself; the songs stop gushing. There is no doubt about the fact, only worry that there is no refuge.

The general romantic conception of inward song was defined by Blake and Goethe, but neither Wordsworth, Shelley, nor Keats could conceive their speculative requirements in the

manner of Blake. Although they accepted Blake's requirement of inward song, they could not adopt the solution of his
forcible vision. They were too much concerned with two cer-
tainties and their dire consequences: the psychic untuning
that accompanied their maturation into full consciousness
and the inevitable depletion of poetic spirit. The two were
parts of one process; and they demanded a unified process of
restoration.

Wordsworth's "Philosophic Song"

Wordsworth had a far more difficult time than Blake restoring his innate powers as a singer, in large part because he was
devoted to a complex process of restoration that confronted
directly the two dire consequences we have been considering.
In ways Blake did not, Wordworth had to confront the conflicting requirements of vision and song.

The goal of romanticism, as Abrams observes, is a "revival
of poetic inspiration," a renovated relationship with nature
that would bring about unencumbered inducements to music.
But Wordsworth was able to accept the loss of this possibility in order to gain something that is, for a poet who has fallen
into consciousness, of greater value. For Wordsworth, a poet's
ability to sing is linked to his ability to acknowledge loss —
especially the loss of spontaneous song. Accepting a burden
repudiated by Blake, Wordsworth's aspiration "tow'rds some
philosophic Song" is a joyous compromise — a form of romantic concession Blake did not need to make and Shelley could
not accept.

For Wordsworth, aspiring toward song requires subsuming
the sporadic achievements of "visionary power" under the
larger quest for renovated *carmine*. One of Wordsworth's great
innovations is his reversal of the speculative requirement of
putting *carmine* first. Wordsworth subsumes speculation
under practice in a way that defines the powers of "philosophic

mind" and the qualities of "philosophic Song." The process of composing poetry becomes a means to restore *carmine* — an ongoing speculative process that confronts the obstacles to song that are presented by consciousness.

Like Blake in his early poems, Wordsworth believed that one becomes aware of "the echoing green" only after one is overtaken by the discord of consciousness and the noisier din of self-consciousness. When he was part of the harmonious music of nature and life, Wordsworth heard and delighted in the song, but was unaware of both the song and his participation. As he writes in "Resolution and Independence": "I heard the woods and distant waters roar;/Or heard them not, as happy as a boy" . . . (17–18), for only the "childhood creed is/ Delight and Liberty" (136). For the child, there is no distinction between the singer and the song, between participating and hearing. The child possesses the "Wisdom and Spirit of the Universe!/ That soul that art the eternity of thought. . . ." Any sound, however, even the most harmonious music of nature, can distract a mature man from the "passionate meditations" that might restore his ability to participate in nature's glorious music. Wordsworth did not suggest that one "forget the glory he hath known" (83), but he saw memory as a painful constraint the imagination would have to turn to delight and liberty. Memory reveals the vacancy — between one's former and present self — that transforms the unheard roar and shout of youth, "the resounding horn,/ The Pack loud-chiming" (*The Prelude* (1.436–37), into a din: then, "not a voice was idle: with the din/ Smitten, the precipices rang aloud" (*The Prelude* 1.439–40). Wordsworth cannot celebrate the loudness of his voice. Whereas Blake aspires to roars, Wordsworth is consistent in trying to quiet them.

Noise is uniformly destructive in Wordsworth, but more important is the capacity of music to defraud — to cover up the noisy struggle of consciousness to sing. In Wordsworth, there is always a need to confront the conflicting aspirations toward actual song and speculative silence. Throughout his poetry, Wordsworth records his movement through various kinds of musical moments: "measured strains," "poetic numbers," "Internal echo," "imperfect sound," "harmony," "harmony dispersed," "straggling sounds," "silence," "utter silence" are but a few. These are starkly different kinds of sound, different kinds of silence; some are propitious, some triumphant, some defrauding.

Throughout *The Prelude* and other poems, Wordsworth qualifies these musical moments in ways that define and examine his spiritual and poetic ambitions and achievements:

> For this didst Thou,
> O Derwent! winding among grassy holms
> Where I was looking on, a Babe in arms,
> Make ceaseless music, that composed my thoughts
> To more than infant softness, giving me,
> Amid the fretful dwellings of mankind,
> A foretaste, a dim earnest, of the calm
> That Nature breathes among the hills and groves.
>
> (1.274–81)

Formerly, outward music could compose the mind; the two could become one. Once thoughts become loud, however, thoughts need to compose themselves — not by an application to outward music, but inwardly. Fifty lines earlier, Wordsworth had articulated his poetic project, examining the spiritual and aesthetic impediments to "ceaseless music." Wordsworth then proceeds to define his aspiration — his glorious goal and its awful burden — in musical terms. I refer to the lines quoted as an epigraph at the beginning of this chapter. The question is whether *The Prelude* constitutes the song to which Wordsworth aspires. And it does not. *The Prelude* is, as Abrams writes, "an involuted poem which is about its own genesis — a prelude to itself."[33] This prelude is a musical process throughout Wordsworth's poetry.

"Resolution and Independence" contemplates this process by focusing on Wordsworth's chief dilemma. He wishes to be included in — resolved by — nature's song, but he wishes at the same time to restore and maintain the independent music that is the original, glorious condition of his soul. The poem considers the poet's inability to achieve such resolution and independence. "There was a roaring in the wind all night," the poem begins. The speaker, it is clear, can neither join nor compete with roaring nature. But he has met a living human example of the condition of music to which he aspires. Affirming his speculative, romantic ideals, Wordsworth praises the almost unheard, natural harmonies of the Leech-gatherer: "His voice to me was like a stream/ Scarce heard; nor word from word could I divide" (107–08). The poet hopes to pursue the kind of "honest maintenance" that would restore to him the condition of music — *carmine* — achieved by the Leech-gatherer. Wordsworth yearns for his own "ceaseless" song, "scarce heard," "word from word" indivisible, but his "honest maintenance," he knows, cannot begin with the kind of honest integrity manifested by the Leech-gatherer.

Once lost, integrity must be restored by labor. A poet must relinquish his hope for spontaneous musical powers and dedicate himself to the "turnings intricate of verse." Where his aspiration to music is concerned, he must devise intricate formulations of what becomes, in the Immortality Ode, "new-fledged hope still fluttering in his breast."

Throughout Wordsworth's poetry, moments of silence are only sometimes moments of truly restorative vision. He calls these moments "spots of time." As we see in *The Prelude*, they are moments "That with distinct pre-eminence retain/ A renovating virtue" (12.208–10). They occur when "The mind is lord and master — outward sense/ The obedient servant of her will. Such moments," writes Wordsworth, "Are scattered everywhere, taking their date/ From our first childhood" (12.222–25). Wordsworth generally qualifies the restorative recollection of such moments with accounts of intervening and present discord. Nature inspires Wordsworth to experience such moments, but such "spots" of *carmine* cannot last.

What is most important, they cannot last long enough to *become* the poem itself. The spiritual goal of punctuating one's life with such moments differs from the goal of producing a poem that prolongs them, a poem one might call harmonious song. This conflict is a real problem for Wordsworth, one that his "philosophic Song" attempts to resolve with a "restored" independent music. In the last books of *The Prelude*, Wordsworth celebrates the triumphs of "the philosophic mind" as it becomes lord over all outward sense, but he also describes the loss of his ability to sing, announcing frequently that he cannot match the songs of nature:

> Oh! that I had a music and a voice
> Harmonious as your own, that I might tell
> What ye have done for me.
>
> (12.29–31)

But what has nature done for him if he cannot tell?

Poems comparing the poet to natural singers who possess *carmine* highlight not only Wordsworth's aspiration to song but also his method of pursuing "philosophic Song." Worse than being unable to match the songs of nature is being unable to sing as well as other human singers. In "The Solitary Reaper": "Whate'er the theme, the Maiden sang/ As if her song could have no ending." In the end the singing dissipates, achieving the quality of silence that constitutes the "ceaseless music" toward which Wordsworth aspires:

> I listened, motionless and still;
> And, as I mounted up the hill,
> The music in my heart I bore,
> Long after it was heard no more.

But the poet is reduced here to passive listening. As he listens, the superiority of music to words becomes clear.

Wordsworth says he wishes to know what the maiden sings: "Will no one tell me what she sings?" Bearing the music of another in his heart, the poet suffers an attack upon his art: the singer's is a "ceaseless music," superior to poetry in part because its words are "scarce heard," indistinguishable, freed of the imperfections of language that are proliferated by consciousness. "The dissociative, agonic quality of song," Kramer observes, "is inherent in the fusion of words and music — so much so that vocal styles are perhaps best described by the ways in which they attack the text."[34] As the list of the third stanza demonstrates, the words are not as important as the voice of the singer and the music of the song. Wordsworth wishes to know not what she sings but how she acquired her ability to sing.

These revealing comparisons between idealized human singers and the poet pervade Wordsworth's poetry. They focus on the problem of restoration. A "voice so thrilling" excels the music of a "philosophic mind," but Wordsworth's "new-fledged hope" — his general poetic program — is to approach such music in a "philosophical Song." "Philosophic Song" renovates hope through a continuous process of mediating speculation and practice.

Wordsworth knows it is a problem when the glorious music in one's heart is not one's own, which is what happens in any process of restoration. But he also knows that there is no way out of this bind. Song cannot satisfactorily be conceived as a process unless it is conceived in speculative terms. Speculation, however, presents its own problem, for a real, audible song of nature is superior to an inaudible, ideal one. A speculative song cannot contain the sounds of the world. What is harmonious to the ears is "straggling sounds" to the mind. Speculation is the only means of achieving "some philosophic Song/ Of Truth that cherishes our daily life," but speculation — "passionate meditation" on the problems of consciousness — brings disquiet, not harmony, to one's soul.

These recognitions led Wordsworth to compromises and resolutions we may now consider further — Wordsworthian forms of triumph inconceivable to Blake and impossible for Shelley. The Immortality Ode is a great example of Wordsworth's speculative compromise. The conflict between inward and outward music, between speculative and practical concerns, is a chief subject of the ode. The poem begins by acknowledging "That there hath past away a glory from the earth," suggesting that the poet's ability as a singer is universally diminished. The third stanza shifts the focus of the ode exclusively to music. Birds still sing their "joyous song." The poet has lost the ability to participate in the "bliss," but the loss is potential, not permanent:

3

Now, while the birds thus sing a joyous song,
   And while the young lambs bound
      As to the tabor's sound,
To me alone there came a thought of grief.
A timely utterance gave that thought relief,
      And I again am strong.

Harmonious music — the ideal, idyllic music of nature — brings about not only a need to avoid music by repairing to thought; it brings a thought of grief. The process of "passionate meditation" offers a means to achieve "A timely utterance." But we need to ask what that "timely utterance" is, and why, precisely, it makes the poet strong again, and how strong, and for how long. Wordsworth knew that failing to face the hard questions would be to relinquish any hope of restoring the conditions necessary for a poet truly to sing. But the ode vacillates in its evaluations of sound and silence, music and thought, memories of his former inclusion in and present feelings of his exclusion from nature's music.

Wordsworth declares, in "Tintern Abbey," "that Nature never did betray/ The heart that loved her." But this is not a plain statement about his harmonious relationship to nature. "What Wordsworth curiously and touchingly predicted when he asserted this," as Kermode remarks, is that "nature can always be made to answer our questions, comply with our fictions."[35] Nature, of course, will betray precisely such a heart, and the Immortality Ode recounts the poet's retaliatory betrayal: "Blank misgivings of a Creature/ Moving about in worlds not realized." Which is followed by Nature's counter-retaliation: "High instincts before which our mortal Nature/ Did tremble like a guilty thing surprised."

Wordsworth's ability to sing is not only linked to his relationship with nature; much like his concept of vision, it is something with which a reader is required to deal at "interminable" length. "It is hard," as Johnston observes, "to tell when ordinary sight transmutes into vision in Wordsworth's poetry — but this difficulty is . . . the very essence of his genius." Wordsworth "is our first and greatest border poet."[36] Wordsworth not only writes peerlessly about borders; he regularly describes his attempts at crossing them in musical terms.

Wordsworth consistently juxtaposes various kinds of musical moments, all of them related to his relationship to nature and his aspiration to both vision and song: (1) two distinct moments of harmony: one is triumphant (spots of *carmine*), the other defeating (ceaseless harmony achieved by others); (2) two (sometimes indistinct) moments of straggling sounds, both defeating: either those he creates (which make him doubt himself) or those he hears (which make him move toward a conception of an irreparably fallen universe); and (3) two distinct moments of silence: one is glorious ("eternal Silence"), indicative of a triumphant harmony restored by the structure of his mind; the other ("utter silence") is a defeating moment of miscarried transition, a failed attempt at restoration. Wordsworth is deeply concerned with the distinction between the two kinds of silence between which his passionate meditations move him.

Such juxtaposition is not only a central element of Wordsworth's poetic style; it is also an example of Wordsworth's
"philosophic mind" engaged in a process of musical speculation. The two must become one. We have begun to see how
this occurs in the Immortality Ode. The second stanza begins
with a call to the birds: "Then sing, ye Birds, sing, sing a joyous song!" But joyous sounds only remind the poet "That there
hath past away a glory from the earth." The third stanza considers the restorative possibility of one's "timely utterance."
But defining and asserting that ability take Wordsworth the
duration of the poem, and this duration identifies the paradox
that is the basis of his awful burden. Accepting the ravages of
time upon utterance is the only way to renovate the ability
for "timely utterance."

Renewed song comes only by accepting the loss of a greater
one. Even after the possibility asserted in the third stanza of
the Immortality Ode, the fourth stanza reveals the conflict
between the fullness of the musical bliss of the natural world
and Wordsworth's reactions to it. The next stanza repeats this
pattern. The poet hears, sees, and feels the "joyous song" of
the world:

> Ye blessed Creatures, I have heard the call
>   Ye to each other make; I see
> The heavens laugh with you in your jubilee;
>   My heart is at your festival,
> The fullness of your bliss, I feel — I feel it all.

Yet the feeling is not full. Wordsworth hears the joyous sounds,
but he cannot participate:

> Oh evil day! if I were sullen
> While Earth herself is adorning
>   This sweet May-morning,
> And the Children are culling
>   On every side,
>   In a thousand valleys far and wide,

> Fresh flowers; while the sun shines warm,
> And the Babe leaps up on his Mother's arm: —
> I hear, I hear, with joy I hear!

Forbidding sullenness, Wordsworth hears with joy, but such joy turns — with an emotional jump indicated by his syntax — to a thought of grief:

> — But there's a Tree, of many, one,
> A single field which I have looked upon,
> Both of them speak of something that is gone:
> The Pansy at my feet
> Doth the same tale repeat:
> Whither is fled the visionary gleam?
> Where is it now, the glory and the dream?

The poem repeatedly tells of loss repeated: "Our birth is but a sleep and a forgetting." "The Youth . . . still is Nature's Priest,/ And by the vision splendid/ Is on his way attended"; but "At length the Man perceives it die away,/ And fade into the light of common day." To confront the "light of common day" one must move "tow'rds some philosophic Song/ Of Truth that cherishes our daily life." Wordsworth sees within the inevitability of loss the possibility for glorious compromise.

The "idea that poetry, or even consciousness, can set one free of the ruins of history and culture is," McGann writes, "the grand illusion of every Romantic poet."[37] But for Wordsworth, the aspiration to song is an awful burden precisely because he realizes not only the illusion in the trope of song, but also the need to harrass it to the point of truth, whatever it might be. "I have been harrassed with the toil of verse,/ Much pains and little progress," he writes in *The Prelude*, "and at once/ Some lovely Image in the Song rose up/ Full-Formed . . ." (4.111–14). Throughout *The Prelude*, only images are fully formed, never the song itself. Hence, celebration of "vision splendid" is subordinated to his speculative musical aspiration.

Throughout his poetry, and especially in *The Prelude*, Wordsworth qualifies the power of his "philosophic mind" fully to achieve the condition of song to which he aspires:

> The power which all
> Acknowledge when thus moved, which Nature thus
> To bodily sense exhibits, is the express
> Resemblance of that glorious faculty
> That higher minds bear with them as their own.
> This is the very spirit in which they deal
> With the whole compass of the universe:
> They, from their native selves, can send abroad
> Kindred mutations; for themselves create
> A like existence; and whene'er it dawns
> Created for them, catch it; — or are caught
> By its inevitable mastery,
> Like angels stopped upon the wing by sound
> Of harmony from heaven's remotest spheres.
>
> (14.86–99)

The decisive difficulty is sustaining the power of "that glorious faculty." "Oh! who is he that hath his whole life long/ Preserved, enlarged, this freedom in himself?" (14.130–31) Wordsworth asks. And who could sustain such integrity within a poem? Unlike Wordsworth, the Leech-gatherer, the Solitary Reaper, birds, and nature itself possess *carmine*. Each sings unpremeditated songs, voicing self-presence. Their glory is their own; they have no need for restoration.

The restorative power of the "philosophic mind" is the subject of the next to last stanza of the Immortality Ode. Mere envy of the joyous songs of birds may cease, for the poet's task is a larger one. Strong enough to hear and be excluded, Wordsworth asks to hear the song of the Birds again:

> Then sing, ye Birds, sing, sing a joyous song!
>   And let the young Lambs bound
>   As to the tabor's sound!
> We in thought will join your throng,

Ye that pie and ye that play
Ye that through your hearts to-day
Feel the gladness of the May!
What though the radiance which was once so bright
Be now for ever taken from my sight,
Though nothing can bring back the hour
Of splendour in the grass, of glory in the flower;
We will grieve not, rather find
Strength in what remains behind;
In the primal sympathy
Which having been must ever be;
In the soothing thoughts that spring
Out of human suffering;
In the faith that looks through death,
In years that bring the philosophic mind.

Silent, speculative music is still inferior to the actual song of the birds, but thought must not, finally, end in grief. Unlike Shelley, Wordsworth can relinquish the hope of restoring fully the sweetness of his youthful voice. It is the resolution of Wordsworth to confront the strength in what remains without imagining it to be either greater or less than it is. Wordsworth is able to celebrate his "philosophic" ability to join in: "We in thought will join your throng." This movement to participatory "thought" indicates a triumphant will to compromise — a solution to actual exclusion that sees illusion for what it is.

In both the Immortality Ode and *The Prelude*, Wordsworth does not announce his arrival at song; he records his moving back and forth between "straggling sounds" and "resolution." One reaches in Wordsworth moments in which the process of aspiring "tow'rds some philosophic Song" is celebrated, not moments in which a final, permanent resolution — speculative and practical — is triumphantly declared. Wordsworth must be content with always moving "tow'rds some philosophic Song." Resolution comes subtly as a means of dealing

forever with the fact of "straggling sounds." "Passionate meditation" is a speculative art; "intricate turnings" offer a practical means of engaging in it. The two work together in a
process of which Wordsworth is exultantly proud.

What results, in both the Immortality Ode and *The Prelude*,
is not merely a poem that speculates upon the prelude to a
transcendent song, but the actual song of his prelude. Wordsworth's project confronts the tragic differences between
inspiration and craft, between "spontaneous poetry" and
"philosophic Song." Restoration confirms loss. "High instincts" bring Wordsworth not only the restorative shock
of recognition that sustains the mind, but also the tragedy
of simultaneous reversal. He is "recognised,/ In flashes, and
with glory not [his] own" (5.605–06). He may not restore his
original music. Restoration itself leads to deeper recognitions of the "vacancy between" the poet and his "self-presence." As Wordsworth writes in his Immortality Ode, the
"Child among his new-born blisses" is painfully remade,
"Shaped by himself with newly-learnèd art . . . And unto this
he frames his song."

In Wordsworth, song cannot be spontaneous; it must
always be in the process of being "remade." This process of
remaking song is related to Wordsworth's comments about
recollection in his *Preface to Lyrical Ballads*. Recollections
in tranquility obtain their own vivid connections and associations with "all that is at enmity with joy" only by losing their
tranquility. To compose calm, one must lose it. Spontaneous
song is not truly possible, contrary to what one of Wordsworth's famous programatic sentences at first suggests: "I
have said that poetry is the spontaneous overflow of powerful
feelings." Wordsworth refines this statement throughout the
Preface. All good poetry "takes its origin from emotion recol-
lected in tranquillity," but true restoration cannot be tranquil:
"the emotion is contemplated till by a species of reaction the
tranquility gradually disappears, and an emotion, kindred
to that which was before the subject of contemplation, is

gradually produced. . . ." Good poetry, it turns out, is not spontaneous; it derives from the "passionate meditation" of a
"philosophic mind." As Wordsworth writes, "poems to which
any value can be attached, were never produced on any vari-
ety of subjects but by a man who, being possessed of more
than usual organic sensibility, had also thought long and
deeply."

As in the Immortality Ode, "soothing thoughts" are part of
"human suffering," acknowledgement of loss. Loss is the root
of our "primal sympathy" and the source of any secondary
symphony. Loss and song are not only linked in Wordsworth;
song is an expression of loss — especially the loss of song.

Wordsworth's aspiration to song leads him throughout
his career to consider two conceptions of restoration, conceptions Wordsworth vividly contrasts in the third book of
The Prelude. The first looks for traces of paradise in outward forms:

> As if awakened, summoned, roused, constrained,
> I looked for universal things, perused
> The common countenance of earth and sky;
> Earth no where unembellished by some trace
> Of that first paradise whence man was driven;
> And sky whose beauty and bounty are expressed
> By the proud name she bears, the name of heaven.
> I called on both to teach me what they might;

The second speaks of turning inward:

> Or, turning the mind in upon herself,
> Pored, watched, expected, listened, spread my thoughts
> And spread them with a wider creeping; felt
> Incumbencies more awful, visitings
> Of the Upholder, of the tranquil Soul
> That tolerates the indignities of Time;
> And, from his centre of eternity
> All finite motions overruling, lives
> In glory immutable.

                                                    (3.108–24)

The second is the one the aspiring singer must choose. "Turning the mind upon itself," producing "Incumbencies more awful" — tolerating the "indignities of Time" — Wordsworth liberates himself precisely to the degree he embraces his "awful burthen."

Just as he inverts older notions of the conflict between speculative and practical music, Wordsworth inverts the definition of a singer offered by Phemios in Homer's *Odyssey*. Wordsworth's new goal — which has replaced all previous aspirations to the present day — was to sing to oneself. What is good for oneself, according to Wordsworth, was also good for humankind. Wordsworth excels Blake in his ability to deal with tragic recognitions of losses of self that require a partial loss of song. Rejecting movements toward speculative silence, Wordsworth's goal is to speak to a version as near as possible to his former self, who as a child "held unconscious intercourse with beauty/ Old as creation, drinking in a pure/ Organic pleasure . . ." (1.562–64). Once fallen into consciousness, he must seek "saving intercourse with his true self," as he writes in his *Preface*.[38] A poet must become his own audience, for in the poet dwells the organic possibility of uniting inward harmony and outward form, subject and object, speculation and practice, individual and society.

Impediments to song are everywhere, but nowhere more than in the poet. In his *Preface*, Wordsworth admits: "so . . . it will be the wish of the poet . . . to let himself slip into an entire delusion, and even confound and identify his own feelings with" feelings he does not have, "feelings of those persons whose feelings he [imaginatively] describes." For Wordsworth, the great danger is in being charmed by one's own practice, or by speculative illusions perpetuated by one's attempts to sing. He must pull himself away not only from the noisy crowds of the city, which disturb his restoration of his inner music; he must also protect himself from any defrauding harmonies of his "philosophic mind." If he does not, as he writes at the end of the first book of *The Prelude*, the consequence is not only the loss of song, but also of hope:

> Meanwhile, my hope has been, that I might fetch
> Invigorating thoughts from former years;
> Might fix the wavering balance of my mind,
> And haply meet reproaches too, whose power
> May spur me on, in manhood now mature,
> To honorable toil. Yet should these hopes
> Prove vain, and thus should neither be taught
> To understand myself, nor thou to know
> With better knowledge how the heart was framed
> Of him thou lovest, need I dread from thee
> Harsh judgments, if the Song be loth to quit
> Those recollected hours that have the charm
> Of visionary things, those lovely forms
> And sweet sensations that throw back our life,
> And almost make remotest infancy
> A visible scene, on which the sun is shining?
>
> (1.621–37)

Trust in "visionary things" and "lovely forms" — whether looking back to "former years" or ahead to "mellower years" — can be illusory and destroy song. To look back to what was (or never was), to look ahead at what will never be, or to fail to "cherish our daily life" would constitute failure — vain hopes. Such failure would issue from an excessive effort to "invigorate" poetic spirit with "a cheerful confidence in things to come," an inability to maintain "honorable toil" within a world too much with us.

Throughout his poetry, Wordsworth subsumes his theory of vision under his broader, speculative aspiration to song. "Ceaseless music," not the sporadic power of vision, is his "last and favourite aspiration." We see this at a climactic moment in book 14 of *The Prelude*:

> There I beheld the emblem of a Mind
> That feeds upon infinity, that broods

> Over the dark abyss, intent to hear
> Its voices issuing forth to silent light
> In one continuous stream; a mind sustained
> By recognitions of transcendent power
> In sense, conducting to ideal form;
> In soul, of more than mortal privilege.

(14.70–77)

Wordsworth's definition of "transcendent power" is rooted in a musical conception: he writes of a mind intent to hear itself speaking to silent light. Here sound replaces some of the divine qualities previously reserved for light, reversing the common conception from the Middle Ages to Wordsworth's day. Whereas for Dante sound gives way to light at the end of *Paradiso*, for Wordsworth, a mind capable of transcendent power fills silence with an integral sound, "one continuous stream" of voices. Without achieving this, the mind of the poet must brood over its own visions of the dark abyss, and yet be content to conduct itself to a music of mortal privilege.

It is Wordsworth's great strength to lay bare his loss of music, as well as his need to keep what remains without merely imagining more. As he writes in one of his sonnets:

> The world is too much with us; late and soon
> Getting and spending, we lay waste our powers:
> Little we see in Nature that is ours.
> We have given our hearts away, a sordid boon!
> This Sea that bares her bosom to the moon;
> The winds that will be howling at all hours,
> And are up-gathered now like sleeping flowers;
> For this, for every thing, we are out of tune;
> It moves us not. — Great God! I'd rather be
> A Pagan suckled in a creed outworn;
> So might I, standing on this pleasant lea,
> Have glimpses that would make me less forlorn.
> Have sight of Proteus rising from the sea;
> Or hear old Triton blow his wreathèd horn.

He may have wished to, but Wordsworth never could give up the idea of the world and man as related forms of potentially harmonious music as an outward creed. He toiled honestly not to give his heart away, and not to see more in nature than was his — for he accepted the "awful burthen" of his "last and favourite aspiration."

Precisely because he is able to confront the loss of his ideal song, Wordsworth is able to make claims for the poet as great, and in some ways greater, than those articulated by Milton: "the poet binds together by passion and knowledge the vast empire of human society, and it is spread over the whole earth, and over all time." Poetry, according to Wordsworth, "is the first and last of all knowledge — it is as immortal as the heart of man" — but only after "purifying thus/ The elements of feeling and of thought," when we "recognize/ A grandeur in the beatings of the heart." "Philosophic mind" must continually purify itself if the heart is to move "tow'rds some philosophic Song." Part of the process of purification is acknowledging the loss of song and ridding one's harp of the power to delude.

Shakespeare wrote as if the Muses were not fragmented. For Milton, only God could finally reattune them. For the Age of Pope, the human poet, by means of reason and decorum (by consummate practical skill), could reattune them. Wordsworth's determination to link musical speculation and practice defined a new burden in English poetry, focusing on new ways to attempt to unify the activities of human consciousness — those fragmented Muses turned awfully inward.

Shelley's "Mute Music"

Shelley internalized the fragmentation of the Muses more beautifully and destructively than any other romantic poet. Discussing the "certain system of traditional forms of harmony of language," an outward languor from which he, like

Blake and Wordsworth, wishes to free poetry, Shelley maintains in his *Defense of Poetry* that "it is by no means essential that a poet should accommodate his language to this traditional form." Shelley embraces instead, in terms close to those of Plato, the necessity of achieving inward harmony before writing a poem:

> The distinction between poets and prose writers is a grave error. The distinction between philosophers and poets has been anticipated. Plato was essentially a poet — the truth and splendour of his imagery and the melody of his language is the most intense that it is possible to conceive. He rejected the measure of the epic, dramatic, and lyrical forms, because he sought to kindle a harmony in thoughts divested of shape and actions, and he forbore to invent any regular plan of rhythm which would include, under determinate forms, the varied pauses of his style.[39]

What matters most is one's devotion to restoring *carmine*. It is for this reason, in contrast to Sidney's, that "verse" is incidental to poetry:

> All the authors of revolutions in opinion are not only necessarily poets as they are inventors, nor even as their words unveil the permanent analogy of things by images which participate in the life of truth; but as their periods are harmonious and rhythmical and contain in themselves the elements of verse; being the echo of the eternal music.[40]

This is Shelley's exultant hope for poetry. It is rooted in his definition of poetry as "'the (expression) of the imagination.'" Poetry, he writes, "is connate with the origin of man. Man is an instrument over which a series of external and internal impressions are driven, like the alternations of an ever-changing wind over an Aeolian lyre, which move it by their motion to ever-changing melody." There is, writes Shelley, "a principle within the human being . . . which acts otherwise than in the lyre, and produces not melody, alone, but harmony, by an internal adjustment of the sounds or motions thus excited to the impressions which excite them."[41] Shelley begins his *Defense of Poetry* by defining imagination in a way that links the ability of the mind to achieve integrity to the ability of the poet to achieve song. The imagination "may be considered . . . as mind acting upon those thoughts so as to colour them with its own light, and composing from them, as from elements, other thoughts, each containing within itself the principle of its own integrity."[42] True poetry, according to Shelley, is an "echo of the eternal music." But Shelley's exultant hope for the imagination and poetry is colored by his rigorous musical definition of success and failure.

Shelley allows himself far less hope than Wordsworth, for he conceives the requirements of speculative restoration without compromise. In "Alastor," for example, he describes the prototypical condition of harmony for which he longs:

> A vision on his sleep
> There came, a dream of hopes that never yet
> Had flushed his cheek. He dreamed a veiled maid
> Sate near him, talking in low solemn tones.
> Her voice was like the voice of his own soul
> Heard in the calm of thought; its music long,
> Like woven sounds of streams and breezes, held
> His inmost sense suspended in its web
> Of many-coloured woof and shifting hues.
> Knowledge and truth and virtue were her theme,
> Thoughts the most dear to him, and poesy,
> Herself a poet.
>
> (149–60)

This is beautiful poetry. Is it coincidental that it expresses Shelley's recipe for failure ever truly to sing? Not at all. The skill of articulation did not have the restorative power for him it had for Wordsworth. Shelley disdained the need for process — especially the process of restoration. He saw it as an increasingly destructive suspension of song. Describing this suspension with poetic skill, rendering it beautifully, revealing the loud force of desire — all are ways of suffering the loss of the voice of his inmost soul "Heard in the calm of thought."

The "long music" to which Shelley aspires he conceives not as merely music but — in the synaesthetic unity of the senses — as a transcendent condition he may never attain. As Shelley writes in his preface to "Alastor," the poem "represents a youth of uncorrupted feelings and adventurous genius led forth by an imagination inflamed and purified through familiarity with all that is excellent and majestic, to the contemplation of the universe." Shelley is writing about an imagination that is purified even before it is corrupted — just as he is writing of a dream of hopes not yet hoped for. Shelley conceives of the voice of one's inmost soul as the voice of a soul that never truly begins the attempt to complete the cosmic circle described by Socrates. Rather, it must begin by completing it. The Chorus in *Oedipus at Colonus* sets the same standard, but with an understanding of its irony: "Not to be born surpasses thought and speech./ The second best is to have seen the light/ And then to go back quickly whence we came."[43] This view, which deems experience part of depletion rather than completion, is central to Shelley's view of his role as a singer. Anything less than an absolute return is unacceptable; and it is this resolute demand for a certain condition of music, this unwillingness to compromise, that most threatens Shelley's ability to sing.

Shelley's famous bird-bard comparison in "To a Sky-Lark" centers on this tension. Shelley's loss of inward "integrity" leads to the destructive outward impulse of romantic envy. Shelley at first imagines the plight of the skylark to be similar to his, but the Skylark's singing turns out to be only a marvel to be hailed, a model to be envied:

> Hail to thee, blith Spirit!
> 　Bird thou never wert,
> That from heaven, or near it,

> Pourest thy full heart
> In profuse strains of unpremeditated art.

The skylark has the very skill a poet needs, not merely a prelapsarian state of artless integrity, but "unpremeditated art." The poet's ability is antithetical to the blithe condition of the bird. The oxymoron "unpremeditated art" describes precisely the music Shelley wishes to achieve — the song of a soul that has begun by completing its cosmic circle ("thou never wert"), not one who has restored that original integrity.

"To a Sky-Lark" consistently compares not only the poet's aspirations and the skylark's ideal achievement, but the consequences of the poet's awareness of the differences. It is Shelley's hope to be:

> a Poet hidden
> In the light of thought,
> Singing hymns unbidden,
> Till the world is wrought
> To sympathy with hopes and fears it heeded not.

His song, however, is too bidden. He divulges his fears more than he elicits ours:

> Chorus Hymeneal
> Or triumphal chaunt
> Matched with thine would be all
> But an empty vaunt,
> A thing wherein we feel there is some hidden want.

The last two lines describe the kind of poetry Shelley always feared writing. With his own "fountain" depleted, Shelley asks to know "What objects are the fountains/ Of thy happy strain?" It is not any particular class of objects but rather "clear keen joyance," Shelley knows, that lets one sing happy strains: "With thy clear keen joyance/ Languor cannot be. . . ."

Given the poet's condition, the skylark simply goes too high for Shelley: "Higher still and higher/ From the earth thou springest/ And singing still dost soar, and soaring ever singest."

Shelley finds himself scorned, a groundling incapable of such singing, not knowing how he "ever should come near":

> Better than all measures
>   Of delightful sound —
> Better than all treasures
>   That in books are found —
> Thy skill to poet were, thou Scorner of the ground!

As if the outcome of the comparison were not enough, Shelley's celebration of its song eventually indicates his weaker impulse to relinquish himself to outward song when his own inner music fails:

> Teach me half the gladness
>   that thy brain must know,
> Such harmonious madness
>   From my lips would flow
> The world should listen then — as I am listening now.

Shelley, like Wordsworth in "The Solitary Reaper," is listening now, not singing. But whereas Wordsworth's moments of passive listening inspire him to create his own moments of triumph, for Shelley such listening becomes a paradigm of spiritual and poetic defeat. He asks for "half" the gladness, an admission of partial defeat at best. He asks, furthermore, to be taught what cannot be learned. Shelley is at his most powerful, and often most musical, when confronting his loss of song. But if defeat brought Shelley to much of his best poetry, the irony was not enough to change his mind about his failure to sing. Unlike Wordsworth, Shelley could not subordinate the pursuit of *carmine* to the practical, heuristic powers of the *cithara*.

When Shelley's aspiration to ceaseless, silent music is not a central subject of his poem, Shelley is a triumphant poet, as in "Prometheus Unbound," "Hymn to Intellectual Beauty," and "Mont Blanc." But when he addresses both his aspiration to song and his status as a singer, Shelley becomes locked in

"mute music," which is the precise anthithesis of his exultant hope.

"Alastor" recounts the manner of Shelley's disappointment
by describing the music of his life: he was once "A lovely
youth, . . ./ He lived, he died, he sung, in solitude. . . ./ And
Silence, too enamoured of the voice,/ Locks its mute music in
her rugged cell" (55, 60, 65–66). The poet's inability to repair
the music of his soul with his free imagination depletes his
spirit. In "Ode to the West Wind," for example, Shelley offers
the "incantation of his verse," but, his spirit overcome by languor, he has "dead thoughts" that are "[l]ike withered leaves."
He needs an outward power, the West Wind, to "scatter" them,
"as from an unextinguished hearth/ Ashes and sparks, my
words among mankind." The need brings "dead thoughts,"
which is different from "the calm of thought." It brings a sad
dirge, "mute music."

When he feels he loses his ability for song, Shelley turns in
weakness to nature, asking it to turn his failure into its success:

> Make me thy lyre, even as the forest is:
> What if my leaves are falling like its own!
> The tumult of thy mighty harmonies
>
> Will take from both a deep, autumnal tone,
> Sweet though in sadness.

With the loss of his ability to produce his own "tumult of . . .
mighty harmonies," Shelley becomes an object, rather than a
singer of song. Exhibiting a death wish, a need to be contained
by music, he asks merely to suffer the powerful song of nature
of which he, now bereft of his own long music, feels he is a
tragic part.

What remains of Shelley's poetic song? What does he ask
us to think of it? With his "lost heart, too soon grown old,"
Shelley describes his song as an "untimely moan":

> Some might lament that I were cold,
>   As I, when this sweet day is gone,

Which my lost heart, too soon grown old,
   Insults with this untimely moan.

Shelley believes he sings in an age too late; and he differs from Milton in having no real hope of instrumentality to effect his reattuning:

         If even
I were as in my boyhood, and could be

The comrade of thy wanderings over Heaven,
As then, when to outstrip thy skyey speed
Scarce seemed a vision; I would ne'er have striven

As thus with thee in prayer in my sore need.

Shelley differs from Wordsworth in having no means to restore spots of *carmine*. Such a poet "seeks in vain," as he writes in his preface to "Alastor," "for a prototype of his conception." Finally, "Blasted by his disappointment, he descends to an untimely grave," first having offered his "untimely moan."

We may have our own, more generous, ways of describing Shelley's poetic rendering of the music of his life, but we must at least consider the poet's truth where he refused to see a mere trope. Combining the important images of the mind as lamp and the heart (or soul) as lute, Shelley considers his status as a singer explicitly in "Lines: When the Lamp is Shattered":

   2
As music and splendor
Survive not the lamp and the lute,
The heart's echoes render
   No song but sad dirges,
Like the wind through a ruined cell,
   Or the mournful surges
That ring the dead seaman's knell.

Having moved devastatingly inward, the heart's movement outward into the world renders no song but sad dirges. The mirror of the mind might become a powerful lamp, but when the lamp is shattered, the lute is broken, and

> When the lute is broken,
> Sweet tones are remembered not. . . .

Time brings Shakespearean indignities. Memory is a wondrous, and potentially restorative faculty, but what it restores for Shelley is a vague memory of his loss of song.

No poet ever suffered his ability to hear the harmonies of nature more than Shelley. No poet ever suffered more the rigorous speculative demands he put upon himself. "By the time Shelley had reached his final phase," as Bloom writes, "he had become altogether the poet of this shadow of ruin, and had ceased to celebrate the possibilities of imaginative relationship." By "giving himself, at last, over to the dark side of his own vision," Bloom writes, Shelley "resolved (or perhaps merely evaded, judgment being so difficult here) a conflict within his self and poetry that had been present from the start." Indeed, the problem of Shelley's failure is remarked even by scholars of his optimism: "As usual, [Shelley] is trying to claim as much as he can while being responsible to his awareness of limiting factors," writes George M. Ridenour.[44] Where Shelley's awareness of limiting factors gives way to his optimism, moreover, he either suffers his evasion of true conflict, as Bloom suggests, or resolves the conflict on the darker side of his vision. As Bloom observes, "though it has become a commonplace of recent criticism and scholarship to affirm otherwise," Shelley appears not to have "changed very much, as a poet, during the last (and most important) six years of his life." Shelley's "two poems of self-discovery," which Bloom defines as his poems "of mature poetic incarnation" ("Mont Blanc" and the "Hymn to Intellectual Beauty"), expose "the two contrary aspects of Shelley's vision that his entire sequence of major poems reveals. The head and the heart, each totally honest in encountering reality, yield rival reports as to the name and nature of reality."[45] They yield, moreover, contrary reports of the possibility of achieving harmony in both the soul of the poet and his poems.

Unlike Wordsworth, Shelley saw no way to write himself into a state of joyous *carmine*. Like Wordsworth, Shelley is a poet of moments, but he qualifies his moments with his more general and gloomy assessment of them, concentrating more on power lost than on what remains. As he explains in his preface to "Alastor,"

> So long as it is possible for his desires to point towards objects thus infinite and unmeasured, he is joyous, and tranquil, and self-possessed. But the period arrives when these objects cease to suffice. His mind is at length suddenly awakened and thirsts for intercourse with an intelligence similar to itself. He images to himself the Being whom he loves.

Whereas Wordsworth could labor to sustain a "saving intercourse" with himself, such solitude led Shelley to a destructive desire to turn outward and find his likeness. Not finding it, his imagination needed to find an image of what never was.

"Alastor" is a poem about the failure of the imagination, and the danger of "imaging" to oneself, as recourse, the being whom one loves. And the poet's last and favorite aspiration becomes his most burdensome failure. For Shelley, the failure incurred by the suffering of *eros* has the effect of ruining the poet's ability to seduce himself with his own song. The attempt of the alienated self to sing of itself to itself is both inevitable and tragic:

> When hearts have once mingled
> Love first leaves the well-built nest;
>   The weak one is singled
> To endure what it once possessed.

Despite his appraisal of his singing, Shelley does, I would argue, turn his loss to a decidedly romantic gain. In the end, a poet who endures the loss of what it once possessed cannot truly be "a ruined cell." However dark his view may be, Shelley can turn "the memory/ Of that which is no more" into "Art and eloquence." Shelley cannot unite the fragmented function of romantic consciousness and produce the tumult of mighty harmonies he desired, but he does express, in remarkable poetry, the tumult of imploding desire.

Writing about the nearly triumphant "Hymn to Intellectual Beauty," and seeing "Alastor" as indicative of "the dark side of [Shelley's] own vision," Bloom describes the triumph of "Alastor." "The mind," he writes, "searching for what would suffice, encountered an icy remoteness, and vacancy of an inadvertent nature. The emotions, visited by delight, felt the desolation of powerlessness, but dared to hope for a fuller visitation." Shelley's rendering of erotic disappointment constitutes a peculiar — and peculiarly musical — triumph. "Shelley chants the apotheosis, not of the poet, but of desire itself," as Bloom writes. "The rhapsodic intensity, the cumulative drive and yet firm control . . . as the high song of humanistic celebration approaches its goal — that seems to me what is crucial in Shelley, and its presence throughout much of his work constitutes his special excellence as a poet."[46] Shelley renders with beauty the apotheosis of a Socratic aspiration to song.

Milton was not the only poet to fear clashing with the very harmony he made it his life's goal to join in echo. Coleridge writes in "Dejection: An Ode" of "the strings of this Aeolian lute,/ Which better far were mute" (7–8). The requirements of song, as he remarks later in the poem, are extreme: "Ah! from the soul itself must issue forth/ A light, a glory . . . A sweet and potent voice, of its own birth,/ Of all sweet sounds the life and element!" We have seen how two conceptions of silence govern romantic aspirations to song. For Wordsworth, consciousness produces sporadic noise; his "eternal silence" is triumphant but fleeting. Shelley's "locked muteness," in contrast, is defeating and lasting.

Keats's "Songs of Spring" and Autumn

Like a number of poets before him, Keats experienced moments when silence seemed better than a failure to achieve the glory of unbidden, natural music. In a letter of 27 February 1818, after listing "a few Axioms" about writing poetry, Keats concludes that "it is easier to think what Poetry should be than to write it — and this leads me on to another axiom. That if Poetry comes not as naturally as the Leaves to a tree it had better not come at all."[47] By the spring of 1819, however, Keats wrote as if it did. We know it did not, but Keats's ripening appears to have come to him in a magical month, as flowers come from seed and rain. Near the end of his short life and shorter poetic career, with larger projects failed, Keats came suddenly to a refuge from the typical romantic burden he expressed in 1818 — most remarkably in *Ode to a Nightingale* and *Ode on a Grecian Urn*.[48] The odes mark not only Keats's astonishing ripening as a poet, but also a triumphant achievement of song that deserves special attention within the history of English poetry. Both of Keats's great odes are triumphant assertions of "silent form," "ditties of no tone," signs of confidence in an ability to construct the "silence and slow time" of poetry.

Keats's famous declaration in *Urn* that "Heard melodies are sweet, but those unheard/ Are sweeter" might at first seem a simple affirmation of the superiority of silence to sound, or of speculative music to actual music: "therefore, ye soft pipes, play on;/ Not to the sensual ear, but, more endear'd,/ Pipe to the spirit ditties of no tone." As Cleanth Brooks observed many years ago, there appears to be a "paradox," namely "the ability . . . of the soundless pipes to play music sweeter than that of the heard melody."[49] The paradox, however, is not that unheard melodies are sweeter than heard melodies; it is that unheard melodies turn out not to be truly sweet. "The beauty portrayed is deathless because it is lifeless" writes Brooks, and he is correct to suggest the "darker implications" of the entire scene.[50] These are not pipes that can reach the sensual ear; these are pipes trapped in silence.

Keats is depicting a scene of action stopped in time. In *Urn*, as Jack Stillinger observes, "the sacrificial procession is stopped forever midway between source and destination."[51] The urn, that is, depicts arrested desire. The ode itself, in contrast, depicts Keats's aspiration in the process of refusing to be arrested: the poem ends with the poet speaking for the urn, on the matter of aspiration. Aspiration, finally, cannot be silent.

Both *Nightingale* and *Urn* assert the value of poetic speech over the competing ideals of natural music and silence. Keats's movement toward this assertion constitutes a large part of his ripening as a poet. And both odes mark this movement. Keats's nightingale is, as Helen Vendler writes, a "natural poet," and it "represents . . . a model for the human poet," for "the nightingale is a voice of pure self-expression."[52] "The most evident thematic structure," Vendler writes, "is the repeated antithesis between the earthbound poet and the free bird."[53] The nightingale occupies "some melodious plot/ Of beechen green" and sings "of summer in full-throated ease," and to attain this condition of music is clearly enviable. *Nightingale*, however, effects a subtle reversal of this antithesis. Keats recognizes that envy is a mere movement outward, and hence a dangerous impediment to harmonious inward song: "Tis not through envy of thy happy lot,/ But being too happy in thine happiness, — / That thou . . . Singst of summer in full-throated ease." Keats represents himself as able not only to listen passively but also to participate. Whereas Shelley's "To a Sky-Lark" emphasizes the disabling function of the poet's envy, Keats's *Nightingale* focuses on the poet's participatory fervor. Keats does not ask in weakness to be taught, nor does he contrast his limitation with the nightingale's freedom. Whereas Shelley is scorned when the skylark goes "higher still and higher," Keats is confident enough in his own ability to tell

the nightingale to go even farther: "Away! away! for I will fly
to thee,/ Not charioted by Bacchus and his pards,/ But on the
viewless wings of Poesy."

Nightingale offers yet another romantic bird-bard comparison, but here the poet gets the advantage. Here irony is
directed against the bird, not against the poet. In *Nightingale*,
the bird's singing is not to be considered a peerless model.
The nightingale, it turns out, cannot match the poet in aspiration, for it does not confront the poet's difficult conditions.

Revealing envy of its easy life of song, Keats expresses his
wish to fade away with the nightingale into the dim forest
and forget the rigors of life. This wish, however, only underscores the depth of painful experience that distinguishes his
human song:

> Fade far away, dissolve, and quite forget
>   What thou among the leaves hast never known.
> The weariness, the fever, and the fret
>   Here, where men sit and hear each other groan;
> Where palsy shakes a few, sad, last gray hairs,
>   Where youth grows pale, and spectre-thin, and dies;
>   Where but to think is to be full of sorrow
>   And leaden-eyed despairs,
>   Where Beauty cannot keep her lustrous eyes,
>   Or new Love pine at them beyond to-morrow.

Wishing to forget what the nightingale has never known is a
way of identifying the limitation of the nightingale in its ideal
nature. Whereas Shelley construes it as a good thing not to be
full of knowledge, Keats, like Wordsworth, sees that experience exalts the poet. Weariness is an inescapable consequence
of human experience. Sorrow is wisdom. Truth is beauty. And
beauty cannot keep her lustrous eyes.

Truth and beauty require a meeting of real and ideal,
and therefore cannot be achieved by the nightingale. When
Keats asserts that he will "fly to thee" on the "viewless wings
of Poesy," he is vaunting the ability of poetry to match the

nightingale in idealism just after he has exposed the nightingale's inability to sing a song that is valuable in the real
world. The nightingale's singing is not commensurate with a
poet's larger task; the nightingale exemplifies an inversion of
"Negative Capability." It is better to be an earthly aspirant to
the higher realm than to be an imaginative ideal.

Stillinger has identified as a basic Keatsian structure "a literally spatial conception of two realms in opposition and a
mythlike set of actions involving characters shuttling back
and forth between them."[54] Most important is Keats's "interest in the dividing line or space *between* the two realms." It is
this interest that the nightingale cannot have.

Unlike the poet, the nightingale can never ripen. The sudden ripening of Keats as a poet must, as Walter Jackson Bate
observed long ago, be explained largely as an attainment of
style; the two great odes of May 1819 doubtless issued from
deep interest in poetic form and firm confidence in practical
skill. But they appear to have come also from profound desire
to integrate experience and speculation — to reconcile a desire to fade into an ideal realm and an acceptance of being
born for death.

This is in large part the subject of the famous "vale of Soul-
making" letter of February 14–May 3, 1819, in which Keats
"repeat[s] Milton's lines"

> How charming is divine Philosophy
> Not harsh and crabbed as dull fools suppose
> But musical as is Apollo's lute —

chiefly to report that he felt "grateful . . . to have got into a
state of mind to relish them properly — Nothing ever becomes
real till it is experienced — Even a Proverb is no proverb to you
till your Life has illustrated it."[55] Keats links his devotion to
speculative concerns and his realization of the value of experience. This section of the letter begins with the observation
of "a rare instance of advantage in the body overpowering the

mind," Keats's version of the consequences of a black eye, which is followed by — not coincidentally — mention of the death of a friend's father and Keats's remark "I shall go to twon tommorrow to see him. This is the world. . . ."[56]

We witness in both *Nightingale* and *Urn* a similar assertion of the need to integrate the experience of groaning and hearing others groan and the quietude of a speculative mind. *Nightingale* offers implicit criticism of the nightingale's ideal song, criticism that is based in Keats's conception of soul-making: "[T]hey are not Souls," Keats writes, "till they acquire identities, till each one is personally itself. . . ." Keats then asks an important question: how are souls to be made "so as to possess a bliss peculiar to each one's individual existence?" And the answer is: "How, but by the medium of a world like this?"[57] The context of this answer is the value of suffering: "The common cognomen of this world among the misguided and superstitious is 'a vale of tears' from which we are to be redeemed by a certain arbitrary interposition of God and taken to Heaven — What a little circumscribe[d] straightened notion! Call the world if you Please 'The vale of Soul-making' Then you will find out the use of the world. . . ."[58]

As a literary nightingale, Keats's nightingale is distinguished by its lack of tears. Keats's poem, in contrast, achieves permanence precisely because it recounts (chiefly in the third stanza, but also in the fifth and seventh) the painful conditions of soul-making: its inscription of aches, pains, and groans establishes the peculiarity of utterance that marks a soul. Keats is explicit in his letter: "Do you not see how necessary a World of Pains and troubles is to school an Intelligence and make it a soul? A Place where the heart must feel and suffer in a thousand diverse ways!"[59] Schooling does irreparable damage to the music of the soul in Shelley. In Keats, it is the source of a poet's insuperable music.

The nightingale, not being born for death, is, paradoxically, not born for life. A soul that is not made by experience cannot truly be immortal. Keats's "immortal Bird" turns out to be immortal only in the limited sense that every nightingale sings the song of the nightingale. It dies, but it is replaced by another indistinguishable singer of that song. Keats's nightingale is immortal in the sense invoked by Shakespeare in Sonnet 18. The "eternal summer" of his poem surpasses the idealized summer of its admired subject. The song of a particular nightingale in a particular tree in 1819 will one day be the song of another, indistinguishable nightingale. It is a universal song (sung by all nightingales), but its universality confirms the insignificance of all of its particular singers. Keats's poetry, in contrast, is lasting in its particularity, and therefore universal in its vision.

Of course, the concluding question of *Nightingale* is urgently rhetorical; it is a profound question — much like the questions of Hamlet — on which the balance of the world seems to depend:

> Was it a vision, or a waking dream?
> Fled is that music: — Do I wake or sleep?

The question strengthens the authority of the poem.[60] Whatever the status of the vision, the poet understands that he must be the mediator of these two realms: he confirms the ability of his mind to inquire into the relationship between the ideal and the real, between beauty and truth.

Keats remarks in his letter of February 14–May 3, 1819 his aspiration to the complete "disinterestedness" of "Mind" exhibited by Socrates and Jesus. Such a state of mind constitutes an ability to be redeemed by — not despite — experience of a world of pains and troubles. Keats's resolve to experience the world is related to his ability to give himself up to the experience of an object, to achieve what Bate describes as "an excitement of the imagination in which the perceptive identification with the object is almost complete, and the living character of the object is caught and shared . . . and given vital expression in art."[61] Here, as in both *Nightingale* and *Urn*, Keats is not attempting an escape from or offering a critique of his "age's dominant cultural illusions," as McGann suggests.[62] Keats's aestheticism embraces the difficult philosophical and experiential task of mediating extreme ideas within the context of human limitation. Neither poem is about the "losses . . . of Ideals (and Ideologies) cherished by the poet."[63] Both poems are triumphant articulations of new ideas about the musical claims poets may make for their poems and art.

Much of Keats's success in 1819 will remain mysterious, for any artistic process, however formulated, is based in mystery. Nevertheless, three general points Bate makes about Keats's career are invaluable to an appreciation of Keats's quick ripening as a poet — as well as of his conception of poetic song in the odes. First, no one "ever learned from Milton more quickly and with greater profit."[64] Second, "In this sudden release and fluency, coming after three months of uncertainty, the first incitements may have had more to do with form and technique than we tend to allow."[65] Third, Keats's "general amassing and condensing of sense-impressions" result in "an imagery that is less 'synaesthetic,' in the ordinary sense, than it is a gifted illustration of what Hazlitt meant by 'gusto.'" Keats's "sympathetic excitement" is special, Bate remarks, because Keats "grasps" the object "as a vital whole."[66]

Let us turn to *Urn* to consider further the importance of these observations. Vendler's analysis of the odes in relation to each other helps us to see that in *Urn* Keats went past his confidence in his ability to "evaporate disagreeables" toward new forms of questioning that acknowledged the pressure put upon Keats by his philosophic mind. As Vendler demonstrates, *Urn* marks Keats's progress toward a fuller accounting of things (as they are, as they may be sensed, imagined, contemplated) by embracing the disagreeables that inevitably confront a philosophic mind. In *Urn*, writes Vendler, "Keats has abandoned his *Nightingale* idea of a suffering world and a pain-free art. Art, on the urn — by including struggle, resistance, and sacrificial procession as well as love and youth — has begun its effort to be all-inclusive, to let in 'the disagreeables.'"[67] Indeed, there is a difference between evaporating disagreeables and "consuming all impediments," to use Virginia Woolf's splendid phrase from *A Room of One's Own*.[68] There is movement toward such consumption in Keats, a movement toward enacting the position he had described earlier in his famous letter of 1817: "The excellence of every Art is its intensity, capable of making all disagreeables evaporate, from their being in close relationship with Beauty & Truth. — Examine King Lear & you will find this examplified throughout."[69] There is, Keats tells us, a vast difference between an evasive aspiration to silence and a heroic embrace of the world. These need to be reconciled — the need being related to both Keats's reaction to *King Lear* and his notion of "Negative Capability."

Keats saw the necessity of embracing the world, but his greater aim was an inward quietness that can extend to contain it. By April of 1819, Keats was moving toward the "quietness" he would achieve with *Urn* in May — the "wide quietness of the untrodden region of my mind." Keats appears to have found the "region" of his mind splendidly restored. But although this quietness suggests a likeness between the condition of Keats's mind and the urn, by the spring of 1819 Keats valued poetry precisely because it is wrought by the poet — because it shows the pains of both his labor and his life. Keats arrived at his quiet condition of mind because he came to accept "hardships and disquietude" with the understanding that "where there is no death there is no life." If the acknowledgment seems simple, we should recall that neither Wordsworth nor Shelley could make it fully; Wordsworth could not fully relinquish his aspiration to a condition of an easy natural song, and Shelley could not relinquish it at all. Keats's triumph in May of 1819 had much to do with his realization that the artifice of poetry had its incomparable power and value.

Vendler locates Keats's development toward affirming artifice over nature in *Urn*, but it is also present, I am suggesting, in *Nightingale*. Vendler reads the two odes as antithetical companion poems clearly marking a clear progression, seeing *Nightingale* as a poem of sense and sound and *Urn* as a poem about thought and vision. These are their subjects, but the poems are companion poems (much like Milton's) that are less different in marking a poetic, aesthetic, or philosophical progression than similar in trying to render (in the various poetic, aesthetic, and philosophic terms that Keats consumed) his larger aspiration toward song.

In both *Nightingale* and *Urn*, the poet seems at first to envy a music he himself cannot achieve: the "full-throated ease" of the nightingale and the "ditties of no tone" depicted on the urn. One might remark conceptual movement from *Nightingale* and *Urn*, as Vendler does, only if one focuses on the difference between their subjects. "In choosing music as its artifact," Vendler writes, *Nightingale* "decides for beauty alone, without truth-content."[70] But we must not see music or the urn as merely the "artifact" or subject of the poem. The relationship between *Nightingale* and *Urn* constitutes a movement in the same direction. The odes focus on different arts, but both render the poet's trials and triumphs as he aspires to his individual conception of poetic song.

In its ability both to experience the ideal song of the nightingale and yet to acknowledge the responsibility of evaluating its status and value in the world, *Nightingale* suggests that poetry is better than natural song. The nightingale, the concluding question of the poem declares, may not exist. And even if it does exist, its song is fled. A chief concern for Keats is the possibility that his imagination might have led him to a vision that will not survive a confrontation with reality. Whatever the status of its subject, the poem exists —

and lasts. Not only the fastness of its rhythms and its rhymes, not only the concreteness of its vision, but also its acknowledgement of reality — and especially of death — make it durable. By acknowledging that time brings decay, a poet can assert, as Shakespeare did before Keats, that the poet — by regulating his readers' experience of time through syntax, rhythm, and rhyme — cannot only make a monument to himself with his poem, but can conquer time. The music of the nightingale fades. The music of the ode — composing meter and marking poetic time — cannot fade in the way the song of the nightingale does.

Keats uses the word *fade* in a number of ways in the two odes. One can wish to "fade" into an ideal realm where one escapes the inevitable "fading" (dying) one experiences in the world of pains. Both *Nightingale* and *Urn* are poems about fading in the former sense so as not to fade in the latter. But although not fading appears at first to be the ideal condition to which Keats aspires in *Urn*, it turns out to be a lifeless state that is utterly to be avoided: cold pastoral. The urn the ode depicts, like the nightingale, might seem at first to be superior to Keats in its artistic ability to attain a state of completeness and permanence. It is because sound fades that "Unheard melodies are sweeter." But the urn does not truly offer unheard melodies. The urn offers a visual depiction of the predicament of being trapped in silence.[71] The poem, at first, appears to be a praise of silence: "Thou still unravish'd bride of quietness,/ Thou foster-child of silence and slow time." But the poem concludes by implying that the actual silence of the urn is not as good as the speaking silence of poetry. Poetry is a special, paradoxical, form of silence. It can use words to mediate the desire toward silence without sucumbing to it.

The second and third stanzas emphasize the poet's rejections of the ideal illusions, and the fourth stanza ends with an explicit description of the consequence of silence. "And, little town, thy streets for evermore/ Will silent be; and not a

soul to tell/ Why thou art desolate, can e'er return." This is
the condition not only of the town but also of the urn itself.
The urn needs to be spoken for.

The ventriloquized speech of the urn is, of course, the great
problem of the poem. We should, unlike Brooks, "be surprised
to have the urn speak." Whatever one's willingness to sus-
pend disbelief, one cannot forget that the urn is praised precisely because it is "silent form." Yet at the end of the ode the
urn must not merely be beautiful but also define beauty; and
this requires linking beauty and truth. Such a link — which
demands a contemplation of *logos* — can only be established
in language. At the end of *Urn*, after praising (yet again) its
ability for silence, Keats must suddenly speak for it: "'Beauty
is truth, truth beauty.'"

Keats's ventriloquism expresses not the urn's ability to link
beauty and truth; it asserts Keats's understanding that there
is a general need to do this that only he can fulfill. After
speaking for the urn, Keats goes on to speak his own words
to us, a comment upon the words he would speak for the
urn: "— that is all/ Ye know on earth, and all ye need to know."
The poem ends with an assertion of "Negative Capability," a
declaration of willingness to persist in a state of continued
aspiration to beauty and truth. Brilliant in its round conci-
sion, the sentence tells us — in a way a walk around the urn
cannot — about the relationship between beauty and truth.

Keats early suggests that the urn leads us out of language
and hence out of thought and time (for words are thought-
bound and syntax is time-bound): "Thou, silent form, dost
tease us out of thought/ As doth eternity." By speaking for the
urn at the end of the ode, however, Keats shows us the value
of poetic language. He shows us what the urn lacks — an ability to complete itself. "The urn's whole and simultaneous
visual art, where everything can be present (and presented)
at once," Vendler suggests, "seemed to Keats, fresh from his
disillusion with the nightingale, sweeter than a temporally

experienced art like music or poetry." But the eye cannot take in the urn "whole and simultaneously," as Vendler herself suggests elsewhere. Keats, she writes, "chooses sculpture over painting as closer (being 'in the round') to representational 'truth' — and chooses bas-relief over statuary as affording more narrative material. He chooses an urn over a frieze," Vendler explains, "because it has no beginning nor end in outline, and can therefore, by its circular form, represent both eternity and the female better than a rectangular form."[72] By speaking for the urn, however, Keats defies the sufficiency of its "silent form." Keats ravishes the "still unravish'd bride of quietness." He affirms the need to sum up the urn, to impregnate it with meaning only language, his language, can declare.

The urn cannot complete itself because it does not confront time — because, unlike poetry, the urn does not engage experience. The last two lines of *Urn* — much like the last two lines of *Nightingale* — engage experience and enact the poet's questioning and defining presence.[73] Whatever is questioned or defined, what is clearly left, in both *Nightingale* and *Urn*, is a durable poem, composed by a poet who excels both the bird and the urn with his ability to confront the need to *define*, to talk about ends. Vendler sees *Urn* as Keats's attempt in part "to assert his own intellectual rights over the urn, saying that his mind must judge and interpret, as well as respond to, the urn's offering of itself."[74] This is the point. Keats must judge; he must mediate. And he must do this in language.

We witness in both *Nightingale* and *Urn* Keats's ability to compose poems that reject actual silence for poetic approximations that excel the rival arts of music and sculpture. Keats asserts the superiority of language over images, not only in its power to pursue the great circular return described by Socrates in *Phaedrus*, but also to create the speculative function of poetic form.

The urn can "express" a "flowery tale more sweetly than our rhyme," says Keats, because it is free of both time and sound. Yet we find out from the beginning to the end of the ode that language excels the "quietness" of the urn. In ways the urn cannot, Keats's poetry can engage the dialectic between sound and silence.

Both *Nightingale* and *Urn* imply the power claimed by Shakespeare in Sonnet 18: the song of the nightingale and the scenes on the urn exist only in the poet's language. And here we come to a complicated matter that is at the heart of both odes. Though she does not consider it further, Vendler exposes this problem in an insightful parenthetical remark: "Keats once again [in *Urn*] plays the part of 'audience,' as he had in *Nightingale*; but he has turned from listener to spectator (or so we at first believe — the terms were always problematic to him, since his own art of written poetry entails in its audience both a seeing and a listening)."[75]

Urn raises a vital question: is the ode to be read silently, or is it to be read aloud, as its own music? Unlike the urn, the poem can offer both. By involving the reader in the choice between silent reading and reading aloud, the poem enacts the crucial conflict between sound and silence that is at the center of the poem. Read silently as a written sign, "O" is the perfect form, even while it connotes nothing, or silence. Read aloud, in contrast, "O" is the heavy, noisy sound of aspiration. In one brief sentence, Keats excels the urn in the ability to perfect round "silent form." The beginning and end of the utterance — "Beauty is truth, truth beauty" — are one, the word *beauty*. Beauty leads us inward in a speculative contemplation of truth, and truth impels us outward to beauty.

Keats is flaunting his poetic powers, demonstrating that he can not only rival the urn in the perfection of (round) form, but also excel its formal rendering of an aspiration to beauty and its erotic devotion to truth. Keats begins the last stanza with "O" and concludes it with "know." The sameness of the sounds suggests completeness, but the differences in meaning (which are related to similarities in sound) link, in a Socratic manner, the limitation of human knowledge and the power of speculative aspiration. Keats appears to have learned a number of lessons from Shakespeare's *King Lear*, as he writes in his letter of February to May 1819, and we might suppose he, too, was consciously playing with the relationship between "O" and "know," alluding to the consequences of saying "nothing."[76]

A silent "flowery tale," like a "leaf-fring'd legend," comes to have less value in the real world than an audible song about the passing of time:

> Where are the songs of spring? Ay, where are they?
>   Think not of them, thou hast thy music too,
> While barred clouds bloom the soft-dying day,
>   And touch the stubble-plains with rosy hue;
> Then in a wailful choir the small gnats mourn
>   Among the river sallows, borne aloft
>   Or sinking as the light wind lives or dies;
> And full-grown lambs loud bleat from hilly bourn;
>   Hedge-crickets sing; and now with treble soft
>   The red-breast whistles from a garden-croft;
>   And gathering swallows twitter in the skies.

To Autumn declares that one may sing truly only while time passes, "while barred clouds bloom the soft-dying day," "as the light wind lives or dies." Songs of death become the only songs of life.

Unlike Shakespeare in Sonnet 73, Keats describes not so much his fire as all the dying songs of nature — the world's choir. Keats's descriptions of gnats, lambs, hedge-crickets, and swallows show them as hardly ruined. He shows them, rather, as noble in their dying. There is a noble gravity in the twittering of gathering swallows that the lone, tearless, ideal nightingale of *Nightingale* does not have. To embrace an ideal is perchance to sleep. To embrace the fact of death is exalting. The spring odes, like the songs of birds in spring, constitute Keats's great music. But dying has its own glorious music. As for Montaigne, "to die well and to live well" must become one goal. When they do, the music of one's life makes one a true poem. One may, finally, open one's mouth and speak honestly, and it will be one's own song.

"To listen to music" is not, for Keats, as Vendler suggests, "very nearly to be dead."[77] It is, rather, to be reminded of death; and, for Keats in the spring of 1819, it is to be prodded to accept the inevitability of one's end. It is to think of death without wishing to escape the beauty of its music. In *Nightingale*, the bird is unaware of its end; hence its natural song does not address it. The urn, moreover, has no end; it needs Keats to sum it up. The poet, in contrast, is profoundly aware of his end; he writes in the attempt — and with consummate skill — to make his artificial song lasting.

Keats ends both *Nightingale* and *Urn* with articulations of a lesson learned by the poet's experience of the work of rival artists. The immortal song of the mortal nightingale fades; the mortal world of the immortal urn refuses to fade. The nightingale's song fades more than the song of the poet; the "ditties of no tone" depicted by the urn, because they are neither heard nor fade, do not sufficiently confront the real obstacles faced by a poet who would make himself a singer of true and beautiful song.

In both *Nightingale* and *Urn*, Keats asserts the ability of poetry to render speculative aspiration better than its rival (sister) arts. *Urn* suggests the need to reject the stasis of visual representation. It is a Socratic point. *Urn* not only puts speculative aspiration before visual representation; it also asserts the value of human speech, and the further value of poetic utterance. As Socrates makes clear in *Phaedrus*, language is the medium of speculative strife. For Keats, the poet and the philosopher are identical. Vendler observes with insight Keats's turn toward Socratic speculation in *Urn*, but she joins a long line of critics in seeing the ending (a turn to abstract philosophical terms) as a poetic flaw.[78] What Vendler sees as a flaw we should see as a strength in Keats — a realization that one has to see not only the necessity but the practical, artistic application of speculation.

Poetry and philosophy are not opposed for Keats. As Keats writes in his letter of February 14–May 3, 1819, speculation must not merely dictate but must become part of experience:

> The whole appears to resolve into this — that Man is originally "a poor forked creature" subject to the same mischances as the beasts of the forest, destined to hardships and disquietude of some kind or other. If he improves by degrees his bodily accommodations and comforts — at each stage, at each accent there are waiting for him a fresh set of annoyances — he is mortal and there is still a heaven with its Stars abov[e] his head. The most interesting question that can come before us is, How far by the persevering endeavours of a seldom appearing Socrates Mankind may be made happy — I can imagine such happiness carried to an extreme — but what must it end in? — Death — and who could in such a case bear with death — the whole troubles of life which are now frittered away in a series of years, would the[n] be accumulated for the last days of a being who instead of hailing its approach, would leave this world as Eve left Paradise — But in truth I do not at all believe in this sort of perfectibility — the nature of the world will not admit of it — the inhabitants of the world will correspond to itself — Let fish philosophise the ice away from the Rivers in winter time and they shall be at continual play in the tepid delight of Summer.[79]

The influence of both the model of Socrates and the figure of Shakespeare's King Lear is clear in both *Nightingale* and *Urn*. Keats had assimilated Socrates' speculative perseverance and Shakespeare's deep insight into the redemptive aspects of tragic *anagnorisis*. *Nightingale* and *Urn* are both redemptive poems; they reject an ideal perfection that Keats comes to doubt. Both affirm Keats's faith in the power of the imagination to attune itself to reality.

Keats was able to deal with loss, whether the loss of his brother, the loss of his health, or the inevitable loss of his life. In *Nightingale, Urn,* and *To Autumn,* we see the beginning of a movement it would take modern poets such as Yeats an entire career to finish: suffering, as Keats had learned from Shakespeare, is ennobling. There need be no loss of great song so long as we understand precisely what the potential of human song is and is not. Singing as an ideal bird is not an option in Keats; neither is silence. We see in Keats the beginning of what would become a modern embrace of the inevitable, noisy descent into a dying sensual body, such as the one Yeats makes in "Byzantium."

Writing about the important subject of silence, Leslie Brisman suggests that "poetry seeming to stand in a silent relationship to itself" is "characteristically Miltonic," and remarks that "[o]ne of the best commentators on the way Miltonic silence points to a higher order redemptive of time is Keats. . . ." Brisman recalls George Steiner's observation that "great silences are to be found wherever there is great literature."[80] As we have seen, we do not find actual silence in great literature; we find various versions of speculative approach, brilliant styles of practical approximation, and, above all, loud resilience.

FIVE

"A Tune Beyond Us As We Are"

೭ಎ

Modernism

"Ennobling Harmony"

"Modern literature begins," writes Denis Donoghue, "not from the seventh book of *The Prelude*, but from the experience of finding its harmonious resolution and its appeal to nature not at all persuasive." Donoghue has in mind the following passage:

> This did I feel, in London's vast domain.
> The Spirit of Nature was upon me there;
> The soul of Beauty and enduring Life
> Vouchsafed her inspiration, and diffused,
> Through meagre lines and colours, and the press
> Of self-destroying, transitory things,
> Composure, and ennobling Harmony.

The passage, Donoghue argues, "is not convincing: it is one of the last occasions on which a poet relies upon a comprehensive sense of nature to encompass the miseries of the city."[1] The larger question I want to consider here is what happens to this notion of "ennobling Harmony" in modern poetry. If in fact it relinquishes its romantic claim to truth, does it nevertheless become a fiction by which modern claims to song may be ennobled?

A modern scrutiny of "ennobling Harmony" does not occur universally in either the period we call *modernism* or the careers of those poets we call *modern*. The inquiry becomes acute, moreover, not when a single poet or a group of poets begins to question the ennobling fictions they inherit from a previous age of poets, but when they begin to question aggressively the ennobling fictions they inherit from themselves — and beyond all others the fiction that they are singers.

What distinguishes *romantic* from *modern* poets is not so much a romantic belief in the power of the imagination to affirm an "ennobling Harmony" as a modern tenacity to ennoble fictions. The way one ennobles fictions depends, of course, on the relation between reality and imagination one conceives. Eventually, the imagination itself can become a fiction; and it does so because what Stevens calls "the pressure of reality" demands that we call what is not real *fiction*. But to the extent fictions become "stubborn and uncompromising" — not only because an autonomous imagination creates them but because a perceiving imagination makes them adhere to what is real, confirming reality with a new pressure — they can vie with reality. And to make a fiction vie with reality is to ennoble it. In this sense, an ennobling fiction is "like/ A new knowledge of reality."[2] When it fails to adhere to reality, however, a fiction can be an ignobling lie.

Stevens knew early in his career that a poet's main task is the endless process of ennobling his fictions, especially the fiction that poetry is song. Throughout his career, in many of his poems, Stevens grounded his theory of poetry in his speculations about the relationship between poetry and song. In "The Man with the Blue Guitar" and "Notes Toward a Supreme fiction," Stevens goes a long way toward articulating his general poetic and theory of imagination, linking clearly his two chief subjects, song and fiction. Both poems are at once songs about fictions and fictions about song.

Stevens is not the first poet for whom the notion of "ennobling harmony" is unequivocally unconvincing, but he is singular in his determination that a poet's status as a singer is fictive, that it may only be imagined, chiefly because the pressure exerted by the desire to sing is a reality that cannot be overcome. This need early became central to modern conceptions of poetic song, and no other modern poet confronted it with the vigor of Stevens.

Like Plato, Stevens understood that the ancient cycle of *eros* is the center of any poet's desire to sing. The matter is the subject of Stevens's essay "The Noble Rider and the Sound of Words." Going back to Plato's *Phaedrus*, that great ancient study of the ancient cycle and its relationship to the aspiration to song, Stevens begins by quoting the passage in which Plato compares a pair of winged horses and a charioteer: "The winged horses and the charioteer of the gods are all of them noble, and of noble breed, while ours are mixed." One is noble, one is not, and Plato compares these horses to two kinds of soul. As Stevens writes, "When perfect and fully winged she soars upward, and is the ruler of the universe; while the imperfect soul loses her feathers, and drooping in her flight at last settles on the solid ground." But "suddenly we remember," Stevens concludes, "it may be, that the soul no longer exists and we droop in our flight and at last settle on the solid ground. The figure becomes antiquated and rustic."[3]

Stevens remarks the "pure poetry" of Plato, at the same time recognizing "what Coleridge called Plato's dear, gorgeous nonsense." Stevens undertook as well as any poet since Hesiod

the complex task of ennobling the trope of song. His conception of song is very much informed by Plato's *Phaedrus*, but
his version of Socratic *eros* is distinguished by his understanding of the need to confront the truth of Plato's "nonsense"
and reject the seemingly "pure poetry" of what are ignobling
lies. Stevens saw that the two kinds of horses represented two
kinds of fictions: one confronts "the pressure of reality" and
can therefore be ennobling; another, because it evades this
pressure, is an ignobling lie.

Plato's noble horse is an antiquated and rustic figure. Stevens
saw that the imperfect had somehow to become our paradise,
for it already was. As he asks in "Sunday Morning,"

> Or do the boughs
> Hang always heavy in that perfect sky,
> Unchanging, yet so like our perishing earth,
> With rivers like our own that seek for seas
> They never find, the same receding shores
> That never touch with inarticulate pang?

The music of heaven is a projection of human desire:

> Why set the pear upon those river-banks
> Or spice the shores with odors of the plum?
> Alas, that they should wear our colors there,
> The silken weavings of our afternoons,
> And pick the strings of our insipid lutes!

It is by accepting ignobling lies, fictional systems of transcendence not of our making, that we make our lutes insipid. The
trope of song has meaning for Stevens, but a singer is one who
manages somehow to keep the soul in flight even while
remembering its existence is a fiction. There will be no singing without this ennobling resolution to settle.

Pure poetry comes to us in the form of myth, and the myth
of our settling that exerts the greatest pressure of reality is
the myth of our birth:

> There was a muddy centre before we breathed.
> There was a myth before the myth began,
> Venerable and articulate and complete.
>
> From this the poem springs: that we live in a place
> That is not our own and, much more, not ourselves
> And hard it is in spite of blazoned days.[4]

Under such conditions, the imagination cannot merely make itself autonomous; even autonomy has, in the end, to be imagined. Stevens felt a persistent need to adhere to reality, to make corrections. And he was always correcting — late with a great effort to account for earlier "ravishments of truth," which is Stevens's way of describing the ennobling of fictions that one does not intend to be one's fictions. The "ravishments of truth" are "so fatal to/ The truth itself, the first idea becomes/ The hermit in a poet's metaphors. . . ."[5]

Desire is its own cyclical reality in Stevens, and the imagination cannot gain complete autonomy from it. As Stevens writes, "not to have is the beginning of desire./ To have what is not is its ancient cycle." To have what is not merely by imagining it is to give away much of the power of imagination: it is to fail to bear the pressure of the ancient cycle.

Every poet has desires, and hence necessary modes of ennobling fictions. Each is likely to have various modes throughout a career, many of them, as in the case of Eliot, neither antique nor rustic, but still evasive. In "The Love Song of J. Alfred Prufrock," Prufrock has heard "the mermaids singing, each to each," yet he does not think that they will sing to him. He doubts not only the "ennobling Harmony" that their singing represents but also his ability to ennoble the fictions with which he tries to give meaning to their singing. Eliot's Prufrock is a failure at the modern agon. He lacks the Nietzschean will to take responsibility for ennobling oneself by means of fictions that mark the movement to modernism.

With the desires of the poet ironically removed, "Prufrock"

suggests that we all, like Prufrock, turn everything into grand
fictions, the most grand of which is the desire to depend on an
"ennobling Harmony" as a basis of "Composure" — a desire
to squeeze the universe into a ball. Prufrock lingers in the
fiction of an "ennobling Harmony" until he realizes that every
human utterance perpetrates some ignobling fiction:

> We have lingered in the chambers of the sea
> By sea-girls wreathed with seaweed red and brown
> Till human voices wake us, and we drown.

Some, like Prufrock, feel as if they are merely lingering in the
real world, and they drown in trying to be buoyed by fictions
not of their making. Others, chiefly poets and other artists,
seek to save themselves by ennobling their own fictions, as
Eliot does later in *The Waste Land*. But in "Prufrock," Eliot
holds himself outside the ancient cycle, looking down, through
the yellow fog, upon those who allow themselves to become
part of it: the ancient desire to roll the universe into one ball
is represented as a tendency to put the dull chiming of an
insensate world of manners into the mannerly composure of
rhyme: "In the Room the women come and go/ Talking
of Michelangelo." In his plays, however, Eliot reveals that he
sees value in an "ennobling Harmony" of manners. Finally,
in *Four Quartets*, Eliot invokes the "ennobling Harmony"
of theology. In the end, as much as he would write about
his beginning, there could be no settling on the solid ground
for Eliot.

Eliot brought a new, solid music to English poetry, but he
did not address the speculative concerns that were crucial to
modernism. Among modern poets, Yeats and Stevens came
to understand best that if they were to avoid both the plight
of Prufrock and the flight of Eliot they were required to take
the risks Prufrock would not take, and refuse the ennobling
harmony Eliot eventually accepted. Yeats and Stevens are
not only the last great singers in English poetry. Not coincidentally, they are also poets who, throughout their careers,

defined their supreme aspirations as poets in musical terms. Among modern poets, Yeats and Stevens display the most intense and speculative interest in the relationship between poetry and song. Both Yeats and Stevens came boldly to reject any ennobling harmonies not of their making. This chapter examines this aspect of their poetry, and of modernism more generally. But before we turn to Yeats and Stevens, it is useful to consider briefly the gradual rejections of "ennobling Harmony" that distinguish modern poetry.

Emerson, Whitman, Dickinson, Pound

Stevens's American precursors still had their notions of "ennobling Harmony," for in America, the problems of discord confronted by the romantics in England seemed temporarily to have disappeared. As F. O. Matthiessen writes, Ralph Waldo Emerson "rejoiced that in the strict reliance of art upon nature, the artist works not as he will but as he must: 'We feel, in seeing a noble building, which rhymes well, as we do in hearing a perfect song, that it is spiritually organic; that is, had a necessity, in Nature, for being; was one of the possible forms in the Divine mind, and is now only discovered and executed by the artist, not arbitrarily composed by him.'"[6] Hence, "Rhythm and rhyme became meaningful for Emerson only when he could trace them to their origins as Pythagoras had done in announcing that 'the world subsists by the rhythmical order of its elements. . . .'"[7] There were reasons to doubt this universal musical order. But nothing, it seems, could vanquish Henry David Thoreau's ability for harmonious resolution — not even a seeming defeat of Nature by industry:

> As I went under the new telegraph-wire, I heard it vibrating like a harp high overhead. It was as the sound of a far-off glorious life, a supernal life, which came down to us, and vibrated the lattice-work of this life of ours.[8]

Thoreau saw an ennobling harmony precisely where one might see a reason to doubt it. The Golden Age symphony

is gone, as is the harp of nature; but for Thoreau the indus-
trial world issues in the wonderful industry of the poet, who,
like humankind in general, becomes an inspired maker of
his glorious lattice-work. How different this is from the defective wind-harp of Coleridge — and from Yeats's conception of
poetic labor. The feeling is specific to Thoreau and his time
and place. As Thoreau's 1851 entry in his journal declares,
song had, once again, "come down to us." It had come down
to Thoreau and Emerson, as well as, in different ways, to Walt
Whitman and Emily Dickinson. But each had at least to consider the matter of settling on the solid ground.

Emerson develops the ennobling harmony of the self
as a "generation of circles," but in "The Poet," he broaches
the ignobling lies modernism would have eventually to
confront:

> 'Tis not in the high stars alone,
> Nor in the cups of budding flowers,
> Nor in the redbreast's mellow tone,
> But in the mud and scum of things
> There alway, alway something sings.[9]

We see in Emerson an inchoate understanding of what becomes
the modernist need to settle, but Emerson did not think to.
Like Blake, he found within himself the soaring composure of
a universal music. "Speak your latent conviction," Emerson
writes in "Self-Reliance," "and it shall be universal sense; for
always the inmost becomes the outmost — and our first
thought is rendered back to us by the trumpets of the Last
Judgement."[10] Emerson had a conception of the cosmic circle
that led him to exclaim what neither Milton nor Wordsworth
could ever think to affirm: "No facts are to me sacred; none
are profane; I simply experiment, an endless seeker with no
Past at my back."[11] For Emerson "the extent to which this
generation of circles, wheel without wheel, will go, depends
on the force of truth of the individual soul." Indeed, "if the

soul is quick and strong it bursts over that boundary on all sides and expands another orbit on the great deep, which also runs up into a high wave, with attempt again to stop and to bind." The matter appears simple: "if the heart refuses to be imprisoned . . . it . . . tends outward with a vast force and to immense and innumerable expansions."[12] Latent convictions are inward manifestations of what is already outwardly, indeed universally, true. Emerson asserts the ennobling harmony of a harmonious universe. His latent conviction, and hence his song, emanates outwardly, but his latent conviction is centered in a romantic and theological dependence upon a fiction not of his making.

Whitman and Dickinson comprise the beginning of modern poetry in America, and they do so, not coincidentally, by experiencing *eros* and defining poetic song in opposing ways. If capable of soulless insensation, we postmoderns might deny — at our peril? — the pure poetry and gorgeous nonsense of each, but modern poets saw a need to confront these contrary manifestations of *eros*.

Whitman is an exemplary singer in tune with himself and in tune with the world. In "Leaves of Grass," he makes the most nearly literal claims to joyous singing to be found in English poetry. There is no division of noble and ignoble riders in Whitman; there is no need for speculation, no need for a theory of "philosophic Song." There is in Whitman no possibility of a broken lute, no envy of any actual sound or speculative condition. There is only love, a kind that appears to put a glorious end to the "ancient cycle" of *eros*. For there is chiefly possession in Whitman. It is Whitman's remarkable characteristic to love with the vigor of erotic desire precisely what he has. Whitman's singing reflects his absolute presence in the sounds of the world, a freedom of the mind to be part of them, and an ability of the body to contain them. Whitman's "I sing a song of myself" recalls, of course, the first line of the Anglo-Saxon poem "The Seafarer," but no poet invokes

the trope with less irony. Whitman is unique in his ability to
enter a world not of his making and be a joyous, harmonious
part of it. He delights in the fact that the world was made
for him; he does not bemoan its need to be remade, neither
by him nor by any god. The sounds Whitman used to make
the inward music of his democratic poetic song came from
without, from the music of the city streets and country roads
into the tuning amplitude of his receptive soul. Despite clear
differences from his dominant culture, Whitman's poetry
shows a personal mythology consonant with a social one. As
Stevens wrote about Whitman, "He is singing and chanting
the things that are part of him,/ The worlds that were and
will be. . . ."[13] His "Song of Myself" is also song of everything
that is *not* him. And as much as any poet writing in English
ever has, Whitman does not see the claim to song as a trope;
he believes he is actually inspired. His "body electric" sings
like the telegraph wires described by Thoreau.

Emily Dickinson achieved a similar confidence. Unlike
Whitman, however, she does not possess the song to which
she aspires. And precisely because she does not possess it
she makes of herself not only a great poet, but one of our
great erotic poets. She renders, in her inimitable way, a soul
caught in the process of erotic expansions and speculative
contractions. What distinguishes Dickinson is her gracious
yet provocative acceptance of the terms of the ancient cycle,
her unremitting aspiration toward a condition of song that
eludes her:

> I shall keep singing!
> Birds will pass me
> On their way to Yellower Climes —
> Each — with a Robin's expectation —
> I — with my Redbreast —
> And my Rhymes —
>
> Late — when I take my place in summer —
> But — I shall bring a fuller tune —

> Vespers — are sweeter than Matins — Signor —
> Morning — only the seed of Noon —

The poem commences a significant mode of modern myth-making. It is marked by personal revision of conventional mythology and by a dearth of explanation, both of which constitute Dickinson's mode of ennobling fictions of her own making. In what way will birds pass Dickinson? In fact, they do not. Contrary to our expectation, Dickinson transfers the burden of expectation to the bird. The Robin's expectations are not poetic, not those of *eros*, but merely impulses of a body ruled by nature. Dickinson's "Redbreast," in contrast, represents a longing for a fullness that the birds — with their expectation — shall never achieve.

Unlike Whitman, Dickinson cannot merely say "I sing"; she cannot yet rejoice in the fullness of her song. She must say, "I shall keep singing!" But she can rejoice in her hope: "I shall bring a fuller tune!" For Dickinson, in contrast to Shelley, suffering completion of the ancient cycle is to be preferred to mere longing for a naive recommencement of it. Dickinson will not trade the song of Vespers for the speech of Matins. Birds will pass her, but so she passes them; as they take their flight, she shall keep singing, keeping the hope of a "fuller tune" that perches in her soul:

> "Hope" is the thing with feathers —
> That perches in the soul —
> And sings the tune without the words —
> And never stops — at all —

Dickinson's conception of poetic song demands her bold movement outward. But there is a special check upon that movement. That check is desire itself, an erotic longing as pure as there is in poetry. Hers is a monumental refusal to assert, as Emerson does, that "the inmost" so seamlessly "becomes the outmost." At the same time, Dickinson hopes for — depends upon — the promise that it might. To imagine the hale desire of Dickinson without her sturdier hope is to approach the erotic penury of a Prufrock.

Much modern poetry is characterized by a fierce desire to dig free one's truly latent convictions; but it can take a poet — Yeats, for example — a career and a lifetime finally to dig free and speak them. For poets such as Yeats and Stevens, a first thought is rendered back to one not by the Last Judgment but by the inspection of one's own mythological circle. Modern poetry begins by attempting the erotic expansions of Emerson and Whitman at the same time it confronts the speculative contractions of Dickinson.

To charm oneself with one's singing, as Whitman does, is a feat that revised the requirements of poetic song, placing new demands on poets. Chief among these was the need to ennoble the personal mythology that identified one as a singer. Ezra Pound saw early that personal mythology is the poet's first, necessary subject. In an early poem, "Cino," he begins by declaring himself responsible for ennobling the fiction that he is a singer:

> Bah! I have sung women in three cities,
> But it is all the same;
> And I will sing of the sun.

Pound begins by debunking love poetry, moving immediately to the subject of singing itself. With an ironic tone new to poetry, Pound begins by revealing the lie behind the claim to song — and the further ignobling that results from trying to make the lie seem true:

> Lips, words, and you snare them,
> Dreams, words, and they are as jewels,
> Strange spells of old deity,
> Ravens, nights, allurement:
> And they are not;
> Having become the souls of song.

Pound's interest in the true, passionate singing of the trouba-
dours leads him to sing a song about singing in which the
pursuit of song replaces the pursuit of the unattainable lover:

> Eyes, dreams, lips, and the night goes.
> Being upon the road once more,
> They are not.
> Forgetful in their towers of our tuneing
> Once for wind-runeing
> They dream us-toward and
> Sighing, say, "Would Cino,
> Passionate Cino, of the wrinkling eyes,
> Gay Cino, of quick laughter,
> Cino, of the dare, the jibe,
> Frail Cino, strongest of his tribe
> That tramp old ways beneath the sun-light,
> Would Cino of the Luth were here!"
>
> Once, twice, a year —
> Vaguely thus word they:
>
> "Cino?" "Oh, eh, Cino Polnesi
> The singer is't you mean?"

Keats had written that poets "are not Souls till they acquire
identities" through experience. For Pound, it is precisely the
poet's identity as a singer that the experience of trying to sing
begins to question or blur:

> I have sung women in three cities.
> But it is all one.
> I will sing of the sun.
> . . . eh? . . . they mostly had grey eyes,
> But it is all one, I will sing of the sun.

He might as well sing about one thing as another, might as
well become indifferent. As Sir Toby Belch says in *Twelfth
Night*, "it is all one." The point, for Sir Toby, is simply to be
singing. But for Pound when "it is all one" the value of singing is threatened.

A poet may struggle with indifference, Pound knew, but he may not become indifferent to his labors to assert his identity as a singer. Like Stevens, Pound thought to go back to the ancient cycle; he must attempt what so far he has not been able to do. He must be honest about his desire to roll the universe into one ball, to turn it into the round music of a perfect poem. "Cino" ends with a song within the poem:

> "I have sung women in three cities.
> But it is all one.
> I will sing of the white birds
> In the blue waters of heaven,
> The clouds that are spray to its sea."

This song within the poem concludes with a promise to sing an imagistic harmony of earth and heaven: heaven will become blue waters, and the clouds will become the spray to its seas. Looking at the horizon, the imagination conjures "the blue waters of heaven"; it asserts harmony where it finds the very division that keeps a poet from singing. It attempts to mitigate what Stevens, surveying the same ancient scene, would call "the indifference of this dividing blue."

Pound's conception of triumphant song is not different from those we see in Dante and Milton: the image of a future singing surpasses the poet's current ability to forge harmony between earth and heaven. Any attempt to sing is full of care and labor, as Pound's translation of "The Seafarer" declares: "May I for my own self song's truth reckon,/ Journey's jargon, how I in harsh days/ Hardship endured oft." Enduring hardship can take one's mind away from soul-making, and from the efforts of speaking unique, perdurable speech. We are all potentially rendered merely "Journey's jargon." When conviction becomes formal, as in "Cino," a singer's identity can become indefinite: "Cino?" "Oh, eh, Cino Polnesi/ The singer is't you mean?" Given these conditions, one must have the strength to endure one's aspiration: "Moaneth alway my mind's lust/ That I fare forth, that I afar hence/ Seek out a foreign fastness."[14] The aspiration to a condition of song can be overwhelmed by the need to ask questions or speculate.

Eventually, there comes the conception of the singer that characterizes Pound's vision of high modernism:

> If she with ivory fingers drive a tune through
> the lyre,
> We look at the process.[15]

There "is no high-road to the Muses."[16] A poet becomes not one who sings but, rather, one who scrutinizes the trope of song. Eventually, Pound became a poet adept at scrutinizing "the fragmentation of the Muses," and the consequences such fragmentation brings:

> What you depart from is not the way
> and olive tree blown white in the wind
> washed in the Kiang and Han
> what whiteness will you add to this whiteness,
> what candor?
> "the great periplum brings in the stars to our shore."

Pound, as here in his *Pisan Cantos*, went far away from Eliot, seeking ever more tenaciously to piece his circle from elusive fragments. Pound went on "with a bang, not a whimper,/ To build the city of Dioce whose terraces are the colour of stars."[17] Having pushed himself in the speculative manner of Hamlet, having made a political career out of his own antic disposition, eventually Pound went mad, much in the manner of Ophelia, singing fragments of songs as if they were the song itself. They were the songs of his self, a disharmony of his making. Eliot, in contrast, went the way of *Four Quartets*, asserting faith in an "ennobling Harmony" not of his making. Both Pound and Eliot, in their starkly different ways, were trying to forestall a loss of song greater than they could bear.

W.B. Yeats: "Singing School"

Embracing fictions not of his making, Yeats long attempted
to forestall the loss of "great song." Eventually, nearing the
end of his career as the great simple singer of his age, Yeats
wrote these remarkable lines about the diminished possibility for song:

> Though the great song return no more
> There's keen delight in what we have:
> The rattle of pebbles on the shore
> Under the receding wave.

One is reminded of Demosthenes, who is said to have achieved
the easy sweetness of his orations by practicing first with a
mouth full of pebbles. Modern poets had, in contrast, never to
spit them out. Yeats's poem "The Nineteenth Century and
After" is a corollary to "Three Movements," a poem also published in *The Winding Stair and Other Poems* in 1933.[18] "Three
Movements" places the modern poet on the shore:

> Shakespearean fish swam the sea, far away from land;
> Romantic fish swam in nets coming to the hand;
> What are all those fish that lie gasping on the strand?

The self-deluding music of the romantics could not return.
The lust for "foreign fastness" had to be seen as destructive. The modern poet, though he "lie gasping on the strand,"
must learn to delight in what he had, even if it were a "rattle
of pebbles." As Edmund Wilson observed long ago, Yeats's
"words, no matter how prosaic, are always somehow luminous and noble, as if the pale pebbles smoothed by the sea
were to take on some mysterious value and become more
precious than jewels or gold."[19] Yeats had this gift, and knew
he had it, but he was interested in the way noble words can
be ignobling. He had to abandon ancient expectations based
on an "ennobling Harmony" and devise a new conception of
ennobling labor.

Yeats's conception of poetic song was rooted in actual voices of Ireland: the easy unpremeditated singing of Irish women, folk songs signifying romantic Ireland. But even before he ceased to appear to be the last of the romantics, 50 years before writing "The Nineteenth Century and After," Yeats understood that sweet, simple song might be an illusory achievement. As early as *The Rose*, Yeats identified song not as a revelry in ease but as a source of valuable discomfort. In "The Man who dreamed of Fairyland," for example, "singing shook him out of his new ease."

By "September 1913" and "Easter 1916," poetic song had become as impossible to achieve as romantic Ireland. For Yeats, the reality of tragic Ireland, as well as the loss of his sexual potency, accompanied the shift from a conception of song as the happy reward given to the good — as in "The fiddler of Dooney," where "the good are always the merry" — to a more deeply speculative conception. Yeats needed to consider what the good may do when they can neither be merry nor enjoy the reward of song.

Many of Yeats's thoughts about poetic song can be explained in biographical terms, although sometimes such terms reduce the poems. A change did occur, as Wilson observed, sometime in the period of *The Green Helmet and Other Poems*. Yeats "still champions, he still puts above everything, the nobility and splendor of the imagination; but he must face life's hard conditions." Hence, he "reduces his verse to something definite and hard — at the same time more severe and more passionate. Now," writes Wilson, "the soap bubble colors vanish; the music of fairyland dies away; we behold only earthly and clear, the bare outlines of 'cold Clare rock and Galway rock and thorn.'" Yeats "no longer hopes from real life any satisfaction other than the triumph of imagination through art."[20] This is true enough, but we must consider what is meant by "the triumph of imagination through art," for it is precisely this — along with Yeats's conception of poetic

song — that changes. Like Ireland, poetry itself became a terrible beauty. Beautiful as a consequence of the severe and
passionate triumph of the imagination and art, but terrible
because devoid of the hope of reality. Wilson suggests that
Yeats carried "the aestheticism of Pater . . . through to its consequences," and that the chief consequence of "living for
beauty" wrought by imagination is to "be thrown fatally out
of key with reality."[21] Yeats resisted this consequence by
examining all his tropes — especially the trope of song.

Yeats first began to examine deeply his status as a singer in
The Green Helmet and Other Poems. Writing poetry is hard,
as Yeats writes in "Adam's Curse," but the "labour to be beautiful" is still necessary, much like the Wordsworthian need to
keep from growing "weary-hearted." But the acceptance of
toil in "Adam's Curse" becomes, as in "All Things Can Tempt
Me," the realization that he is merely accustomed to his work.
The toil of poetry ceases in some crucial way to be real, but
the consequences of performing "accustomed toil" become,
as in "All Things Can Tempt Me," disturbingly real:

> Now nothing but comes readier to the hand
> Than this accustomed toil. When I was young,
> I had not given a penny for a song
> Did not the poet sing it with such airs
> That one believed he had a sword upstairs;
> Yet would be now, could I but have my wish,
> Colder and dumber and deafer than a fish.

The realization that the poet has no magic power, no sword
upstairs — but only airs — complicates an already terrible
choice: "perfection of the life or of the art." Eventually, establishing a link between life and art becomes the greater part of
a poet's toil. His desire becomes stronger as his vigor dissipates, as Yeats puts the matter in these vigorous lines:

> The fascination of what's difficult
> Has dried the sap out of my veins, and rent

> Spontaneous joy and natural content
> Out of my heart.

As Yeats writes in "Words": "I might have thrown poor words away/ And been content to live." Unlike Milton, and the romantics, Yeats could not link the completion of a speculative circle and the living of life. He thought he had to choose, thinking that it is devotion to the toil of poetry, not some deeper crisis of consciousness, that upsets a happy life. When Shelley, in contrast, alludes to the inevitable despondency of the poet, he is not suggesting there is any other way to live a life.

In accepting his task as a poet, Yeats is niggardly in identifying rewards. The reward for toil is only more arduous toil, more deep fascination with what is difficult. Or mere delusion. In "A Woman Homer Sung" "life and letters seem/ But an heroic dream." As the connection between life and art becomes tenuous, so Adam's curse seems to be not so much the labor as the loss of conviction that such labor can cause. In *Responsibilities*, Yeats writes of "Poets with whom I learned my trade." Labor must not lead to a misconception of the requirements of song. As the epigraph to the collection says, "In dreams begins responsibility." To sing is the poet's dream, and it is also his chief responsibility. He must keep "the Muses' sterner laws," much like those steadfast people celebrated in the poem that stands as a prologue to the collection, including that "silent and fierce old man" whom "the daily spectacle" stirs but does not confound.

Yeats was stirred by daily and historical spectacle, as he relates in *The Wild Swans at Coole*, and he had to mediate the requirements of song and life, as in "Ego Dominus Tuus":

> Hic. Yet surely there are men who have made their art
>   Out of no tragic war, lovers of life,
>   Impulsive men that look for happiness
>   And sing when they have found it.

Ille.   No, not sing,
>   For those that love the world serve it in action,
>   Grow rich, popular and full of influence,
>   And should they paint or write, still it is action:
>   The struggle of the fly in marmalade.
>   The rhetorician would deceive his neighbours,
>   The sentimentalist himself; while art
>   Is but a vision of reality.

This crucial dialogue is always running in Yeats. What seems to have become increasingly clear to Yeats is that song was an "ennobling Harmony" that could suit the sentimentalist. He would have to ennoble "the struggle of the fly in marmalade." But how to conceive the struggle as singing? The question was: is it only merry men — happy, deceived sentimentalists — who can sing?

The last poem in *Responsibilities*, "A Coat," is about the sentimentality that hinders any attempt at self-ennobling. The poet has made his "song a coat/ Covered with embroideries/ Out of old mythologies/ From heel to throat." The poem moves with speed and force to a renunciation of his former means of fashioning himself as a singer:

> Song, let them take it,
> For there's more enterprise
> In walking naked.

To Yeats, the art of song is something very different from the enterprise of fools who catch a thing and wear it "in the world's eyes,/ As though they wrought it." The poem ends in an angry tone. Like Lear on the heath, Yeats is considering his own foolishness in wearing his covering as if he had wrought it. With rhythm and syntax indicating reluctance, Yeats relinquishes his singing robe, knowing he must maintain a sterner conception of song. There is more enterprise in singing naked.

The poem that serves as an epigraph to *Responsibilities*, a sonnet beginning with a description of the poet's changed condition as a singer, poses deep questions about the value of poetry in its relation to a speculative affirmation of the value of life. "A sterner conscience" must become a "friendlier home." Otherwise, "priceless things" will only be defiled. Fourteen years after *Responsibilities*, in *The Tower*, Yeats's examination of value continues. His examination returns to romantic urges, as well as a modern lust to embroider oneself with fragments of mythology. Finally, the mythology is so old and common that it reveals the nakedness inherent in fictions — especially the claim to song.

"Sailing to Byzantium" is a poem about many things, but largely a poem about the poet's aspiration to an illusive condition of music:

> That is no country for old men. The young
> In one another's arms, birds in the trees,
> — Those dying generations — at their song. . . .

Byzantium "is no country for old men," but neither, Yeats subtly reveals, is it a country for the young. The young, "like birds in the trees . . . at their song," are themselves but "dying generations." The graphic word order separating birds from their song is poignant. For a poet who seeks a permanent song, it is fruitless to pine for youth or envy the song of birds. Whatever is begotten and born eventually dies. What is important is the monument one may build before the inevitable date. But "Caught in that sensual music all neglect/ Monuments of unageing intellect." The practical music of life — as opposed to the speculative music of a man's life — is a distraction by which fools catch themselves, much as Yeats, earlier in his life, was caught in the sensual music of the Irish countryside, Maude Gonne, and the Dublin street. What can be worse for an aging poet who thinks only of his monument, however, is neglecting a speculative music of his making, living as if he might be happy in an ancient musical ceremony.

The second stanza addresses a danger: that the poet may attribute an ennobling harmony to himself and his poem. It offers a brilliant revision of "The Coat":

> An aged man is but a paltry thing,
> A tattered coat upon a stick, unless
> Soul clap its hands and sing, and louder sing
> For every tatter in its mortal dress,
> Nor is there singing school but studying
> Monuments of its own magnificence;
> And therefore I have sailed the seas and come
> To the holy city of Byzantium.

Eros and logos meet in mythos. Myth may either reveal or evade a monument of one's magnificence. One must examine the construction of one's monuments, for they are fictions. Man is mortal, and mortality brings its ineluctable clothing — especially the brilliant threads of fictive evasion. Man can never hope to get truly naked; he *is* a "tattered coat." Nakedness itself became a fiction. Here, the redeeming nakedness of "The Coat" becomes an ignobling fiction. Man is a fictive animal. But he is also a truth-seeking animal, able to discern that even his nakedness is a tattered coat.

Yeats has come to Byzantium to learn how monuments are built. The first two stanzas of "Sailing to Byzantium" express the poet's desire to turn himself honestly into the monument he already is. But the third stanza moves against the wisdom of bodily decrepitude, turning instead to mythological constructions of transcendence. The first and second stanzas of "Sailing to Byzantium" affirm the knowledge of Keats in *Ode to a Nightingale*: the poet must build his own monument. But Yeats then moves, in the third and fourth stanzas, not merely to a weak romantic desire, but even to the kind of "ennobling Harmony" that sustained religious poets of the Renaissance. Looking for an outward force to repair him ("O sages . . . / Come from the holy fire"), Yeats seeks others to "be the singing-masters of my soul." The third stanza subtly acknowledges that the invocation of sages is made in weakness, and in error, but Yeats's desire overwhelms the deeper awareness that there is no "singing school." The first and second stanzas make clear the need to become the singing-master of one's own soul, but in the third stanza the poet is unwilling to accept anything less than transcendent song. The fiction of inspiration is a powerful distraction from Yeats's need to build a monument to his own magnificence. Yeats speaks as if he needs purging he may not perform himself, much in the manner of John Donne's request at the conclusion of the holy sonnet that begins "Batter my heart . . .":

> Consume my heart away; sick with desire
> And fastened to a dying animal
> It knows not what it is; and gather me
> Into the artifice of eternity.

The transport hoped for here is archetypical: to join the "artifice of eternity." But the phrase suggests the two meanings that express the central crisis of the poem: (1) the wish to be gathered into the work of a supreme artificer; and (2) the conviction that eternity is itself an artifice, and hence something a poet must create himself. Yeats does not believe in the first; but he relinquishes his responsibility in the second.

In Byzantium, the poet finds sages who stand in "God's holy fire/ As in the gold mosaic of a wall." But such fire, if like gold frozen in a wall, is paradoxically cold — colder even than Keats's "cold pastoral," for what is frozen here is "God's holy fire." Indeed, Byzantium is a place where "God's holy fire" may be reduced to craft. Rather than magical, Byzantium turns out to be a place of mere enterprise — a "singing school" that offers only commonplace forms of inspiration. As George Steiner suggests in *Real Presences*, Byzantium itself, like Alexandria, signifies "the imperialism of the second- and third hand," represents a "dominion of secondary and parasitic

discourse over immediacy, of the critical over the creative."[22]
Byzantium has this association for Yeats. As Yeats writes in
another poem from *The Tower*, "Among School Children,"
even the putatively firsthand singing-masters are secondhand:

> Plato thought nature but a spume that plays
> Upon a ghostly paradigm of things;
> Soldier Aristotle played the taws
> Upon the bottom of a king of kings;
> World-famous golden-thighed Pythagoras
> Fingered upon a fiddle-stick or strings
> What a star sang and careless Muses heard:
> Old clothes upon old sticks to scare a bird.

The best of singing-masters are only purveyors of ghostly para-
digms — old clothes upon old sticks, just like Yeats. They are
decked out with the embroidery of myth. Yet however much
their function is exposed, these "old clothes" remain frightening to birds and bards, those rare beings among us who
can establish their being only by singing. Just as awareness of
one's mortal tatter leads one to embroider, the great anxiety
about having no originary music leads one to invoke secondhand singing-masters. In "Sailing to Byzantium," even after
seeing what should send him away, the poet still wishes to be
gathered in.

Truly to sing one needs to create moments in which one
becomes the singing-master of one's soul. Such moments, as
Yeats expresses in "Among School Children," are moments
in which one's refusal to be taken out of one's nature brings
one to the "Presences/ That passion, piety or affection knows."
One must stop worshiping perfect images, stop putting stock
in transcendence; one must begin, rather, to animate one's
life with the things of one's life:

> Both nuns and mothers worship images,
> But those the candles light are not as those
> That animate a mother's reveries,

But keep a marble or a bronze repose.
And yet they too break hearts — O Presences
That passion, piety or affection knows,
And that all heavenly glory symbolise —
O self-born mockers of man's enterprise. . . .

One does well to be a self-born mocker of human enterprise, as Yeats is, for mere enterprise, when it turns symbolic, takes one out of one's nature, and leaves one brokenhearted.

Nevertheless, it is hard to remain strong. The third stanza of "Sailing to Byzantium" depicts a speaker so fearful of dying that he becomes eager to give up his real presence for a secondary one. The inspiration he seeks would take him out of himself, render him secondary: a secondhand flame lacking the fury of determination, desire in the futile act of trying to quell itself. One cannot achieve such quelling. To attempt this is to manifest the destructive romantic urge to be subsumed into something other than oneself: "swimming into nets coming to the hand." The nets become attractive merely for the vain comfort they promise. "The secondary," as Steiner writes, "is our narcotic. Like sleepwalkers, we are guarded by the numbing of . . . the theoretical, from the often harsh, imperious radiance of sheer presence."[23]

In "Sailing to Byzantium," not even sages can intercede in Yeats's experience of the ancient cycle, and the point of the poem is that Yeats seeks their intervention anyway; it is an outward movement that might obscure the suffering of desire. Yeats depicts *eros* as if it were a tangible demon that makes him "sick." But it is "being sick with desire/ And fastened to a dying animal," as the second stanza suggests, that makes one a singer.

In the last stanza of "Sailing to Byzantium," Yeats retreats further from the bold — modern — solution articulated in the second stanza. In its movement (from the first two stanzas to the last two), "Sailing to Byzantium" does not declare Yeats a grand artificer; it posits him as an imperfect maker imperfectly made. Whereas Keats celebrates his power to create his Grecian urn, Yeats imagines that he himself must be remade into a wrought object. He wishes that he might be taken out of his nature, even though it is the only potential monument of his magnificence:

> Once out of nature I shall never take
> My bodily form from any natural thing,
> But such a form as Grecian goldsmiths make
> Of hammered gold and gold enamelling
> To keep a drowsy Emperor awake;
> Or set upon a golden bough to sing
> To lords and ladies of Byzantium
> Of what is past, or passing, or to come.

"Sailing to Byzantium" depicts the confrontation between a modern tenacity to ennoble oneself and a romantic retreat to an "ennobling Harmony." The poem recounts a poet's over-determined refuge from a world inimical to song.

Whatever the lies on which it is based, the trope of transcendent song is by necessity the "last and favorite" trope of any great poet. Refusing to say it is something else, Yeats at least acknowledges his desire for what it is. Such desire, however rooted in ancient and romantic fictions not of his making, is less dangerous than its repression by fictions also not of his making. Whatever the distrust of mythology suggested in the first two stanzas, unstoppable desire, as in the third and fourth stanzas, constitutes the poet's soul trying to clap its hands.

"Sailing to Byzantium" is a great modern poem in part because it is an expression of the decidedly modern necessity of perpetuating, against all pressures of reality, a romantic desire to sing. Yeats pursues this crucial subject in his next collection of poems, moving from weak confrontation to luminous enactments of a uniquely modern agon. In "Byzantium," "The unpurged images of day recede," and Yeats depicts the wished-for place of transcendence as secondary, lacking being, a place where the images disdain "All that man is." The world is a sea of such images, a "gong-tormented sea." The phrase is Yeats's way of exposing not only the ennobling harmony of transcendent song, but, what is more important, the tragic wish to live by it. If they are acknowledged as "mere complexities,/ The fury and the mire of human veins," then there is real value in such images. But when the false images cease to answer reality,

> all complexities of fury leave,
> Dying into a dance,
> An agony of trance,
> An agony of flame that cannot singe a sleeve.

To look for singing-masters in Byzantium is to do more than invoke a dead metaphor; it is to try to live by one, risking spiritual death and artistic failure.

In "Among School Children," Yeats articulates his monumental conception of the modern artist:

> Labour is blossoming or dancing where
> The body is not bruised to pleasure the soul,
> Nor beauty born out of its own despair,
> Nor blear-eyed wisdom out of midnight oil.

This is the strong assertion the speaker of "Sailing to Byzantium" cannot make. Yeats formulates his exemplary vision of the process in which the creator and his creation must become indistinguishable:

> O chestnuttree, greatrooted blossomer,
> Are you the leaf, the blossom or the bole?
> O body swayed to music, O brightening glance,
> How can we know the dancer from the dance?

If one can distinguish the singer from the song, the singer has failed utterly. Yeats's disputes between body and soul are evidence not so much of failure as an insistence on dealing with the conflict, as well as its permutations: imagination and reality, eternity and time.

The aspiration to song has always been an aspiration to triumph over — or evade — time. To triumph over time, one cannot evade it. One must, like Milton, have a theological belief that time resolves all conflicts, unifying the self and everything the self is not. Or one must have an ability to live in moments — in the manner of Pater and the Symbolists. Yeats's refusal to evade time is fundamental to his modernist aspiration to song. As Donoghue writes, arguing against a point made by Kermode in *Romantic Image*, "The Yeatsian dance seems much more severe, much stricter than the Symbolist dance of Loie Fuller." The main point, as Donoghue writes, is that although "Yeats and many of his artistic contemporaries were fascinated by this dancer," nevertheless, "the description does not seem quite in keeping with the dance-climaxes of Yeats's own later plays, which do not try to evade time at all."[24] Yeats knew that song, if it were to be in any way at all transcendent, had to exist in time.

One can read Yeats's *Collected Poems*, as Donoghue does, "as dramatizing a great dispute between Self and Soul; Self being all those motives which tie one to earth and time, Soul being the freedom of imagination transcending the finite," a dispute, as Donoghue points out, that "was never resolved." Donoghue is right to "quarrel with those who would read the Byzantine poems as if they were written by Wallace Stevens," for "these poems are not parables about the free imagination." Indeed, "they are poems about the dispute of Self and Soul at a time when old age and approaching death seem to vote resoundingly for Soul."[25] But while old age and death weigh heavily in "Sailing to Byzantium," the poet does not, I would argue, "vote resoundingly for soul." There is, rather, an attempt to reveal the fictions about the soul that have clouded the dispute, and to acknowledge the truths about the body that might help to resolve it, or at least to make it a more valuable dispute.

Yeats's idiom, as Donoghue writes, is "the acknowledgement of conflict within the single state of man, and at the same time the further acknowledgement that value resides in the conflict itself." As Donoghue points out, "Eliot, in these circumstances, would tend to resolve the dispute by direct appeal to a higher authority: Yeats made most of his poems from the dispute itself."[26] I would locate in *The Tower* Yeats's further acknowledgement that the urge to turn to a higher authority is great. It is precisely this acknowledgement, absent in Eliot, that allowed Yeats to live in the dispute. *The Tower* is a continuation of a movement toward "the living text of the world," a movement Donoghue sees as stronger in *The Wilde Swans at Coole*.

As Donoghue writes, Yeats chooses "the living world for text." His poems are "poems of place, time, memory, voice, conflict, personality." Donoghue does "not find there a single poem in which Yeats releases himself from these obligations: he never composed a Supreme fiction." That Yeats "occasionally wished to do so," Donoghue "would not deny: the poems that spring to mind at once are, of course, the two Byzantium poems."[27] There is more we can say about "Sailing to Byzantium," however, than what it wishes. What is crucial, what makes it such a fine poem, is the manner of its wish.

Yeats's aspiration to a condition of song had, clearly, very much to do with the time and place in which he lived: a musical and poetic nation whose sense of nationhood was always reflected in the music of its poetry and the poetry of its music. A loss of "great song" was, for Yeats, tied to the loss of a great Ireland. Indeed, we should not fail to consider Joyce's treatment of the subject. Joyce also published in 1914 a great work that linked the spiritual dying of romantic

Ireland with the death of song. His concerns are similar, but his conclusions are different. He sees psuedo-speculation as the gravest danger to the power of actual song.

Having early given up poetry — his quintessentially lyric poetry — to pursue the music of his prose, Joyce offered a terribly beautiful conception of "the music of man's life" in "The Dead."[28] Like Yeats, Joyce at once exalted the refusal to give up lyricism in an unmusical world and warned subtly against parlous forms of false refusal. "The Dead" reduces the trope of song to the literal act of singing and reveals that romantic Ireland is so dead and gone that even the actual singers can no longer sing. "Listening to-night to the names of all those great singers of the past it seemed to me, I must confess," says Gabriel Conroy, "that we were living in a less spacious age. . . ." For Gabriel, musical cosmology fuses with the social condition. The problem has nothing to do with a failure of artistic technique or the Irish larynx; it has to do with a failure of the Irish soul, the failure of a "less spacious age." Gabriel, however, is the character who embodies this failure. He sees no way to revive the song, and he has no idea that his plea "still [to] cherish in our hearts the memory of those dead and gone great ones whose fame the world will not willingly let die" will confirm his own slow death when his wife reveals her unwillingness to allow the song of her life to die.

As much as one may have a critical understanding that the art of singing is dying, as Gabriel does, without an understanding of its basis in the ancient cycle, one renders one's own musical death. While others remark the still-strong voice of his aging aunt Julia, which looks proleptically to the heroic singing of the dying boy, Gabriel refuses to agree, thinking them, rather than himself, to be caught in the sensual music of dying. Caught in the psuedo-speculation of his own neglect, Gabriel allows himself to dismiss the loud singing of others. Such dismissal attends the tragic noises of one's own slow dying, of one's own death march, which is marked, in "The Dead," always by the rhythm of feet: squeaking galoshes, the feet of dancing guests, the footsteps of one's wife as she ascends the stairs.

Many things are dead in Joyce's story, and the death of the impulse to song is symbolic of a collective deadness of the Irish soul — and in a more general way the modern soul. The triumphant hero of "The Dead," seen in contrast with Gabriel, is a young boy who was the last of the great singers, rushing recklessly, without galoshes, into the rain that would bring about his quick glorious death. Such passion, it eventually becomes clear to Gabriel, is the only means of securing life in a world of spiritual death. Speculative delusions of safety, in contrast, bring Gabriel more quickly to his spiritual death. Gabriel never had "the full glory of such passion," which, however romantic, is better than the refusals of life he makes his custom. Finally, Gabriel recognizes that "[o]ne by one they were all becoming shades," and, though it appears too late for action, he can finally assert: "Better pass boldly into that other world, in the full glory of some passion, than fade and wither dismally with age."

"The Dead" is a story of musical enclosure, a story about the ways people in a less spacious age consign themselves to smaller and feebler music, cadences of spiritual death. It focuses on every last enclosure: windows, galoshes, coats. Love of a woman and love of song must be correlative forms of *eros*. The young boy brings his naked self, and he comes in the rain, his voice a pure instrument that can express his soul — even through a window. Gabriel has an epiphany when he hears his wife describe what true love is — a devotion to possibility, a willingness to die for song: "Generous tears filled Gabriel's eyes. He had never felt like that himself toward any woman. . . ." Gabriel sees himself as one of the living dead. He ends, as does the boy in "Araby," derided by his vanity. Gabriel knows he has obscured the truth of his mortal tatter under the safety of embroidery. He knows he has refused to allow his soul to clap its hands and sing.

Yeats began in *Responsibilities* to concentrate on the

potentially disastrous vanity of the singer. Throughout his career, Yeats's strong reaction against his own vanity as a poet and a man intensified. Joyce, in contrast, was able, in prose, to make himself more and more successfully vain. Joyce turned the defeating vanity of "Araby" into the potentially useful vanity of Stephen Dedalus in *Portrait of the Artist as a Young Man*. In *Ulysses*, we find destructive vanity objectified in characters; the vanity of Joyce's style, however, becomes a triumphant music that vies with the sweet but vainglorious singing of Dublin's streets.

It took Yeats longer than Joyce to turn both his vanity and the vanity of his style completely to ironic gain. In "All Things can tempt Me," Yeats opposes devotion to the craft of verse with foolish action: "All things can tempt me from this craft of verse:/ One time it was a woman's face, or worse — / The seeming needs of my fool-driven land. . . ." By the end of Yeats's life, the craft of verse itself seemed a manifestation of foolish desire, but he knew well that desire itself comprised the most nearly naked and hence ennobling truth.

"The Circus Animals' Desertion" sends us back to Yeats's other poems, bringing all of the weight of the failure he attributes to them to the success of this poem. Yeats examines the relationship between the music of his life and the music of his poems:

> I sought a theme and sought for it in vain,
> I sought it daily for six weeks or so.
> Maybe at last being but a broken man
> I must be satisfied with my heart. . . .

Not at all in vain, of course. But we must try to take the poet at his word when he appears to us this way. By declaring his earlier desires thwarted by the indirection of his heart, Yeats attaches another level of meaning to them. He achieves a yet more terrible — and durable — beauty:

>   although
> Winter and summer till old age began
> My circus animals were all on show,
> Those stilted boys, that burnished chariot,
> Lion and woman and the Lord knows what.

"What can I but enumerate old themes," Yeats asks, "Vain gaiety, vain battle, vain repose,/ Themes of the embittered heart, or so it seems,/ That might adorn old songs or courtly shows?" But if Yeats is disquieted, it is his disquiet that ennobles him:

> Those masterful images because complete
> Grew in pure mind but out of what began?
> A mound of refuse or the sweepings of a street,
> Old kettles, old bottles, and a broken can,
> Old iron, old bones, old rags, that raving slut
> Who keeps the till. Now that my ladder's gone
> I must lie down where all the ladders start
> In the foul rag and bone shop of the heart.

Yeats had earlier relied upon his conception of cyclical history. But here there is no other truth, no ennobling harmony. There is no totalizing aesthetic, psychic, theological, or mythological principle with which to ennoble the trope of song. There is only the terrible, beautiful truth about where the ancient cycle begins and ends. Complete images of pure mind must give way to a mind of refuse, for images are never complete, and mind is never pure. The voice, therefore, may never be pure, and neither may song.

The oral tradition to which Yeats belonged was one in which, as Donoghue remarks, "it is easier to reconcile oneself to the temporal, the limited, the finite, because these are the very conditions of Voice."[29] Song, in this sense, is what is indelibly present, not "what is past, or passing, or to come." In the end, one cannot want a Grecian goldsmith to hammer one out of one's nature. One may complete one's musical circle only by allowing reality to hammer one's ladder into a circle, joining with disquiet one's beginning and one's end.

"The Circus Animals' Desertion" makes one of the great careerist renunciations in English poetry — along with Chaucer's retraction, if we take it to be genuine, and Shakespeare's renunciation of his "rough magic," if we take Prospero for the playwright. It took Yeats until the end of his life to confront the consequences of "living for beauty." He could only slowly document his refusal to give up lyricism even when he found the world inimical to a lyre.

Wallace Stevens: "Silence Made Still Dirtier"

Stevens writes in "Peter Quince at the Clavier" that he has a mind to write not only about actual music, not only about actual sounds, but about a deeper aspect of life inconceivable without speculative musical terms to describe it:

> Just as my fingers on these keys
> Make music, so the selfsame sounds
> On my spirit make a music, too.
>
> Music is feeling, then, not sound.

Stevens early had a mind to get past sounds; but he had a better (sensual) sense not to. Stevens was devoted to the sensual music of life and sounds, but he was also determined to justify their value through speculation.

Stevens speculated early in his career about joining his beginning and his end:

> Jove in the clouds had his inhuman birth.
> No mother suckled him, no sweet land gave
> Large-mannered motions to his mythy mind
> He moved among us, as a muttering king;
> Magnificent, would move among his hinds
> Until our blood, commingling, virginal,

With heaven, brought such requital to desire
The very hinds discerned it, in a star.
Shall our blood fail? Or shall it come to be
The blood of paradise? And shall the earth
Seem all of paradise that we shall know?
The sky will be much friendlier then than now,
A part of labor and a part of pain,
And next in glory to enduring love,
Not this dividing and indifferent blue.[30]

Stevens saw the present strife of *eros* as greater in glory than any future resolution of division: even when it ceases to be dividing, the sky shall be next in glory to "enduring love." Stevens could accept the bittersweetness of *eros* — or, as Anne Carson observes, the sweetbitterness (γλυκύπικρον).[31] The sky is unfriendly now not merely because it is dividing, but because it is also indifferent to the poet's enduring love; it finds his labors and pains of no consequence. The phrase "dividing and indifferent blue" emphasizes with irony the etymological meanings of *in-different*: without difference, hence "not-dividing." The sky is dividing (it excludes the poet from its realm), but is itself harmonious, without differences. It is also cruelly indifferent to the consequences of the division it enforces.

Poets, like philosophers and theologians, have for a long time encountered in the briefest perusal of the sky these various manifestations of indifference. Old and new questions about the Muses arise: are they harmoniously banded against the labors of human beings? are they fragmented? are they merely a human invention, a further displacing rationalization of our human feeling that we live in a place not our own? Perhaps Jove has a "mythy mind" only because people do, and poets to excess. Myth is a way for the self to carry out war with anything that is not the self, a way of bringing everything that is not the self into a relationship with it.

Much like Shakespeare, Stevens is not concerned to settle

on one consistent mythology. He is interested, rather, in using myths to make his meticulous accounts of desire, as well as the possibility of its requital. The sky represents at once both the mythological fragmentation of the Muses that keeps a poet from singing and the haughty mythological harmony of the heavens from which the poet is excluded. This antagonism, however much based in competing mythologies, seems real. It is a pressure of reality felt by every poet who would become a singer.

Stevens found a good deal of pure poetry in Plato's *Phaedrus*, but where Plato sees two kinds of souls, the "noble" soul and the "imperfect," Stevens sees only one, imperfect soul, and it is the task of the singer to ennoble its settling to a place not its own. For Stevens, the imperfect is the noble — and the possible. "The imperfect is so hot in us." To be imperfect is to be as yet unmade, which is a good thing.[32] A singer is "a shadow hunched/ Above the arrowy, still strings" of his blue guitar, "The maker of a thing yet to be made." Song cannot be a transcendent existence beyond our being; it must be wrought of our imperfection. It is our task as singers not so much to perfect ourselves as to ennoble our imperfection — by means, of course, of our imagination.

"To the One of Fictive Music" is an important programmatic poem in which Stevens offers an early articulation of the relationship between the imagination and his aspiration to song:

> Now, of the music summoned by the birth
> That separates us from the wind and sea,
> Yet leaves us in them, until earth becomes,
> By being so much of the things we are,
> Gross effigy and simulacrum, none
> Gives motion to perfection more serene
> Than yours, out of our imperfections wrought,
> Most rare, or ever of more kindred air
> In the laborious weaving that you wear.

For so retentive of themselves are men
That music is intensest which proclaims
The near, the clear, and vaunts the clearest bloom,
And of all vigils musing the obscure,
That apprehends the most which sees and names,
As in your name, an image that is sure,
Among the arrant spices of the sun,
O bough and bush and scented vine, in whom
We give ourselves our likest issuance.

Yet not too like, yet not so like to be
Too near, too clear, saving a little to endow
Our feigning with the strange unlike, whence springs
The difference that heavenly pity brings.
For this, musician, in your girdle fixed
Bear other perfumes. On your pale head wear
A band entwining, set with fatal stones.
Unreal, give back to us what once you gave:
The imagination that we spurned and crave.[33]

Fictions must be "not so like as to be too near." The imagination is at once implicated in the ancient cycle and responsible for creating it. Birth still displaces us, separates us from wind and sea, and we wish to be more near; the imagination can do this, but it must be sure to "endow/ Our feigning with the strange unlike." Forging identity is false. When the imagination is responsible for division, however, "difference" is not cruel; it is brought by heavenly pity. We were right to spurn the romantic intonings, but the imagination can make the world friendlier.

Stevens continued to work out the relation between imagination and reality, defining as their proper balance the kind of song to which he aspired throughout his career, especially in the long poems "The Man with the Blue Guitar" and "Notes Toward a Supreme fiction." One must imagine everything, according to Stevens, and yet one must not merely imagine anything; for one must imagine things as they are.[34] Hence, the differences between an ennobling and an ignobling fiction — as between "pure poetry" and "gorgeous nonsense" — become fine. This tension is a subject of "The Man with the Blue Guitar":

> I cannot bring a world quite round,
> Although I patch it as I can.
>
> I sing a hero's head, large eye
> And bearded bronze, but not a man,
>
> Although I patch him as I can
> And reach through him almost to man.
>
> If to serenade almost to man
> Is to miss, by that, things as they are,
>
> Say that it is the serenade
> Of a man that plays a blue guitar.[35]

Stevens could listen to himself in the process of "almost" singing. Unlike the romantics, he could listen with delight to the stubborn sounds of an imperfect world. The achievement of song is never complete for Stevens, and we must take delight in the incompletion, the imperfection.

Knowing the mind is at war with reality, and that the war is endless, Stevens knows that all a poet can do is "patch." He must not, however, do merely the kind of patching that would make him the kind of "joiner" described by Plato; he must be an erotic dialectician:

> Soldier, there is a war between the mind
> And sky, between thought and day and night. It is
> For that the poet is always in the sun,
>
> Patches the moon together in his room
> To his Virgilian cadences, up down,
> Up down. It is a war that never ends.[36]

When he looked at the sky, he thought to turn it into a "friendlier" home. But as Stevens sees it, the war between the mind

and the sky is unending, and merely to keep up with its altercations is an interminable labor, a form of enduring love, full
of bitterness — and also full of delight.

Stevens could accept the "dividing and indifferent blue,"
but he also sought to mitigate it, usually within the terms of
related dichotomies: eternal and temporal; heavenly and
earthly; universal and particular; objective and subjective; and
so on — day and night; sun and moon; up and down. These
dichotomies — the crucial subjects of critical ages from Plato
to poststructuralism — appear to be obvious distinctions made
here on earth by a creature who posits (whether on account of
divine illumination or the logic and rhetoric of a mythy mind)
that earth is different from heaven, and also in some ways
similar. The trope of song is a comprehensive way to conceive of the world and the self. It allows a poet to translate
every conceivable philosophical and aesthetic dichotomy into
the classes of action and being poets strive to achieve for themselves and their works.

These altercations about one's beginning and one's end
assert a real pressure on language — and on a poet's aspiration
to song. As Stevens writes in "The Poems of Our Climate":

> The imperfect is our paradise.
> Note that, in this bitterness, delight,
> Since the imperfect is so hot in us,
> Lies in flawed words and stubborn sounds.[37]

Our climate may be cold, as Milton and Shelley thought, but
it is cold for reasons other than those Milton and Shelley knew.
And it is precisely because our climate is cold that we are still
hot, especially in our attempts to sing. The conditions of music
to which Milton and Shelley aspire are, in Stevens, only ennobling harmonies, ignobling fictions that make it seem

> As if, as if, as if the disparate halves
> Of things were waiting in a bethrothal known
> To none, awaiting espousal to the sound

> Of right joining, a music of ideas, the burning
> And breeding and bearing birth of harmony,
> The final relation, the marriage of the rest.[38]

Stevens is the master of reading "as if" without believing in transcendence — of ennobling fictions while being a "harassing master,"[39] proving that "the theory/ Of poetry is the theory of life,/ As it is, in the intricate evasions of as."[40]

Stevens had moments when he wished to believe in a music beyond life, a speculative music that confirmed the goodness of the world:

> Here in New England at the very moment, nothing but good seems to be returning; and in that good, particularly if we ignore the difference between men and the natural world, how easy it is suddenly to believe in the poem as one has never believed in it before, suddenly to require of it a meaning beyond what its words can possibly say, a sound beyond any giving of the ear, a motion beyond our previous knowledge of feeling.[41]

But Stevens could not ignore the "difference between men and the natural world"; and going "beyond" would therefore be difficult. Rather, a poet must engage in a Hamlet-like struggle to ennoble a place not one's own, a place of ignobling fictions to which the poet has ineluctably settled. Unlike Hamlet, however, one must begin, if holding any hope for an immaculate end, to take delight in the imperfect. To do this, the poet must give up the hope of achieving "a sound beyond any giving of the ear." The poet must discern, among countless others, "the difficult difference" between "flawed words" and "stubborn sounds." To be imperfect is to be unmade; hence, it remains for us to make our paradise. This the imagination must do, according to Stevens, but it must keep its vitality by adhering to what is real.

Music, it would seem, because free of "stubborn words," "flawed sounds," and the "pressure of reality," exceeds poetry in its ability to achieve perfection, but Stevens took special delight in the burden of turning language into the perfection of song. Delighted to be a chattering poet of the imperfect, Stevens is the first poet to insist that poetry must exceed music:

Poetry

Exceeding music must take the place
Of empty heaven and its hymns,

Ourselves in poetry must take their place,
Even in the chattering of your guitar.

VI

A tune beyond us as we are,
Yet nothing changed by the blue guitar;

Ourselves in the tune as if in space,
Yet nothing changed. . . .[42]

If, however, the task of a poet is at once to sing "a tune beyond us as we are" and to sing "things as they are," with "nothing changed," then that task will demand what Stevens calls "the difficultest rigor" of catching the being of things. As Donoghue remarks, Stevens tries frequently "to render essence by deploying existents in lithe relationships. It is the relationship, the movement of energy between the objects, that certifies their participation in the act-of-being."[43] The mind, as Stevens beheld, sees relation everywhere: "Life's nonsense pierces us with strange relation."[44] The mind both creates relations that are not there and perceives relations that are. To find where relations begin and end is to sing.

In his aspiration to song, Stevens returns again and again to the supreme myth of our displacing — the myth of our beginning — attempting always, while adhering to the pressure of reality, to patch an immaculate end. Myths are partial explanations of the world by people (or peoples) who can consider only their parts in it. In *Parts of the World*, the collection he published after *The Man with the Blue Guitar*, Stevens includes a number of poems that consider why our beginning and our end can be approached only by a subtle appreciation of the daily, detectable beginnings and ends — the strange relations — that might tell us more about how the myth of our beginning first began. As Stevens makes clear in "The Pure Good of Theory," abstract theory must give way to the necessity of detection:

> Man, that is not born of woman but of air,
> That comes here in the solar chariot,
> Like rhetoric in a narration of the eye —
>
> We knew one parent must have been divine,
> Adam of beau regard, from fat Elysia,
> Whose mind malformed this morning metaphor,
>
> While all the leaves leaked gold. His mind made morning,
> As he slept. He woke in a metaphor: this was
> A metamorphosis of paradise,
>
> Malformed, the world was paradise malformed . . .
> Now, closely the ear attends the varying
> Of this precarious music, the change of key
>
> Not quite detected at the moment of change
> And, now, it attends the difficult difference.[45]

With the supreme truth of his creation in God's image, John Donne could both revel that his God is metaphorical and feel justified in being metaphorical himself. Stevens could revel that "The imperfect is our paradise" and thus remains to be made. But "The Pure Good of Theory" is a poem about the danger of malforming it. The word *theory* has here its older meaning of "looking at," contemplating or speculating in an empirical sense, rather than in the modern sense of theory as pure speculation. Pure theory imposes. Stevens's poem declares not the good of pure theory but the pure good of Stevens's empirical theory. With his use of the dash and ellipsis in this passage, Stevens asserts — at those critical moments — the difficulty of making associations after the moment of change. The music of his poem must follow the changes of the music of life. But there is a precarious dilemma . . . the changes are *now* difficult to detect. Stevens is determined to combine — empirically — the related concerns of speculation and practice.

Stevens saw metaphysical questions about identity and an interest to discern it as central to his conception of himself as a singer. The ability to reveal in-difference (identity) is an ability to forge true harmony, to turn speech into music. But difference, what Stevens calls the "strange unlike," is what makes music "intensest." Indifference (or disinterest), in contrast, leads one to see as identical things that are different, which is to see things as they are not — and this is to lose the power of song.

Poets who see them must come to terms with differences, the most important of which is the difference between poetry and song. If one is indifferent, one will likely reject the serenade of a blue guitar for what it is and accept it for what it is not. That is the way of the human mind, of language, and, therefore, of life:

> Slowly the ivy on the stones
> Becomes the stones. Women become
>
> The cities, children become the fields
> And men in waves become the sea.
>
> It is the chord that falsifies.
> The sea returns upon the men,
>
> The fields entrap the children, brick
> Is a weed and all the flies are caught,
>
> Wingless and withered, but living alive.
> The discord merely magnifies.
>
> Deeper within the belly's dark
> Of time, time grows upon the rock.[46]

Stevens had a rare ability to reveal "the difficult difference" where indifferent people see only resemblances; and he saw a need to resist evasive metaphors of transcendence and false identities — especially those inherent in claims to song:

> Ah, ké! the bloody wren, the felon jay,
> Ké-ké, the jug-throated robin pouring out,
> Bethou, bethou, bethou me in my glade.
>
> There was such idiot minstrelsy in rain,
> So many clappers going without bells,
> That these bethous compose a heavenly gong.

In Yeats's "Byzantium," a gong torments precisely those people who wish to attribute to it a value it cannot have. For Stevens, the "bethous compose" a gong rather than the desired song, a parody of Shelley's pleas, a travesty of Milton's "heavenly tune":

> One voice repeating, one tireless chorister,
> The phrases of a single phrase, kéké,
> A single text, granite monotony. . . .

Birds sing and fly effortlessly through the blue sky, indifferent to its division:

> These are of minstrels lacking minstrelsy,
> Of an earth in which the first leaf is the tale
> Of leaves, in which the sparrow is a bird
>
> Of stone, that never changes. Bethou him, you
> And you, bethou him and bethou. It is
> A sound like any other. It will end.[47]

They lack minstrelsy because they lack mythology; they lack the war that never ends between mind and sky.

The trope of song is antiquated, but Stevens knows he must use it to define himself:

> Where
> Do I begin and end? And where,

> As I strum the thing, do I pick up
> That which momentously declares
>
> Itself not to be I and yet
> Must be. It could be nothing else.

There can be no distinction between the singer and his song. They must become one: "Tom-tom, c'est moi. The blue guitar/ And I are one."[48] Yet Stevens sees himself chiefly as a singer in the process of becoming his song:

> And the color, the overcast blue
> Of the air, in which the blue guitar
>
> Is a form, described but difficult,
> And I am merely a shadow hunched
>
> Above the arrowy, still strings,
> The maker of a thing yet to be made. . . .[49]

In the act of singing — which is an act of making — the imperfect may become a paradise.

In Stevens, the perfection of any thing generally requires that it become a musical manifestation of what it is. Though Stevens bases the power of poetry in imagination, he defines that power in musical terms. Hence, the completion he seeks requires more than *mimesis*. The process of *mimesis*, for reasons Plato expressed, is doomed to incompletion. One must engage in empirical theorizing, what Stevens calls "universal intercourse":

> Poetry is the subject of the poem,
> From this the poem issues and
>
> To this returns. Between the two,
> Between issue and return, there is
>
> An absence in reality,
> Things as they are. Or so we say.
>
> But are these separate? Is it
> An absence for the poem, which acquires

Its true appearances there, sun's green,
Cloud's red, earth feeling, sky that thinks?

From these it takes. Perhaps it gives,
In the universal intercourse.[50]

It is obvious in many of Stevens's poems that he was influenced by what Steiner describes as Mallarmé's "disjunction of language from external reference" and "Rimbaud's deconstruction of the first person singular." Stevens was aware that these poets "splinter the foundations of the Hebraic-Hellenic-Cartesian edifice" upon which relationship between word and world is built.[51] But Stevens was no deconstructionist; he believed in the relationship between word and world as much as any poet writing in English. Stevens did not believe that linguistic undecidability meant that language could only declare the absence of things. He believed, rather, that language and imagination together could invest the world and things as they are with too much meaning, much of it false, and much of it true. It is not language itself that creates absence and confusion, according to Stevens. Rather, "The loss of a language creates confusion or dumbness."[52]

Stevens is aware of what Steiner describes as the "circularities, of the processes of infinite regression implicit in any invocation of a writer's or artist's motives and stated intentions."[53] But Stevens refuses to claim either that meaning is fixed or that it is as easily destroyed as Mallarmé claims. Stevens sees absence itself as a totalizing fiction. The kind of absence declared by Mallarmé would itself have to be imagined, and to be sustained by language. Hence, Stevens refuses to trade the Hebraic-Hellenic-Cartesian edifice for an abyss of meaning and a world of absence. That "The first idea was not our own" is the first fact, and it may not be refuted. "Adam/ in Eden was the father of Descartes. . . ."

Whereas pastoral singers of classical antiquity may see themselves in a universe created as a condition of music,

Stevens found himself in a modern agon. As Stevens wrote in 1942, "The poetry of a work of the imagination constantly illustrates the fundamental and endless struggle with fact. It goes on everywhere, even in the periods that we call peace. But in war, the desire to move in the direction of fact as we want it to be and to move quickly is overwhelming."[54] Language can be used to assert the power of the imagination over the discordant realities of the world. The mind can choose either to take or give "in the universal intercourse." But a singer must at once do both — must acknowledge both the power of the self to create and the stubbornness of the world to be. "What does a man do when he delineates the images of reality?" asks Stevens in a short essay in which he sees such delineations as "rubbings of reality." "Obviously," he answers,

> the need is a general need and the activity a general activity. It is of our nature that we proceed from the chromatic to the clear, from the unknown to the known. Accordingly the writer who practices in order to make perfect is really practicing to get at his subject and, in that exercise, is participating in a universal activity.[55]

As Donoghue remarks, "For Stevens's poems we have his own theories, fabulous in their resource, with only this disability, that they are neater than the poems themselves in the matter of consistency. The poems flout the essays time and again, as perhaps they should."[56] This flouting, this avoidance of consistency is part of Stevens's theory of the relationship between the fictive and the real; it constitutes his participation in a "universal intercourse."

For Stevens, there is no real hope of effecting a cosmic reattuning with the blue sky, nor of our taking the place of the gods; but neither is there any movement toward nihilism. We shared, writes Stevens, the experience of the annihilation of the gods, but "[i]t was their annihilation, not ours, and yet, it left us feeling that in a measure we, too, had been

annihilated. It left us feeling dispossessed and alone in a solitude. . . ."[57] The trouble with a time of disbelief, Stevens saw,
is that it is "a time in which the frequency of detached styles
is greatest." By "detached" Stevens means "the unsuccessful,
the ineffective, the arbitrary, the literary, the nonumbilical,
that which in its highest degree would still be words." When
detachment occurs, the singer is not his song. Stevens's basic
idea here is speculative: "For the style of the poem and the
poem itself to be one there must be a mating and a marriage,
not an arid love-song."[58] There must be not mere lyricism
or verbal groping, but erotic possession, if not of the object
itself, at least of the difficulty one confronts in trying to
apprehend it.

Though he sometimes could, Stevens could not universally
assert the imagination as the only reality; nor could he assert
an absolute power of the mind to sing. Combining practice
and speculation is the only way for Stevens to pursue at once
the world and the realities that imagination makes of it. This
conviction was made strong both at Harvard and at the Hart-
ford Insurance Company, where Stevens thought and wrote
enthusiastically about actuarial things.[59]

There is in Stevens another crucial conviction, which,
unlike the traceable making of a pragmatic upper-middle-class
idealist, is rooted in the mysterious process that makes a poet
born rather than made. Like Shakespeare, Stevens was too
much in love with the physicality of language (the saying
of it, the listening to it) to believe what Steiner calls the "severance or distancing of speech from the empirical, from the
historical, from the Cratylean bias which quickens all poetics."[60] A poet who asserts that our paradise "lies in flawed
words and stubborn sounds" does not distrust language; but
that poet only trusts it to the extent he uses it to adhere to
what is real. Song occurs only when imagination and reality
are inextricably linked.

Stevens spent a career trying to ground the noble rider in

the "pressure of reality" and the sound of words; only by doing so could he turn the trope of song into an ennobling fiction. His poetic is rooted deeply in the Pythagorean-Platonic tradition of musical speculation. Sound and idea — indeed, hearing and thinking — must become one, as Stevens writes in "Of Modern Poetry." The poet of "The poem of the mind in the act of finding/ What will suffice" is Stevens's modern version of Plato's "true musician." Such a poem, born of such a poet, must

> like an insatiable actor, slowly and
> With meditation, speak words that in the ear,
> In the delicatest ear of the mind, repeat,
> Exactly, that which it wants to hear, at the sound
> Of which, an invisible audience listens,
> Not to the play, but to itself, expressed
> In an emotion as of two people as of two
> Emotions becoming one. The actor is
> A metaphysician in the dark, twanging
> An instrument, twanging a wiry string that gives
> Sounds passing through sudden rightnesses, wholly
> Containing the mind, below which it cannot descend,
> Beyond which it has no will to rise.[61]

The maker of a thing yet to be made twanging a wiry string is Stevens's revision of Pythagoras and his monochord. Stevens's musical metaphysician seeks "Sudden rightnesses," but there are limits "beyond which" the mind, bearing itself in reality, can have no will to rise. Stevens seeks "A tune beyond us as we are,/ Yet nothing changed by the blue guitar." Stevens means "beyond us" not in the sense that we go beyond ourselves as we are but, rather, in the sense that we change and transcend ourselves by apprehending ("passing through sudden rightnesses") with a will to go no farther.

Change is necessary. But the will not to change is the basis of Stevens's conception of poetic song. It is a necessary response to a stronger desire: "Desiring the exhilarations of changes," which Stevens calls

> The motive for metaphor, shrinking from
> The weight of primary noon,
> The A B C of being,
>
> The ruddy temper, the hammer
> Of red and blue, the hard sound —
> Steel against intimation — the sharp flash,
> The vital, arrogant, fatal, dominant X.[62]

Sounds can pass "through sudden rightnesses" when there is no will to go further, but when such a will fails, replaced by the desire for exhilarating change, there is "the hard sound" of identity and "the sharp flash" of recognition. "[T]he hard sound" is the sound of reality, but given the motive for metaphor, one must attend to it with "the delicatest ear of the mind." To shrink from the "weight of primary noon" and "The A B C of being" is to shrink from the pressure of reality, the "vital, arrogant, fatal, dominant X." And yet, even when one resists the motive for metaphor, there is difficulty: the mind is always behind reality, and language is frequently ahead of the mind. It is largely for this reason that "the imagination is always at the end of an era. What happens," writes Stevens, "is that it is always attaching itself to a new reality, and adhering to it.[63]

Imaginative language — fiction — can be used to move ever closer toward vital apprehension of "what is real." A supreme fiction will be the most vital fiction, being at once the most imaginative and the one that most adheres to what is real. As Stevens writes, "The final belief is to believe in a fiction, which you know to be a fiction, there being nothing else. The exquisite truth is to know that it is a fiction and that you believe in it willingly."[64]

But the endless process of aspiring to a condition of song requires an endless process of ennobling fictions by bearing them under the pressure of reality:

> The romantic intoning, the declaimed clairvoyance
> Are parts of apotheosis, appropriate
> And of its nature, the idiom thereof.
>
> They differ from reason's click-clack, its applied
> Enflashings. But apotheosis is not
> The origin of the major man. He comes,
>
> Compact in invincible foils, from reason,
> Lighted at midnight by the studious eye,
> Swaddled in revery, the object of
>
> The hum of thoughts evaded in the mind,
> Hidden from other thoughts, he that reposes
> On a breast forever precious for that touch,
>
> For whom the good of April falls tenderly,
> Falls down, the cock-birds calling at the time.
> My dame, sing for this person accurate songs.[65]

Stevens's aspiration to "accurate songs" constitutes the imagination in the simultaneous acts of freeing itself and adhering to what is real. It is for this reason the conclusion of "Notes Toward a Supreme fiction" offers the following advice:

> How simply the fictive hero becomes the real;
> How gladly with proper words the soldier dies,
> If he must, or lives on the bread of faithful speech.

The poet is a soldier in a war of the fictive against the real. By striving to use "proper words" and "faithful speech" he strives to achieve a supreme fiction — which is song.

It is not a poet's actual singing that constitutes "a tune beyond us as we are," but the speculative process of catching objects in the act of singing themselves:

> To sing jubilas at exact, accustomed times,
> To be crested and wear the mane of a multitude
> And so, as part, to exult with its great throat,

To speak of joy and to sing of it, borne on
The shoulders of joyous men, to feel the heart
That is common, the bravest fundament,

This is a facile exercise.

One must never abandon the sensual, but one must perceive
the world, and oneself in it, "in more than sensual mode":

> Jerome
> Begat the tubas and the fire-wind strings,
> The golden fingers picking dark-blue air:
>
> For companies of voices moving there,
> To find of sound the bleakest ancestor,
> To find of light a music issuing
>
> Whereon it falls in more than sensual mode.
> But the difficultest rigor is forthwith,
> On the image of what we see, to catch from that
>
> Irrational moment its unreasoning,
> As when the sun comes rising, when the sea
> Clears deeply, when the moon hangs on the wall
>
> Of heaven-haven. These are not things transformed.
> Yet we are shaken by them as if they were.[66]

To encounter a metaphor that evades reality can be frightening, but it is more frightening if we fail to be shaken by things
when they are not transformed. As Stevens writes in "Prologues to What Is Possible": "The metaphor stirred his fear.
The object with which he was compared/ Was beyond his
recognizing."[67] The metaphor is "frightening because," as
Jacqueline Vaught Brogan writes, "unity or 'one-ness' would
be more than human speech."[68] One would have to be quiet.
Or to be purely musical.

Poetry may exceed music because to be purely musical
is to fail to be shaken. Stevens had long understood the danger of illusory harmony: "It is the chord that falsifies. . . . The
discord merely magnifies."[69] He is writing about the power of

language both to unify and to fragment, as he explains in a letter to Hi Simons: "the chord destroys its elements by uniting them in the chord. . . . On the other hand, discord exaggerates the separation between its elements." Whereas discord "merely" magnifies what is, the chord "falsifies." The problem is part of the battle between reality and imagination: "As between reality and the imagination, we look forward to an era when there will exist the supreme balance between the two."[70] To achieve such balance is to achieve song. But the balance is itself a supreme fiction. Song is a fiction — but it is a supreme fiction. Once one bears the burden of ennobling oneself by ennobling one's fictions, song, thus defined, becomes possible.

There is, moreover, the need to resist the illusion of immaculation, of merely imagined balance, or harmony. Late in his life, Stevens had this advice:

> Be orator but with an accurate tongue
> And without eloquence. . . .[71]

Stevens is writing of the need to subsume one's heart and tongue to the tongue that is the world in the process of singing itself. "When the sky is so blue," Stevens writes, "things sing themselves." The imagination makes it at once possible and difficult to hear them. The debris of life and mind puts one in the condition of being "not quite able to sing."[72]

It is by experiencing the slow movement of vanishing points that we become who we are, much like Achilles and Priam at the end of *The Iliad*, able to sing ourselves and to hear things sing themselves. Stevens, whose first published collection he called *Harmonium*, moves in his last collection, "The Rock," ever more resolutely toward an accurate tongue, toward things singing themselves, toward what Stevens calls "a plain sense of things":

> After the leaves have fallen, we return
> To a plain sense of things. It is as if

We had come to an end of the imagination,
Inanimate in an inert savoir.

It is difficult even to choose the adjective
For this blank cold, this sadness without cause.
The great structure has become a minor house.
No turban walks across the lessened floors.

The greenhouse never so badly needed paint.
The chimney is fifty years old and slants to one side.
A fantastic effort has failed, a repetition
In a repetitiousness of men and flies.

Yet the absence of the imagination had
Itself to be imagined. The great pond,
The plain sense of it, without reflections, leaves,
Mud, water like dirty glass, expressing silence

Of a sort, silence of a rat come out to see,
The great pond and its waste of the lilies, all this
Had to be imagined as an inevitable knowledge,
Required, as a necessity requires.[73]

A plain sense of things is Stevens's grandest "as if." "The plain sense," as Kermode observes, "is itself metaphorical: there is no escape from metaphor; univocity in language is no more than a dream." Hence, there is "the extraordinary effort required to imagine, to find language for, the plain sense of things and hold the language there for the briefest moment."[74] Vanishing points may show us that the greenhouse needs to be painted, may show us what necessity is, as if we did not truly know. "The Planet on the Table," a late poem, discusses the matter plainly. The more considerable a poet's ability to give words value, the more, inevitably, the poet will see only the poverty of words, which are poor oftentimes precisely because they are so rich, so full of metaphorical meanings of which they may not be emptied.[75] It is difficult to choose adjectives not only because the plainest language is itself metaphorical but because as part of our defense against the "vitality" of language we are always going to seek a figurative evasion of those evasions in which even the plainest language traps us.

Evasion leads to a loss of song, and Stevens is as much concerned with destructive attempts at evasion as any poet since Shakespeare. *King Lear* is a play concerned with the need for moral, psychological, epistemological, and, finally, linguistic movement toward recognition of "the thing itself." Lear tries to keep the name of king even when the word no longer identifies him. "Fetch me a better answer" is Lear's reply to truth. Hence, as the best abusers know, Lear is "apt/ To have his ear abused." The play climaxes with the "recognition" of identities that simultaneously bring one joy and pain.[76] Which is why, as Kent says, "To be acknowledged is . . . o'erpaid."[77] Kent, whose "occupation" is "to be plain," knows it is more than enough to say, "Fellow, I know thee." But Kent, needing no evasions for himself, forgets the reason for his disguise, exposing the plucky nature that got him banished. "I will teach the differences," he tells the fool, within earshot of Lear. Then the fool has to teach Kent a lesson about differences — namely, not to teach them with such ruthless indifference: "We'll set thee to school to an ant, to teach thee there's no laboring i' the' winter."[78] The fool discerns the differences between a part of labor and a part of pain, and understands, too, the impossibility of discerning them. In *King Lear* the ability to see "the difficult difference" where once there appeared to be none makes one at once too fit and unfit for life in this world.

Hamlet offers a corollary lesson. Throughout the play, Rosencrantz and Guildenstern serve as gibes to anyone who is set upon observing differences, an easy amusement of no consequence to anyone who is indifferent. Unlike Claudius, Hamlet and his mother can tell apart "the indifferent children of the earth."[79] Whereas Claudius, Polonius, and Laertes do not see ready differences, Hamlet, Horatio, and Gertrude see them well. Ophelia, like Hamlet, discerns more than she or language can articulate; unlike Hamlet, she cannot bear herself in a life devoted to the labor and pain of scrutinizing the differences between labor and pain, as between "slings and arrows." She cannot bear the precision of such laborious speaking. Hamlet can seem to amuse himself with it, but his "antic disposition" is a feigned indifference by a man to whom difference (and indifference) matter too much. Throughout the play, our ears — like Hamlet's — become too attuned to "the difficult difference." Hard sounds pass through sudden rightnesses; song becomes impossible in Hamlet's life. Finally, Hamlet cracks, as Horatio says. Next comes the awesome crack of a drum march announcing the entrance of Fortinbras. It is a musical entrance — into an unmusical world. Horatio offers hope for an orderly world that makes a world of differences: "And let me speak to th'yet unknowing world. . . ." And Fortinbras, ending the play, perceives the jarring nature of the incommensurate: "Such a sight as this/ Becomes the field, but here shows much amiss." Then he bids the soldiers shoot. This shooting enforces an awful truth, that in a world of inescapable faction, it is best to confront discord for what it is. It is good to care deeply, good to try to forge harmony, but best to know when the chord merely falsifies, for a well-intentioned forgery of illusive harmony is always a lurking danger. As Ophelia says to Gertrude: "O, you must wear your rue with a difference."[80]

Like Homer and Shakespeare, Stevens was a poet obsessed with "the difficult difference" between in-difference (identity) and indifference (disinterest in difference). He was a master of discerning "the difficult difference," but to come as close as one might possibly come to expressing "the plain sense" of a thing requires laborious speaking, a slow process of achieving plain, accurate speech that manages to account for difference even as it strives to record the strange relations with which life pierces us. This, for Stevens, is the labor of turning speech into song — a conception of poetic song that revises all previous aspiratons to music.

To move from speech to song is to make one's beginning meet one's end — immaculately. But there is no immaculation in Stevens, and this is part of his definition of poetic song. Whereas for Wordsworth song is a last and favorite aspiration, for Stevens song is merely a fiction — but it is a necessary fiction, the "fiction of an absolute." It is grounded in the "ancient cycle," in one's irreducible desire, if only for a moment, to sing:

> The poem refreshes life so that we share,
> For a moment, the first idea . . . It satisfies
> Belief in an immaculate beginning
>
> And sends us, winged by and unconscious will,
> To an immaculate end. We move between these points:
> From that ever-early candor to its late plural
>
> And the candor of them is the strong exhilaration
> Of what we feel from what we think, of thought
> Beating in the heart, as if blood newly came,
>
> An elixir, an excitation, a pure power.
> The poem, through candor, brings back a power again
> That gives a candid kind to everything.[81]

Stevens's theory of language meets his conception of *eros*; candor is the only power capable of completing the ancient cycle. And candor tells us that there is no immaculate end. There is only honest maculation — the thought of the imperfect within us beating in the heart. We may complete ourselves only by refusing the greater desire to impose completion. In Stevens, dissonance therefore flows into and, finally, out of resolution. Anything else would be a forfeit of any possibility of achieving song.

In Ben Jonson's wonderful description of the Brave infant of Seguntum, it is plainly noble to piece one's circle, brave to impose order in a disorderly world:

> Thou looking then about,
> Ere thou wert half got out,

> Wise Child, didst hastily return,
> And mad'st thy mother's womb thine urn.
> How summed a circle didst thou leave mankind
> Of deepest lore, could we the center find.

Jonson was invoking the "ennobling Harmony" of his day. He was happy to use a trope of rhetoric when it could celebrate the reality of a hyperbolic life:

> All offices were done
> By him, so ample, full, and round,
> In weight, in measure, number, sound,
> As though his age imperfect might appear,
> His life was of humanity the sphere.[82]

Shakespeare can seem as compelled by the circle of perfection as Jonson, but Shakespeare liked to expose it as a trope. Stevens saw that to impose an idea of perfection is to mar any aspect of perfection that might, in fact, be sought; it is to put a false and ugly end to the ancient cycle of desire. This is one lesson of *King Lear*. Lear's first speech expresses his wish to make an immaculate end: "'tis our fast intent/ To shake all cares and business from our age . . . while we/ Unburdened crawl toward death." By trying to make an immaculate end, he mars it, and in the process begins randomly to curse beginnings.

Stevens had his own "fast intent," but he knew that to impose an immaculate end is not immaculate. Stevens, like Shakespeare, embraced his earthy mold, seeing value in discovering the "luminous melody of proper sound." There is a celebration of sensuous sounds that is absent in Yeats, and a replacement of "vacillation" with what Stevens could call an "amassing":

> He had to choose. But it was not a choice
> Between excluding things. It was not a choice
>
> Between, but of. He chose to include the things
> That in each other are included, the whole,
> The complicate, amassing harmony.

To impose order, Stevens knew, is "a brave affair."

> But to impose is not
> To discover. To discover an order as of
> A season, to discover summer and know it,
>
> To discover winter and know it well, to find,
> Not to impose, not to have reasoned at all,
> Out of nothing to have come on major weather,
>
> It is possible, possible, possible. It must
> Be possible. It must be that in time
> The real will from its crude compoundings come,
>
> Seeming, at first, a beat disgorged, unlike,
> Warmed by a desperate milk. To find the real,
> To be stripped of every fiction except one,
>
> The fiction of an absolute — Angel,
> Be silent in your luminous cloud and hear
> The luminous melody of proper sound.[83]

Early in his career Stevens saw that the possibility of song is rooted in myth of one's beginning. And "There was a myth before the myth began." "Apotheosis is not the origin of the major man." The "major man" may know himself only in major weather, may know himself, may become a singer, only by writing the poems of his climate. One is born into a muddy world of sounds, and one may make an end only by embracing them. It is therefore a powerful moment for a poet when it is possible to renounce the transcendental mythology of a heavenly music that excludes the poet and confidently tell an Angel to be silent and listen to the poet's supreme fiction — when the Angel becomes a fiction subservient to the poet's absolute fiction, and the "proper sound" of the poet becomes the only reality.

The circularity of Stevens's musical speculations throughout his career declares both his experience of the ancient cycle and his conception of the possibility of achieving song. The

trope of song is a wish for transcendence as it meets a determination to practice seeing "things as they are":

> A tune beyond us as we are,
> Yet nothing changed by the blue guitar;
>
> Ourselves in the tune as if in space,
> Yet nothing changed, except the place
>
> Of things as they are and only the place
> As you play them, on the blue guitar,
>
> Placed, so, beyond the compass of change,
> Perceived in a final atmosphere;
>
> For a moment final. . . .[84]

A poet who wishes to sing tries to create moments that seem
for a moment final, when being is "momentously" declared —
or "placed." But when one identifies it, thinking it final, one
realizes it is only a moment. What had seemed momentous is
suddenly only momentary. And one is sent back to the question of origin: "Where/ Do I begin and end?/ And where,/ As
I strum the thing, do I pick up/ That which momentously
declares/ Itself not to be I and yet/ Must be." A tune beyond
us as we are is *beyond* us precisely because it is "beyond the
compass of change." But things will change, and this is
Stevens's point. Things will change, but the blue guitar must
change nothing. It must perceive in a final atmosphere, real-
izing that anything perceived in a final atmosphere is only for
a moment final.

In the end, there is no final moment, no immaculate end —
except death. Death is the vital, arrogant, fatal, dominant X;
it is the only vanishing point that is final. It brings completion, and it marks the end of one's ability to complete oneself.
Death silences one, closing the ancient musical circle of desire described by Socrates. But as much as one aspires to
completion, so one aspires not to be silenced.

What distinguishes Stevens's conception of poetic song, along with its rejection of falsifying by chords, is its refusal to retreat to any aspiration toward silence. What distinguishes Stevens from his fellow moderns — as from his romantic precursors — is his refusal to be suspicious of sounds. At the same time, he is suspicious of any theoretical (speculative) trust in a perfect music, whether it originates outside oneself or from within. Unlike Milton and unlike Shelley, Stevens saw clashing as the only possible singing. The only possible music, finally, is the music of speech, with all of its dirty employment:

> If the poetry of X was music,
> So that it came to him of its own,
> Without understanding, out of the wall
>
> Or in the ceiling, in sounds not chosen,
> Or chosen quickly, in a freedom
> That was their element, we should not know
>
> That X is an obstruction, a man
> Too exactly himself, and that there are words
> Better without an author, without a poet,
>
> Or having a separate author, a different poet,
> An accretion from ourselves, intelligent
> Beyond intelligence, an artificial man
>
> At a distance, a secondary expositor,
> A being of sound, whom one does not approach
> Through any exaggeration. From him, we collect.
>
> Tell X that speech is not dirty silence
> Clarified. It is silence made still dirtier.
> It is more than an imitation for the ear.[85]

If only Michel Foucault were correct, if only there were no author, then poetry might conceivably be immaculate. Stevens knew that the romantics were wrong, that authors themselves are the obstacle to song — especially the unity of the author's consciousness to the point where the author is "too exactly himself." The title of this poem is "The Creations of Sound" (not "The Creation of Sounds"). The point is not that there are different sounds but that there are different ways to create them. Stevens insists on choice; the worst sounds are "sounds not chosen." This point is not something the romantics, or Yeats, ever considered. Sounds chosen "too exactly" are destructive, for by putting his obstinate self before the stubborness of sounds, X becomes an obstruction to what must be a "being of sound." For Stevens, this must be at once an objective and subjective genitive.

As we have seen, Stevens's speculative conception of speech, song, and silence brings about a new conception of poetic song. Whereas others had still hoped to make immaculate ends, Stevens saw the unremitting need for laborious speaking, the ennobling one does while settling on the solid ground. His dedication to settling is the basis of his refusal to ennoble silence in answer to the loss of "ennobling Harmony." There is, for Stevens, no song except earthly song. Earthly song is speech. And speech is not dirty silence clarified but silence made still dirtier.

Speech, Silence, Song

To join an immaculate beginning and an immaculate end is the chief part of any aspiration to a condition of music. But our beginning is not immaculate, and one cannot aspire to song without prizing the laborious middle of things:

> An unaffected man in a negative light
> Could not have borne his labor nor have died
> Sighing that he should leave the banjo's twang.[1]

Stevens brings us to, and helps us to see, a number of conclusions.

Modernism is widely distinguished by an understanding that there is no "ennobling Harmony," but modern aspirations to song are so strong they become marked by a desire to retreat to immaculation. Silence replaces the denuded fiction of transcendent harmony. Consider, for example, a remarkable contemporary of Stevens, Arnold Schoenberg. "Schoenberg once ironically mentioned," as Theodor Adorno remarks, "that musical theory is always concerned only with the beginning and the end and never with what comes between, namely, with the music itself."[2] As another remarkable contemporary of Stevens, Ludwig Wittgenstein, wrote: "what can be said at all can be said clearly, and what we cannot talk about we must pass over in silence." Wittgenstein was attempting to sum up "the whole sense of" his *Tractatus Logico-Philosophicus* in his preface, which iterates the last sentence of the work, the only one published in his lifetime: "What we cannot speak about we must pass over in silence."[3] As radically as Wittgenstein developed Western metaphysics and epistemology, this inclination to silence is not new. As Edward Rothstein observes in his study of the relationship between music and mathematics, when the Greeks "discovered that numbers exist which are neither integers nor ratios of integers — numbers which confounded all their notions of harmony and rationality — they were so horrified that the discovery was kept secret. *Alogon* — the unutterable — these numbers were called." The Greek philosopher Proclus related that "those who brought these numbers out of hiding perished in a shipwreck: 'For the unutterable and the formless must needs be concealed.'"[4]

An immaculate end can be achieved only by uttering and forming the unutterable and formless, only, that is, by dealing resourcefully with the middle, as in Sonata form. In theory, one may think about excluding or concealing the middle — abandoning sound, passing things over in silence. But to do this is to abandon life, and art. Some paths, as Heinrich Schenker observed, "must be traversed." But the traversing can damage the art, as Schoenberg suggests when writing not about the theory of harmony but about his *Theory of Harmony*: "My *Theory of Harmony* is obviously much too long. Once its author is out of the way — the living obstacle to judicious cutting — three quarters of the text must then surely go by the board."[5]

Both life and art, whether for a Renaissance Christian or a modern aesthete, are obstacles to an immaculate end.

Schoenberg knew that the closer he got to perfect form the more he would approach silence. "Mature music," writes Adorno in his essay on Schoenberg,

> becomes suspicious of real sound as such.... [T]he end of musical interpretation becomes conceivable. The silent, imaginative reading of music could render actual playing as superfluous as, for instance, speaking is made by the reading of written material; such a practice could at the same time save music from the abuse inflicted upon the compositional content by virtually every performance today.[6]

But although the stubbornness of sounds may recommend the theoretical refuge of silence, in practice — and so, too, in theory — concealment becomes an unacceptable resolution.

In Schoenberg's 12-tone theory, the desire for theoretical perfection confronts the practical need to minimize imperfections. One not only chooses sounds; one embraces their flaws and stubbornness. One must use every tone before repeating any one. Schoenberg could not allow the listener to be an "unaffected man." "It is precisely because of its seriousness, richness and integrity," as Adorno writes, "that his music arouses resentment. The more it gives its listeners, the less it offers them." As Adorno explains, "It requires the listener spontaneously to compose its inner movement and demands of him not mere contemplation but praxis. In this, however, Schoenberg blasphemes against the expectation, cherished despite all idealistic assurances to the contrary, that music will present the comfortable listener with a series of pleasurable sensations."[7] Shakespeare, similarly, knew how to make an audience discomforted by its comfort; as we saw in examining *Merchant*, he makes his audience compose the imagistic patterns of his plays, forcing them in the process to recompose their expectations. Shakespeare knew that the only way truly to affect people is to please them in a manner contrary to the one in which they are used to being unaffected. As any expert on the ancient cycle knows, one can only want more by possessing less.

"The imperfect is our paradise," and a modern composer such as Schoenberg, like a modern poet such as Stevens, must compose the songs of his climate, taking delight in the bitterness of silence made still dirtier. In the end, there is no resting in the fictions of pure theory; pure theory must reject itself. For there can be no resting in concealment, no resting in the fiction of sounds clarified:

> Say even that this complete simplicity
> Stripped one of all one's torments, concealed
> The evilly compounded, vital I
> And made it fresh in a world of white,
> A world of clear water, brilliant-edged,
> Still one would want more, one would need more,
> More than a world of white and snowy scents.
>
> III
>
> There would still remain the never-resting mind,
> So that one would want to escape, come back
> To what had been so long composed.[8]

One must escape from evasive fictions of simplicity, returning to the beginning and middle, "what had been so long composed." Stevens's conception of *eros* exceeds the Platonic conception by maintaining the ancient cycle of desire but rejecting the fiction of an immaculate end. There can be no perfection of one's circle — only the endless process of ennobling and correction.

Schoenberg, like Stevens, knows he must have a theoretical practice. His *Theory of Harmony* attempts "not to set up new eternal laws. If I should succeed in teaching the pupil the handicraft of our art as completely as a carpenter can teach his," he writes, "then I shall be satisfied. And I would be proud if . . . I could say: 'I have *taken* from composition pupils a bad *aesthetics* and have *given* them in return a good *course in handicraft*." The musical theoretician, Schoenberg tells us, must be "compelled by [his] errors." What is most important, he writes, "I have never tried to talk my pupils into believing me infallible — only a 'Gesangsprofessor' (professor of singing) finds that necessary."[9] It is necessary, goes the joke, because singers are fatuous. But then there is the truth that they have to be, the requirements of singing being what they are. Schoenberg's preludial jest at the expense of singers reveals that the scruple of a theoretician exalts the theoretician above an actual singer. But where the ability to assert perfection is concerned, the theoretician cannot match the singer. The modern singer, like all singers of all times, must believe in his or her authority — must have *ethos* — if nothing else.

Despite the threat to their authority brought by the failure of romanticism, neither the modern theorist nor the modern singer could be silent. Singers cannot acknowledge the shame of their imperfection; conversely, theoreticians' pursuit of their errors diminishes — by ennobling — their shame. As Adorno writes, Schoenberg's "warm, free, sonorous voice was untroubled by the fear of singing which is burned into the civilized mind and which makes the pseudo-nonchalance of the professional singer all the more distressing."[10]

Yeats and Stevens are the last great singers of the English language, but both scrutinize the aspiration to song; both see an immaculate end as an unachievable musical condition about which one must speak. "Speech after long silence; it is right," writes Yeats. And the subject of such speech? Art and song. It is right

> That we descant and yet again descant
> Upon the supreme theme of Art and Song:
> Bodily decrepitude is wisdom; young
> We loved each other and were ignorant.

To turn the decrepitude of life into the clean wisdom of art one must, as Aristotle concluded, take Platonic dialectic through a new course.

Plot involves *mimesis*, and is achieved by the art of dialectic. One must design — arbitrarily, but in accordance with what is probable — a beginning, a middle, and an end. We broach here the crucial concerns of the art of plot. One must begin in the middle of things. A plot must begin *in medias res*, offering a beginning full of clashing tensions that the middle develops and the end resolves. An imitation of life, narrative unfolds in time. And inevitable clashing makes the life and work of a speculative poet even more full of tensions, even more glaringly identified with a discordant middle. In the end, created resemblances must give way to created vanishing points.

A poet's aspiration to song pits a Platonic belief in the "ancient cycle" of eros against an Aristotelian belief in the powers of *praxis*; it pits Plato's "true musician" against Sidney's "little maker." As Stevens shows us, the Aristotelian notion of narrative completion clashes with any speculative desire for an immaculate end — for the transcendent perfection of harmonious music or undiscording silence. Speculative aspiration rejects the practical (Aristotelian) use of dialectic, clinging instead to a Platonic aspiration for something more than *mimetic*. The tensions between life and art comprise the differences between Aristotelian *praxis* and Platonic speculation: between plot and harmony, between the noisy intonations of earthly music and the immaculation of transcendent song. It is by embracing such tensions, rather than evading them that speculative poets aspire to sing their "fuller" tunes.

Aristotelian dialectic is a process of patching middles, a process of reconciling beginnings and ends.[11] The speculative aspiration toward a loud ennobling harmony or a fuller tune, whether in Milton or Dickinson, is an aspiration toward a transcendent end of dialectic. If a tune can be "fuller," it is not yet full — and especially if a poet needs to invoke an outside power that "makes prose song" — whether that power is a divine muse or an ennobling fiction. One is not yet "part both of the choir, and song," where one "receives, and gives addition," to use John Donne's wonderful phrases in *The Anniversaries*. "'Tis such a full, and such a filling good." This, for Donne, is what it is, or would be, to get up to the "watchtower" and "see things despoiled of fallacies," when one "shalt not peep through lattices of eyes,/ Nor hear through labyrinths of ears, nor learn/ By circuit, or collections to discern." Rather, "in heaven thou straight know'st all, concerning it,/ And what concerns it not, shalt straight forget." One will forget disagreeables, will forget the effort to achieve a plain sense of things as well as the impulse to evade, will forget the ancient cycle of desire, the burden and shame of trying to sing. One will forget beginning and middle — and will not experience the end as an end, but as a beginning of "endless rest." As Donne writes in "La Corona": "The ends crown our works, but thou crown'st our ends,/ For, at our end begins our endless rest."[12] One will forget, as in Donne, the tension between harmony and plot (between God's song and God's plan), or, as in Yeats, the vacillation between one's song and one's life:

> *The Soul*. Seek out reality, leave things that seem.
> *The Heart*. What, be a singer born and lack a theme?
> *The Soul*. Isaiah's coal, what more can man desire?[13]

A full tune will be a full forgetting of *eros* itself. Only amnesia can make the end immaculate.

This insight is not peculiar to modernism. It was regnant in the Renaissance, when some people tried to imitate an immaculate end before the end. According to Ben Jonson, who was singularly able to imitate immaculation, "[T]he just canon of [Master Vincent Corbet's] life" was immaculate:

> A life that knew nor noise, nor strife:
> But was by sweetening so his will,
> All order, and disposure, still.
> His mind as pure, and neatly kept,
> As were his nurseries; and swept
> So of uncleanness. . . .[14]

Jonson had a fond aspiration to wrest from the trope, by urbane employment, a real truth therein. As a poet, if not as a man, he could conduct any happening, with *sprezzatura*, to a neat end. But to do this, to stay clean, one must refuse immersion in *eros* and keep a courtly distance from life. To love is to get dirty, for "Love has pitched his mansion in/ The place of excrement." This is true, as Yeats knew, of the purest form of *eros*. The movement from love to *eros*, from concern for the body to concern for the soul, brings one, much in the manner of Donne in "The Ecstasy," not out of the body as much as back down to it: "Else a great prince in prison lies." One must live, and act; there can be no ennobling without settling on the solid ground.

Noise and strife are enemies of art, dirty aspects of life, countenances of time. An aspiration toward silence, as in Shelley, marks a reluctance to continue in a world of spiritual noise and bodily strife, a wish to have the chance to make a refusal to begin. As the Brave Infant of Seguntum would have known, one may attune one's beginning and one's end only by not beginning, thus thwarting time.

Not only must a poet serve the two masters of plot and song; a poet must also contend with the problem that harmony itself presents. One seeks silence, as the romantics came to know, because sound reminds us of time, ruining the inward purity the mind seeks. Harmony itself — when audible — is a form of discord. In Bach, as Adorno writes, "the stringency of the polyphony distracts attention from the *continuo* schema with which it operates." In Schoenberg, "stringency ultimately makes all chord schemas and all facades superfluous: his is music of the intellectual ear."[15]

It is the nature of harmony to reveal discord as time passes. The longer one listens, the more harmony appears to be discordant. "The fundamental tone and the fifth — the C and G — have a very close consonant relation, but there is also a tension between them," as Rothstein observes. "For if we create a string vibrating with a fundamental of G, its *own* strongest overtones do not overlap closely with the overtones of C. . . ."[16]

"It is the chord that falsifies," writes Stevens. Hence, poetry may exceed music, but only when one is free of the fiction of the perfection of song. The modern ennobling of silence is a secular version of the ennobling of amnesia Renaissance Christians conceived as marking the transition from life and art to an immaculate, endless rest. It is for this reason Stevens demands "the delicatest ear of the mind" — but not at the expense of a sensual ear. Stevens could not accept the ennobling harmony of Emerson, or the ignobling regret of Nietzsche.

Silence is preferable to speech, according to Emerson, because speech (or discourse) is shameful:

> Good as is discourse, silence is better, and shames it. The length of the discourse indicates the distance of thought betwixt the speaker and the hearer. If they were at a perfect understanding in any part, no words would be necessary thereon. If at one in all parts, no words would be suffered.[17]

Such distance is greatest when the speaker avoids all acknowledgment of the speaker's own shame. For the important distance, as Stevens knew, is not between speaker and audience but between the speaker and self — between the would-be singer and what could become a candid aspiration to song.

Song, according to Nietzsche in his 1886 preface to *The Birth of Tragedy*, is better than silence, but silence, he acquiesces, is preferable to speech:

> People would hint suspiciously that there was a sort of maenadic soul in this book, stammering out laborious, arbitrary phrases in an alien tongue — as though the speaker were not quite sure himself whether he preferred speech to silence. And, indeed, this 'new soul' should have *sung*, not spoken.[18]

Laborious, arbitrary, alien. Antithetical in three ways to the romantic requirements. The "awful burthen" is difficult to shrug off, whatever one's will to power. In offering this opinion of his 1872 work on the Apollonian and Dionysian spirits in his 1886 preface, Nietzsche acknowledges a distance he regrets, a shame he still feels. Strife is noisy. "Man speaks," as Martin Heidegger put it.[19] But wishes to sing.

The world "has already grown so destitute, it can no longer discern the default of God as a default," writes Heidegger. "The word for abyss — *Abgrund* — originally means the soil and ground towards which, because it is undermost, a thing tends downward. But in what follows we shall think of the *Ab-* as the complete absence of the ground."[20] Stevens does muse that it would be best to speak "without speech,/ The loftiest syllables among loftiest things." It would be best if the world were calm, if everything were in the silent stasis of its being. Silence would be better than speech, better than sound. But, just as the world is made of things, we are made out of words; indeed, "Life consists/ Of propositions about life."[21] Why is it we never find Stevens expressing Nietzsche's regret? Not because Stevens is one of the last and most stubborn of logocentrists, but because his bold unwillingness to replace the shame of speech with the ignobling harmony of silence accompanies his unwillingness to replace the enigma of presence with the ennobling harmony of absence.

Nietzsche feels frustration in his refusals to settle on the solid ground. This frustration is partly a manifestation of an unwillingness to acknowledge the inability of philosophical theory to help one to escape the ancient cycle. This is also true of Paul Valéry. Nietzsche and Valéry attacked received wisdom, scrutinized facile fictions, antagonized ennobling harmonies, but neither could keep from invoking the ennobling harmony of silence when the ennobling harmony of song appeared illusory. Valéry believed that pure poetry would be music and that pure music would be silence:

> The aim, then, is to create the kind of silence to which the *beautiful* responds. Or the pure line of verse, or the luminous idea . . . Then the line seems to be born of itself, born of

necessity — which is precisely my state — and finds that it is memory.[22]

Stevens learned a good deal from Valéry, but he thought to ground his luminous ideas in necessity. Speech, says Stevens, is all we have, and it reveals the effect of the limitation of human perception upon the trajectory of human desire. Clouds are still pedagogues, and we are still mimics, but speech is "more than mimesis for the ear" — precisely because it is less than purely mimetic:

> We are the mimics. Clouds are pedagogues
> The air is not a mirror but bare board,
> Coulisse bright-dark, tragic chiaroscuro
>
> And cosmic color of the rose, in which
> Abysmal instruments make sounds like pips
> Of the sweeping meanings that we add to them.[23]

Speech is not an imitation for the ear. Nor is silence its transcendent *telos*. There are, moreover, only evasive approaches to silence, attempts to conceal the gloriously abysmal nature of our instruments.

Stevens was writing about the old relationships, between sight and sound, light and song. In "The Plain Sense of Things," Stevens rejects the conceptions of both mind as mirror and mind as pure lamp; he links these rejections to a greater need to disavow the ignobling fiction of clarified silence. The dirty reflections of Stevens's "great pond" express only "silence/Of a sort, silence of a rat come out to see." This rat is a supreme artist, a being of the solid ground that, in Woolf's phrase, "consumes all impediments."

The absence of dirty reflections, much like the presence of transcendent ones, may only be imagined. What remains is the necessity of imagining — with an abysmal instrument that seems to be both as reflective as a mirror and as luminous as a lamp — the absence of reflections, and the absence of the

sweeping mimetic meanings we add to sounds. Stevens sees
that there can be no "awaiting espousal to the sound of right
joining, a music of ideas . . . The final relation, the marriage
of the rest." Stevens is not suspicious of sounds themselves,
but he does tell us they are flawed and stubborn, that they
burden us with time, recording our settling on solid ground,
to speech, to silence made still dirtier.

Wittgenstein conceived time as a muddle experienced as a
problem. The experience of hearing is an emphatic reminder
of the problem of time. The eye, in contrast, can seem to resolve it — especially the mind's eye. The eye is the noblest
sense, nobler than the ear because vision is instantaneous,
whereas hearing is slow. The flashing speed of light shames
the lumbering speed of sound. During the Renaissance, as perhaps also today, one might look at a painting and discern its
plot at once. There once was, but no longer is, an earthly *synopsis* for the ear. The problem is expressed so well by Milton.

Milton's God is a musician who takes his sweet time to
tune the world. Earthly time (the middle of God's plot) is subject to divine time (the beginning and end of God's plot). Earthly
(practical) music must therefore be subjected to God's (speculative) music. So, too, for George Herbert, as in "Deniall":

> O cheer and tune my heartlesse breast,
> Deferre no time;
> That so thy favours granting my request,
> They and my minde may chime,
> And mend my rhyme.

The deeply speculative Renaissance conviction that the problem of time is a good thing — making for better music — gave
Herbert many moving lines, as in "The Temper":

> Yet take thy way; for sure thy way is best:
> Stretch or contract me, thy poore debter:

> This is but tuning of my breast,
>> To make the musick better.

Herbert believed that his discordant middle was the glory of God's music.

In the speculative cosmology of poets such as Herbert and Milton, however, a concern for plot clashes with the speculative desire for the transcendent perfection of harmonious music. As we have seen, there is tension between the desire to sing and devotion to join God's better music. Although God is the only being capable of making an immaculate end, Herbert thought to mend his own ways (as both man and poet). In the end, however, Herbert deferred to God's ennobling harmony, as in "The Thanksgiving":

> For thy predestination I'le contrive,
>> That three yeares hence, if I survive,
> I'le build a spittle, or mend common wayes,
>> But mend mine own without delayes.
> Then I will use the works of thy creation,
>> As if I us'd them but for fashion.
> The world and I will quarrell: and the yeare
>> Shall not perceive, that I am here.
> My musick shall finde thee, and ev'ry string
>> Shall have his attribute to sing;
> That all together may accord in thee,
>> And prove one God, one harmonie.

Herbert can quarrel with the world, contemplating perfection of art and life. But as "The Holdfast" states, "We must confess that nothing is our own." Herbert cannot mend his delay. The reattuning is for God to accomplish:

> If thou shalt give me wit, it shall appeare,
>> If thou hast giv'n it me, 'tis here.[24]

The radical paradox of Christian life puts a Protestant poet who aspires to sing God's "one harmonie" in a predicament:

it is perhaps better to wait. Free of this radical Christian paradox, as the romantics were, one confronts an "awful burthen": gone is the future of a promised *synopsis* for the ear: song is no longer made sweeter as one is waiting. Time destroys music.

"The default of God," as Heidegger wrote, "means that no god any longer gathers men and things unto himself. . . ." And it is hard for human beings to roll the universe into one ball. "Not only is there no guarantee of the temporal immortality of the human soul," Wittgenstein writes. What is more important, "The solution of the riddle of life in space and time lies *outside* space and time."[25]

Whether in an age when the only possibility is a leap of faith, or in an age of disbelief, once there is no ennobling harmony, no available *synopsis* for the ear, one has vigorously to endeavor to defeat time — head on, in temporal terms. And there are two ways to do this: to slow the mind to a halt, to an eternal moment; or to speed up the mind to the point where it may "catch from" an "Irrational moment its unreasoning." The romantics think to slow speech and hearing to a triumphant halt, to the perfection of stasis achieved by vision. Hearing is slow, but never slow enough for the romantics; it keeps up too well with the passing sounds of a world too much with us. Hearing is too slow, in contrast, for Stevens; it cannot keep up with either reality or the imagination.

In any age, one's conceptions of speech, song, and silence depend on one's conception of time. Waiting can lead to the good musical end of time in both Shakespeare and Milton. Shakespeare offers us in *King Lear* a patient character who thought that silence was best. Cordelia can wait, for "Time shall unfold what plighted cunning hides." She is one character who early recognizes things as they are. Kent is another. Unlike Kent, Cordelia knows also that language falsifies and that a plain sense of things disheartens men (by revealing that the great structure has become a minor house). Hence,

Cordelia chooses to say nothing. For Cordelia, moreover, saying nothing is not a refusal to begin. It is an insistence upon enduring. Cordelia knows she is in the middle of things — no play gets *in medias res* as quickly as *King Lear*. So much in the middle, she knows, nothing save time itself can make an immaculate end.

Cordelia lives in a fictive world created by Shakespeare, a fictive world based in temporal and theological time and made for a world that appreciated the nice unfolding of theatrical, as well as temporal and theological, time. In this world, not only is Father Time an eater of things (*tempus edax rerum*); truth is also the daughter of time (*veritas filia temporis*).[26] There is a compelling contrast between the silent suffering of Cordelia and the grandiloquent power of Shakespeare's plot. Unlike Herbert, Shakespeare could play God, manipulate time, reveal truth. By creating vanishing points of resemblance, Shakespeare could make dramatic time the father of theological truths. In time, he could turn things happy, or at least to order, and hence to good. For all of these reasons, as bad as things might be, the character of Cordelia believes that time will make her happy; and, in its way, it does.

As both a modern poet and a diligent actuary, Stevens could not wait for a good end of time. By Stevens's era, time has become a "hooded enemy." It is "The inimical music." It will not unfold truth, and it will not make one happy:

> Felicity, ah! Time is the hooded enemy,
> The inimical music, the enchantered space
> In which the enchanted preludes have their place.

Stevens refuses the notion that "The solution of the riddle of life in space and time lies *outside* space and time." Any evasion of the problem of time is as much an enemy as time is:

> It is time that beats in the breast and it is time
> That batters against the mind, silent and proud,
> The mind that knows it is destroyed by time.[27]

For Stevens, time does not reveal truth; the mind does. But it may do so only in time. And time batters and destroys the mind. It is the greatest desire of the mind to be silent and proud. But time beats and batters it. The measure of our moments, time marks our strife, making a plot of our movement toward the final, fatal dominant X. Time makes us notice moments in a way that forces us to mark them, rather than to experience them as ends in themselves, instances of gemlike flame, success in life. And when we mark our moments, making a plot of them, or theories about them, they become merely moments.

Pater, experiencing moments as ends in themselves, endeavored to put a good modern end to time, and hence to the shameful tension between speculation and practice. As Pater writes, "Not the fruit of experience, but experience itself, is the end." Anti-Aristotelian, disinterested in the fruit of *praxis*, Pater is nevertheless not Platonic, for Pater sees Socratic dialectic, the putting off of being until the completion of a cosmic circle, as nonsense — and not gorgeous. There must be something more than "enchanted preludes." In a moment, thought Pater, one's beginning and one's end must cohere. Pater saw no need to wait for an end of moments, no need to repair to theory, but rather continuous moments of opportunity:

> Not to discriminate every moment some passionate attitude in those about us, and in the very brilliancy of their gifts some tragic dividing of forces on their ways is, on this short day of frost and sun, to sleep before evening. With this sense of the splendour of our experience and of its awful brevity, gathering all we are into one desperate effort to see and touch, we shall hardly have time to make theories about the things we see and touch.[28]

We see in Pater the importance of the etymology of *theory*. We hardly have time to make theories; we have only time enough to look at things. To go to sleep before evening is to be like dry birds fluttering in blue leaves, as in the subtitle of the last section of Stevens's "The Pure Good of Theory." Here Stevens combines a Paternian notion of splendor with his own dedication to turning the "devastations" of the mind into "divertisments." The end of the poem speaks of the need to be

> Touched suddenly by the universal flare
> For a moment, a moment in which we read and repeat
> The eloquences of light's faculties.[29]

Stevens differs from Pater in his battle with time, in his requirement that in such a moment we must not only "read" but also "repeat." In Stevens's poetry, a Paternian hunger for moments converges with a Platonic manner of deferring momentous declarations of being. There is necessary value in "enchanted preludes." Stevens is "merely a shadow hunched/ Above the arrowy, still strings,/ The maker of a thing yet to be made." He can neither wait for the good end of time nor be satisfied with a life of moments. He must make his own end — and knows he must not malform it.

Some theories, such as speculative music, will have a claim on this act of making. "The Pure Good of Theory" not only makes poetic use of philosophy; it addresses the specific role Pater had in mind for philosophy, as well as its relation to any aspiration toward song:

> What we have to do is to be for ever curiously testing new opinions and courting new impressions, never acquiescing in a facile orthodoxy, of Comte, or of Hegel, or of our own. Philosophical theories or ideas, as points of view, instruments of criticism, may help us to gather up what might otherwise pass unregarded by us. "Philosophy is the microscope of thought." The theory or idea or system which requires of us the sacrifice of any part of this experience, in consideration of some interest into which we cannot enter, or some abstract theory we have not identified with ourselves, or of what is only conventional, has no real claim upon us.[30]

Stevens excels at speculation, in rendering theories of what we see and touch, but he also sees the practical value — neglected by Plato's speculative account of the ancient cycle — of seeing and touching. "No theory, not even that which is true, is safe from perversion into delusion once it has renounced a spontaneous relation to the object," as Adorno writes.[31] A poet must be, as Stevens urges, a severe master harassing his craft to supply the "more urgent proof that the theory/ Of poetry is the theory of life/ As it is, in the intricate evasions of as. . . ."

Symbolism offers "As" as a means to transcend the epistemological limitations put upon us by time. But Yeats and Stevens both came to see that it cannot. "All could be known or shone/ If Time were but gone." So says crazy Jane. But time is never gone, and there is better wisdom, Yeats writes, "learned in bodily lowliness."[32] Symbolism offers a silent *synopsis* for the eye. In Yeats, however, noisy vacillation is the only constancy, for symbolism must confront the musical component of the body in the dance. And this is a component that changes — and embraces change — rhythmically, melodically, in time and space.

Yeats was rooted in "[a]n oral culture" that "commit[ted] itself to the human situation in a sense that Symbolism tries to evade." "Unless it somehow touched and stirred that deep, primitive sense of life," high art "was bound to be meagre, superficial." As Donoghue puts it, Yeats was part of a culture that "assume[d] the integrity of the Person and the validity of temporal life," and which had "no interest in the inscrutable silence of Symbolism."[33]

Modern humanity, not God, is responsible for revelations. And if we cannot sing, we have to speak, to make propositions about temporal life, which we reveal — in an endless process — always to be fictive, but never untrue. As Yeats writes in "Those Dancing Days are Gone":

> I thought it out this very day,
> Noon upon the clock,
> A man may put pretence away
> Who leans upon a stick,
> May sing, and sing until he drop,
> Whether to maid or hag:
> *I carry the sun in a golden cup,*
> *The moon in a silver bag.*

In Yeats there is always pretence; in Stevens, intricate evasion. And they know it. But for both, time at once batters the motive for metaphor and quickens the aspiration to song.

Stevens urged that poetry had to exceed music precisely in its ability to ennoble its chattering. John Cage had the idea to join an immaculate beginning to an immaculate end by composing silence for a measured number of minutes and seconds. In "4'33," the abandonment of music impels an audience to listen to silence. And while we might uphold, and even revel in, this ennobling of silence, the silence is sure to remind us of the terms against which it is wrought. It is likely to distract us into thought, whether mundane or deep: the need to do one's laundry, or the need to contemplate one's beginning and end. The silence is framed by life, and so it becomes life: ushers, squeaky theater seats, bouffant hair, aftershave lotions. It reminds us that we are in the middle of noise and strife — something laborious, arbitrary, alien. One might even have the disruptive thought of wishing to listen more comfortably at home — where one used to hear, on vinyl, the crackle of *mimesis*, where one may now think about the absence of that crackle offered by a CD. Cage's composition may, if all goes well, keep us from counting time, but he must, alas, measure the duration of his imposition — "4'33." A live performance of "4'33" is an enlightening event. Cage, like Stevens, is after "more than an imitation for the ear."[34] Cage's palpable aspiration to silence makes us aware not of the absence of sound but of sound itself. Sound reminds us of our imperfection — especially the sound of dirty silence in the process of being clarified. A listener will not be unaffected. Silence offers no refuge. Indeed, it is when he was deaf that Beethoven composed his dirtiest music.

George Steiner writes that "music is, indeed, time made free of temporality."[35] It is not, as we have seen. The impossibility of freeing time of its temporality is a chief problem facing anyone who aspires to a condition of song — composers, philosophers, and poets alike.

The attempt to sing, Hart Crane knew as well as anyone, is an attempt to "condense eternity." Crane could not espouse the belief in toil that sustained Yeats for so many years:

> O harp and alter, of the fury fused,
> (How could mere toil align thy choiring strings!)

Crane saw, both in "The Bridge" and "Voyages," the world divided into two kinds of music, and he saw himself, like so many before him, on the wrong side of that great divide. The Brooklyn Bridge has an "[u]nfractioned idiom":

> Again the traffic lights that skim thy swift
> Unfractioned idiom, immaculate sigh of stars,
> Beading thy path — condense eternity:
> And we have seen night lifted in thine arms.

Whereas the sky — "the dividing and indifferent blue" — is the source of much poetic attention, it is the sea, of course, that concerns Crane. Listening to all of its sounds, Crane writes that the sea, unlike the poet, provides a "great wink of eternity":

> Take this Sea, whose diapason knells
> On scrolls of silver snowy sentences,
> The sceptered terror of whose sessions rends
> As her demeanors motion well or ill. . . .

Like Milton, Crane is obsessed with the unifying aspect of the diapason. Unlike Milton, Crane reports that he has heard it, and been rent by its power:

> and where death, if shed,
> Presumes no carnage, but this single change, —
> Upon the steep floor flung from dawn to dawn
> The silken skilled transmemberment of song;
> Permit me voyage, love, into your hands . . .[36]

Crane obtained what he asks for here: the sea subsumes every earthly sound into its music, including the sounds of the rent poet. We return, again, as did Milton in *Lycidas*, to the exemplary fate of Orpheus, "Whom Universal nature did lament,/ When by the rout that made the hideous roar,/ His gory visage down the stream was sent. . . ."

In Crane we see a solemn modern example of a speculative musical poetic conceived so individually and strictly as to bring the poet the only appropriate means for him to complete the music not only of his art but of his life. The verse bears the lineaments of so much shame: there is no possibility even of "immaculate sighs." Crane could succumb to death, as to the difficult terms of life, only by seeing them in the speculative musical terms of the ancient cycle.

A great interpreter of nature, Plato was remarkable to link the nature of desire to an aspiration to a condition of music, and to link the ancient cycle of *eros* to speculative rather than Sophistic dialectic. While the worst have ignored it, the best theorists of our time have tried to reconceive the ancient cycle, finding joy in the fragmentation of the muses. For Roland Barthes, to take one example, speculative concerns are subsumed under practical ones: the fragmentation of human language is a "*Babel heureuse*," the fiction of "*le texte de plaisir*" that is the basis of the ennobling harmony of "*le plaisir du texte.*" The pleasure is rhetorical, but it is said to lead to the more nearly speculative "*possibilité d'une dialectique du désire, d'une imprévision de la jouissance: que les jeux ne soient pas faits, qu'il y ait un jeu.*"[37] With no solid ground to which to settle, the abyss, it is suggested, becomes a linguistic playground. But even for us postmoderns, there is much reason to go the way of Yeats, to keep a fascination with what is difficult. And to go the way of Stevens, joining all pleasures of the text to the labor of settling on the solid ground.

One recent revision of Plato's ancient cycle, advanced by Derrida, involves succumbing to the death of the letter, and to the further deaths of full speech, of presence, of the self.[38] Derrida refuses as a fiction the idea that we may ever truly begin. Hence we need never desire to make an immaculate end. Against our death by the letter, Derrida, like Barthes, asserts the joy we may take in the freeplay of signifiers, the speaking middle into which, by language, we are arbitrarily positioned. Platonic *eros*, appears, from this view, a naive aspiration. But in a protracted argument over the translation of his work ("*L'Affaire Derrida*") carried out during recent years in the *New York Review of Books*, Derrida himself disclosed a more nearly Platonic position, admitting to having intended — or striven toward, hence seeing the need to stand up for — his own originary meanings, none of which, in his opinion, are lightly to be played with by those whose misprisions keep them from discerning Derrida's peculiar ability to keep language from unspeaking them, and thus him. Even if "the indefinite process of supplementarity has always already . . . inscribed . . . the splitting of the self,"[39] no speaker, no writer, whatever the danger of supplying the supplement, can willingly allow themselves to be put *en abyme*, as Derrida has revealed — even if it is only the circle of one's own career that one wishes to complete with one's peculiar evasion of plain sense.

Perhaps it is untrue that there will be no laboring in the winter, as long as age brings us, against the blinding insight of language, all too near to a desire for our own plain sense of things. In the trajectory of his career as a writer, Derrida moved boldly from *difference* to *differance*, but he has recently confronted the ultimate power of indifference — if of a reader more than the blue sky. Either way, one cannot remain unaffected.

Virginia Woolf wrote long ago that it is not a trust in

language that is so much to be guarded against as a trust in readers. As she writes in *A Room of One's Own*: "If opinions upon any of these matters had been chalked on the pavement, nobody would have stooped to read them. The nonchalance of the hurrying feet would have rubbed them out in half an hour."[40] It was indifference, the indistinguishable maenads, not theory, that killed Orpheus. It is the nonchalant world, not language, that will turn us into traces. And yet, it is also language, for the reasons Derrida has expressed. In the last section of *To the Lighthouse*, "Time Passes," Woolf has Lily Brisco, who is ashamed of her art, express her wish "to say not one thing, but everything." For "Little words that broke up the thought and dismembered it said nothing. 'About life, about death; about Mrs. Ramsey' — no, she thought, one could say nothing to nobody."[41] It is not only language, but also a shameless love of real speech coupled with a powerful aspiration to song, that refuses the death of the letter, that can in some way keep us from death, since nothing can.

Why is song a condition toward which not only poets but also composers aspire without frequent or final announcements of arrival? Because, until recently, as Kramer writes in the preface of *Classical Music and Postmodern Knowledge*, "music has figured familiarly in Modern Western culture as the vehicle for everything that cannot be represented or denoted." Not only in modern Western culture, we should point out, but also for Plato, Milton, and Wordsworth. In this sense, music — in ways unlike writing and painting — is always about desiring to go beyond the wish "to say." Postmodernism does not unsay this truth, but it changes the way we look at aspiration and the forms it takes. According to Kramer, "the resistance to signification once embodied by music now seems to be an inextricable part of signification itself."[42] Doubtless, this is part of the struggle of music to be musical, a valuable insight of postmodern musicology. Unfortunately, postmodernism also mischaracterizes modern aspirations toward music and submissions to desire.

Writing about Stevens's "remarkable but little-known" poem "Anglai Mort à Florence," Kramer writes that "Stevens's insight is that music acts as a substitute for a blissful sense of full presence felt to have been lost." It can act as such; as we have seen, however, music is never a "substitute" for Stevens. "The only thing this exemplary Modernist text misses," writes Kramer, "is the further insight that the lost presence, the time when one stood alone, is itself a musical fiction."[43] Kramer offers this as an insight of postmodern critical practice. But it is precisely what Stevens shows. For Stevens, song is a fiction grounded in the "ancient cycle," a "fiction of an absolute." And as Stevens writes, "the final belief is to believe in a fiction, which you know to be a fiction, there being nothing else."

In recent music history, the Beatles provide us with the example of an absolute belief in music running a full course in only seven years. In the early 1960s, the Beatles became lovable for their ability to sing "Yeah, yeah, yeah!" as if they were naive angels assenting not only to the truth of their musical creations, but also to the universal belief in the musical power of *eros*: "She loves you, yeah, yeah, yeah." Some seven years later, when various forms of "no" had crept into their aura, the Beatles stopped singing "Yeah, yeah, yeah." By the time they recorded *Abbey Road*, the title of which indicates an absolute return to a finite place, the members of the band could no longer love each other for what they were. But even as they were beating up on each other, aware that they would split, they could, in the sweet songs, bring out their vocal harmonies perhaps better and more selflessly than ever. And that is the point. The album had to make, at once, its return and departure. In "Polythene Pam," doubtless the precursor of punk rock, with Ringo's keeping of time on the tom-tom rather than a cymbal, Lennon and McCartney intone the last "Yeah, yeah, yeah" of the Beatles, the first in a long while. Unlike earlier intonations, which pushed the beat forward with rhythmical prospect, it rides the back of the musical beat. Its tone is unlike all the others, a dismissive acknowledgement of many kinds of loss, none more than the innocent ability to make beautiful music together. The first song of *Abbey Road* is "Come Together." The last song is entitled "The End." "The End" begins with solos, first drums, and then guitars, the only group improvisation the Beatles every recorded. The raucous improvisation — or "jam" — ends abrubtly, and the music gets sweet again. "And in the end," sings Paul McCartney, "the love you take is equal to the love you make." Then the band split, and none of its young ex-members could keep silent, however fragmented their muses.

For the Beatles, just as for Milton and Stevens, music must inevitably be seen as a reminder of a blissful sense of full presence thought to be lost. As Kramer writes, "that presence arises only as an echo thrown in retrospect by the music that supposedly recalls it. Music so construed is more fantasized than heard."[44] Perhaps sometimes true, but we must not impeach what is heard simply because it has a relation to fantasy. Whereas modernism ennobled silence, postmodernism tends to silence music, transforming it into the a-musical circumstances of its production. Rather than bear the awful, romantic burden of aspiring toward a condition of music, postmodernism puts it safely — in a new mode of dissociative repression — between quotation marks: "'Music' in this context refers not so much to an acoustic phenomenon as to an object constituted in representation. It is music as a cultural trope produced by muscial aesthetics, imaginative literature, and reflexively, by musical composition."[45] Kramer mentions these last three arts as if they were bad and dangerous things, even though he sees his postmodern knowledge as part of an attempt to revive the value of classical music. Kramer appears to see his ambivalence as merely a part of the praxis of critique, but he seems more like Prufrock caught in indecision than Stevens "Above the arrowy, still strings,/ The maker of a thing yet to be made."

As we have seen, Stevens's aspiration toward a condition of music rejects both the notion that music can be either "immaculate" or "beyond." Stevens could keep from both the modern and postmodern snares. He attempts neither to ennoble silence nor to evade the sounds of ineluctable music. He saw the threat to order, but he could not ennoble the fiction of an ennobling abyss. That he would leave to postmodernism.

In looking at "Anglai Mort à Florence," Kramer does not account for another poem from the same collection, or for the larger context that *Ideas of Order* builds. "A Postcard from the Volcano" begins, "Children picking up our bones/ Will never know that these were once/ As quick as foxes on the hill. . . ." Postmodern historicism seeks to show only how slow those bones were. And perhaps a later age will declare that postmodernism was too quick in doing this. As he stood at the opening of the volcano, Stevens was prescient in knowing that children would push him into an abyss once he was gone:

> Children,
> Still weaving budded aureoles,
> Will speak our speech and never know,
>
> Will say of the mansion that it seems
> As if he that lived there left behind
> A spirit storming in blank walls,
>
> A dirty house in a gutted world,
> A tatter of shadows peaked to white,
> Smeared with the gold of the opulent sun.

The end of the last poem in *Ideas of Order*, "Delightful Evening" leaves us with "The twilight overfull/ Of wormy metaphors." We have not yet gotten to the worminess of the metaphors of postmodernism. That will take the unfolding of time.

Postmodernists suggest not only that the abyss is the only case, but also that it is good, and that the act of pushing people of the past into it is an even greater good. "The truth (sic) is that we listen, and with feeling, only as we read and act, as speaking subjects in a world of contingencies," writes Kramer, and "the thesis of [my] book is simply that it is a good thing for music."[46] The kind of good Stevens saw in a world of contingency is in some ways similar, but also crucially different. While in an early poem from *Harmonium* called "Negation" Stevens could assert that "we endure brief lives,/ The evanescent symmetries/ From that meticulous potter's thumb," he was also able to continue the assertions of "Peter Quince at the Clavier." And as he continued writing poetry, he began to see his aspiration toward song within the context of his own revealing symmetries and meticulous thumbprints.

Postmodernism largely invalidates — in an aggressive evasion of ego by the desire of a superanalytical id — artistic articulations of what that music "supposedly" recalls, for, as Kramer writes, it "problematiz[es] the great ordering principles of rationality, unity, universality, and truth" — favorite terms of Stevens — and "recasts them as special cases of contingency, plurality, historicity, and ideology."

In such a context, we must not only appraise the aspirations of those who tried to sing in olden days, but also assess any dismissal of the value of those attempts. Postmodernism is a collocation of new confrontations with losses — losses that modern writers had already confronted, such as center and self. Modernism and postmodernism are deeply related on these subjects. Postmodernists see modernists as clinging to something that had been lost. But it is frequently the case that postmodernists merely cling to these attributions of clinging.

Let us, for a moment, go back to where we began, and let me suggest that the matter is similar to Cicero's blaming Socrates for servering truth and eloquence. Postmodernists accuse modernists of yoking truth and eloquence — being and form — violently together. And while this is sometimes the case, more often, as we have seen, it is not.

There is a need to examine postmodernism's inadequacies in dealing with the modernist concepts that brought it about — and none more than loss and desire. Loss and desire, as concepts, give postmodernism its beginning, but as realities in life and forms in art, loss and desire present postmodernists with trouble. They see loss and desire everywhere, but they cannot confront honestly the consequences that Renaissance, romantic, and modern artists attribute to these. Of course, they do not allow for the notion of honesty, seeing it as equally naive in Wordsworth and Stevens. And in doing this, postmodernists appear to pose as if they might remain "unaffected" people "in a negative light."

Let us not forget that the moderns generally knew that there is no possession. If there is one fact about which Renaissance, romantic, and modern poets agree, it is that desire is rooted in an inability to possess and that human nature aspires to possess anyway. The "critical practice" of reducing desire to the radical social terms of new historicisms, while it can illuminate the conditions of artistic production in ways that go beyond the now defunct forms of superficial biography, has its pitfalls. Chief among them is the attempt to flee the consequences of one's own desires by attributing "false consciousness" or other failures to others, championing the fulfillments of one's own "social" desires while debunking — "demystifying" — the mysterious desires of others from the past, by overdetermining, after the fashion of Foucault, dichotomies that provide fodder for current "critical practice." Postmodern musicology points us toward the body parts of singers, or the social circumstances of their audiences — away, that is, from the music itself, and away from the universal aspiration identified by Pater.[47]

The allures and pressures of postmodernism should not make us think that we can abandon — or "reify" as essentially social — aspiration itself, especially aspiration toward a means of musical transcendence. Ralph Ellison, who turned from an early interest in music to a long interest in letters, had this to say in a 1961 interview: "I came to understand . . . that all that stood between me and writing symphonies was not simply a matter of civil rights — even though the civil rights struggle was all too real."[48] The desire to achieve a condition of music cannot itself be adequately historicized. We know how Stevens kept his house, but this tells less about his poetry than his intense aspiration toward a condition of song.

Recent critics see music as merely something that "functions to empower the persons, institutions, and social groups in control of its production." According to Kramer, belief in the power of "musical immediacy . . . can become a powerful means of ideological seduction or coercion, not least for those who find it most empowering or liberating."[49] What postmodern critics seem not to understand — in a similar way, ironically, to Christian humanists — is that poets have not found the aspiration to song solely liberating. Nevertheless, as the poet Jack Gilbert insists in almost all his courageous poems, there is little value in the evasion of grand aspirations, especially during one's own special moments in history. In "Orpheus in Greenwich Village," he asks these questions: "What if Orpheus,/ confident in the hard-/found mastery,/ should go down into Hell?" What if "then, surrounded/ by the closing beasts," he "should notice, suddenly,/they had no ears?"[50] May an aspiring singer not conclude that the audience is hopelessly deaf? And may the singer not feel, in conclusion, oppressed by such an audience?

It would be enlightening to gain such honesty from postmodern critiques. In addition to hearing about the importance of race, class, and gender in the concert halls, it would be good to hear about universal hopes for transcendence that music and thoughts about music will, it appears, always engender. Postmodernism has yet to give an account of its

own evasions — and their consequences. Indeed, the consequence of failure appears to be removed from postmodernism,
for particular forms of aspiration are conspicuously denounced.
But there will be no art without a belief in life. No belief in
the value of life without a musical desire for a fiction of what
might be. This desire is as universal as any desire can be. It
may not be historicized into the local, personal perversities of
any particular age — not even our own.

Twentieth century criticism has not yet accounted for the
practical and theoretical value of musical speculation in the
history of poetry. "When it speaks of music, language is lame,"
suggests Steiner. Among modern critics, Steiner has made
some of the most insightful comments about the relationships
that obtain between speech and silence, as well as between
music and time. But he has heedlessly slighted numerous
poets, as if they had nothing of value to say on the matter.
Steiner grants that there "are kindlings of discursive revelation in Plato, in Kierkegaard, in Schopenhauer, Nietzsche and
Adorno." According to Steiner, "The messianic intimation in
music is often manifest. But attempts to verbalize it," he concludes, "produce impotent metaphors."[51] What Steiner might
see, though he does not say it, is the value of language when it
speaks of musical speculation. That is, whereas language cannot speak of actual music, language is itself a vigorous speculative pursuit of the music of the speaker's life. As Stevens
writes, "Music falls on the silence like a sense,/ A passion
that we feel, not understand."[52] Similarly, Milton's Adam,
having, in the words of the angel, "attain'd the sum/ Of wisdom," becomes humble enough to say: "beyond is all abyss,/
Eternity, whose end no eye can reach." As Stevens writes,
"to meditate for us a reality not ourselves . . . is what the
poet does"; and "the virtue here is humility."[53] This kind of

humility, if often lacking in philosophers and critics, is promi-
nent in many poets — especially poets who aspire to sing.

Steiner reaches his conclusions in part because he pays
more attention to philosophers who examine (and sometimes
kill) metaphors than to poets who make them live by living
by them. Adorno had remarked such lameness of language
about music. The pitfall of all kinds of criticism, Adorno makes
clear, is the failure to see "the lameness of a thought." Much
of Adorno's analysis is keen, but even he, like Spitzer, fails to
heed his own cautions about the potential failings of criticism.
Both Adorno and Steiner fall into the harmonizing tendency
this book cautions against. Consider, for example, Adorno's
attempt to give caution to critics: "Immanent criticism of
intellectual and artistic phenomena," according to Adorno,
"reveals the truth or untruth of a perception, the consequence
or lameness of a thought, the coherence or incoherence of a
structure, the substantiality or emptiness of a figure of speech."
Furthermore, "a successful work, according to immanent criticism, is not" writes Adorno, "one which resolves objective
contradictions in a spurious harmony, but one which expresses
the idea of harmony negatively by embodying the contradictions, pure and uncompromised, in its innermost structure."
Adorno describes a noble pursuit, but one cannot, as Stevens
says, be unaffected in a negative light, seeing — or hearing —
pure and uncompromised contradictions.

Theory, as Adorno wrote, led to a sense of "artistic maturity and intellectualization" that seeks to "abolish not only
sensuous appearance, but, with it, art itself."[54] Theory, or criticism, can do this, likely because theoretical notions of maturity neglect the notions we find in poets as dissimilar as Milton
and Stevens — because, in other words, theory replaces desire
with "intellectualization," and hence cannot "catch from" an
"Irrational moment its unreasoning." To make oneself a singer,
as Stevens shows us, one must balance one's confidence in

speculative theory and one's devotion to practical methods. An evasion of this necessity by going over to one side is the greatest obstacle to song. Poets cannot put all their hope in an idea, nor all their store in practical skill.

"[I]mmanent criticism holds in evidence," writes Adorno, "the fact that the mind has always been under a spell."[55] Indeed, diverse critics in this century have been under the spell cast by the idea of harmony. Adorno and Spitzer differ radically as critics, but their comments on harmony are astoundingly similar. A spell is, after all, a spell. And the idea of harmony casts a powerful one. When the subject is Schoenberg's triumph, Adorno becomes metaphorical, even trite, grabbing hackneyed expressions from high culture. Consider, for example, the following comments on the *Second Kammersymphonie*:

> The last movement . . . in song once again, sounds as though it came from another world, from the realm of freedom; it is the new music through and through, despite the F sharp major at the end, its first unadulterated manifestation, more utopian in its inspiration than any thereafter. The instrumental introduction of this 'withdrawal' has the sound of truth, as though music had been freed of all chains and was soaring above and beyond enormous abysses towards that other planet invoked in the poem.[56]

The last sentence sounds very much like the versions of Milton constructed by those scholars who merely applied Neoplatonism to the passage about "*Lydian* Airs" in "L'Allegro." Adorno's life and education in Vienna would, of course, make any other kind of description unlikely.

But there is an important point here. Is this not the way we all speak, and truly wish to speak, after hearing music that seems actually to *transport* us? Are we not happy to make instrumental music the occasion for ennobling the motive for metaphor, for the lame language — "freedom," "new," "unadulterated," "truth," "soaring," "above and beyond" —

we cling to when expressing the dreams that begin in our responsibilities? Whitman exuded freedom. Pound said to "make it new." But Stevens is quick to show us that there is nothing truly free, truly new, truly unadulterated. As for soaring above and beyond, as Stevens declares, it is only our full and filling adoration of "empty heaven and its hymns." There is truth, as Schoenberg taught, chiefly in our compelling errors. Yet still, we all have an exceeding will to evade. And only a poet is likely to have the desire and skill to intervene in inevitable cycles, turning intricate evasion toward a plain sense of things.

Finally, we may conclude that speculative poets do not claim to have achieved song. At least where aspirations to song are concerned, recent criticism is wrong to see poets as people who falsely protect themselves as part of a privileged class of singing prophets. Writing on what causes cultures to constitute "the poetic" and privilege certain kinds of "literariness," Derek Attridge observes the habit of poets to value in self-serving ways the oppositional terms with which writers define their poetics:

> [a]lthough the acquisition of [decorum] is often presented as though it were merely a matter of industry and application on the part of the individual, it nevertheless combines a first-order discrimination on the basis of class (proper breeding is essential) with a finer discrimination on the basis of individual and inborn capacities (only a few of the dominant class will be favored by nature or, we might say, biology). There is always, therefore, a *je ne sais quoi* beyond the reach of rules and imitation, a something that cannot be taught and that protects the small caste of true poets.[57]

This can be true of an Englishman writing in the sixteenth century, for whom speculative music was of little concern. What is compelling about the ways speculative poets use the trope of song, we have seen, is that by resisting the power of a spell they universally conceive song as "beyond the reach

of rules and imitation." Poets who aspire to speculative harmony — beginning most noticeably with Milton — do not invoke the trope to protect themselves as parts of any caste.
Rather, they invoke it to exclude themselves from the very
condition to which they most aspire. Perhaps Wordsworth
put it best: it is a "last and favorite aspiration . . . an awful
burthen." And if our age and culture, in which critics acknowledge themselves as legislators, cannot allow particular people,
especially poets, to see themselves as particularly marked by
a burden of their own choosing, then we have clearly reached
at least the temporary end of art.

After Shakespeare, almost all great poets writing in English
who examine their aspiration to music express, in speculative terms, their limitations as singers and the means by which
they may — and in many cases may not — transcend them.

It might seem that, under such conditions, the aspiration
to song should have long ago abated. As Keats declares in "Ode
to Psyche," the trope of song had long been antiquated:

> O brightest! though too late for antique vows,
>   Too, too late for the fond believing lyre. . . .

There is excessive emphasis: the vows are "antique" the
belief "fond"; it is "too too late." But as fond Sappho (the
mother of believing lyres) taught, a poet's chief subject is
desire, and the secondary subject therefore time. Precisely
because the ear is slow, a poet's desires are best expressed in
musical terms. In the end, Stevens knew, the aspiration to a
condition of music exists, and it must be ennobled by fictions
that confront the pressure of reality — if by nothing else, then
by the aspiration itself.

I have been writing about the attempts of poets to escape
what they perceive to be their conditions, predicaments, or
limitations, precisely without resorting to what Adorno calls
"the language of escape." For Milton, the language of Neoplatonism was a language of illusory escape, a language of

metaphors that failed to resist the real pressures of theology that distinguished poetry from song. For Stevens, singing constitutes the most difficult rigor of tracing back one's intricate evasions of *as*, of knowing a trope that is not a trope from a trope that is.

The trope of song did not devolve into exhaustion or escape in the thousands of years between Homer and Milton or the hundreds of years between Milton and Stevens, and it will survive postmodernism. It sustained Milton in both 1633 and 1674 as the center of his conception of himself as both a man and a poet. It sustained Stevens from 1915 to 1955. Whatever the obvious and more subtle differences between philosophy and poetry, Susanne K. Langer's conception of "generative ideas" offers a way of thinking about the history of thought that helps us to think about the history of aspirations to song. "Generative ideas," writes Langer, are "not theories; they are the terms in which theories are conceived." They are not theories or new answers according to old theories but "new questions . . . specific questions." "Generative ideas" are new questions that attempt to discover new problems. They arise not because old problems and questions have been adequately solved or answered — or escaped — but because genius insists upon finding better (larger or deeper) questions. "The end of a philosophical epoch comes with the exhaustion of its [generative ideas]".[58] "It is the mode of handling problems, rather than what they are about, that assigns them to an age," as Langer writes. "Their subject-matter may be fortuitous, and depend on conquests, discoveries, plagues, or governments; their treatment derives from a steadier source."[59] The way poets animate by scrutiny the trope of song assigns them not only to an age but to themselves. This is likely always to be so.

Since before the time of Hesiod, poets have lived by the terms of speculative music. They have not produced impotent metaphors. They have excelled philosophers — and literary

critics — in both their inventive use and critical scrutiny of
the trope of song. Going back far enough in time, of course,
we know that philosophers themselves were the great aspir-
ants to song. They were at once actual singers and thinkers
who spoke about the difficulty of achieving a condition of song.
"So Thales, Empedocles, and Parmenides sang their natural
philosophy in verses; so did Pythagoras," writes Sidney.[60]
Orpheus, Thales, Pythagoras were singers. Then, at some point,
philosophers became philosophers; song ceased to be a primary aspiration. The love of eloquence and the love of wisdom seemed to be split. Poets, however, could never allow
them to be. Song could never cease to be the favorite aspiration of poets. A poet, as Sidney knew, is a maker of fictions,
and one may make fictions without verse. To be a poet is to
be more than a philosopher. But to be a singer is to be more
than a poet.

Notes

Notes to Introduction

1. Homer, *The Iliad*, trans. Richmond Lattimore (Chicago: Chicago UP, 1951) 59; Hesiod, *Theogony*, in *Hesiod, the Homeric Hymns and Homerica*, trans. Hugh B. Evelyn-White (1914; Cambridge: Harvard UP, 1980) 79; Virgil, *Aeneid*, my translation; John Milton, *Paradise Lost*, book 7, line 24; Walt Whitman, "Song of Myself," *Leaves of Grass*, ed. Malcolm Cowley (1959; New York: Viking, 1982); Emily Dickinson, "250," *Final Harvest*, ed. Thomas H. Johnson (Boston: Little, Brown, 1961) 32.

2. Michel de Montaigne, "Of Experience," *The Complete Essays of Montaigne*, trans. Donald M. Frame (1958; Stanford: Stanford UP, 1965) 815.

3. E. Talbot Donaldson, trans., *Beowulf* (New York: Norton, 1966) 1, 16.

4. Wesley Trimpi, *Muses of One Mind* (Princeton: Princeton UP, 1983) ix.

5. Trimpi xvi.

6. Plutarch, *Moralia*, trans F. H. Sandbach, vol. 9 (London, Loeb Classical Library, 1961) 271–75.

7. John Caldwell, "The *De Institutione Arithmetica* and *De Institutione Musica*," *Boethius*, ed. Margaret Gibson (Oxford: Basil Blackwell, 1981) 145, explains: "The line of demarcation between the latter two was often misunderstood by later writers, who (perhaps because the instances given of instrumental music do not include the voice) understood human music as vocal. But the description of it by Boethius makes it clear that it is to be understood as a metaphor of the parts of the soul and of the body, and of

their relation to each other." Cf. Boethius, *De Institutione Musica*, ed. Godofredus Friedlein (1867; Frankfurt: Minerva, 1966).

8. See Trimpi xvii. "It is the purpose of [his] study," Trimpi writes, "to describe the nature of [the] restrictions placed upon the literary analysis of experience and of the ever-recurring efforts to overcome them."

9. John Milton, *Complete Poetry and Major Prose*, ed. Merritt Y. Hughes (New York: Macmillan, 1957) 79–80. All quotations of Milton are from this edition; I refer parenthetically to line numbers for the poems, page numbers for the prose.

10. Sir Thomas Browne, *Religio Medici, Selected Writings*, ed. Sir Geoffrey Keynes (Chicago: Chicago UP, 1968) 40.

11. William Butler Yeats, "Adam's Curse," *The Poems of W. B. Yeats* ed. Richard J. Finneran (New York: Macmillan, 1983).

12. Susanne K. Langer, *Philosophy in a New Key: A Study in the Symbolism of Reason, Rite, and Art* (Cambridge: Harvard UP, 1957) x–xi.

13. The emphasis is mine.

14. Homer, *The Iliad* 447, 488.

15. I. A. Richards, *The Philosophy of Rhetoric* (1936; Oxford: Oxford UP, 1976) 127.

16. See Frank Kermode's fine essay on the subject, "The Plain Sense of Things," in *An Appetite for Poetry* (Cambridge: Harvard UP, 1989) 172–88, to which I am greatly indebted.

17. Lawrence Kramer, *Music and Poetry: The Nineteenth Century and After* (Berkeley: U California P, 1984) 6–7.

18. Kramer 129.

19. Sir Philip Sidney, *An Apology for Poetry*, ed. Forrest G. Robinson (Indianapolis: Bobbs-Merrill, 1970) 21.

20. Derek Attridge, *Well-Weighed Syllables* (Cambridge: Cambridge UP, 1974) 2.

21. Sidney 53.

22. Attridge, *Well-Weighed Syllables* 2.

23. See Umberto Eco, *Semiotics and the Philosophy of Language*, (Bloomington: Indiana UP, 1984); Max Black, *Models and Metaphors* (Ithaca: Cornell UP, 1962); and Nelson Goodman, *Of Mind and Other Matters* (Cambridge: Harvard UP, 1984) especially 71–77.

24. George Lakoff and Mark Turner, *More than Cool Reason: A Field Guide to Poetic Metaphor* (Chicago: U Chicago P, 1989) 50.

25. Thomas Campion, *The Works of Thomas Campion*, ed. Walter R. Davis (New York: Norton 1970) 48.

26. S. Schoenbaum, *Shakespeare's Lives* (Oxford: Oxford UP, 1991) 26.

27. W. B. Yeats, *Essays and Introductions* (New York: Macmillan, 1961) 98.

28. Ruth Wallerstein, *Studies in Seventeenth-Century Poetic* (Madison: U Wisconsin P, 1961) 3.

29. James Hutton, "Some English Poems in Praise of Music," *English Miscellany* 2 (1950): 1, 4–5.

30. See John Hollander, *The Untuning of the Sky* (1961; New York: Norton, 1970), especially 150–53 and S. K. Heninger, *Touches of Sweet Harmony* (San Marino, California: The Huntington Library, 1974).

31. A relevant example is Merritt Y. Hughes, *John Milton: Complete Poems and Major Prose*, 602, who writes, in a footnote to "On the Music of the Spheres," that "the Platonic conception, which inspired *Music* and *Arcades*, entered Renaissance literature with the authority of the Florentine Neoplatonists."

32. Leo Spitzer, *Classical and Christian Ideas of World Harmony*, ed. Anna Granville Hatcher (Baltimore: The Johns Hopkins Press, 1963) 4.

33. John H. Long, *Shakespeare's Use of Music: The Histories and Tragedies* (Gainesville: U Florida P, 1971) 1.

34. Heninger, *Touches of Sweet Harmony* 4.

35. Cf. Marc Berley, "Milton's Earthy Grossness," *Milton Studies* 30 (1993): 149–62.

36. Frank Kermode, *Forms of Attention* (Chicago: U Chicago P, 1985) 87.

37. Wallace Stevens, "The Man with the Blue Guitar," *The Collected Poems of Wallace Stevens* (New York: Vintage, 1954).

38. Cf. Lawrence Kramer, *Classical Music and Postmodern Knowledge* (Berkeley: U California P, 1995).

39. See Tilottama Rajan, *Dark Interpreter: The Discourse of Romanticism* (Ithaca: Cornell UP, 1980) 13–14.

Notes to Chapter One

1. M. L. West, "The Singing of Homer and the Modes of Early Greek Music," *Journal of Hellenic Studies* 101 (1981): 113–14.

2. Nan Cooke Carpenter, *Music in the Medieval and Renaissance Universities* (1958; New York: Da Capo Press, 1972) 7.

3. It is not possible to distinguish with any degree of certainty the contributions of Socrates and Plato. In the following pages I refer to them separately only for the purpose of recalling the two historical figures, the teacher who wrote nothing and the pupil who wrote a lot. I refer to Socrates as a speaker in Plato's dialogues, and to Plato as the writer, and to both as developers of the speculative musical tradition. I am concerned here with the writings of Plato, not with whether Socrates or Plato is responsible for certain doctrines.

4. On Pythagoras and Pythagoreanism see Isidore Levy, *Recherches sur les sources de la légende de Pythagore* (New York:

Garland, 1987); Dominic J. O'Meara, *Pythagoras Revived* (Oxford: Clarendon Press, 1989); Robert Navon, ed., *The Pythagorean Writings*, trs. Kenneth Guthrie and Thomas Taylor (New York: Selene Books, 1986); W. D. Ross, *Plato's Theory of Ideas* (Oxford: Oxford UP, 1951). Most direct influence is untraceable, but Socrates is believed to have had relations to Pythagoras and early Pythagoreans and to have carried on certain aspects of Pythagorean teachings. Much of the teaching of Pythagoras that comes down to us from other sources is more lore than philosophy. G. S. Kirk, J. E. Raven and M. Schofield, *The Presocratic Philosophers* (1957; Cambridge: Cambridge UP, 1983) 214–38, state the problem well: "Pythagoras wrote nothing. Hence a void was created which was to become filled by a huge body of literature, much of it worthless as historical evidence of Pythagoras's own teachings. It included accounts of Pythagorean physics, ethics and political theory as well as metaphysics; biographies of Pythagoras; and several dozen treatises (many still extant) whose authorship was ascribed to early Pythagoreans — although all of them (excepting some fragments of Philolaus and Archytas) are nowadays judged to be pseudonymous fictions of later origin. . . . The three major *Lives* by Diogenes Laertius, Porphyry and Iambilichus . . . are scissors-and-paste compilations of the Christian era. But they contain, together with some extremely credulous matter, extracts or epitomes of authors of the period 350–250 B.C. who had access to fairly early traditions about Pythagoras and the Pythagoreans: notably, Aristoxenus, Dicaearchus and Timaeus." I will be referring to the tradition as Pythagorean, Socratic, and Platonic — with the intention of acknowledging both the probable contribution of all three philosophers and the difficulty of sorting out all relevant questions concerning intellectual property.

5. Ernest G. McClain, *The Pythagorean Plato: Prelude to the Song Itself* (New York: Nicolas-Has Inc., 1978), makes an important contribution to the study of Plato by establishing music and mathematics as the foundation of Plato's philosophy. Cf. Robert S. Brumbaugh, *Plato's Mathematical Imagination* (Bloomington: Indiana UP, 1954).

6. Plato, *Republic*, trans. Paul Shorey, in *The Collected Dialogues of Plato*, ed., Edith Hamilton and Huntington Cairns (Princeton: Princeton UP, 1961) 401d–402a. All translations of Plato, except where indicated, are from this edition. I will hereafter refer first to the name of the translator, the work, and the numbers of Stephanus; thereafter only to the work and the numbers of Stephanus.

7. The emphasis is mine.

8. See *Phaedrus* 247c3–4: "Τὸν δε ὑπουράνιον τόπον οὔτε τις ὕμνησέ πω τῶν τῇδε ποιητὴς οὔτε ποτὲ ὑμνήσει κατ'ἀξίαν." All citations

of *Phaedrus* are from Ioannes Burnet, ed., *Platonis Opera* (Oxford: Oxford UP, 1901).

9. Cf. Plato, *Timaeus* 32c–37c.

10. See *Phaedrus* 248e1–3. Cf. *Phaedrus* 248d3–4: "ἀλλὰ τὴν μὲν πλεῖστα ἰδοῦσαν εἰς γονὴν ἀνδρὸς γενησομένου φιλοσόφου ἢ φιλοκάλου ἢ μουσικοῦ τινος καὶ ἐρωτικοῦ. . . ." Eros is the subject on which the dialogue will end, having made a transition from Socrates' critique of a rhetorical love letter to his formulation of dialectical philosophy that has its basis in *eros*.

11. See *Phaedrus* 248e1–3: "ἕκτῃ ποιητικὸς ἢ τῶν περὶ μίμησίν τις ἄλλος ἁρμόσει, ἑβδόμη δημιουργικὸς ἢ γεωργικός, ὀγδόη σοφιστικὸς ἢ δημοκοπικός, ἐνάτῃ τυραννικός."

12. Cf. Ernst Robert Curtius, *European Literature and the Latin Middle Ages*, trans. Willard R. Trask (1953; Princeton: Princeton UP, 1973) 544–46.

13. McClain 10 links speculative music and mathematics to temperament: "In the circle beginning and end coincide so that the reference tone, D, actually *functions visually* as *geometric* mean between the symmetrically located arithmetic and harmonic means — whose own positions alternate according to whether numbers are thought of as multiples or submultiples, and attached to tones which rise and fall. By this device we have acquired a Socratic 'seat in the mean' (*Republic* 619a) which never changes, for the tone-field will develop symmetrically. . . ."

14. *Phaedrus* 248d3–4.

15. Carpenter 6.

16. Hesiod, *Theogony*, line 1, in *Hesiod: The Homeric Hymns and Homerica* 78–79. See also *Theogony* line 36.

17. Pindar, *The Odes of Pindar*, trans. Sir J. E. Sandys (1915; Cambridge: Harvard UP, 1978).

18. *Republic* 531d.

19. Plato, *Republic*, trans. G. M. A. Grube (Indianapolis: Hackett, 1974) 183.

20. *Phaedrus* 273e3–4: "οὔ ποτ' ἔσται τεχνικὸς λόγων πέρι καθ' ὅσον δυνατὸν ἀνθρώπῳ."

21. Montaigne, *Essais*, vol. 2., ed. M. Rat (Paris: Éditions Garnier Frère, 1962) 577.

22. Frame, *The Complete Essays of Montaigne* 857.

23. *Phaedrus* 277a3–4: "καὶ τὸν ἔχοντα εὐδαιμονεῖν ποιοῦντες εἰς ὅσον ἀνθρώπῳ δυνατὸν μάλιστα."

24. Dickinson 34.

25. Trimpi 3.

26. *Republic* 531d. I have substituted the word "song" where

Shorey has "strain" as a translation for νόμου in the phrase "ἡ οὐκ ἴσμεν ὅτι πάντα ταῦτα προοίμια ἐστιν αὐτοῦ τοῦ νόμου ὅν δεῖ μαθεῖν." See Grube 183.

27. Cf. Plato, *Laws*, books 6 and 7; cf. Aristotle, *Politics*, books 7 and 8.

28. Carpenter 154. Cf. Sir Charles Mallet, *History of the University of Oxford* (London, 1924) II, 120 and Strickland Gison, *Statua antiqua Vniversitatis Oxoniensis* (Oxford, 1920–21) 390.

29. Homer, *The Odyssey*, trans. Richmond Lattimore (New York: Harper and Row, 1967) 36.

30. Homer, *The Odyssey* 330.

31. In his *Metaphysics*, trans. Richard Hope (1952; Ann Arbor: U Michigan P, 1960) 43–44, Aristotle makes the distinction between *philosophia theoretica* and *philosophia practica*, which is the basis of his defense of rhetoric and poetry, and the imagination in general, and which is related to the distinction between speculative and practical music: "the science of primary being, inasmuch as it treats by definition of first factors and of what is the most intelligible, would be wisdom. . . . However, we know how things or acts or changes come about when we know their source or generation (the opposite of their end). Thus, any one of these types of scientific explanation would seem to be a different type of knowledge and yet may give us wisdom." Aristotle defends mimesis (indeed, all practical "arts") because it deals with the sphere of human action, not "primary being," and may therefore instruct, on a "practical" but not "theoretical" level.

32. See Kathy Eden, *Poetic and Legal Fiction in the Aristotelian Tradition* (Princeton: Princeton UP, 1986) 30–31.

33. Aristotle, *On Poetry and Style*, trans. G. M. A. Grube (Indianapolis: Hackett Publishing Co., 1989) 3–4: "Our subject is the art of poetry in general and its different genres, the specific effect of each genre, the way to construct stories to make good poetry, the number and nature of its constituent elements, and all other matters which belong to this particular inquiry. And let us begin as is natural, with basic principles. The epic, tragedy, comedy, dithyrambic poetry, most music on the flute and on the lyre — all these are, in principle, imitations. They differ in three ways: they imitate different things, or imitate them by different means, or in a different manner. Some people imitate and portray many things by means of color and shape (whether as conscious artists or through force of habit); others imitate by means of the voice. So all the arts we have mentioned produce their imitations by means of rhythm, speech, and melody, using them separately or together. For example, melody and rhythm are the two means used when playing the flute or the lyre,

or other instruments which may have a similar effect, such as the pipes. The art of dancing uses rhythm only, without melody, yet its rhythmic patterns, too, imitate character, emotions, and actions."

34. Aristotle, *The Art of Rhetoric*, trans. J. H. Freese (1926; Cambridge: Harvard UP, 1982) 19.

35. Aristotle, *The Art of Rhetoric* 17.

36. Quintilian, *Institutio Oratoria*, trans. H. E. Butler, Vol. 1, (1920; Cambridge: Harvard UP, 1980) 40–41: "I hold that no one can be a true orator unless he is also a good man and, even if he could be, I would not have it so."

37. Quintilian, *Institutio* 63–65.

38. E. D. Hirsch, Jr., *Cultural Literacy* (Boston: Houghton Mifflin Company, 1987).

39. Quintilian, *Institutio* 160–77.

40. Carpenter 7.

41. This and following quotations of this letter are from Marsilio Ficino, *The Letters of Marsilio Ficino*, Vol. 1, trans. by the Language Department of the School of Economic Science, London, (London: Shepheard-Walwyn, 1975) 42–48.

42. Cf. Plato, *Republic*, 450d–e.

43. Plato, *Apology*, 22e–24b, in G. M. A. Grube, trans., *The Trial and Death of Socrates* (Indianapolis: Hackett, 1975). Hereafter I will refer parenthetically only to the work and the numbers of Stephanus.

44. Richard Rorty, *Philosophy and the Mirror of Nature* (Princeton: Princeton UP, 1979), observes that almost all philosophers after Descartes, whatever their claims to the contrary, are trained as foundationalists, which is to say they are trained to establish the foundations of belief and "true knowledge." Hence, one may regularly encounter today — in print, in lectures — the opinion that Socrates is a "true knower." Such an opinion misses the point of Socrates' assertion that he is a lover of wisdom or philosopher, not a true knower or wise man. It is this error that got the first true philosopher killed — the error, perhaps, that made philosophy into a profession. Cf. Gregory Vlastos, "Socrates' Disavowal of Knowledge," *Philosophical Quarterly* 35 (1985): 1–31.

45. Ficino, *The Letters of Marsilio Ficino* 43.

46. Ficino, *The Letters of Marsilio Ficino* 45.

47. See McClain 3: "Although the ear cannot verify results with any accuracy beyond the first few subdivisions of the 'fifth' 2:3, 'fourth' 3:4, and perhaps the 'major third' 4:5 and 'minor third' 5:6, yet even micro-intervals can be readily calculated by the number theorist, to whatever limits please him, by continued operations with these same first six integers. And the tuner can follow, generating each tone from the last one, never daring to omit intermediate steps."

48. In the Middle Ages and Renaissance, speculative music was confused with certain aspects of practical music; the ability to read music and the knowledge necessary to teach schoolboys to sing, for example, was considered theoretical and therefore speculative. Al-Farabi, one of the most important translators of Aristotle in the Middle Ages, seems to have played a large role in the conflation of speculative and practical music. See Baron Rodolphe d'Erlanger, *La Musique Arabe, Grand traité de la musique* (Paris: Librairie Orientaliste Paul Geuthner, 1930), a translation of Al-Farabi's treatise on music. In the introduction Al-Farabi makes the new distinction, which loses the Pythagorean distinction, based on his disagreement with the ancient philosopher (28): *"L'opinion des pythagoriciens que les planètes et les étoiles, dans leur course, font naître des sons qui se combinent harmonieusement est eronée. En physique, il est démontré que leur hypothèse est impossible, que le mouvement des astres et des étoiles ne peut engendrer aucun son. Presque tout ce qui appartient à la théorie musicale est un produit de l'art, étranger à la nature. On croit que la musique est un art à la fois théorique et pratique, par la confusion que fait naître l'emploi du même mot (musique) pour ces deux arts [qui sont distincts]."*

49. C. A. Patrides, *Milton and the Christian Tradition* (Oxford: Clarendon Press, 1966) 29.

50. Plato, *Timaeus* 47a.

51. Cf. *Republic* 443c–e.

52. Ficino, *The Book of Life*, trans. Charles Boer (Irving, Texas: Spring Publications, 1980) 159.

53. See Gary Tomlinson's study of Ficino's theories of music, *Music in Renaissance Magic* (Chicago: U Chicago P, 1993). See also Eric Sven Ryding, *In Harmonie Framed: Musical Humanism, Thomas Campion, and the Two Daniels*, Sixteenth Century Essays & Studies, vol. 21 (Kirksvill, Missouri: Sixteenth Century Journal Publishers, 1993) 11–12: "In his *De Vita* (1489), a study of health and medicine, Ficino discusses, among other things, the salutary influence of the planets and the effects of music on man. Stressing the occult to a surprising degree. . . . Numerous ancient authorities — Origen, Synesius, Al-Kindi, Zoroaster, Iamblichus, and others — have agreed (Ficino tells us) that words, especially chanted words, have great power. This belief was also held by the Pythagoreans, 'who used to perform wonders by words, songs, and sounds in the Phoebean and Orphic manner. . . .' The power, Ficino argues, can still be harnessed. One should try, by playing the right music, to draw the beneficial influence from the heavens. After observing how certain kinds of music are played by certain kinds of people, one can determine what kind of music draws what celestial effects." In the words of

Ficino, in *The Book of Life* (160–61), one should observe the "location and aspect of the stars, and under these explore which speeches, songs, movements, dances, customs, and actions usually excite people, so that you may be able to imitate such things for the sake of the powers that are in these songs, which pleases some heavenly object." Writing chiefly about the practice of music as it influenced the poetry of three Renaissance poets who composed lute songs, Ryding demonstrates the general influence of Ficino's mythical ideas about music on some practicing Renaissance poets and musicians. The same influence, we will see, may not be established in the case of Milton.

54. The important work done by scholars such as D. P. Walker and Francis Yates, although very useful for a reading of Ronsard, is, as we will see, misleading in the case of Milton. See for example D. P. Walker, "Musical Humanism in the 16th and Early 17th Centuries," *The Music Review* 2 (1941): 1–13, 111–21, 220–27, 288–308 and *The Music Review* 3 (1942): 55–71; "The aim of Baïf's *Académie de Poésie et de Musique*," *Journal of Renaissance and Baroque Music* 1 (1946): 91–100; "The Influence of *musique mesurée à l'antique*, particularly on the *airs de cour* of the Early 17th Century," *Musica Disciplina* 2 (1948): 141–63; "*Le chant orphique de Marsile Ficin*," *Colloques internationaux du CNRS* (Paris: Editions du CNRS, 1954); "Ficino's *spiritus* and Music," *Annales Musicologiques* 1 (1953): 131–50; and Francis Yates, *The French Academies of the Sixteenth Century* (London: The Warburg Institute, 1947).

55. Thomas Morley, *A Plain and Easy Introduction to Practical Music*, ed. R. Alec Harman (1963; New York: Norton, 1973) 101: "Music is either speculative or practical. Speculative is that kind of music which, by mathematical helps, seeketh the causes, properties and natures of sounds, by themselves and compared with others, proceeding no further, but content with the only contemplation of the art. Practical is that which teacheth all that may be known in songs, either for the understanding of other men's, or making of one's own. . . ."

56. We may examine the link between practical musical study and the study of rhetoric in the Renaissance by comparing the various rhetorical manuals with the manuals on practical music, some chief examples of which are: Thomas Wilson's *The Arte of Rhetorique* (1560); Scaliger's *Poetics* (1561); Ascham's *The Schoolmaster* (1570); Thomas Lodge's *Defence of Poetry* (1579); Puttenham's *The Arte of English Poesie* (1589); Sidney's *An Apology for Poetry* or *The Defense of Poesy* (1595). On music: Zarlino's *Istituzioni armoniche* (1558); William Bathe's *A Briefe Introduction to the True Art of Musicke* (1584) and *A Brief Introduction to the Skill of Song* (1600); John Case's or anonymous *The Praise of Music* (1586); Thomas

Morley's *A Plain and Easy Introduction to Practical Music* (1597) and *The First Book of Consort Lessons* (1599; 1611); John Dowland's translation in 1609 of Ornithoparcus's *Micrologus* (1609) and *Varietie of Lute-Lessons* (1610).

57. Sir Philip Sidney, *An Apology for Poetry*, ed. Forrest G. Robinson (Indianapolis: Bobbs-Merrill, 1970). I use this edition for all quotations of Sidney and refer parenthetically to page number.

58. Baldassare Castiglione, *The Courtier*, trans. Thomas Hoby (New York: Everyman, 1961) 75.

59. *Touches of Sweet Harmony* 3. The emphasis is mine.

60. The emphasis is mine.

61. Edward W. Tayler, *Milton's Poetry* (Pittsburgh: Duquesne UP, 1979) 5–7.

62. Cf. Aristotle, *Politics*, books 7 and 8.

63. Boethius, *The Consolation of Philosophy*, trans. Richard Green (Indianapolis: Library of Liberal Arts, 1962) 25.

64. *The Consolation of Philosophy* 25.

65. Or perhaps misundertood as less prohibitive than it is. Hence, even those who champion Plato as a defender of poetry can also miss the point of his speculative musical program. See, for example, Julius A. Elias, *Plato's Defense of Poetry* (London: Macmillan, 1984).

66. Cf. Cicero, *De Oratore*, book 3, trans. H. Rackham (1942; Cambridge: Harvard UP, 1982) 47–49.

67. We have as evidence of this Cicero's claim, in *Tusculanne Disputationes*, 1.2, that the "highest education [is] found in instrumental and vocal music." If translated into Boethian terms familiar to writers in the Renaissance, Cicero's claim would be that *musica instrumentalis* is the highest form of education.

68. Trimpi xi. See Trimpi 117–19 for further disussion of theoretical versus practical arts.

69. Trimpi 3, xvii.

70. Plato, *Apology* 22e–23b.

71. Cicero, *De Oratore*, book 3, 47–49.

72. Percy Bysshe Shelley, "On the *Symposium*," *The Works of Percy Bysshe Shelley* ed. Carlos Baker (New York: Random House, 1951) 493.

73. Mythology tells us there was no distinction between heavenly and earthly music during the Golden Age. Later, in the writings of the Presocratic philosophers — and earlier too, we must presume — metaphor becomes the way to put the universe together, just as it becomes the way to explain how it fell apart.

74. Dante Alighieri, *Paradiso: Text and Commentary*, ed. Charles S. Singleton (Princeton: Princeton UP, 1975) canto 10, lines 142–48.

75. Rachel Jacoff, preface, in John Freccero *Dante: The Poetics of Conversion* (Cambridge: Harvard UP, 1986) xi.

76. The difficulty of drawing conclusions about the significance of the phrase is perhaps remarked best by Singleton's glib commentary, Dante Alighieri, *Purgatorio: Text and Commentary*, trans. Charles S. Singleton (Princeton: Princeton UP, 1973) 570–71: "this is . . . the phrase which has become the chapter heading in so many histories of Italian literature.

77. Edmund Spenser, "In Honour of Love," *Fowre Hymnes, The Yale Edition of the Shorter Poems of Edmund Spenser*, eds. William A. Oram, Einar Bjorvand, Ronald Bond, Thomas H. Cain, Alexander Dunlop, Richard Schell (New Haven: Yale UP, 1989) 705.

78. Hollander, *The Untuning of the Sky* 4.

79. Kramer, *Classical Music and Postmodern Thought* 16.

80. Lionel Trilling, "The Sense of the Past," *The Liberal Imagination* (New York: Viking Press, 1950) 184–185.

81. Denis Donoghue, *Walter Pater: Lover of Strange Souls* (New York: Alfred A. Knopf, 1995) 8.

82. Augustine, *On Music*, trans. Robert Catesby Taliaferro, in *Writings of Saint Augustine*, Vol. 2, ed. Ludwig Schopp (New York: CIMA Publishing Co., 1947) 163.

83. Augustine, *On Music* 324–25.

84. Augustine, *On Music* 163.

85. Kenneth Burke, *The Rhetoric of Religion* (1961; Berkeley: U California P, 1970) 49.

86. Augustine, *On Music* 375–76.

87. George Herbert, "Deniall," *The Works of George Herbert*, ed. F. E. Hutchinson (1941; Oxford: Clarendon Press, 1967).

88. Montaigne, *The Complete Essays of Montaigne* 828.

89. Plato, *Phadrus* 278c–e.

90. Edward Rothstein, *Emblems of Mind: The Inner Life of Music and Mathematics* (New York: Avon, 1995) 23.

91. Quoted by W. H. Auden in *The Dyer's Hand* (New York: Vintage, 1968) 23.

92. Cf. Kramer 129.

93. Quoted by Kramer, 3.

94. Kramer 3.

95. Theodor W. Adorno, "Music, Language, and Composition" (1965), trans. Susan Gillespie, *Musical Quarterly* 77 (1993): 402.

Notes to Chapter Two

1. James Hutton, "Some English Poems in Praise of Music," *English Miscellany* 2 (1950): 1–63.

2. Hutton 1–5.

3. See John Hollander, *The Untuning of the Sky* (Princeton: Princeton UP, 1961); S. K. Heninger, *Touches of Sweet Harmony* (San

Marino, California: The Huntington Library, 1974); Lawrence Danson, *The Harmonies of the Merchant of Venice* (New Haven: Yale UP, 1978).

4. See, for example, Nan Cooke Carpenter, *Music in the Medieval and Renaissance Universities* (New York: Da Capo Press, 1972) 147.

5. See Marc Berley, "Milton's Earthy Grossness: Music and the Condition of the Poet in 'L'Allegro' and 'Il Penseroso,'" *Milton Studies,* ed. Albert C. Labriola, Vol. 30 (Pittsburgh: U Pittsburgh P, 1993): 149–61.

6. C. L. Barber, *Shakespeare's Festive Comedy* (Princeton: Princeton UP, 1959) 187.

7. I quote throughout from William Shakespeare, *The Complete Plays,* ed. Alfred Harbage (New York: Viking, 1969).

8. Irene Dash, *Wooing, Wedding* and *Power* (New York: Columbia UP, 1981), mentions neither Jessica nor *Merchant;* in *The Woman's Part: Feminist Criticism of Shakespeare,* eds. Carolyn Ruth Swift Lenz, Gayle Greene, and Carol Thomas Neely (Urbana: U Illinois P, 1983), Jessica is mentioned in only one essay, and only once, in a typical sentence linking her choice of Lorenzo to her father's misfortune; Lisa Jardine, *Still Harping on Daughters* (1983; New York: Columbia UP, 1989), mentions Jessica only once, to remark only the matter of her cross-dressing; *Women's Re-Visions of Shakespeare,* ed. Marianne Novy (Urbana: U Illinois P, 1990) is a collection in which Jessica is not mentioned at all; in the few allusions to *Merchant* throughout the volume, it is Portia who is the subject.

9. Cynthia Lewis, "Antonio and Alienation in *The Merchant of Venice,*" *South Atlantic Review* 48 (1983) 20.

10. Frank Kermode, *Shakespeare, Spenser, Donne* (London: Routledge & Kegan Paul, 1971) 210–15.

11. Maynard Mack, "Engagement and Detachment in Shakespeare's Plays," reprinted in *Everybody's Shakespeare* (Lincoln: U Nebraska P, 1993) 25.

12. Robin Headlam Wells, *Elizabethan Mythologies* (Cambridge: Cambridge UP, 1994) 5.

13. John Gross, *Shylock: A Legacy and Its Legend* (New York: Simon & Schuster, 1992) 99.

14. Shakespeare, *Cymbeline* 2.3.11–31.

15. Hutton 4.

16. Hutton and Hollander do not not consider how Capella and Zarlino differ from Pythagoras and Plato on the subject of music. See Hutton (36–37), where he observes an abruptness but fails to remark its significance; also (6–7), where he does not distinguish the writings of Plato from the work of later writers such as Aristotle,

Quintilian, "Heraclides Ponticus, Theophrastus, and others [who] had further extended the subject," for according to Hutton, "the whole was reduced by the Hellenistic schoolmen to simple statements illuminated by suitable *exempla*." A weakness of Hutton's "sketch" is the irrelevance of many of the *exempla* he adduces to a meaningful dramatic analysis of Lorenzo's speech. Hutton considers neither Jessica nor the important questions raised by the dramatic context.

Similarly, the conclusion of Hollander's analysis of Lorenzo's "troping of the doctrine" (151–52), fails to take Jessica into account: "This is the vision of Plato's Er and Cicero's Scipio. It is significant that the one instance of Shakespeare's troping of the doctrine is Lorenzo's explanation of the inaudible character of the heavenly music. Neither of the traditional reasons (acclimatization, or the physical thresholds of perception) is given. Instead, the unheard music is related to immortality, and by extension to a prelapsarian condition, a world which, like heaven, need not conceal its ultimate gold, which even Belmont must do. This approaches Milton's treatment of the subject in *At a Solemn Music*." Hollander points to Ronsard and then, remarking no difficulties in Lorenzo's exchange with Jessica, writes that "Lorenzo retorts with a traditional disquisition on music and the affections, ending on a note of *musica humana* with all of its ethical and political connotations." Hollander concludes his analysis without stating what the connotations are: "Innuendoes of *musica mundana*, golden, silent, and inaccessible, are intimated at Belmont, where actual music is heard, and where the Venetian incompatibilities of gold and love are finally reconciled, almost as much in the golden music as in the golden ring."

17. See Plato's *Phaedrus*, especially 247c–d.

18. See Marsilio Ficino, *The Book of Life*; also Gary Tomlinson's study of Ficino in *Music in Renaissance Magic*.

19. Gross 91.

20. The subject is too large for the length of this chapter, but I would turn the reader to the recent articles and books written from Marxist, Cultural Materialist, and New Historicist perspectives that might shed further light on Jessica's "exchange." I would point out, however, that even these studies do not give Jessica the attention she commands. See, for example, Karen Newman, "Portia's Ring: Unruly Women and Structures of Exchange in *The Merchant of Venice*," *Shakespeare Quarterly* 1987 (38) 19–33. Newman offers intelligent analysis of the role of Portia's ring, as well as of "exchange" more generally. But Newman does not even mention Jessica's "exchange" as a point of comparison or contrast.

21. Shakespeare's learning has always been in question. But his

ability to take commonplaces from various traditions and make them both his own and dramatically relevant suggests not only more learning than we can account for but also a kind of learning it is impossible to quantify. Cf. E. M. W. Tillyard, "The Cosmic Background," *Shakespeare's History Plays* (London: Chatto & Windus, 1944). Tillyard argues that Shakespeare was "learned," but he qualifies what is meant by "learned." "For proofs," Tillyard writes (3) "take for example Lorenzo on music. . . ." Tillyard quotes lines four to eleven and makes the following argument: "This has been called 'an unlearned man's impression of Plato's sublime dream'. . . . Shakespeare, it is alleged, gets Plato wrong. . . . It is true that he garbled the above passage from the *Republic* by substituting cherubim for sirens and vastly enlarging the revenge of the heavenly music, but Lorenzo's general doctrine shows an accurate knowledge of a part of Plato's *Timaeus*. . . . Shakespeare reproduces the gist of this doctrine."

22. Hollander 151–52; Danson 177.

23. Danson 170, 175, 186.

24. Danson 188–89.

25. See Danson 186.

26. Charles Mosely, "Portia's Music and the Naughty World," *The Merchant of Venice*, Eds. Linda Cookson and Bryan Loughrey (Essex: Longman, 1992) 22.

27. Danson 178–84.

28. Kermode, *Shakespeare, Spenser, Donne* 215.

29. Gross 72.

30. Catherine Belsey, "Love in Venice," *Shakespeare Survey* 44 (1991): 41–53.

31. Belsey 43. Belsey writes that all of the characters in the play look "back to a world, fast disappearing in the late sixteenth century, where love was seen as anarchic, destructive, dangerous." Belsey does not uphold, apparently, Jessica's distinction between false and true vows, between destructive and true love. She argues instead that the play — hence Shakespeare, hence Lorenzo — speaks nostalgically (historically) about a desire that, in accordance with historical indicia, can no longer be fulfilled. In Belsey's view, Jessica and Lorenzo, an otherwise harmonious couple, are deprived of an allegorical harmony, or granted only a trace of it — for in the late sixteenth century, just as now, one may get no more than a trace of anything. It is certainly true that *Merchant* reveals a dark side of love in Venice, as Belsey writes — true, too, that Shakespeare is an expert on the subject of desire. But *Merchant* does not concern a general crisis in the history of desire as much as it treats the particular problems that the women in the play have with particular men.

32. James Shapiro, *Shakespeare and the Jews* (New York: Columbia UP, 1996) 158–59, remarks briefly the possibility that Jessica "might revert to her Jewish nature." The possibility, of course, is only hinted at, and it is part of Shakespeare's skill here to resist closure. To consider the matter fully, one has to pay more attention to the dramatic structure of the play than Shapiro does.

33. He has Lorenzo himself mock his claim to such a title: "I must be one of these same dumb wise men,/ For Gratiano never lets me speak" (1.1.105–06).

34. Norman Rabkin, *Shakespeare and the Problem of Meaning* (Chicago: U Chicago P, 1981) 28–29.

35. Keith Geary, "The Nature of Portia's Victory: Turning to Men in *The Merchant of Venice*," *Shakespeare Survey* 37 (1984): 55.

36. See Michael W. Shurgot, "Gobbo's Gift and the 'Muddy Vesture of Decay' in *The Merchant of Venice*," *Essays in Literature* 10:2 (1983): 139–148.

37. Harry Berger, Jr., "Marriage in *The Merchant of Venice*," *Shakespeare Quarterly* 32:2 (1981): 161.

38. On this general subject, see James Shapiro, *Shakespeare and the Jews*.

39. Even before his "problem plays," Shakespeare likes to set up patterns that suggest the closure the play refuses to provide. A. P. Rossiter, *Angel with Horns* (London: Longmans, 1961), offers a general discussion of the reasons "problematical" plays might be given the title "Problem Plays" and suggests that perhaps we ought "no longer be content with an eternal triangle of three "Problem Plays." The matter is beyond the scope of this chapter, but I am suggesting a number of problems, as well as a central one large enough to include *Merchant* in the general discussion.

40. Rabkin 28.

41. One exception to the "harmonizing habit" is offered by John Picker, "Shylock and the Struggle for Closure," *Judaism* 43:2 (1994): 174–89, who considers with insight the dramatic context that forces us to consider Jessica's response to Lorenzo's "musical illusion of happiness." Picker's consideration of music, however, is general and brief, for his subject is the more general one of closure. He concludes, moreover, by bringing Jessica too close to Shylock's worldview.

42. Cf. Newman 32.

43. Edward S. LeComte, *Yet Once More* (New York: Liberal Arts Press, 1953) 16.

44. Shakespeare, *The History of Troilus and Cressida* 3.3.296–99, 5.1.74–75.

45. In *King Lear* and in *Pericles*, Shakespeare does invoke the medicinal (Neoplatonic) powers of music. Cf. F. D. Hoeniger,

"Musical Cures of Melancholy and Mania in Shakespeare," *Mirror Up to Shakespeare: Essays in Honour of G. R. Hibbard*, ed. J. C. Gray (Toronto: U Toronto P, 1984) 55–67. In late plays such as *Cymbeline* and *The Winter's Tale*, Shakespeare depicts the magical power of music.

46. See Kermode, "Cornelius and Voltemand: Doubles in *Hamlet*," *Forms of Attention* 35–63; also "George T. Wright, "Hendiadys and *Hamlet*," *PMLA* 96 (1981): 168–94.

47. Kermode, *Shakespeare, Spenser, Donne* 152.

48. Jonathan Dollimore, *Radical Tragedy* (Chicago: U Chicago P, 1984) 5.

49. Shakespeare, *Pericles* 1.1.80–86.

Notes to Chapter Three

1. For general discussions of speculative music relevant to Milton see Heninger, Hollander, Hutton, and Spitzer; also Marjorie Hope Nicolson, *The Breaking of the Circle* (Evanston: Northwestern UP, 1950). For specific treatment of Milton, see Sigmond Spaeth, *Milton's Knowledge of Music* (1913; Ann Arbor: U Michigan P, 1963). On Milton's sources of contemporary musical techniques and theories and his acquisition of books during his stay in Italy, see Ernest Brennecke, Jr., *John Milton the Elder and His Music* (New York: Columbia UP, 1938).

2. Merritt Y. Hughes, ed. *John Milton: Complete Poetry and Major Prose*. All quotations of Milton's poetry are from this edition. I hereafter refer parenthetically to line numbers.

3. Cedric C. Brown, *John Milton's Aristocractic Entertainments* (Cambridge: Cambridge UP, 1985) 153, 156.

4. *Musica instrumentalis* is both voice and instrumental music, and also poetry. As Caldwell writes (152): "Vocal music and speech . . ., together with an intermediate category appropriate to epic recitation, are dealt with . . . with the clear implication that all three fall within the category of 'musica instrumentalis.'"

5. Joan S. Bennett, *Reviving* Liberty: *Radical Christian Humanism in Milton's Great Poems* (Cambridge: Harvard UP, 1989) 192.

6. See, for example, William Riley Parker, *Milton: A Biography* (Oxford: Clarendon Press, 1968); A. S. P. Woodhouse, *The Heavenly Muse* (U of Toronto P, 1972); and James Holly Hanford, *John Milton, Poet and Humanist* (Cleveland: Western Reserve UP, 1966).

7. E. M. W. Tillyard, *Milton* (New York: Dial Press, 1930); F. W. Bateson, "The Money-lender's Son: 'L'Allegro' and 'Il Penseroso,'" *English Poetry: A Critical Introduction* (London: Longmans, 1950) 149–64.

8. Noise is melodious in heaven, discordant on earth. In Paradise,

according to Milton, there are no negative terms; all words effect only their positive meanings, which appear in their pejorative sense only to the fallen narrator and the reader. See Freud's essay "The Antithetical Meaning of Primal Words," *Standard Edition of the Complete Psychological Works*, ed. and trans. James Strachey, vol. 19 (New York: Norton, 1961) 235–39.

9. Marjorie Nicolson, *The Breaking of the Circle* 164.

10. Hollander, *The Untuning of the Sky* 331, concludes his discussion of "At a Solemn Music" by reading Milton as a poet concerned chiefly with practical music: "Milton's combination of the praise of music generally, in the fashion of the previous century, with the figurative equivalence of song and prayer of the contemplative tradition, the whole finally turned to a consideration of public prayer and public utterance (it is not so much the jarring of disproportioned *musica humana* that is bemoaned, but of customs and practices) represents to some extent a synthesis of these conventions."

11. Denis Saurat, *Milton: Man and Thinker* (1925; New York: Haskell House, 1970) v, long ago asserted that "Neo-Platonism offered much too easy, and much too loose, an explanation" of much of "Milton's thought." But many scholars have since identified in the early poems moments of Neoplatonic ascent, musical ecstasy, purgation by means of divine music. See, for example, Kester Svendsen, "Milton's L'Allegro and Il Penseroso," *The Explicator* 8 (1950) item 49; and Rosemond Tuve, "Structural figures of 'L'Allegro' and 'Il Penseroso,'" *Images and Themes in Five Poems by Milton* (Cambridge: Harvard UP, 1957). See also the work by Norman B. Council, Gerald Cox, William A. Darkey Jr., S. K. Heninger, and James Hutton cited in this chapter.

12. Hutton, "Some English Poems in Praise of Music" 10.

13. Bennet, *Reviving Liberty* 185.

14. Lines 50–51: "And now, to sum it all up, what pleasure is there in the inane modulations of the voice without words and meaning and rhythmic eloquence?"

15. See William Haller, *The Rise of Puritanism* (New York: Columbia UP, 1938), especially 150–51; also Louis L. Martz, *The Poetry of Meditation* 168. Martz suggests that a "deeper explanation seems more likely, perhaps the explanation provided by Haller," than the "matter of [Milton's] years." For a reading of the poem very different from mine, one that resolves the very tension that is Milton's chief subject, see William Kerrigan, *The Prophetic Milton* (Charlottesville: UP of Virginia, 1974) 195–200.

16. Hughes, *John Milton: Complete Poetry and Major Prose* 604–05. All quotations of Milton's prose are, unless otherwise noted, from this edition. I hereafter refer parenthetically to page numbers.

17. Cf. Spaeth 61: "The expression 'measurable music' represented an idea, based upon the Pythagorean theory, that correct music could be composed through a mere knowledge of the mechanical laws governing the art. . . . It was an idea analogous to the prevalent modern theory that technical correctness is sufficient to create art, whether it be in music, painting, or literature."

18. Cf. Spaeth 99.

19. Spaeth 96.

20. See Gerard H. Cox, "Unbinding 'The Hidden Soul of Harmony': *L'Allegro, Il Penseroso,* and the Hermetic Tradition," *Milton Studies* 18 (1983): 45–62; Norman B. Council, "*L'Allegro, Il Penseroso* and 'The Cycle of Universal Knowledge'" *Milton Studies* 9 (1976): 203–20; both claim Milton is writing about a music he contemplated. Christopher Grose, in "The Lydian Airs of 'L'Allegro' and 'Il Penseroso'," *JEGP* 83 (1984): 183–99; Spaeth, *Milton's Knowledge of Music;* Hutton, and Hollander, *The Untuning of the Sky,* write that Milton was writing about music he both contemplated and heard. William A. Darkey, Jr. "Milton's 'At A Solemn Musick,'" unpublished Master's essay, Columbia University, 1949, considers all of Milton's references to music as references to music Milton heard. See also Raymond B. Waddington, "A Musical Source for 'L'Allegro'?" *Milton Quarterly* 27.2 (May 1993): 72–74.

21. Peter Le Huray, "The Fair Musick That All Creatures Made," *The Age of Milton,* eds. C. A. Patrides and Raymond B. Waddington (Totowa, NJ: Barnes and Noble, 1980) 268, even suggests that "there is precious little evidence of any very serious concern for music."

22. Much criticism has followed either the letter or the spirit of Merritt Hughes's note about the Lydian mode, in *John Milton: Complete Poetry and Major Prose* 71. Hughes, however, misstates Hutton, who writes, in "Some English Poems in Praise of Music" (46): "the commentators inform us that Milton dissents from Plato's condemnations of the Lydian mode; but that is beside the point." The important thing, Hutton argues, is the claim about piercing put forth by Cassiodorus. By paying too much attention to the Lydian mode and too little to piercing and the condition of grossness, critics miss Milton's point.

23. *Phaedo,* trans. Hugh Tredennick, in *Plato: The Collected Dialogues* 68.

24. Edward LeComte, *Yet Once More* 16.

25. Cicero, *De Republica,* trans. Clinton Walker Keys (1928; Cambridge: Harvard UP, 1988) 273.

26. See Kester Svendsen, "Milton's L'Allegro and Il Penseroso" and Rosemond Tuve, "Structural Figures of 'L'Allegro' and 'Il Penseroso.'"

27. Samuel Johnson, *Lives of the English Poets*, ed. G. B. Hill, Vol. 3 (Oxford, 1905). Others have remarked the hypothetical nature of the delights and pleasures, but none with attention to music and the ear that may or may not hear it. Thomas M. Greene, "Four Studies in Milton: The Meeting Soul in Milton's Companion Poems," *ELR* 14 (1984): 159–74, is the only critic who has written of the conditional elements with any concern about the impossibility of fulfilling them, although with an emphasis different from mine. Greene is interested in the way conditionals make it "not easy to gauge the reality of what does or might or might not happen."

28. This is especially true of readings that view the poems either as a progress or as the actualization of choice. See D. C. Allen, *The Harmonious Vision: Studies in Milton's Poetry* (Baltimore: Johns Hopkins UP, 1954) 10, who writes that "'Il Penseroso' . . . is 'more accomplished' and 'more mature' than 'L'Allegro'. . . . . 'Il Penseroso' is the poem of a poet that has found his way." See Leslie Brisman, *Milton's Poetry of Choice* (New York: Cornell UP, 1973) who identifies not only progress but choice implicit in that progress: "The poems are about choice, and they make that choice as they move along. . . . In moving from the first poem to the second a choice is being actualized." Cf. Rosemond Tuve, "Structural Figures of 'L'Allegro' and 'Il Penseroso,'" who writes against the argument of progression, emphasizing instead the unity of the poems, which she demonstrates by a study of images.

29. Tuve writes, for example, in *Images and Themes in Five Poems by Milton* 32: "The poem ends firmly, with a climactic last representative of those who taste Melancholy's pleasures in the pursuit of wisdom; for certainly the hermit who spells out the secrets of the physical universe in his solitary cell is no concession to religiosity but the very type of the withdrawn seer who experiences the last pleasure: to know things in their causes and see into the hidden harmonies of the cosmos." See also Thomas M. Greene, "Four Studies in Milton" (169) on "the 'ecstasies' which dissolve il penseroso as he hears the full-voiced choir"; Kester Svendsen, "Milton's L'Allegro and Il Penseroso": "For the pensive man in his ecstasy experiences what Milton said in the nativity hymn could happen through the 'holy Song' of the spheres and the angels."

30. Cf. *Comus* 453–58.

31. Stanley Fish, in "What It's Like to Read *L'Allegro* and *Il Penseroso*," *Milton Studies* 7 (1975): 77–99, has written unpersuasively that "the poems *mean* the experience they give; and because they so mean, the conditionals with which they end are false. . . . These conditionals are false because the conditions they specify have already been met."

32. Arthur Barker, "The Pattern of Milton's Nativity Ode." *UTQ* 10 (1941): 171–72.

33. See Edward Tayler, *Milton's Poetry* 32–33, on the poetic *nunc stans* and Milton's awareness of writing *sub specie aeternitatis*, of which the grammatical enactment of waiting is, in striking contrast, not an example. It rather expresses "what do I do now?" Milton here is, like other Christians, a man in human history waiting for grace.

34. Tayler, *Milton's Poetry* 36.

35. The emphasis is mine.

36. Christopher Marlowe, *Complete Plays and Poems*, ed. E. D. Pendry (1909; London: Everyman, 1983). Robert Ny, ed., *Sir Walter Raleigh's Verse* (London: Faber and Faber, 1972).

37. See, for example, William Kerrigan, *The Prophetic Milton* (Charlottesville: UP of Virginia, 1974) and Joseph Anthony Wittreich, Jr., *Visionary Poetics* (San Marino, CA: Huntington Library, 1979).

38. See James L. Kugel, ed., *Poets and Prophets* (Ithaca: Cornell UP, 1990) 1ff.

39. See Kerrigan 198: "With moderate joy and impeccable taste, [Milton] joins the divine celebration. His inspired voice divides the singing with angels and does us proud: the collective speech of humanity enters the angelic choir without disgrace, with only self-imposed humiliation."

40. See Harris Francis Fletcher *Milton's Rabbinical Readings* (1930; New York: Gordian Press, 1967); Denis Saurat, *Milton: Man and Thinker*; and E. C. Baldwin, "Some Extra-Biblical Semitic Influences Upon Milton's Story of the Fall of Man," *JEGP* 28 (1929) 366–401. Jason P. Rosenblatt, "Milton's Chief Rabbi," *Milton Studies* 24 (1988): 43–71, argues persuasively against skeptical scholars who "in part because they are more familiar with the primary sources" unfairly conclude "that Milton's scholarship is 'dubious'." As Rosenblatt writes, while John Selden provided Milton with much of his Hebrew learning, "Milton's competence in biblical Hebrew" allowed him to be "more than a one-stop shopper in Selden's supermarket of Hebraic materials." Cf. Golda Werman, *Milton and Midrash* (Washington, D.C.: The Catholic U of America P, 1995).

41. Abraham Joshua Heschel, *Maimonides: A Biography*, trans. Joachim Neugroschel (1935 in German; New York: Farrar, Straus, Giroux, 1982) 25.

42. Heschel, *Maimonides* 26.

43. Moses Maimonides, *Guide for the Perplexed*, trans. M. Friedländer (1904; New York: Dover, 1956) 219–20.

44. Maimonides 220.

45. See Kerrigan 10–11. Kerrigan does not mention Maimonides, and Joseph Anthony Wittreich Jr., *Visionary Poetics* (San Marino:

Huntington Library) 80–81, only mentions Maimonides once, in a general statement about *Lycidas* that fails to account for the significance of his writings within Milton's conception of prophecy.

46. Maimonides 220.

47. William G. Riggs, *The Christian Poet in Paradise Lost* (Berkeley: U California P, 1972) 5, offers a useful summary of the ways in which Milton must exert such control. In the four times the narrator presents himself to us in the invocations, "he appears 'with his garland and singing robes about him,' but he is also recognizably John Milton. . . . On each of these occasions his concern is with the relation between the poet as human singer and the superhuman subject of his song. This relation is a formative matter in *Paradise Lost*: it controls Milton's sense of poetic decorum. Milton's cautious consideration of his own strengths and weaknesses as inspired poet is expressed not just in the poem's four prologues but through his narrative — the argument of *Paradise Lost* and its aesthetic principles are inseparable."

48. Maimonides 221–22.

49. Rosenblatt 44.

50. Rosenblatt 59.

51. Cf. Rosenblatt 59.

52. See Rosenblatt 62–65, where he writes, "Milton cites the Edenic prohibition formula as part of a demonstration that the divine decree of predestination is conditional."

53. Kerrigan 161.

54. See Kerrigan 200, where he quotes Milton on poetry, remarking the "power" of poetry "to allay the perturbations of the mind, and set the affections in right tune, to celebrate in glorious and lofty Hymns the throne and equipage of Gods Almightinesse." Kerrigan elides, I would point out, the first part of Milton's sentence.

55. Maimonides 222.

56. Kerrigan 80.

57. Isaiah 6.7–8.

58. Heninger *The Touches of Sweet Harmony* 3.

59. See Kathleen Swaim, *Before and After the Fall: Contrasting Modes in Paradise Lost* (Amherst: U Massachusetts P, 1986).

60. Tayler, *Milton's Poetry* 5–7.

61. See book 1, line 263.

62. For further discussion of similarities between the narrator and Satan, see William Riggs, "The Poet and Satan in *Paradise Lost*," *Milton Studies* 2, ed. James D. Simmonds (Pittsburgh: University of Pittsburgh Press, 1970) 59–82.

63. For a relevant analysis of anadiplosis, anaphora, analepsis, and other figures in Milton's poetry see LeComte, *Yet Once More* 19–47.

64. Anne Davidson Ferry, *Milton's Epic Voice: The Narrator in Paradise Lost* (Cambridge: Harvard UP, 1967) 20–22.

65. D. Masson, ed. *The Poetical Works of John Milton*, Vol. III (London, 1882) 335.

66. Woodhouse, *The Heavenly Muse* 55.

67. Kerrigan 32.

68. J. Max Patrick and Roger H. Sundell, *Milton and the Art of Sacred Song* (Wisconsin: U. of Wisconsin P, 1979) ix.

69. Kerrigan 4.

70. Kerrigan 261.

71. William Madsen, *From Shadowy Types to Truth* (New Haven: Yale UP, 1968) 74–75.

72. Kerrigan 187.

73. Kerrigan 161.

74. See Kerrigan 18 and 30.

75. Kerrigan 200–01.

76. Kerrigan 144–46.

77. Kerrigan 151.

78. Barbara Kiefer Lewalski, *Paradise Lost and the Rhetoric of Literary Forms* (Princeton: Princeton UP, 1985) 7.

79. Madsen 75.

80. See, for example, Roy Flannagan, *The Cambridge Companion to Milton*, ed. Dennis Danielson (Cambridge: Cambridge UP, 1989): "The poetic style of *Comus* is youthful, skillful, and exuberant, it is the poetry of a young and joyful virtuoso just discovering the power and the music of his poetry. Milton as always takes himself very seriously as prophetic poet in touch with divine forces of harmony, but he also knows the power of good poetry to influence its listeners or readers, as when Orpheus made stones weep or sang Eurydice out of Hades, and he knows, as did the Shakespeare of the sonnets, the power of poetry to confer immortality on the poet" (29). This misses the importance of Milton's allusions to music: "Another ideal of the masque genre was to create beauty on stage, to combine the talents of painter, poet, and musician in a philosophical drama that would demonstrate world order and universal harmony. Plato was the philosopher of choice, lending the notion of musical harmony philosophical respectability" (22).

81. S. K. Heninger, "Sidney and Milton: The Poet as Maker," in *Milton and the Line of Vision* ed. Joseph Anthony Wittreich, Jr. (Madison: U Wisconsin P, 1975) 67–68.

82. See Heninger, "Sidney and Milton: The Poet as Maker" 67–68. Heninger writes further: "One final point which has pervasive significance for reading *Paradise Lost* is the fiction of a poetic maker: just as God made the universe and is immanent in every portion of

His creation, so the poet is immanent throughout the universe of his poem. . . . I think we must read *Paradise Lost* as a personal as well as universal statement. Milton is immanent in every component of the poem, and conversely the poem in its entirety is a comprehensive projection of the poet. Milton is Adam. . . . Milton wishfully identifies with Christ. . . . And Milton further identifies with both God and Satan. . . . Milton is also Eve and Raphael and even Michael . . . but there is no need to labor the point. Just as God provides the continuum wherein the multifarious items of the universe subsist, so also the poet encompasses the multeity of his poem" (94–95).

83. Northrop Frye, *A Study of English Romanticism* (Chicago: University of Chicago Press, 1968) 22.

84. Harold Bloom, *Ruin the Sacred Truths* (Cambridge: Harvard UP, 1989) 91.

85. Bloom, *Ruin the Sacred Truths* 98, writes: "Between Milton and God no mediation was necessary, which I again suggest puts Milton's Christianity into question." Milton's Christianity — his steadfast refusal to stop looking for mediation, his refusal to become, in effect, the nearly romantic poet Bloom mistakes him for — is, I would argue, what makes Milton the imposing poet he is.

86. Cf. Kathleen Williams, *Spenser's Fairie Queene: The World of Glass* (London: Routledge and Kegan Paul, 1966).

87. J. H. Hanford, "That Shepherd, Who First Taught the Chosen Seed: A Note on Milton's Mosaic Inspiration," *University of Toronto Quarterly* 8 (1939) 403–19.

88. Hanford 405.

89. J. H. Hanford, *A Milton Handbook* (New York: F. S. Crofts, 1938) 4.

90. Denis Donoghue, *Walter Pater: Lover of Strange Souls* 7.

Notes to Chapter Four

1. William Wordsworth, *The Prelude*, 1.227–37. All quotations of Wordsworth are from *A Norton Critical Edition* ed. Jonathan Wordsworth, M. H. Abrams, and Stephen Gill (New York: Norton, 1979).

2. Samuel Taylor Coleridge, *Biographia Literaria, The Oxford Authors*, ed. H. J. Jackson (Oxford: Oxford UP, 1985) 160.

3. Cited by M. H. Abrams in "The Correspondent Breeze: A Romantic Metaphor," *English Romantic Poets: Modern Essays in Criticism*, ed. M. H. Abrams (Oxford: Oxford UP, 1960) 37.

4. Abrams, "The Correspondent Breeze" 40.

5. See M. H. Abrams, *Natural Supernaturalism* (New York: Norton 1971) 91–92: Demonstrating the way "the subject, mind, or spirit which is primary and takes over the initiative and the functions which had once been the prerogatives of deity," as Abrams writes, Wordsworth offers a fine example of what "we can justifiably call Romantic philosophy."

6. Abrams, *Natural Supernaturalism* 123, 120, 123.

7. Tilottima Rajan, *Dark Interpreter* (Ithaca: Cornell UP 1980) 16.

8. Hartman, ed. *New Perspectives on Coleridge and Wordsworth: Selected Papers from the English Institute* (New York: Columbia UP, 1972) viii.

9. See, for example, *Natural Supernaturalism* 95: "Wordsworth's paradise, however, can be achieved simply by a union of man's mind with nature, and so is a present paradise in this world, capable of being described 'by words/ Which speak of nothing more than what we are.'"

10. Kenneth R. Johnston "The Idiom of Vision," in Geoffrey Hartman, ed. *New Perspectives on Coleridge and Wordsworth* 7. Cf. David Perkins, *The Quest for Permanence* (Cambridge: Harvard UP, 1959), where he suggests, for example, that "one finds [Wordsworth] was seeking to ease a suffocating, almost panicky fear that man is doomed to isolation from the healthful influence of his natural surroundings. In the poetry, this fear expresses itself, first of all, in situations where man is pictured as an actual intruder, whose 'restless thoughts' and impulsive actions violate the harmonious 'calm of nature.'"

11. Geoffrey Hartman, *Wordsworth's Poetry* (1964; New Haven: Yale UP, 1971) xi.

12. Hartman, *Wordsworth's Poetry* 18.

13. Jerome J. McGann, *The Romantic Ideology: A Critical Investigation* (Chicago: U Chicago P, 1983) 40.

14. McGann 40.

15. McGann 71.

16. McGann 109.

17. McGann 134.

18. As Abrams writes in his study of the Romantics' attempts to "reconstitute the grounds of hope," (*Natural Supernaturalism* 12–13), "Much of what distinguishes writers I call 'Romantic' derives from the fact that they undertook, whatever their religious creed or lack of creed, to save traditional concepts, schemes, and values which had been based on the relation of the Creator to his creature and creation, but to reformulate them within the prevailing two-term system of subject and object, ego and non-ego, the human mind or consciousness and its transactions with nature."

19. William Blake, *The Complete Poetry and Prose*, ed. David V. Erdman (1965; New York: Doubleday, 1982). All quotations of Blake are from this edition.

20. Harold Bloom, "The Internalization of Quest-Romance," in *Romanticism and Consciousness: Essays in Criticism* ed. Harold Bloom (New York: Norton, 1970) 5.

21. Hartman, *Wordsworth's Poetry* xiii.

22. "Sweet" is not a word reserved to describe the music of heaven, as it is for Milton. By 1806, as Hollander points out, "Wordsworth and Collins imply a post-Renaissance meaning for 'sweet' in a musical context — in the seventeenth century it still means only 'in tune' (cf. modern residual 'sour notes') — moving toward 'dear.'" "Sweet" song is still a poet's chief goal, but we must mark this lexical shift. See Hollander, "Wordsworth and the Music of Sound," in *New Perspectives on Coleridge and Wordsworth*, 49. An informative essay, it is, however, more a catalogue of various treatments of the trope by different poets than a consideration of the deep meanings the trope has for any particular poets.

23. Lord Byron, *The Complete Poetical Works*, ed. Jerome J. McGann (Oxford: Oxford UP, 1980–86). All quotations of Byron are from this edition.

24. See William Crisman, "Songs Named 'Song' and the Bind of Self-Conscious Lyricism in Blake," *English Literary History* 61:3 (1994) 622. Crisman reads the poems as a sequence, offering a persuasive analysis of the poems within it.

25. See Northrop Frye, *Anatomy of Criticism* (Princeton: Princeton UP, 1957) 293–302.

26. Crisman 623.

27. Abrams, *Natural Supernaturalism* 54.

28. Blake, "The Marriage of Heaven and Hell" 21.

29. C. M. Bowra, *The Romantic Imagination* (Cambridge: Harvard UP, 1949) 14.

30. Blake, "Jerusalem: To the Public" 145.

31. Blake, "Jerusalem: To the Public" 153.

32. Johann Wolfgang von Goethe, *Faust*, trans. Peter Salm (New York: Bantam, 1962), lines 138–47, and 184–87.

33. Abrams, *Natural Supernaturalism* 79.

34. Kramer 129.

35. Frank Kermode, *The Sense of an Ending* (Oxford: Oxford UP, 1966) 37.

36. Johnston, "The Idiom of Vision" 3.

37. McGann 137.

38. *Preface* 147.

39. Percy Bysshe Shelley, *Shelley's Poetry and Prose* ed. Donald H. Reiman and Sharon B. Powers (New York: Norton, 1977) 484. All

quotations of Shelley are from this edition; I refer to page numbers for the prose, line numbers for the poetry.

40. Shelley 485.

41. Shelley 480.

42. Shelley 480.

43. Sophocles, *Oedipus at Colonus*, trans. Elizabeth Wyckoff (Chicago: U Chicago P, 1954) lines 1224–26.

44. George M. Ridenour, "Shelley's Optimism," *Shelley: A Collection of Critical Essays*, ed. George M. Ridenour (Englewood Cliffs, NJ: Prentice-Hall, 1965) 7.

45. Bloom, "The Unpastured Sea: an Introduction to Shelley," *Romanticism and Consciousness* 376–77.

46. Bloom, "The Unpastured Sea: an Introduction to Shelley" 375–77.

47. John Keats, *The Letters of John Keats*, ed. Maurice Buxton Forman (1931; Oxford: Oxford UP, 1952) 107.

48. John Keats, *John Keats: Complete Poems*, ed. Jack Stillinger (Cambridge: Harvard UP, 1978). All quotations of Keats are from this edition.

49. Cleanth Brooks, *The Well Wrought Urn* (New York: Harcourt, Brace and Co., 1947) 162.

50. Brooks 157.

51. Stillinger, *John Keats: Complete Poems* xx.

52. Helen Vendler, *The Odes of John Keats* (Cambridge: Harvard UP, 1983) 81.

53. Vendler 83.

54. Stillinger xvi.

55. *The Letters of John Keats* 316.

56. *The Letters of John Keats* 314.

57. *The Letters of John Keats* 335.

58. *The Letters of John Keats* 334–35.

59. *The Letters of John Keats* 335.

60. Cf. Susan J. Wolfson, *Romantic Self-Questioning* (Ithaca: Cornell UP, 1986).

61. Walter Jackson Bate, *John Keats* (Cambridge: Harvard UP, 1964) 244.

62. McGann 133; see also 110. Keeping the distinction between early and late romanticism, McGann identifies in the "despair" of Coleridge in his "'secondary' poetic phase" what he calls "the sign of its ideological truthfulness." McGann sees such "truthfulness" as greatest in the "third phase" of romanticism, that of Shelley and, chiefly, of Byron, whose "ideology — in contrast to Blake, Wordsworth, and the early Coleridge — has to be defined in negative terms: nihilism, cynicism, anarchism." The aspirations to song by various

romantic poets clouds the general distinction between early and late romanticism, setting apart Keats from fellow late-romantics Byron and Shelley.

63. McGann 132.

64. W. Jackson Bate, "Evolution Toward Qualities of Permanent Value," *English Romantic Poets: Modern Essays in Criticism*, ed. M. H. Abrams (Oxford: Oxford UP, 1960) 347.

65. Bate, *John Keats* 498.

66. Bate, "Evolution Toward Qualities of Permanent Value" 346.

67. Vendler 142.

68. Virginia Woolf, *A Room of One's Own* (1929; New York: Harcourt Brace Jovanovich, 1957) 68.

69. *The Letters of John Keats* 70.

70. Vendler 78.

71. Numerous readers have remarked the negative aspects of the urn, as well as the poet's slow rejection of the ideal escapes they seem at first to offer. See, for example, Brooks and Stillinger.

72. Vendler 310.

73. See Wolfson.

74. Vendler 145.

75. Vendler 118.

76. See Edward W. Tayler's brilliant discussion of "no," know," and "nothing," in "*King Lear* and Negation," *English Literary Renaissance* 20.1 (1990) 17–39.

77. Vendler 85.

78. Vendler 145.

79. *The Letters of John Keats* 334.

80. Leslie Brisman, *Milton's Poetry of Choice and Its Romantic Heirs* 85, 93.

Notes to Chapter Five

1. Denis Donoghue, *The Old Moderns* (New York: Alfred A. Knopf, 1994) 8.

2. Stevens, "Not Ideas About the Thing but the Thing Itself," *The Collected Poems* 534. Hereafter *CP*.

3. Stevens, "The Noble Rider and the Sound of Words," *The Necessary Angel* (New York: Vintage, 1951) 3–4. Hereafter *NA*.

4. Stevens, "Notes Toward a Supreme Fiction," *CP* 383.

5. Stevens, "Notes Toward a Supreme Fiction," *CP* 381.

6. F. O. Matthiessen, *American Renaissance* (Oxford: Oxford UP, 1941) 135.

7. Matthiessen 137.

8. Henry David Thoreau, *Journal: 1848–1851*, ed. Robert Sattlemayer, Mark R. Ratterson, and William Ross, Vol. 3 (Princeton: Princeton UP, 1990) 247.

9. Ralph Waldo Emerson, *Collected Works*, ed. Alfred Ferguson (Cambridge: Harvard UP, 1971).

10. Ralph Waldo Emerson, "Circles," *Essays* (1926; Thomas Y. Crowell, 1951) 31–32.

11. Emerson, *Essays* 225.

12. Emerson, *Essays* 214.

13. Stevens, "Like Decorations in a Nigger Cemetery," *CP* 150.

14. Ezra Pound, "The Seafarer," *Personae* (New York: New Directions, 1971) 64–66.

15. Pound, "Homage to Sextus Propertius," *Personae* 217.

16. Pound, "Homage to Sextus Propertius," *Personae* 207.

17. Ezra Pound, *The Cantos* (1973; New York: New Directions, 1986) 425.

18. W. B. Yeats, *The Poems of W. B. Yeats*, ed. Richard B. Finneran (New York: Macmillan, 1983). All quotations of Yeats's poetry are from this edition.

19. Edmund Wilson, *Axel's Castle* (1931; New York: W. W. Norton, 1984) 36.

20. Wilson 34–35.

21. Wilson 33–34.

22. George Steiner, *Real Presences* (Chicago: U Chicago P, 1989) 26, 38.

23. Steiner 49.

24. Denis Donoghue, *The Ordinary Universe* (1968; New York: Ecco Press, 1987) 118.

25. Donoghue, *The Ordinary Universe* 141–42.

26. Donoghue, *The Ordinary Universe* 138.

27. Donoghue, *The Ordinary Universe* 141.

28. James Joyce, *Dubliners* (New York: Viking, 1968) 203.

29. Donoghue, *The Ordinary Universe* 136.

30. Stevens, "Sunday Morning," *CP* 67–68.

31. See Anne Carson, *Eros: The Bittersweet* (Princeton: Princeton UP, 1986).

32. Stevens, "The Man with the Blue Guitar," *CP* 169, 194.

33. Stevens, "To the One of Fictive Music," *CP* 87–88.

34. Frank Doggett, *Wallace Stevens: The Making of the Poem* (Baltimore: Johns Hopkins UP, 1980) xii, offers a fine description of Stevens's general view: "That the truth of poetry should be a sense of objective reality and that such a reality could never be known in itself was an ideal that gave his poems the uncertainty he believed they must have to be objects of enduring contemplation."

35. Stevens, "The Man with the Blue Guitar," *CP* 165–66.

36. Stevens, "Notes Toward a Supreme Fiction," *CP* 407.

37. Stevens, "The Man with the Blue Guitar," *CP* 194.

38. Stevens, "Study of Images II," *CP* 464–65.

39. See Jacqueline Vaught Brogan, *Stevens and Simile: A Theory of Language* (Princeton: Princeton UP, 1986). Writing that critics have ignored simile in favor of metaphor, Brogan documents that in "periods that correspond to what may be called major poetic breakthroughs" there are "dramatic increases" in Stevens's use of "like," "as," and "as if." Her observation supports her point that "Stevens came to resolve the latent tension of language" by sustaining "both poles of language simultaneously." She defines these poles as "essentially a unitive/ realist/ or logocenric conception of language" and, conversely, "a disjunctive/ nominalist/ even deconstructive conception . . ." 19, 21. ix.

40. Stevens, "An Ordinary Evening in New Haven," *CP* 486. Cf. Doggett 152.

41. Wallace Stevens, *Opus Posthumous* (1957; New York: Alfred A. Knopf, 1989) 262. Hereafter *OP*.

42. Stevens, "The Man with the Blue Guitar," *CP* 167.

43. Donoghue, *Ordinary Universe* 28.

44. Stevens, "Notes Toward a Supreme Fiction," *CP* 383.

45. Stevens, "The Pure Good of Theory," *CP* 331–32.

46. Stevens, "The Man with the Blue Guitar," *CP* 170.

47. Stevens, "Notes Toward a Supreme Fiction," *CP* 394.

48. Stevens, "The Man with the Blue Guitar," *CP* 171.

49. Stevens, "The Man with the Blue Guitar," *CP* 169.

50. Stevens, "The Man with the Blue Guitar," *CP* 176–77.

51. Steiner 94.

52. Stevens, *OP* 202, 185.

53. Steiner 174.

54. Stevens, *OP* 242.

55. Stevens, *OP* 245.

56. Donoghue, *The Ordinary Universe* 28.

57. Stevens, *OP* 260.

58. Stevens, *OP* 264.

59. See Frank Lentricchia's chapter on Stevens, "Writing After Hours," in *Ariel and the Police* (Madison: U of Wisconsin P, 1988); see also Samuel French Morse, "The Native Element," *Kenyon Review* 20 (1958): 446–65.

60. Steiner 106.

61. Stevens, "Of Modern Poetry," *CP* 240.

62. Stevens, "The Motive for Metaphor," *CP* 288.

63. Stevens, "The Noble Rider and the Sound of Words," *NA* 22.

64. Stevens, *OP* 189.
65. Stevens, "Notes toward a Supreme Fiction," *CP* 387.
66. Stevens, "Notes Toward a Supreme Fiction," *CP* 398–99.
67. Stevens, "Prologues to What Is Possible," *CP* 515–17.
68. Brogan 18–19.
69. Stevens, "The Man with the Blue Guitar," *CP* 171.
70. Wallace Stevens, *Letters of Wallace Stevens*, ed. Holly Stevens (New York: Alfred A. Knopf, 1966) 363. See Brogan 117–19, where, analyzing this poem and letter, she links Stevens's desire for a "supreme balance" to his placing of "restraints" on both realist or logocentric and nominalist or deconstructive theories of language.
71. Stevens, "To an Old Philosopher in Rome," *CP* 509.
72. Stevens, "Debris of Life and Mind," *CP* 338.
73. Stevens, "The Plain Sense of Things," *CP* 502–03.
74. Kermode, "The Plain Sense of Things," *An Appetite for Poetry* 172–73.
75. See Kermode, "The Plain Sense of Things," *An Appetite for Poety* 172–88.
76. On this aspect of *anagnorisis* see Edward W. Tayler, "*King Lear* and Negation" 17–39.
77. Shakespeare, *King Lear*, 4.7.4.
78. Shakespeare, *King Lear*, 1.4.85; 2.4.67.
79. Shakespeare, *Hamlet*, 2.2.224.
80. Shakespeare, *Hamlet*, 4.5.181–82.
81. Stevens, "Notes Toward a Supreme Fiction," *CP* 382.
82. Ben Jonson, "To the Immortal Memory and Friendship of that Noble Pair, Sir Lucius Cary and Sir H. Morison," *The Complete Poems*, ed. George Parfitt (New Haven: Yale UP, 1975).
83. Stevens, "Notes Toward a Supreme Fiction," *CP* 403–04.
84. Stevens, "The Man with the Blue Guitar," *CP* 167–68.
85. Stevens, "The Creations of Sound," *CP* 310–11

Notes to Conclusions

1. Stevens, "Notes Toward a Supreme Fiction," *CP* 393.
2. Theodor W. Adorno, "Arnold Schoenberg 1874–1951," *Prisms*, trans. Samuel and Shierry Weber (Cambridge: MIT Press, 1981) 157.
3. Ludwig Wittgenstein, *Tractatus Logico-Philosophicus*, trans. D. F. Pears and B. F. McGuinness (1961; Atlantic Highlands, NJ: Humanities Press, 1974) v, 74.
4. Edward Rothstein, *Emblems of Mind: The Inner Life of Music and Mathematics* (New York: Times Books, 1995) 28–29.
5. Arnold Schoenberg, *Theory of Harmony*, trans. Roy E. Carter (1911; Berkeley: U California P, 1978) xiii.

6. Adorno, "Arnold Schoenberg 1874–1951," *Prisms* 169.

7. Adorno, "Arnold Schoenberg 1874–1951," *Prisms* 150.

8. Stevens, "The Poems of Our Climate," *CP* 193–94.

9. Schoenberg 1.

10. Adorno, "Arnold Schoenberg 1874–1951," *Prisms* 151.

11. See Kermode's *The Sense of an Ending*, to which my consideration of these general questions is greatly indebted.

12. John Donne, *The Complete Poems*, ed. A. J. Smith (New York: Viking Penguin, 1971).

13. Yeats, "Vacillation," *The Poems of W. B. Yeats* 252.

14. Ben Jonson, "An Epitaph on Master Vincent Corbet" 142.

15. Adorno, "Arnold Schoenberg 1874–1951," *Prisms* 157.

16. Rothstein 27.

17. Emerson, *Essays* 220.

18. Friedrich Nietzsche, *The Birth of Tragedy and the Genealogy of Morals*, trans. Francis Golffing (New York: Doubleday, 1956) 7.

19. Martin Heidegger, "Language," *Poetry, Language, Thought*, trans. Albert Hofstadter (New York: Harper and Row, 1971) 189.

20. Heidegger, "What Are Poets For?" *Poetry, Language, Thought* 92.

21. Stevens, "Men Made Out of Words," *The Collected Poems* 355.

22. Paul Valéry, *The Art of Poetry*, trans. Denise Folliot (1958; Princeton: Princeton UP, 1985) 175.

23. Stevens, "Notes Toward a Supreme Fiction," *CP* 384.

24. All quotations of George Herbert are from *The Works of George Herbert*, ed. F. E. Hutchinson (1941; Oxford: Clarendon Press, 1967).

25. Wittgenstein 72.

26. See Erwin Panofsky, "Father Time," *Studies in Iconology* (Oxford: Oxford UP, 1939) and Fritz Saxl, "Veritas Filia Temporis," *Philosophy and History* (Oxford: Oxford UP, 1936). See also Tayler, *Milton's Poetry*.

27. Stevens, "The Pure Good of Theory," *CP* 329.

28. Walter Pater, *The Renaissance*, in *Walter Pater: Three Major Texts*, ed. William E. Buckler (New York: New York University Press, 1986) 219–20.

29. Stevens, "The Pure Good of Theory," *CP* 333.

30. Pater 219.

31. Adorno, "Culture Criticism and Society," *Prisms* 33.

32. Yeats, *The Poems of W. B. Yeats* 257, 259.

33. Donoghue, *Ordinary Universe* 133. Cf. Kermode, *Romantic Image* (London: Routledge & Kegan Paul, 1957).

34. Stevens, "The Creations of Sound," *CP* 310–11.

35. George Steiner, *Real Presences* (Oxford: Oxford UP, 1989) 27.

36. Hart Crane, *The Collected Poems and Selected Letters and Prose of Hart Crane* (New York: Liveright, 1966).

37. Roland Barthes, *Le plaisir du texte* (Paris: Éditions du Seuil, 1973) 10–11.

38. Jacques Derrida, *Of Grammatology*, trans. Gayatri Chakravorty Spivak (Baltimore: Johns Hopkins UP, 1976) especially pages 6–26 and 97–164.

39. Derrida, *Of Grammatology* 163.

40. Virginia Woolf, *A Room of One's Own* 95.

41. Virginia Woolf, *To the Lighthouse* (1927; New York: Harcourt, Brace, Jovanovich, 1981) 178.

42. Kramer, *Classical Music and Post Modern Knowledge* xii.

43. Kramer xiii.

44. Kramer xiii.

45. Kramer 35. Cf. Kramer 17: "From a postmodernist perspective, music as musicology has conceived it simply does not exist."

46. Kramer xiii.

47. See Kramer 234; see also Susan McClary, *Feminine Endings: Music, Gender, and Sexuality* (Minneapolis: U Minnesota P, 1991).

48. Ralph Ellison, *Shadow and Act* (1964; New York: Vintage, 1995) 13.

49. Kramer 17.

50. Jack Gilbert, *Monolithos* (New York: Knopf, 1982) 25.

51. Steiner 19.

52. Stevens, "Notes Toward a Supreme Fiction," *CP* 392.

53. Stevens, "About One of Marianne Moore's Poems," *NA* 99.

54. Adorno, "Arnold Schoenberg 1874–1951," *Prisms* 170.

55. Adorno, "Cultural Criticism and Society," *Prisms* 33.

56. Adorno, "Arnold Schoenberg 1874–1951," *Prisms* 159.

57. Derek Attridge, *Peculiar Language: Literature as Difference from the Renaissance to James Joyce* (London: Methuen, 1988) 47–48.

58. Susanne K. Langer, *Philosophy in a New Key* 8–9.

59. Langer 1.

60. Sidney, *An Apology for Poetry* 8.

Works Cited

Abrams, M. H. "The Correspondent Breeze: A Romantic Metaphor." *English Romantic Poets: Modern Essays in Criticism*. Ed. M. H. Abrams. Oxford: Oxford UP, 1960.

———. *Natural Supernaturalism*. New York: Norton, 1971.

Adorno, Theodor W. "Music, Language, and Composition." 1965. Trans. Susan Gillespie *Musical Quarterly* 77 (1993).

———. *Prisms*. Trans. Samuel and Shierry Weber. Cambridge: MIT Press, 1981.

Allen, D. C. *The Harmonious Vision: Studies in Milton's Poetry*. Baltimore: The Johns Hopkins Press, 1954.

Alighieri, Dante. *Paradiso*. *The Divine Comedy*. Trans. Allen Mandelbaum. New York: Bantam, 1984.

———. *Paradiso: Text and Commentary*. Trans. Charles S. Singleton. Princeton: Princeton UP, 1975.

———. *Purgatorio: Text and Commentary*. *The Divine Comedy*. Trans. Charles S. Singleton. Princeton: Princeton UP, 1973.

Aristotle. *On Poetry and Style*. Trans. G. M. A. Grube. 1958. Indianapolis: Hackett, 1989.

———. *The Art of Rhetoric*. Trans. J. H. Freese. 1926. Cambridge: Harvard UP, 1982.

———. *Metaphysics*. Trans. Richard Hope. 1952. Ann Arbor: U Michigan P, 1960.

———. *Politics*. Trans. Ernest Barker. 1946. Oxford: Oxford UP, 1958.

Ascham, Roger. *The Schoolmaster*. London 1560.

Attridge, Derek. *Peculiar Language: Literature as Difference from the Renaissance to James Joyce*. London: Methuen, 1988.

———. *Well-Weighed Syllables*. Cambridge: Cambridge UP, 1974.

Augustine. *On Music.* Trans. Robert Catesby Taliaferro. *Writings of Saint Augustine.* Ed. Ludwig Schopp. Vol. 2. New York: CIMA Publishing Co., 1947.

Baldwin, E. C. "Some Extra-Biblical Semitic Influences Upon Milton's Story of the Fall of Man." *Journal of English and German Philology* 28 (1929) 366–401.

Barber, C. L., *Shakespeare's Festive Comedy.* Princeton: Princeton UP, 1959.

Barker, Arthur. "The Pattern of Milton's Nativity Ode." *University of Toronto Quarterly.* 10 (1941): 167–81.

Barthes, Roland. *Le plaisir du text.* Paris: Éditions de Seuil, 1973.

Bate, Walter Jackson. "Evolution Toward Qualities of Permanent Value." *English Romantic Poets: Modern Essays in Criticism.* Ed. M. H. Abrams. Oxford: Oxford UP, 1960.

———. *John Keats.* Cambridge: Harvard UP, 1964.

Bateson, F. W. "The Money-lender's son: 'L'Allegro' and 'Il Penseroso.'" *English Poetry: A Critical Introduction.* London: Longmans, 1950.

Bath, William. *A Brief Introduction to the True Arte of Musicke.* London, 1584.

———. *A Brief Introduction to the Skill of Song.* London, 1600.

Belsey, Catherine. "Love in Venice." *Shakespeare Survey* 44 (1991): 41–53.

Bennett, Joan S. *Reviving Liberty.* Cambridge: U Harvard P, 1989.

Berger Jr., Harry. "Marriage in *The Merchant of Venice.*" *Shakespeare Quarterly* 32.2 (1981): 155–62.

Berley, Marc. "Milton's Earthy Grossness." *Milton Studies* 30. Ed. Albert C. Labriola. Pittsburgh: U Pittsburgh P, 1993.

Black, Max. *Models and Metaphors.* Ithaca: Cornell UP, 1962.

Blake, William. *The Complete Poetry and Prose.* Ed. David V. Erdman. 1965. New York: Doubleday, 1982.

Bloom, Harold. *The Anxiety of Influence.* Oxford: Oxford, UP, 1973.

———. Ed. *Romanticism and Consciousness: Essays in Criticism* New York: Norton, 1970.

———. *Ruin the Sacred Truths.* Cambridge: Harvard UP, 1989.

Boethius. *The Consolation of Philosophy.* Trans. Richard Green. Indianapolis: Library of Liberal Arts, 1962.

———. *De Institutione Musica.* Ed. Godofredus Friedlein. 1867. Frankfurt: Minerva, 1966.

Bowra, C. M. *The Romantic Imagination.* Cambridge: Harvard UP, 1949.

Brennecke, Ernest, Jr. *John Milton the Elder and His Music.* New York: Columbia UP, 1938.

Brisman, Leslie. *Milton's Poetry of Choice and Its Romantic Heirs.* Ithaca: Cornell UP, 1973.

Brogan, Jacqueline Vaught. *Stevens and Simile: A Theory of Language.* Princeton: Princeton UP, 1986.

Brooks, Cleanth. *The Well Wrought Urn.* New York: Harcourt, Brace and Co., 1947.

Brown, Cedric C. *Milton's Aristocratic Entertainments.* Cambridge: Cambridge UP, 1985.

Browne, Sir Thomas. *Selected Writings.* Ed. Sir Geoffrey Keynes. Chicago: Chicago UP, 1968.

Brumbaugh, Robert S. *Plato's Mathematical Imagination.* Bloomington: Indiana UP, 1954.

Burke, Kenneth. *The Rhetoric of Religion.* 1961. Berkeley: U California P, 1970.

Byron, George Gordon, Lord. *The Complete Poetical Works.* Ed. Jerome J. McGann. Oxford: Oxford UP, 1980–86.

Caldwell, John. "The *De Institutione Arithmetica* and *De Institutione Musica*," *Boethius.* Ed. Margaret Gibson. Oxford: Basil Blackwell, 1981.

Campion, Thomas. *The Works of Thomas Campion.* Ed. Walter R. Davis. 1967. New York: Norton, 1970.

Carpenter, Nan Cooke. *Music in the Medieval and Renaissance Universities.* New York: Da Capo Press, 1972.

Carson, Anne. *Eros: The Bittersweet.* Princeton: Princeton UP, 1986.

Case, John, or anonymous. *The Praise of Music.* Oxford, 1586.

Castiglione, Baldassare. *The Courtier.* Trans. Thomas Hoby. New York: Everyman, 1961.

Cicero. *De Oratore.* Trans. H. Rackham. 1942. Cambridge: Harvard UP, 1982.

———. *De Republica.* Trans. Clinton Walker Keys. 1928. Cambridge: Harvard UP, 1988.

Coleridge, Samuel Taylor. *Biographia Literaria. The Oxford Authors.* Ed. H. J. Jackson. Oxford: Oxford UP, 1985.

Council, Norman B. "*L'Allegro, Il Penseroso* and 'The Cycle of Universal Knowledge.'" *Milton Studies 9.* Ed. James D. Simmonds. Pittsburgh: U Pittsburgh P, 1976.

Cox, Gerard H. "Unbinding 'The Hidden Soul of Harmony': *L'Allegro, Il Penseroso*, and the Hermetic Tradition." *Milton Studies 18.* Ed. James D. Simmonds. Pittsburgh: U Pittsburgh P, 1983.

Crane, Hart. *The Collected Poems and Selected Letters and Prose.* New York: Liveright, 1966.

Crisman, William, "Songs Named 'Song' and the Bind of Self-Conscious Lyricism in Blake," *English Literary History* 61.3 (1994): 619–33.

Curtius, Ernst Robert. *European Literature and the Latin Middle Ages*. Trans. Willard R. Trask. 1953. Princeton: Princeton UP, 1973.

Danielson, Dennis. Ed. *The Cambridge Companion to Milton*. Cambridge: Cambridge UP, 1989.

Danson, Lawrence. *The Harmonies of The Merchant of Venice*. New Haven: Yale UP, 1978.

Darkey, William A., Jr. "Milton's 'At A Solemn Musick.'" Unpublished Master's Essay, Columbia U, 1949.

Dash, Irene. *Wooing, Wedding* and *Power*. New York: Columbia UP, 1981.

Derrida, Jacques. *Of Grammatology*. Trans. Gayatri Chakravorty Spivak. Baltimore: Johns Hopkins UP, 1976.

———. *Speech and Phenomena*. Trans. David B. Allison. Evanston: Northwestern UP, 1973.

Dickinson, Emily. *Final Harvest*. Ed. Thomas H. Johnson. Boston: Little, Brown, 1961.

Doggett, Frank. *Wallace Stevens: The Making of the Poem*. Baltimore: Johns Hopkins, UP, 1980.

Dollimore, Jonathan. *Radical Tragedy*. Chicago: U Chicago P, 1984.

E. Talbot Donaldson. Trans. *Beowulf*. New York: Norton, 1966.

Donne, John. *The Poems of John Donne*. Ed. A. J. Smith. New York: Viking Penguin, 1971.

Donoghue, Dennis. *The Ordinary Universe*. 1968. New York: Ecco Press, 1987.

———. *The Old Moderns*. New York: Knopf, 1994.

———. *Walter Pater: Lover of Strange Souls*. New York: Knopf, 1995.

Dowland, John. Trans. *Micrologus*. London, 1609.

———. *Varietie of Lute-Lessons*. London, 1610.

Eco, Umberto. *Semiotics and the Philosophy of Language*. Bloomington: Indiana UP, 1984.

Eden, Kathy. *Poetic and Legal Fiction in the Aristotelian Tradition*. Princeton: Princeton UP, 1986.

Elias, Julius A. *Plato's Defense of Poetry*. London: Macmillan, 1984.

Emerson, Ralph Waldo. *Collected Works*. Ed. Alfred Ferguson. Cambridge: Harvard, UP, 1971.

———. *Essays*. 1926. New York: Thomas Y. Crowell, 1951.

d'Erlanger, Baron Rudolphe. *La Musique Arabe. Grand traite de la musique*. Paris: Librairie Orientaliste Paul Geuthner, 1930.

Ferry, Anne Davidson. *Milton's Epic Voice: The Narrator in Paradise Lost*. Cambridge: Harvard UP, 1967.

Ficino, Marsilio. *The Book of Life*. Trans. Charles Boer. Irving, Texas: Spring Publications, 1980.

———. *The Letters of Marsilio Ficino*. Trans. The Language Department of the School of Economic Science, London. Vol. 1. London: Shepheard-Walwyn, 1975.

Finney, Gretchen. "Ecstasy and Music in Seventeenth-Century England." *Journal of the History of Ideas* 8 (1947): 153–186.

———. *Musical Backgrounds for English Poetry 1580–1650*. New Brunswick, New Jersey: Rutgers UP, 1962.

Fish, Stanley E. "What It's Like to Read *L'Allegro* and *Il Penseroso*. *Milton Studies* 7. Ed. Albert C. Labriola and Michael Lieb. Pittsburgh: U Pittsburgh P, 1975.

Fletcher, Angus. *The Prophetic Moment: An Essay on Spenser*. Chicago: U Chicago P, 1971.

Fletcher, Harris Francis. *Milton's Rabbinical Readings*. 1930. New York: Haskell House, 1970.

Freccero, John. *Dante: The Poetics of Conversion*. Ed. Rachel Jacoff. Cambridge: Harvard UP, 1986.

Freud, Sigmund. *Standard Edition of the Complete Psychological Works*. Ed. and Trans. James Strachey. Vol. 19. New York: Norton, 1961.

Frye, Northrop. *A Study of English Romanticism*. Chicago: University of Chicago Press, 1968.

———. *Anatomy of Criticism*. Princeton: Princeton UP, 1957.

Geary, Keith. "The Nature of Portia's Victory: Turning to Men in *The Merchant of Venice*." *Shakespeare Survey* 37 (1984): 55–68.

Goodman, Nelson. *Of Mind and Other Matters*. Cambridge: Harvard, UP, 1984.

Greene, Thomas M. "Four Studies in Milton: The Meeting Soul in Milton's Companion Poems." *English Literary Renaissance* 14 (1984) 159–174.

Grose, Christopher. "The Lydian Airs of 'L'Allegro' and 'Il Penseroso.'" *Journal of English and German Philology*. 83 (1984): 183–199.

Gross, John. *Shylock: A Legacy and Its Legend*. New York: Simon & Schuster, 1992.

Hanford, James Holly. *A Milton Handbook*. New York: F. S. Crofts, 1938.

———. *John Milton, Poet and Humanist*. Cleveland: Case Western Reserve UP, 1966.

———. "That Shepherd, Who first Taught the Chosen Seed: A Note on Milton's Mosaic Inspiration." *University of Toronto Quarterly* 8 (1939) 403–19.

Haller, William. *The Rise of Puritanism*. New York: Columbia UP, 1938.

Hartman, Geoffrey. Ed. *New Perspectives on Coleridge and Wordsworth: Selected Papers from the English Institute*. New York: Columbia UP, 1972.

———. *Wordsworth's Poetry*. 1964. New Haven: Yale UP, 1971.

Heidegger, Martin. *Poetry, Language, Thought*. Trans. Albert Hofstadter. New York: Harper and Row, 1971.

Heninger, S. K. *The Touches of Sweet Harmony.* San Marino, California: The Huntington Library, 1974.

———. "Sidney and Milton: The Poet as Maker." *Milton and the Line of Vision.* Ed. Joseph Anthony Wittreich, Jr. Wisconsin: U Wisconsin P, 1975.

Herbert, George. *The Works of George Herbert.* Ed. F. E. Hutchinson. 1941. Oxford: Clarendon Press, 1967.

Heschel, Abraham Joshua. *Maimonides: A Biography.* Trans. Joachim Neugroshel. 1935. New York: Farrar, Straus, Giroux, 1982.

Hesiod. *Hesiod: The Homeric Hymns and Homerica.* Trans. Hugh B. Evelyn-White. 1914. Cambridge: Harvard UP, 1950.

Hirsch, E. D., Jr. *Cultural Literacy.* Boston: Houghton Mifflin Company, 1987.

Hoeniger, F. D. "Musical Cures of Melancholy and Mania in Shakespeare." *Mirror Up to Shakespeare: Essays in Honour of G. R. Hibbard.* Ed. J. C. Gray. Toronto: U Toronto P, 1984.

Hollander, John. *The Untuning of the Sky.* 1961. New York: W. W. Norton, 1970.

Homer. *The Iliad.* Trans. Richmond Lattimore. Chicago: U Chicago P, 1951.

———. *The Odyssey.* Trans. Richmond Lattimore. Chicago: U Chicago P, 1967.

Hutton, James. "Some English Poems in Praise of Music." *English Miscellany* 2 (1950): 1–63.

Jardine, Lisa. *Still Harping on Shakespeare's Daughters.* 1983. New York: Columbia UP, 1989.

Johnson, Samuel. *Lives of the English Poets.* Ed. G. B. Hill. Vol. 3 Oxford, 1905.

Johnston, Kenneth R. "The Idiom of Vision." *New Perspectives on Coleridge and Wordsworth.* Ed. Geoffrey Hartman. New York: Columbia UP, 1972.

Jonson, Ben. *The Complete Poems.* Ed. George Parfitt. New Haven: Yale UP, 1975.

Joyce, James. *Dubliners.* 1914. Reprint, New York: Viking, 1968.

Keats, John. *John Keats: Complete Poems.* Ed. Jack Stillinger. Cambridge: Harvard UP, 1978.

———. *The Letters of John Keats.* Ed. Maurice Buxton Forman. 1931. Oxford: Oxford UP, 1952.

Kermode, Frank. *An Appetite for Poetry.* Cambridge: Harvard UP, 1989.

———. *Forms of Attention.* Chicago: U Chicago P, 1985.

———. *Shakespeare, Spenser, Donne.* London: Routledge & Kegan Paul, 1971.

———. *Romantic Image.* London: Routledge & Kegan Paul, 1957.

————. *The Sense of an Ending.* Oxford: Oxford UP, 1963.

————. *Wallace Stevens.* 1960. Reprint, New York: Chip's, 1979.

Kerrigan, William. *The Prophetic Milton.* Charlottesville: UP Virginia, 1974.

Kirk, G. S., J. E. Raven, and M. Schofield. Eds. *The Presocratic Philosophers.* 1957. Reprint, Cambridge: Cambridge UP, 1983.

Kramer, Lawrence. *Classical Music and Postmodern Thought.* Berkeley: U California P, 1995.

————. *Poetry and Music: The Nineteenth Century and After.* Berkeley: U California P, 1984.

Kugel, James L. Ed. *Poets and Prophets.* Ithaca: Cornell UP, 1990.

Lacoff, George and Mark Turner. *More Than Cool Reason.* Chicago: U Chicago P, 1989.

Langer, Susanne K. *Philosophy in a New Key.* Cambridge: Harvard UP, 1957.

LeComte, Edward S. *Yet Once More.* New York: Liberal Arts Press, 1953.

Le Hurray, Peter. "The Fair Musick That All Creatures Made." *The Age of Milton.* Eds. C. A. Patrides and Raymond B. Waddington. Totowa, NJ: Barnes and Noble, 1980.

Lentricchia, Frank. *Ariel and the Police.* Madison: U of Wisconsin P, 1988.

Lenz, Carolyn Ruth Swifl, Gayle Greene, and Carol Thomas Neely. Eds. *The Woman's Part: Feminist Criticism of Shakespeare.* Urbana: U Illinois P, 1983.

Lewalksi, Barbara Kiefer. *Paradise Lost and the Rhetoric of Literary Forms.* Princeton: Princeton UP, 1985.

Lewis, Cynthia. "Antonio and Alienation in *The Merchant of Venice*," *South Atlantic Review* 48 (1983): 19–31.

Levy, Isadore. *Recherches sur les source de la légende de Pythagore.* New York: Garland, 1987.

Lodge, Thomas. *Defence of Poetry.* London, 1579.

Long, John H. *Shakespeare's Use of Music.* Gainsville: U Florida P, 1971.

Mack, Maynard. *Everybody's Shakespeare.* Lincoln: U Nebraska P, 1993.

Madsen, William. *From Shadowy Types to Truth.* New Haven: Yale UP, 1968.

Maimonides, Moses. *Guide for the Perplexed.* Trans. M. Friedländer. 1904. Reprint, New York: Dover, 1956.

Marlowe, Christopher. *Complete Plays and Poems.* Ed. E. D. Pendry. 1919. Reprint, London: Everyman, 1983.

Martz, Louis L. *The Poetry of Meditation.* 1954. Reprint, New Haven: Yale UP, 1962.

Masson, D. Ed. *The Poetical Works of John Milton*. Vol. 3. London, 1882.

Matthiessen, F. O. *American Renaissance*. Oxford: Oxford UP, 1941.

McClain, Ernest G. *The Pythagorean Plato: Prelude to the Song Itself*. New York: Nicolas-Has Inc., 1978.

McClary, Susan. *Feminine Endings: Music, Gender, and Sexuality*. Minneapolis: U Minnesota P, 1991.

Milton, John. *Complete Poetry and Major Prose*. Ed. Merritt Y. Hughes. New York: Macmillan, 1957.

Montaigne, Michel de. *The Complete Essays of Montaigne*. Trans. Donald M. Frame. 1958. Reprint, Stanford: Stanford UP, 1965.

———. *Essais*. Ed. M. Rat. Paris: Éditions Garnier Frère, 1962.

Morley, Thomas. *A Plain and Easy Introduction to Practical Music*. London, 1597.

———. *The First Book of Consort Lessons*. 1599. Reprint, London, 1611.

Morse, Samuel French. "The Native Element." *Kenyon Review* 20 (1958): 446–65.

Mosely, Charles, "Portia's Music and the Naughty World." *The Merchant of Venice*. Eds. Linda Cookson and Bryan Loughrey. Essex: Longman, 1992.

Navon, Robert, ed. *The Pythagorean Writings*. Trans. Kenneth Guthrie and Thomas Taylor. Kew Gardens: Selene Books, 1986.

Newman, Karen. "Portia's Ring: Unruly Women and Structures of Exchange in *The Merchant of Venice*." *Shakespeare Quarterly* 1987 (38): 19–33.

Nicolson, Marjorie Hope. *The Breaking of the Circle*. Evanston: Northwestern UP, 1950.

Nietzsche, Friedrich. *The Birth of Tragedy and the Genealogy of Morals*. Trans. Francis Golffing. New York: Doubleday, 1956.

Novy, Marianne. Ed. *Re-Visions of Shakespeare*. Urbana: U Illinois P, 1990.

O'Meara, J. *Pythagoras Revived*. Oxford: Clarendon Press, 1989.

Ornithoparcus. *Micrologus*. Trans. John Dowland. 1609.

The Oxford English Dictionary. Oxford: Oxford UP, 1971.

Panofsky, Erwin. *Studies in Iconology*. 1939. Reprint, New York: Harper, 1962.

Parker, William Riley. *Milton: A Biography*. Oxford: Clarendon Press, 1968.

Pater, Walter. *The Renaissance. Walter Pater: Three Major Texts*. Ed. William E. Buckler. New York: New York UP, 1986.

Patrick, J. Max and Roger H. Sundell. Eds. *Milton and the Art of Sacred Song*. Wisconsin: U Wisconsin P, 1979.

Patrides, C. A. *Milton and the Christian Tradition*. Oxford: Clarendon Press, 1966.

Perkins, David. *The Quest for Permanence.* Cambridge: Harvard UP, 1959.

Picker, John. "Shylock and the Struggle for Closure." *Judaism* 43.2 (1994): 174–89.

Pindar, *The Odes of Pindar.* Trans. Sir J. E. Sandys 1915. Reprint, Cambridge: Harvard UP, 1978.

Plato. *The Collected Dialogues of Plato.* Ed. Edith Hamilton and Huntington Cairns. Princeton: Princeton UP, 1961.

———. *Apology. The Trial and Death of Socrates.* Trans. G. M. A. Grube. Indianapolis: Hackett, 1975.

———. *Plato's Republic.* Trans. G. M. A. Grube. Indianapolis: Hackett, 1974.

———. *Plato in Twelve Volumes.* Ed. Goold, G. P. 1930. Reprint, Cambridge: Harvard UP, 1982.

Plutarch. *Moralia.* Trans. F. H. Sandbach. Vol. 9. Reprint, London: Loeb Classical Library, 1961.

Pound, Ezra. *Cantos.* 1973. Reprint, New York: New Directions, 1986.

———. *Personae.* 1926. Reprint, New York: New Directions, 1971.

Puttenham, George. *The Arte of English Poesy.* London, 1589.

Quintilian. *Institutio Oratoria.* Trans. H. E. Butler. 1920. Reprint, Cambridge: Harvard UP, 1980.

Rabkin, Norman. *Shakespeare and the Problem of Meaning.* Chicago: U Chicago P, 1981.

Rajan, Tilottama. *Dark Interpreter.* Ithaca: Cornell UP, 1980.

Raleigh, Sir Walter. *Sir Walter Raleigh's Verse.* London: Faber & Faber, 1972.

Richards, I. A. *The Philosophy of Rhetoric.* 1936. Reprint, Oxford: Oxford UP, 1976.

Ridenour, George M. "Shelley's Optimism." *Shelley: A Collection of Critical Essays.* Ed. George M. Ridenour. Englewood Cliffs, NJ: Prentice-Hall, 1965.

Riggs, William G. *The Christian Poet in Paradise Lost.* Berkeley: U California P, 1972.

———. "The Poet and Satan in *Paradise Lost.*" *Milton Studies* 2. Ed. James D. Simmonds. Pittsburgh: U Pittsburgh P, 1970.

Rorty, Richard. *Philosophy and the Mirror of Nature.* Princeton: Princeton UP, 1979.

Rosenblatt, Jason P. "Milton's Chief Rabbi." *Milton Studies* 24 (1988): 43–71.

Ross, W. D. *Plato's Theory of Ideas.* Oxford: Oxford UP, 1951.

Rossiter, A. P. *Angel with Horns.* London: Longmans, 1961.

Rothstein, Edward. *Emblems of Mind: The Inner Life of Music and Mathematics.* New York: Times Books, 1995.

Ryding, Eric Sven Ryding. *In Harmonie Framed: Musical Humanism, Thomas Campion, and the Two Daniels.* Sixteenth Century

Essays & Studies, Vol. 21. Kirksville, Missouri: Sixteenth Century Journal Publishers, 1993.

Saurat, Denis. *Milton: Man and Thinker*. 1925. New York: Haskell House, 1970.

Saxl, Fritz. *Philosophy and History*. Oxford: Oxford UP, 1936.

Scaliger, Julius Caesar. *Poetics*. London, 1561.

Schoenbaum, S. *Shakespeare's Lives*. Oxford: Oxford UP, 1991.

Schoenberg, Arnold. *Theory of Harmony*. Trans. Roy E. Carter. 1911. Berkeley: U California P, 1978.

Shakespeare, William. *The Complete Works*. Ed. Alfred Harbage. New York: Viking, 1969.

Shapiro, James. *Shakespeare and the Jews*. New York: Columbia UP, 1996.

Shelley, Percy Bysshe. *Shelley's Poetry and Prose*. Ed. Donald H. Reiman and Sharon B. Powers. New York: Norton, 1977.

———. *The Works of Percy Bysshe Shelley*. New York: Random House, 1951.

Shurgot, Michael W. "Gobbo's Gift and the 'Muddy Vesture of Decay' in *The Merchant of Venice*." *Essays in Literature*. 10.2 (1983): 139–48.

Sidney, Sir Philip. *An Apology for Poetry*. Ed. Forrest G. Robinson. Indianapolis: Bobbs-Merrill, 1970.

Sophocles. *Oedipus at Colonus*. Trans. Elizabeth Wyckoff. Chicago: U Chicago P, 1954.

Spaeth, Sigmond. *Milton's Knowledge of Music*. 1913. Ann Arbor: U Michigan P, 1963.

Spenser, Edmund. *The Yale Edition of the Shorter Poems of Edmund Spenser*. Eds. William A. Oram, Einar Bjorvand, Ronald Bond, Thomas H. Cain, Alexander Dunlop, and Richard Schell. New Haven: Yale UP, 1989.

Spitzer, Leo. *Classical and Christian Ideas of World Harmony*. Ed. Anna Granville Hatcher. Baltimore: The Johns Hopkins Press, 1963.

Steiner, George. *Real Presences*. Chicago: U Chicago P, 1989.

Sternfeld, F. W. "Shakespeare and Music." *A New Companion to Shakespeare Studies*. Ed. Kenneth Muir and S. Schoenbaum. Cambridge: Cambridge UP, 1971.

Stevens, Wallace. *The Collected Poems*. New York: Vintage, 1954.

———. *Letters of Wallace Stevens*. Ed. Holly Stevens. New York: Alfred A. Knopf, 1966.

———. *The Necessary Angel*. New York: Vintage, 1951.

———. *Opus Posthumous*. 1957. Reprint, New York: Alfred A. Knopf, 1989.

Svendsen, Kester. "Milton's L'Allegro and Il Penseroso." *The Explicator*. 8 (1950) item 49.

Swaim, Kathleen. *Before and After the Fall*: *Contrasting Modes in Paradise Lost*. Amherst: U Massachusetts P, 1986.

Tayler, Edward W. "*King Lear* and Negation." *English Literary Renaissance* 20.1 (1990): 17–39.

———. *Milton's Poetry*: *Its Development in Time*. Pittsburgh: Duquesne UP, 1979.

Thoreau, Henry David. *Journal*: *1848–1851*. Eds. Robert Sattlemayer, Mark R. Ratterson, and William Ross. Vol. 3. Princeton: Princeton UP, 1990.

Tillyard, E. M. W. *Milton*. New York: Dial Press, 1930.

———. *Shakespeare's History Plays*. London. Chatto & Windus, 1944.

Tomlinson, Gary. *Music in Renaissance Magic*. Chicago: U Chicago P, 1993.

Trilling, Lionel. *The Liberal Imagination*. New York: Viking, 1950.

Trimpi, Wesley. *Muses of One Mind*. Princeton: Princeton UP, 1983.

Tuve, Rosemond. *Images and Themes in Five Poems by Milton*. Cambridge: Harvard UP, 1957.

Valéry, Paul. *The Art of Poetry*. Trans. Denise Folliot. 1958. Princeton: Princeton UP, 1985.

Vendler, Helen. *The Odes of John Keats*. Cambridge: Harvard UP, 1983.

———. "The Qualified Assertions of Wallace Stevens." *The Act of the Mind*: *Essays on the Poetry of Wallace Stevens*. Eds. J. Hillis Miller and Roy Harvey Pearce. Baltimore: Johns Hopkins UP, 1965.

Virgil. *Aeneid*. *Œuvres de Virgile*. Ed. F. Plessis and P. Lejay. Paris: Librairie Hachette, 1920.

Vlastos, Gregory. "Socrates' Disavowal of Knowledge." *Philosophical Quarterly* 35 (1985) 1–31.

Von Goethe, Johann Wolfgang. *Faust*. Trans. Peter Salm. New York: Bantam, 1962.

Waddington, Raymond B. "Musical Source for 'L'Allegro'?" *Milton Quarterly* 27.2 (1993): 72–74.

Walker, D. P. "Musical Humanism in the 16th and Early 17th Centuries." *The Music Review* 2 (1941): 1–13, 111–21, 220–27, 288–308 and *The Music Review* 3 (1942): 55–71.

———. "The aim of Baïf's *Académie de Poésie et de Musique*." *Journal of Renaissance and Baroque Music* 1 (1946): 91–100.

———. "The Influence of *musique mesurée à l'antique*, particularly on the *airs de cour* of the Early 17th Century." *Musica Disciplina* 2 (1948): 141–63.

———. "Le chant orphique de Marsile Ficin." *Colloques internationaux du CNRS* (Paris: Editions du CNRS, 1954).

———. "Ficino's *spiritus* and Music." *Annales Musicologiques* 1 (1953): 131–50.

Wallerstein, Ruth. *Studies in Seventeenth-Century Poetic*. Madison: U Wisconsin P, 1961.

Wells, Robin Headlam. *Elizabethan Mythologies*. Cambridge: Cambridge UP, 1994.

Werman, Golda. *Milton and Midrash*. Washington, D.C.: The Catholic U of America P, 1995.

West, M. L. "The Singing of Homer and the Modes of Early Greek Music." *Journal of Hellenic Studies* 101 (1981): 113–29.

Whitman, Walt. *Leaves of Grass*. Ed. Malcolm Cowley. 1959. Reprint, New York: Viking, 1982.

Williams, Kathleen. *Spenser's Fairie Queene: The World of Glass*. London: Routlege and Kegan Paul, 1966.

Wilson, Edmund. *Axel's Castle*. 1931. Reprint, New York: Norton, 1984.

Wilson, Thomas. *The Arte of Rhetorique*. London, 1560.

Wittgenstein, Ludwig. *Tractatus Logico-Philosophicus*. Trans. D. F. Pears and B. F. McGuinness. 1961. Reprint, Atlantic Highlands, NJ: Humanities Press, 1974.

Wittreich Jr., Joseph Anthony. "All Angelic Natures Joined in One: Epic Convention and Prophetic Interiority in the Council Scenes of *Paradise Lost*." *Milton Studies* 17. Eds. Richard S. Ide and Joseph Wittreich. Pittsburgh: U Pittsburgh P, 1983.

———. *Visionary Poetics*. San Marino, CA: Huntington Library, 1979.

Wolfson, Susan J. *Romantic Self-Questioning*. Ithaca: Cornell UP, 1986.

Woodhouse, A. S. P. and Douglas Bush. *A Variorum Commentary on the Poems of John Milton. The Minor Poems*. New York: Columbia UP, 1970.

Woodhouse, A. S. P. *The Heavenly Muse*. Toronto: U Toronto P, 1972.

Woolf, Virginia. *A Room of One's Own*. 1929. Reprint, New York: Harcourt Brace Jovanovich, 1957.

———. *To The Lighthouse*. 1927. Reprint, New York: Harcourt, Brace, Jovanovich, 1981.

Wordsworth, William. *A Norton Critical Edition*. Eds. Jonathan Wordsworth, M. H. Abrams, and Stephen Gill. New York: Norton, 1979.

Wright, George T. "Hendiadys and *Hamlet*." *PMLA* 96 (1981): 168–94.

Yates, Frances. *The French Academies of the Sixteenth Century*. London: The Warburg Institute, 1947.

Yeats, W. B. *The Poems of W. B. Yeats*. Ed. Richard J. Finneran. New York: Macmillan, 1983.

———. *Essays and Introductions*. New York: Macmillian, 1961.

Zarlino, Gioseffe. *Istituzioni armoniche*. Venice, 1558.

INDEX

prophecy, 169; and Renaissance, 20,
28, 34, 141; Socrates on, 34–35; and
speculative music, 19–21, 28–29;
Valéry on, ix–x
Postmodernism, 212, 359–60
Pound, Ezra, 189, 282–85; translations
by: "Seafarer," 284–85; works by:
"Cino," 282–84; *Pisan Cantos*, 285
Practical Music. *See also* Music,
Speculative music, 5–7, 20, 40–41, 50,
62, 87, 291, 376n48
The Prelude (Wordsworth), 206–10, 216–
17, 219–21, 228–30, 235–38, 241–42,
271
Prophecy, 143, 169–70
Pythagoras: and mathematics, 28–29;
and Plato, 8; and Socrates, 28, 61;
teachings of, x, 5, 7–8, 46–48, 371–
72n4; theories of, x, 22, 29, 44–45, 52,
85, 152–53, 277, 319, 368; Yeats on,
294

Quintilian, 43–45

Rabkin, Norman, 88, 114, 121
Real Presences (Steiner), 293–94
*Reason of Church Government Urged
against Prelaty, The* (Milton), 170–74
Redbreast (Dickinson), 281
Renaissance: and England, 35, 38–41, 45;
music of, 5–6, 85, 98; and
neoplatonism, 48–52; poetry of, 18,
20, 28, 34, 125, 141, 334, 339, 360;
and speculative music, 24
Republic (Plato), 29–31, 35, 38–41, 46,
382n21
Richards, I. A., 13–14
Ridenour, George M., 251
Romantic Ideology, The (McGann),
214–15
Romantic Image (Kermode), 298
Romantics, romanticism, xi, 24–25,
207–08, 213–15, 272, 286, 308, 331–
32, 337, 346, 392n18
Romeo and Juliet (Shakespeare), 115
Ronsard, Pierre de, 20, 49–50, 85–86, 96
A Room of One's Own (Woolf), 261, 355
Rothstein, Edward, 78, 334, 340–41

Samson Agonistes (Milton), 204
Schenker, Heinrich, 334
Schoenberg, Arnold, xi, 333–37, 340, 365
Schwartz, Delmore, 134–35
"The Seafarer," 279–80, 284
"The Sense of the Past" (Trilling), 71
Shakespeare, William: and Christianity,
118–19; on Cleopatra, 106; and
dramatic conflict, 83, 88, 121–22;
Gross on, 95; Hutton on, 20–21, 84–

86; influence of, 21–22, 39, 318, 366;
Kermode on, 137; and language, x–xi,
24–25, 94, 270, 326; Long on, 22;
Mack on, 90; and music, x, 19–22, 83,
88–89, 95, 108, 124–30; and neoplatonism, 49–50, 84–86, 93, 96, 128–
33; Schwartz on, 134–35; and speculative music, x, 45, 82, 87; themes of,
84, 106, 110–11, 126–28, 305–06, 328–
29, 381–82n21; tragedies, 134–35;
works by: *Cymbeline*, 96; *Hamlet*,
127, 133–34, 136, 140, 285, 310, 325–
26; *King Lear*, 112, 140, 261, 267, 290,
325, 328, 346–47; *Love's Labor's Lost*,
96, 129; *Measure for Measure*, 101,
118–19, 130; *Merchant of Venice*, 7,
19–20, 85–86, 92, 97–98, 104–05, 117,
123–24, 335; *Romeo and Juliet*, 115;
Sonnets, 88, 138–40, 259, 266–67;
Taming of the Shrew, 125, 129; *The
Tempest*, 136; *Tragedy of King
Richard the Second*, 130; *Troilus and
Cressida*, 95, 106, 129; *Twelfth
Night*, 115–17, 125, 129, 283
Shelley, Percy Bysshe: Bloom on, 251–
53; on music, x, 246–48; Ridenour on,
251; and Socrates, 63–64, 246; themes
of, 24, 66–67, 289, 309–10, 331, 340;
works by: "Alastor," 245–46, 249–50,
252–53; *Defense of Poetry*, 244–45;
"Hymn to Intellectual Beauty," 248,
251, 253; "Mont Blanc," 248, 251;
"Ode to the West Wind," 249–50;
Oedipus at Colonus, 246;
"Prometheus Unbound," 248; "To a
Sky-Lark," 246–48, 255
Sidney, Sir Philip: on Aristotle, 50–59;
Attridge on, 15–16; Heniger on, 52;
theories of, x, 66, 368; works by: *An
Apology for Poetry*, 15–16, 50–60, 64
Socrates: aspiration to song, 31–33; and
Cicero, 61–63, 65; on muses, 46; and
music, 31–32, 38, 44; and Plato, x, 3–
5, 28–32, 35–41, 45–47, 61, 64–65 99,
265, 273–74, 371n3; on poetry, 35–35;
and Pythagoras, 28, 61; and Shelley,
63–64, 246; and speculative music,
30; theories of, 38, 46, 62–66, 330
Song. *See* Music
Spaeth, Sigmond, 153–54
Speculative music. *See also* Music,
Practical music: definition of, 5–7, 82;
poetry of, 19–21, 24, 28–29; and
Shakespeare, x, 45, 82, 87; and
Stevens, 45, 82, 310–11k; uses of, 44–
45, 84, 373n13, 376n48, 384n1
Spencer, Edmund, 67–68
Spitzer, Leo, 22–23
Steiner, George, 270, 293–95, 316, 318,